PREFACE.

THE following account of the Church's general progress, from the close of the age of Heathen persecution to the doctrinal settlement effected by the Fourth Œcumenical Council, is based substantially on what I had formerly occasion to prepare for my pupils at Trinity College, Glenalmond. I would fain hope that it may to some extent enable the younger students of Ecclesiastical History, and general readers interested in the subject, to increase their knowledge of a period which is second in importance to the Apostolic age alone.

Those who study such a period may be warned against two extremes, disguised in the garb of reverence and of candour. It is possible to make facts give way to an ideal, to forget that wrong is wrong in the orthodox, and to judge their opponents without equity. It is also possible, in reaction from this unfairness, to approach the subject as it were *ab extra*, to be cold or hostile to the great Church leaders, and to reserve one's tenderness for heresiarchs. Modern tendencies run strongly against the first of these two methods, but give some encouragement to the second. I trust that in these pages there will be found no trace of either.

One brief but most majestic Psalm, which contributes to our Easter gladness, may well be in our thoughts as we contemplate the early triumphs of Christ's kingdom. "When Israel came out of Egypt, and the house of Jacob from among the strange people," there was in it far more of unfaithfulness to a high vocation than in the Church of Athanasius and Augustine, of Chrysostom and Leo. Yet "the sea saw and fled, Jordan was driven back," because "Judah was His sanctuary, and Israel His dominion." And so the Church held on her way,—not without spot or blemish, not without struggle and suffering,—yet still beautiful and "terrible as an army with banners," victorious by the strength of her faith in one royal and world-redeeming Name.

Michaelmas, 1860.

A History of the Church

From the Edict of Milan, A.D. 313, to the Council of Chalcedon, A.D. 451

William Bright

Alpha Editions

This edition published in 2019

ISBN : 9789353975029

Design and Setting By
Alpha Editions
email - alphaedis@gmail.com

A History of the Church,

FROM

THE EDICT OF MILAN, A.D. 313,

TO

THE COUNCIL OF CHALCEDON, A.D. 451.

BY

WILLIAM BRIGHT, M.A.,

FELLOW OF UNIVERSITY COLLEGE, OXFORD;
LATE PROFESSOR OF ECCLESIASTICAL HISTORY IN THE SCOTTISH CHURCH.

Oxford & London:

J. H. AND JAS. PARKER.

1860.

CONTENTS.

CHAPTER I.

MARTYRS.—The Church has rest.—Donatism.—Death of Maximin.—Ancyra.—Neocæsarea.—Council of Arles.—Quiet Days.—Licinian Persecution.—Arius.—His Argument.—Athanasius.—The Power of Arianism.—Recall of Donatists.—The Eusebii.—Alexander's Encyclic.—The "Thalia."—Constantine's aspect towards Christianity.—The Homoousion.—Council of Nicæa meets.—Arius examined.—Trickery of Eusebians.—The Creed.—Other Questions.—The Council closed . . . . page 1—26

CHAPTER II.

Death of S. Alexander.—Helena at Jerusalem.—The Cross and the Sepulchre.—Consecration of S. Athanasius.—S. Frumentius.—S. Nina.—Recall of Arius.—Deposition of Eustathius.—Charges against Athanasius.—Case of Ischyras.—Case of Arsenius.—Council of Tyre.—The Mareotis Commission.—Council of Jerusalem.—First Exile of Athanasius.—Marcellus.—Death of Arius.—Death of Constantine.—Return of Athanasius.—Council of the Dedication.—Gregory at Alexandria.—Second Exile of Athanasius.—Persecution in Persia.—Theophilus the Indian.—Council of Sardica.—Secession of Eusebians.—Acts of the Council . . . . 27—55

CHAPTER III.

Photinus condemned.—Donatus.—The "Macarian Times."—Council of Carthage.—Letter of Pope Julius.—Flavian and Diodore.—Return of Athanasius.—Death of Constans.—Martyrdom of Paul.—The Anomoion.—New Accusations.—The Homoiousion.—The Homoion.——Council of Arles.—Council of Milan.—Weakness of Bishops.—Persecution.—Liberius exiled.—Hosius exiled.—Death of S. Antony.—Syrianus' Irruption.—Outrages at Alexandria.—Intrusion of George.

—Exile of S. Hilary.—Egyptian Monasteries.—Retreat of S. Athanasius . . . . page 56—84

CHAPTER IV.

Fall of Hosius.—Fall of Liberius.—S. Basil in Pontus.—Cyril deposed. Council of Ancyra.—Hilary's "De Synodis."—The Dated Creed.—Council of Ariminum.—Deputations to Constantius.—Council of Seleucia.—Conference at Nicè.—Council of Ariminum yields.—Triumph of Acacianism.—Council of Constantinople.—Eudoxius at Constantinople.—Macedonianism.—Hilary in Gaul.—Meletius.—Arian Creeds.—Aerius.—Death of Constantius . . . . 85—108

CHAPTER V.

Julian's Apostasy.—His treatment of Christians.—Christian Zealots.—Murder of George.—Return of S. Athanasius.—Council of Alexandria.—Lucifer at Antioch.—The Peace-makers.—Donatists recalled.—Donatist Tyranny.—Julian at Antioch.—Fourth Exile of Athanasius.—The Attempt at Jerusalem.—Death of Julian.—Council of Alexandria.—Jovian and the Arians.—Jovian's Policy.—Valentinian and Valens.—Council of Lampsacus.—Deputation to Liberius.—Easterns conform.—Damasus and Ursinus.—Ursinus expelled.—Council of Tyana.—Edict of Valens . . . . 109—136

CHAPTER VI.

Fifth Exile of S. Athanasius.—Council of Laodicea.—Council of Rome.—Epistle "ad Afros."—S. Basil consecrated.—Persecution.—Athanasius and Basil.—Basil and Modestus.—Basil and Valens.—Apollinarianism.—Gregory consecrated.—Death of S. Athanasius.—His Character.—Persecution at Alexandria.—Labours of Martin.—Basil and Eustathius.—Exile of Eusebius.—Ambrose consecrated.—Troubles of Basil.—Gratian.—Ulphilas.—Epiphanius.—Question of "the Hypostases."—Jerome and Damasus.—"Tome of the Westerns."—Recall of Exiles.—Death of S. Basil . 137—163

CHAPTER VII.

S. Gregory at Constantinople.—Council of Gangra.—Edict of Theodosius.—Priscillian.—Council of Saragossa.—Gregory in S. Sophia.—Chrysostom.—Council of Constantinople.—Gregory resigns.—Nectarius.—The Creed re-edited.—Canons.—The Hierarchy.—Rome and Constantinople.—Council of Aquileia.—Jerome at Rome.—The altar of Victory.—Augustine at Rome.—Manicheism.—Augustine at Milan. —Ambrose and Symmachus.—Priscillian executed.—Justina's first attempt.—The Portian Church.—Jerome leaves Rome.—Progress of Augustine.—Justina's second attempt.—Discovery of Relics.—Conversion of S. Augustine . . . . . . page 164—194

CHAPTER VIII.

S. Martin at Treves.—Sedition at Antioch.—Flavian's Pleading.—Baptism of S. Augustine.—S. Ambrose at Treves.—Theodosius at Milan. Theodosius at Rome.—Jerome at Bethlehem.—Jovinian.—Massacre at Thessalonica.—Penance of Theodosius.—Penitential Usages.—Theodosius absolved.—The Serapeum.—The Massalians.—Murder of Valentinian II.—Great Law against Idolatry.—The Maximianists.—Jerome and Ruffinus.—Epiphanius in Palestine.—Origenistic Controversy.—Battle of Aquileia.—Paulinus at Nola.—Death of Theodosius.—Augustine as a Pastor.—His Consecration.—Death of S. Ambrose . . . . 195—223

CHAPTER IX.

S. Ninian.—Third Council of Carthage.—Death of S. Martin.—"Candida Casa."—S. Chrysostom consecrated.—The "De Principiis."—"Fourth Council of Carthage."—Eutropius.—Theophilus abandons Origenism.—First Council of Toledo.—Writings of S. Augustine.—S. Chrysostom at Ephesus.—The Tall Brothers.—Theophilus at Constantinople.—Council of the Oak.—Chrysostom's Ejection and Return.—Death of Paula.—Sacrileges at Constantinople.—Chrysostom's Second Exile.—Persecution of Joannites.—Donatist Outrages.—Pelagius.—Chrysostom at Cucusus.—Atticus.—Joannites in Exile.—Vigilantius.—Pagans invade Gaul.—Death of S. Chrysostom 224—255

CHAPTER X.

Theodosius II.—Siege of Rome.—Cœlestius.—Paulinus.—Synesius.—Taking of Rome.—Andronicus.—Conference of Carthage.—Council of Braga.—Trial of Cœlestius.—His Condemnation.—Augustine and the Pelagians.—Death of Theophilus.—End of Antiochene Schism.—Violences at Alexandria.—Orosius.—Conference at Jerusalem.—Council of Diospolis.—Theodore.—Council of Carthage.—Council of Milevum. —Letter of S. Innocent.—His Death . . . . . 256—282

CHAPTER XI.

Cyril and Atticus.—Cœlestius at Rome.—Pelagius' Confession.—Zosimus deceived.—He is resisted.—Council of Carthage.—S. Germain.—Letter of Zosimus.—Julian condemned.—Predestinarianism.—Boniface and Eulalius.—Case of Apiarius.—Gaudentius.—Death of S. Jerome.—Persecution in Persia.—Dispute as to Illyricum.—Antony of Fussala.—Case of Apiarius closed.—Disputes at Adrumetum.—Semi-Pelagianism.—Leporius.—Nestorius.—Vandals in Africa.—Teaching of Gallicans.—Augustine's Statements.—Grace and Free-Will . . . . page 283-309

CHAPTER XII.

Origin of Nestorianism.—"Theotocos."—Sermon of Proclus.—Reply of Nestorius.—The Question at Issue.—S. Cyril's Letter to the Monks.—His First Letter to Nestorius.—Cassian's Treatise.—S. Germain in Britain.—Second Letter to Nestorius.—His Reply.—Cyril writes to Theodosius.—Council of Rome.—Death of S. Augustine.—Third Letter to Nestorius.—A General Council summoned.—Nestorius and Theodoret.—Bishops at Ephesus.—The Council opened.—First Session.—Nestorius condemned.—John of Antioch arrives.—The Roman Legates.—Definition of Doctrine.—The "Rights of Cyprus."—Canons . . . . 310—339

CHAPTER XIII.

Count John.—Dalmatius.—Cyril's Explanations.—The Deputies.—Maximian consecrated.—S. Palladius.—Death of Cœlestine.—Council at Antioch.—Eastern Dissensions.—S. Patrick.—Paul of Emesa.—Formulary of Union.—Paul's Sermons.—S. Cyril and John united.—Anger of Nestorianizers.—Perplexity of Cyril's friends.—"One Incarnate Nature."—Vincent of Lerins.—S. Proclus.—Exile of Alexander.—Nestorianism in Persia.—Tome of S. Proclus.—The Memory of Theodore.—Taking of Carthage.—Council of Riez.—Death of Sixtus.—Accession of S. Leo . . . . 340—365

CHAPTER XIV.

First Council of Orange.—Manicheans at Rome.—Death of S. Cyril.—Dioscorus.—Death of Nestorius.—Case of Celidonius.—Claims of Leo.—He breaks with Hilary.—Rescript of Valentinian.—S. Germain again in Britain.—Priscillianists.—The "Eranistes."—Letters of Theodoret.—His Confession of Orthodoxy.—Ibas of Edessa.—Eutyches accused.

—"Two Natures."—Trial of Eutyches.—He is condemned.—Trial of Ibas.—A General Council summoned.—Death of S. Hilary.—The Council meets at Ephesus.—Eutyches acquitted.—Martyrdom of S. Flavian.—The "Latrocinium" . . . . . page 366—393

CHAPTER XV.

Synod of Rome.—Theodoret writes to S. Leo.—Arguments of S. Leo.—Pulcheria and Marcian.—Attila in Gaul.—A New Council summoned.—It meets at Chalcedon.—Theodoret admitted.—First Session.—Trial of Dioscorus.—He is deposed.—S. Leo's Tome approved.—Egyptian Suffragans.—"Of Two Natures."—"In Two Natures."—Theodoret and Ibas.—Canons.—Twenty-eighth Canon.—The Legates object to it.—It is confirmed.—Synodal Letters.—Position of S. Leo . . . . 394—417

APPENDIX.

I. The Canons of Nicæa 418
II. From the Tome of S. Leo 424
III. Principal Events 428

INDEX 431

CHAPTER I.

From the Edict of Milan to the Council of Nicæa.

"No weapon that is formed against thee shall prosper, and every tongue that shall rise against thee in judgment thou shalt condemn."

Isa. liv. 17.

IN the spring of A.D. 313 the universal Church was enjoying rest from the last of the great persecutions.

This deadly struggle between the worldly and spiritual kingdoms had begun in the February of 303; but since the abdication of Diocletian in 305 it had been mainly confined to the East. It had reinforced the "white-robed host of martyrs" from all classes of Christians, and by all forms of agonizing death. The Church had been full of those grand endurances which S. Ambrose calls "æterna Christi munera;" wherein

"... the yearning faith of saints,
The unconquered hope that never faints,
The love of Christ that knows not shame,
The prince of this world overcame [a]."

Among the martyred bishops were Anthimus of Nicomedia, beheaded; Tyrannio of Tyre, drowned; Sylvanus of Emesa, flung to wild beasts; Irenæus of Sirmium, whose faith withstood the entreaties of wife and children; Felix of Tubiza, who, being commanded to surrender the Scriptures, persisted in answering, "Habeo, sed non do," and thanked God that, after a virginal life of fifty-six years, he was now in Christ's cause to bend his neck to the slaughter; Phileas of Thmuis, who has left a vivid picture of Egyptian martyrdoms, and in the moment of his own gave glory to the "spotless and infinite One, the First and the Last [b];" Peter of Alexandria, whose humility would not let him sit down on "the throne of the Evangelist," and whose wisdom and charity are embodied in his Penitential Canons. Among

---

[a] From Mr. Neale's noble version of this hymn.

[b] Ruinart, Act. Sinc., pp. 433, 391, 521.

the clergy were Vincent of Saragossa,—as noble a deacon-martyr as S. Laurence; Romanus of Cæsarea, a deacon and exorcist; Zenobius, a priest who expired under torture; Pamphilus, renowned for his learning and his intimacy with the Church-historian Eusebius; Valens, a venerable deacon who had Scripture laid up in his memory [c]; Lucian of Antioch, the editor of the Septuagint, who had for some time been connected with heresy, but lived to be a martyr in the Church; Saturninus, an African, who, when tortured with other Christians for celebrating the Sunday service, replied to the proconsul, "It is the command of our Law." Among the people were Alban, the British proto-martyr: Peter the chamberlain, and others of "Cæsar's household;" George, (if we may trust the obscure tradition,) a military officer; Sebastian, who held a similar rank; Genesius, an actor, who is said to have been converted while engaged in a mimicry of baptism [d]. Among the women, youths, and children, were Agnes at Rome, Eulalia in Spain, Theodora in Egypt, Ennathas in Palestine, illustrious as virgin-martyrs; Afra, a penitent at Augsburg, whose thoughts recurred to the Feet that had been washed with tears; Pancras, a boy of fourteen, at Rome; Apphianus, a youth of twenty, at Cæsarea; Porphyry, the young servant of Pamphilus; Cyriac, a child who shared in his mother's martyrdom.

Many also there were whose sufferings came short of death, but who were maimed, or blinded, or sent to the mines or into dreary exile, or sold as slaves, or expelled from the army, or deprived of property or of civil rights. If there were some apostates, as Stephen, bishop of Laodicea, a man of more learning than faith [e], and others who became "traditors," that is, gave up the sacred books and vessels or other church furniture,—there were, on the other hand instances of that over-forwardness which the Church condemned in general as a virtual tempting of God. It is im-

[c] Cf. Eus. Mart. 11. [d] S. Aug. c. Don. vii. 53; Ruinart, p. 312. [e] Eus. vii. 32.

possible for us fully to conceive the varied trials which a persecution brought to bear upon men's faith: the rending asunder of family ties, the perpetual insecurity, the anticipations of intense agony, the "horrible dread" of giving way under its pressure; the actual inflictions which became a routine with Roman magistrates,—the iron hooks that laid the bones bare, the "little horse" that wrenched them asunder, and drew forth such cries as "Gratias Tibi ago, Domine; pro nomine Tuo da sufferentiam[f];" the boiling pitch, the melted lead, the fire, the wild beasts, and other tortures too hideous to describe. In their eagerness to uproot the faith, the persecuting rulers took pains to fill the schools with text-books which insulted its Author[g], and the markets with food that had come in contact with idolatrous sacrifices. They had, in short, left nothing untried; and a monument in Spain had prematurely boasted of their success:—"Diocletian Augustus," it was said, "had abolished the superstition of Christ." "Against whom hast thou exalted thy voice, and lifted up thine eyes on high? even against the Holy One of Israel."

And now He had made the storm to cease. Galerius had died, in 311, by the fearful disease that smote Antiochus and Agrippa: his last act had been an edict of toleration and an entreaty for Christian prayers. Constantine had won Rome,—by his own account to Eusebius, after the vision of the luminous cross,—and Maxentius had been "swept away" by the Tiber. Diocletian had died of grief on hearing the news. Constantine and Licinius had proclaimed toleration of all religious sects, apparently under certain conditions; whereupon Maximin, the sovereign of the East, pre-eminent for his savage hatred of Christianity, issued an order[h] that no force should be used against it. The edict of the two Western emperors having failed to re-assure all persons, a second edict was framed at Milan, in the spring

---

[f] Ruinart, p. 417. [g] The "Acts of Pilate," a blasphemous forgery.
[h] Eus. ix. 9.

of 313, which proclaimed an absolute and unconditional toleration [i], alike of Christianity and of all other religions,—and added a special order for the restoration of all buildings and places which had belonged to "the Christian body;"—the individuals who were thus to restore them were to be rewarded by the government. No profession of Christianity was made by the emperors; they trusted by this decree to win the favour of "whatever divinity might reign in heaven."

The Edict of Milan, then, did not establish Christianity as the state-religion; its effect was to annul all legal hindrances to liberty of worship, and to recognise the Christians as a body known to the law. A separate ordinance, addressed to Anulinus, proconsul of Africa, interpreted "Christian body" to mean the Catholic Church. This was to exclude the new sect, afterwards called that of the Donatists, which had sprung up in the preceding year, and had separated from the communion of Cæcilian, bishop of Carthage, on the ground that his consecrator, Felix of Aptunga, had been a traditor, and that he himself had cruelly punished the confessors who had courted persecution by preventing their friends from coming to relieve their wants. Instead of him the schismatics acknowledged Majorinus as bishop of Carthage. The moral groundwork of this Numidian sect was a gloomy zeal, without humility or love, for the purity of the Church; a zeal which could ally itself with the grossest violence and injustice, and with personal spite of the basest kind. Constantine ordered the African government to proceed against all who "persevered in this madness, seducing the Catholic people by an unprincipled imposture:" while he made over a large sum to Cæcilian for the use of the clergy of the "legitimate and most holy" religion, and exempted them from burdens of public office, that they might be free to serve the Empire by their prayers [k]. The schismatics, on their part, sent in an

[i] De Mort. Pers. 48; Eus. x. 5.

[k] See Eus. x. 6, 7. For a list of similar exemptions, see the note in Oxf. edition of Fleury, vol. i. p. 162.

accusation of Cæcilian, and supplicated the "best of emperors" to have the case tried by judges from Gaul[l]: an appeal to the civil power which for many years gave point to the invectives of the Catholics.

Meantime, the career of Maximin was hastening to its end. He had not allowed to the Christians, whom his recent order had secured from violence, any liberty of assembling for worship; and now, throwing off the mask, he declared war. Licinius overthrew him at Hadrianople on May 1. In his despair, Maximin put forth an edict equivalent to that of Milan[m]; slew many of the pagan diviners who had assured him of victory; and, finally, took poison at Tarsus. His death was a long agony; in his frenzy he dashed his head against the wall, and the Christians believed that at length, when his sight was gone, a vision of Divine judgment made him cry out as one under torture, "God is there, with attendants in white, giving sentence against me. It was not I—it was the others!" At length—so runs the Christian story—his anguish wrung from him a confession of guilt, and a piteous appeal to the mercy of the Saviour[n].

Constantine had now leisure to attend to the case of the African schism. At his desire, Melchiades, bishop of Rome, with several other prelates, held a Council in the Lateran palace at Rome[o], (Oct. 10, 313,) before which appeared Donatus, bishop of Casæ Nigræ, and other accusers of Cæcilian. The question as to Felix of Aptunga was not entertained; as to the personal charges against Cæcilian, the Council insisted on distinct, tangible evidence, and this was not forthcoming; while, on the other hand, Cæcilian accused Donatus of having reiterated, in some cases, baptism and imposition of hands. The Council set aside the judgment pronounced against Cæcilian in his absence by Numidian bishops in the interest of his enemies, affirmed

[l] "Rogamus te, . . . optime imperator, quoniam de genere justo es."—(Aug., tom. ix. p. 778.)

[m] Eus. ix. 10. [n] De Mort. 49. [o] Aug., tom. ix. p. 779.

him to be innocent and worthy of communion, but condemned Donatus alone of his accusers, and offered to recognise, in cases of rival bishops, the prelate who might be senior in consecration[p]. Cæcilian, for the sake of peace, was detained by Constantine in Italy; while two bishops, after making enquiry into the case in Africa, pronounced his adherents to be the true African Church. The case of Felix was examined on the spot by the proconsul, who found the evidence for his having been a traditor to be the forgery of a malignant scribe. The schismatics, still dissatisfied, asked for a council of all the Western bishops; and such an assembly was summoned to meet at Arles. Before it assembled, a small council was held (about Easter, 314,) at Ancyra in Galatia, chiefly on the case of those who had lapsed in the persecution. Its most important canon, the thirteenth, forbids an inferior class of consecrated bishops, named *chorepiscopi*, to ordain priests or deacons, still less to ordain city-priests, except by written leave from the bishop[q]. The Council also speaks of the three higher classes of penitents, the Hearers, the Kneelers, and those who were allowed to join in the prayers of the Eucharist, without actually receiving the oblation, and who are commonly known as the "Consistentes." The lowest class was that of "Weepers." The tenth canon of Ancyra forbids deacons who marry to keep their offices, unless at ordination they intimated their intention to marry. Another Council, contemporaneous with this, was that of Neocæsarea, the capital of Cappadocia, where S. Gregory the Wonder-worker had in the former century been bishop. This assembly decreed that a priest who should marry must lose his office[r]; de-

[p] Aug. Ep. 43.

[q] See Routh, Rell. Sac. iv. 214. There is a question as to whether some chorepiscopi were not, in fact, equivalent to rural deans. Those who think so urge the thirteenth canon of Neocæsarea, which compares them to the Seventy. Bingham considers that all the chorepiscopi were bishops, i. 183, (b. 2. c. 14. §. 4.)

[r] The ancient Church allowed married men to become priests and retain their wives; but disapproved of marriage after ordination. Socrates, i. 11.

nounced the marriage of a woman with two brothers successively; forbade, in ordinary cases, the ordination of one who had been "illuminated" (i. e. baptized) during illness, because such a person's faith "is of constraint, not of free will;" spoke of "offering" (the Eucharist) as the great priestly duty[s]; asserted the superiority of city-priests to country-priests, and, on the ground of Acts vi., fixed seven as the maximum for the deacons of every city.

The Council of Arles met on Aug. 1, 314. Sylvester, now bishop of Rome, was represented by four clergy, but Marinus of Arles was president. About four hundred bishops appeared; among whom were Eborius of York, Restitutus of London, and Adelphius of Lincoln[t]. Again Cæcilian's cause was triumphant. Besides the sentence against his enemies, twenty-two canons were passed, the most important of which were,—the first, which ordained that Easter should be kept by all on one day, and that the Bishop of Rome should write to all, according to usage, respecting that day in each year; the eighth, which ordained that converts from heresy, who could shew that they had been baptized in the Name of the Trinity, should "receive the Holy Spirit by the laying on of hands," but that those who could *not* should receive baptism[u]; and the fifteenth, which emphatically prohibited deacons from "offering" the Holy Eucharist.

To Constantine's extreme disgust, the defeated schismatics appealed to him against the Council. "The judgment of bishops" (so he wrote to the members of the Council) "ought to be regarded as a judgment of the Lord Himself. To ignore the heavenly sentence and to demand

---

[s] Compare S. Hilary, Fragm. 2. 16:—"Sacrificii opus sine presbytero esse non potuit."

[t] "De civitate Coloniæ Londinensium:" probably a mistake for *Lindi*, Lincoln. Routh, iv. 296.

[u] This was the point contended for by Stephen of Rome against S. Cyprian, on the ground that the holy Name of the Trinity gave reality to an administration of baptism even by a person of unsound belief.

a secular one," was, in his view, an insane imitation of heathen fashions. What could these men think of Christ their Saviour? The act, of itself, stamped them as traitors. Yet he consented to receive their appeal, "intending afterwards to make his excuses to the bishops[y]," and being minded to leave the appellants without excuse for further obstinacy. After some changes of purpose as to the scene of this new hearing, he confronted Cæcilian with the appellants at Milan in 316. The result was that he wrote, on Nov. 10, to Eumalius, the "Vicar[z]" of Africa:—"I have found Cæcilian to be a person thoroughly innocent, and faithfully observant of all the duties of his religion. It plainly appeared that no crime could be proved against him[a]."

In the first moments of his indignation against the accusers, Constantine thought of putting them to death[b]. But he contented himself with issuing decrees of banishment, and expelling the schismatics from the churches. It is uncertain at what time the schismatical episcopate at Carthage began to be held by the second and more eminent Donatus, from whom the party took its name[c].

While the African Church was harassed by Donatism, in other provinces the faithful had an interval of tranquil sunshine between the storm of persecution that had passed away and the more terrible storm of heresy that was at hand. "There sprang up for us all," says Eusebius, "a heaven-sent joy[d]." It seemed a fulfilment of the prophecy, "My people shall dwell in a peaceable habitation." The worship of the Church was celebrated with all that stateliness which even in earlier times, whenever she had the op-

---

[y] S. Aug. Ep. 43.

[z] Under the Prætorian Præfect of Italy were *Vicars* of Rome, Italy, and Africa. The title of prætorian præfect, originally belonging to the commander of the prætorian guards, was given under Constantine to the chief magistrates of the East, Illyricum, Italy, and Gaul.

[a] S. Aug. c. Cresc. iii. c. 71; Brev. Coll. 3. 37; P. Collat. i. 33.

[b] S. Aug. c. Ep. Parm. i. 8. [c] Hooker, b. 5. 62. 7. [d] Eus. x. 2.

portunity, was the natural expression of her faith and love[e]. —She could worship, if need were, in catacombs; but even in her days of depression, the rich lamps and the golden altar-vessels witnessed for the principle of sacred splendour, and prophesied of the cathedrals that were to be. There had been magnificent churches in the Christendom of the third century; but now the sanctuaries that arose were like "high palaces," and all the skill of sculptor and architect was tasked to make them a glorious thank-offering. Such was the new cathedral at Tyre, erected by the Bishop Paulinus and his flock, the dedication of which was marked by a florid sermon from Eusebius[f].

But in those Eastern provinces which Licinius still retained, after his unsuccessful war with Constantine in 314, the Church had new sufferings to undergo. Licinius, who hated Christianity, began to impede the action of the Church system by forbidding the bishops to hold synods, and thus compelling them, as Eusebius says[g], either to violate his commands or to nullify the institutions of the Church; "for no otherwise than by synods could great questions be settled." Gradually he went further in the path of persecution: forbidding Church services within cities, "because the country air was purer;" forbidding women to worship with men, "lest public morality should suffer;" casting off his loyal Christian servants, and at length commanding all his soldiers to sacrifice on pain of dismissal. Then came an outbreak of the old persecutors' fury: bishops were again, as formerly, the special victims of an emperor's hatred. One was cut in pieces; another, Paul of Neocæsarea, had his hands disabled with hot iron. At Sebaste forty Christian soldiers were stripped and ex-

---

[e] See Hooker, b. 5. c. 15; ib. c. 79. s. 14. See also Routh, Rell. Sac. iv. 323, for the list of gold and silver chalices, lamps, &c., surrendered by Silvanus and others. See Mill's Univ. Serm., p. 316.

[f] See Eus. viii. 1; x. 2. 4.

[g] Eus. Vit. Const. i. 51.

posed to the piercing Armenian winter[h]. According to the story, they kept on praying, "As forty have entered the stadium, O Lord, let forty win the crown!" One of them gave way, and sought the warm shelter which was offered to apostates; whereupon the guard, suddenly converted, took his place, and completed the roll of the Forty Martyrs.

This trouble, however, was soon to pass away. Not so that other affliction then beginning, so terrible in its early strength, so wonderfully enduring in its consequences, which was brought upon the Church by the heresy of a priest at Alexandria.

Several years before the martyrdom of Bishop Peter, a schism had been formed in Egypt under Meletius, bishop of Lycopolis, which took for its watchword the purity of Church discipline. The character of Meletius is to this day a problem[i]. Among his adherents was a Libyan named Arius, who on returning to Church unity was ordained deacon by Peter, and afterwards, on giving fresh proofs of spiritual disloyalty, was excommunicated. Peter, we are told, refused in his last days to take off the censure, foreseeing that Arius would rend the Church. Achillas, who succeeded Peter in 312, was so indulgent as to re-admit Arius into communion, and ordain him priest for the most important charge in Alexandria: the name of this church was Baucalis. Achillas was succeeded by Alexander in 313; and Arius continued under him to hold a high position among the parish priests, as we should call them, of the

---

[h] S. Basil does not say that they were exposed on a frozen lake, but that the lake near *the city in which they suffered* was frozen. In the same context he says that they suffered in the midst of the city. Hom. 20. His family held them in special veneration.

[i] According to Epiphanius, he was a brave confessor who never himself seceded, and who deemed Peter too gentle to those who had lapsed. According to the far higher authority of Athanasius, Apol. c. Ar. 59, he was condemned by Peter in a council for various crimes, and amongst others for actual apostasy. The Nicene Fathers say nothing about his apostasy, nor does a letter of contemporary bishops which remonstrates with him for schismatical proceedings.

city. The notion that he resented Alexander's election seems to rest on insufficient evidence[j].

In the year 319, the sixth of Alexander's prelacy, he addressed his clergy, at some length[k], on the supreme mystery of the Triune Godhead. The Father and the Son, he insisted, were of one essence and co-equal majesty. Arius protested against this statement, as amounting to that Sabellian heresy which had confounded the Persons, and been denounced by Dionysius, one of the greatest of Alexander's predecessors. He then proceeded to argue:—The Father is a Father, the Son is a Son. Therefore the Father must have existed before the Son. Therefore, *once the Son was not*. Therefore, He was *made*, like all creatures, *of a substance that had not previously existed.*

This was the essence of Arius' teaching. Trained in the schools of disputatious logic at Antioch, and by temperament devoid of reverence, he had accustomed himself to think nothing too majestic for the grasp of a syllogistic formula. He took his stand on the assumption that such a formula could comprehend the Infinite; that he could argue irresistibly from human sonship to divine. And yet his argument, to thoughtful minds, was self-destructive; for it began by insisting on the truth of our Lord's Sonship, and ended by making Him wholly alien from the essence of the Father.

Before this public avowal of his opinions, it appears that Arius had disseminated them in private. We can form, by means of the descriptions which have come down to us[l], a vivid image of the great heresiarch. There might be seen in Alexandrian streets and houses a tall, elderly man, in a half-cloak and a short tunic, with a worn, pallid face, and downcast eyes. The quiet gravity of his bearing,—the

---

[j] Theodoret, i. 2, says that he acted from jealousy; Philostorgius, that he waived his claims in favour of Alexander.

[k] Soc. i. 5.

[l] Epiph. Hær. 69, with Constantine's Ep. to Arius.

sweet persuasive voice, with its ready greetings and its fluent logic,—had a wonderful fascination for several of his brother-clergy, a large body of laymen, and many of the consecrated virgins. Alexander at first endeavoured to reclaim him by holding conferences in which the subject was discussed. But these proved ineffectual: so that the Archbishop, who had already been blamed for too great forbearance,—on the ground of which a priest named Colluthus had actually set up a sect of his own, and pretended to confer holy orders,—was obliged to employ the censures of the Church. He pronounced the Arian doctrine an impiety; commanded Arius to retract, and on his refusal, excommunicated him. He wrote a letter to Arius' partisans, exhorting them to submit to the faith[m]; and the great majority of the priests and deacons subscribed this letter. Among the deacons was a young man of twenty-four or thereabouts, who had been carefully educated for the service of the Church, and had already distinguished himself by treatises "against the Gentiles," and "on the Incarnation." His name was Athanasius[n].

The excitement was rather increased than abated by this proceeding. The Arian party grew daily in strength and boldness; the women especially were in the forefront of the faction, and were employed to support the accusations which its leaders brought before the civil courts, against the Archbishop and the faithful. There seemed to be every prospect of an Alexandrian sedition, with all its terrible phenomena, in behalf of a doctrine which amounted to apostasy from Christ[o]. Alexander summoned a council of nearly a hundred bishops, who owed obedience to his see[p]. It was ascertained by this assembly that, in Arius' view,

[m] See Ath. Hist. Tracts, p. 297.

[n] The story about his having attracted Alexander's notice by "shewing his mates how saints baptize and bless," is against chronological and other probabilities, and may safely be set aside, although given by Ruffinus, and after him by Socrates and Sozomen.

[o] Theod. i. 4.

[p] Soc. i. 6.

the Son of God was the first of creatures, and in that sense the Only-begotten; created after the image of the Divine Wisdom, and therefore called the Word; created in order that by His means God might create us; incapable of thoroughly knowing either the Father's nature or His own. One awful question remained. The Arians were asked whether this exalted creature could change from good to evil? They answered, "*Yes, He can.*" The Council replied to this fearful utterance by a solemn anathema against Arius, with two bishops who adhered to him, Secundus and Theonas, five priests, and six deacons.—Two other priests and four other deacons were either then or soon afterwards included in the condemnation.

We can never understand the history of an error until we to some extent appreciate its attractions. What was the charm that Arianism possessed, during so many years, for adherents so diverse both in race and character? First, it was a form of rationalism, and therefore a relief to minds that shrunk from so awful a mystery as the Incarnation of the Eternal. Secondly, it was a vague, elastic creed, congenial to those who disliked all definite doctrine. Thirdly, it appealed to many by its affinity to older heresies. Fourthly, its assertion of a created and inferior godhead would come home to persons in transition from polytheism to Christianity [q]. Fifthly, the scope which it practically allowed to a profane and worldly temper was agreeable to the multitudes for whom the Church was too austere, who desired a relaxed and adapted Gospel. Lastly, who

---

[q] Hence the Fathers often taunt the Arians with formal idolatry, as worshippers of *one believed to be a creature*. S. Ath. ad Ep. Æg. 4, 13; Or. c. Ar. i. 8. Hilar. de Trin. viii. 28: "O heretic, who declarest Christ to be a creature, understand what thou art,—thou who canst not but know that to worship a creature is accursed." Ambr. de Fide, i. c. 11: "If they think the Son foreign to the Father, why do they adore Him? . . . . Or if they do not adore Him, let them say so, and there is an end of it." The worship of Christ was a thing so ingrained in ancient Christianity, that the Arians durst not say, "We adore Him not."

can tell how many simple souls were allured by the promise of a safeguard against Sabellianism, or against "carnal views" of the nature of God?

These events happened in 320 and 321. At the same time, the regions westward of Alexander's patriarchate (if we may here apply that term by anticipation) were again disturbed by the Donatist troubles. One of the schismatic prelates, Silvanus of Cirta, was denounced before the civil court as a traditor and a simonist[r]. The accuser was Nundinarius, a deacon whom he had deposed, and whom he had refused to receive again into favour. Zenophilus, who tried the case, found Silvanus guilty, and sent him into banishment. Another officer named Ursacius seems to have acted with Zenophilus, and incurred the hatred of the party. But shortly afterwards the Donatists requested Constantine to stop the persecution which they had endured for disowning "that worthless bishop of his." The Emperor, by a letter of May 5, 321, recalled them from exile, at the same time expressing his detestation of their violence, and declaring that he left them to the judgment of God[s]. And it was probably about this time that he exhorted the Catholics to wait patiently for a Divine relief from their afflictions[t]. The extraordinary audacity of the Donatists is shewn by his own words: "Whatever sufferings may be inflicted by their fury will be counted as martyrdom in the sight of God." It can hardly be doubted that he refers to the outrages of those wild fanatical peasants who derived from their original habits of begging from cottage to cottage the name of *circumcellions*[u]. We shall hear more of them at a later period; it may suffice to say that the strange frenzy which made them, in many cases, rush upon their death in the cause of Donatism, had previously led them to court mar-

---

[r] See S. Aug. c. Creso. iii. 32; Routh, Rell. Sac. iv. 320.

[s] S. Aug. ad Don. post coll. 54, 56. The letter was to Verinus, the vice-præfect.

[t] See S. Aug., tom. ix. 791.

[u] S. Aug. c. Gaud. i. 32.

tyrdom at the hands of pagans on festivals of the gods[x]. Their organization, as a Donatist force, became more perfect afterwards; but they seem to have been in these early days of the schism a terror to the defenceless Catholics. Encouraged by the revocation of penal edicts, the Donatists sent a bishop named Victor to Rome[y]. He could not gain admission into any church, and was reduced to assemble his small flock of Africans outside the city, in a cavern on a hill, whence they derived the contemptuous epithet of "Montenses."

To return to the Arian history. Deprived of a home in Alexandria, Arius wrote to the Bishop of Nicomedia, who had been bred in the same school with him at Antioch[z]. His name was Eusebius. He had procured by court interest a translation from the see of Berytus; and he now possessed the ear of Constantine. Arius complained to this unprincipled and ambitious man that he was "unjustly persecuted by the Pope Alexander[a]" for denying the eternity of the Son. The Son, he insisted, must be a creature, although He might be entitled "perfect God."

Having quitted Egypt, Arius visited Palestine. Eusebius the historian, bishop of Cæsarea, was one of the prelates on whom he relied; and although the extent of his sympathy with Arianism has been disputed, it may be truly said that "his acts are his confession[b]." Nor did he "scruple to say plainly that Christ was not true God;" a saying which has been coupled with that of a thoroughgoing Arian, Athanasius of Anazarbus, that Christ was "one of the hundred sheep[c]." Macarius of Jerusalem, and Philogonius the patriarch of Antioch, would have nothing

[x] See Aug. Ep. 185. 12. [y] Optatus, lib. ii. [z] Theod. i. 5.

[a] The term Pope was at this time more specifically applied to the Archbishop of Alexandria than to any other prelate, although it rightfully belonged to all.

[b] Newman's Arians, p. 150. ed. 1854.

[c] See S. Ath. de Syn. s. 17. This latter impiety was in a letter to Alexander.

to say to Arianism. Alexander sent letter after letter to the Syrian bishops[d], some of whom answered as if agreeing with his view, while others avowed their feeling for Arius. But if Palestine was doubtful, Nicomedia was committed to his side; and there he found a welcome from Eusebius, who had written to him, "Since your sentiments are good, pray that all may adopt them: for it is plain to any one that *what has been made was not, before its generation*[e]."

Arius and his companions wrote to their Archbishop[f], from Nicomedia, a letter which has been reckoned the first of the Arian creeds. They addressed him respectfully as their "blessed Pope," and referred to his own alleged teaching. They spoke of the Son as "God's *perfect creature*, but *not as one of the creatures*." He was not, they affirmed, of the Father's essence—for that would imply a materialistic view. He was said to be generated before all time, but still to have come into existence, so that He was not before His generation. Eusebius urged Paulinus of Tyre to declare himself[g], and insisted that Prov. viii. 22[h] made the Son a creature, and that even the dewdrops were called the offspring of God. The bishops of Bithynia, under the guidance of Eusebius, pronounced Arius worthy of their communion, and put forth a circular letter to all prelates, requesting them to mediate between Alexander and the friends of Arius[i]. The Archbishop of Alexandria, on his side, issued an encyclic to all Catholic bishops, in which he gave a history of the schism; set forth the Arian propositions with a comment which became proverbial, "Who ever yet heard such things?" and arrayed Scripture texts against them, with the Scriptural predictions of an apostasy which the faithful must abhor[k]. He caused his own priests and deacons to

---

[d] Epiph. Hær. 89.

[e] S. Ath. l. c.

[f] S. Ath. de Syn. 16.

[g] Theod. i. 6.

[h] ἔκτισέ με, LXX. S. Ath. applied this text, thus rendered, to Christ's Body. Some Fathers "had the acuteness to find out the mistranslation of the original—ἔκτισε for ἐκτήσατο."—(Bp. Forbes on Nic. Cr., p. 158.)

[i] Soz. i. 15.

[k] Soc. i. 6.

subscribe this letter, as they had subscribed the one addressed to the Arians. Arius, wishing by all means to popularize his views, embodied them in a poem called *Thalia*, in a metre which had very evil associations. Describing himself as a "well-known sufferer for God's glory," he spoke of the Son as "not equal, no, nor one in essence with the Father," but a creature of His will, called into existence at a certain period, capable of knowing Him only in part[l]. From this "store of all irreligion[m]," and from the songs which he wrote for sailors, travellers, and millers, arose in great measure that storm of Arian irreverence, which varied the talk of the shop or the bath by flippant denials of the Co-equality, and assailed the very boys and women in the market with scoffing questions about an Eternal Son[n].

After this Arius returned to Palestine, and was permitted by Eusebius of Cæsarea and other bishops to form a distinct congregation, on condition that he did his utmost to be reconciled to Alexander[o]. This permission is alluded to in a long letter from Alexander to his namesake of Byzantium, preserved by Theodoret[p], which may be taken as a sample of the mass of letters which he wrote against Arianism. He denounces the Arians for their heathenish and Judaic views of Christ, for their persecuting violence, their intellectual arrogance, their disingenuous pretences. He insists on the doctrine of an Eternal Father and an Eternal Son, whose sonship is by essence, and not by adoption. This doctrine involves no Sabellianism, no Ditheism, no partition of the Divine essence, no denial of the Father's prerogative as the Unbegotten. One remarkable point in this letter is that it speaks of Mary as "the Mother of God[q];" another, that it

[l] S. Ath. de Syn. s. 15; Or. c. Ar. i. 5. 6.
[m] S. Ath. c. Ar. i. 10.
[n] Ibid. i. 22.
[o] Soz. i. 15.
[p] Theod. i. 4.
[q] As does S. Ath., Or. c. Ar. iii. 14, ἐπὶ τῆς Θεοτόκου Μαρίας. Ib. 29, 33. So S. Cyril of Jerusalem, Catech. x. 19, "The Virgin Mother of God is His witness."

avows the inadequacy of human language for the full expression of a transcendant mystery [r]. It appears from the letter that Alexander had framed a formulary of doctrine, which he requested the Byzantine prelate to subscribe [s].

While the controversy was thus raging, Constantine had been at war with Licinius. The latter was overthrown in 323, and the conqueror then assumed a more distinctively Christian attitude. Priests had accompanied him in the late campaign; he had been wont to pray, before a battle, in a tent where the cross was erected; he wrote letters [t], acknowledging that the only true God had given him victory. It would be monstrous that "God's servant" should be neglectful of His confessors; therefore the Emperor recalled all Christian exiles, readmitted Christian soldiers to the army, set free all who had been enslaved, restored property to confessors and heirs of martyrs, and to the Church as a corporation. He caused himself to be painted as in the act of prayer, and with a cross over his head and a transfixed serpent under his feet. In a letter to the Eastern provincials, he pointed out the judgments which had fallen on the persecutors; but while recommending the religion which God had visibly supported, he promised that it should be forced upon none. Hence we must suppose that the edicts which he issued against sacrifices had reference to some magical rites, and to the offerings made in the Emperor's name [u]. He shewed himself zealous against impure idolatries, and earnestly desirous of the Church's extension. Having already commanded "Sunday" observance [x], he gave

---

[r] Compare S. Aug. de Trin. v. 9, that as to what is meant by Three in the Godhead, "magnâ prorsus inopiâ humanum laborat ingenium." See, too, his Serm. 117. 5.

[s] The Benedictines would identify this "tome" with S. Alexander's letter to all bishops.

[t] Eus. V. C. ii. 24—42.

[u] See Milman's Hist. Christ. ii. 463. Still, he did not refuse the title of Pontifex Maximus.

[x] All work in towns was to cease on "the venerable day of the sun:" but country people might "freely pursue agricultural work."

an example of attendance on other festivals, and supplied a blaze of lights for the Paschal vigil [y]. He built churches, and contributed to their splendour: crosses bright with precious stones, and probably stone altars, began to appear under his encouragement [z]. The Emperor became a lecturer on religion, and spoke in grave and solemn tones on the Divine unity, on salvation, and on the account to be rendered. Was he sincere in all this? Most probably he had a genuine belief in the Christian system, so far as he understood it: but he knew little of its teaching as a dogma, or of its demands as a law. Hence, while he gave much to his religion, he did not give himself. A strange inconsistency distinguished his religious position; and bishops, too ready to become courtiers, allowed a prince who had not asked for baptism to dogmatize on things pertaining to God, and to call himself "a bishop for the external relations" of the Church [a].

Public peace was Constantine's first object; and now, after all his trouble with the Donatists, he was sorely disappointed to find in the East a wider and deadlier schism. In a letter to Alexander and Arius [b], he expressed his natural longing for "tranquil days;" but he also exhibited his ignorance of the real bearings of the controversy, and his imperial self-confidence in pronouncing upon it. The strife, he said, had arisen from an unpractical question stirred by the one, and an inconsiderate opinion expressed by the other. Let them indulge no more in such intellectual exercises; or, at any rate, keep them from publicity.

---

[y] For the antiquity of this solemn observance of that night, "the sanctification of which," in the words of the Paschal "Præconium," "restores innocence to the fallen and joy to the sorrowful," see the story of Narcissus in Euseb. vi. 9.

[z] See Bingham, b. viii. c. 5. s. 15. We shall see that wooden altars were still in use after the days of Constantine. The ancients did not consider that the reality of an altar depended on its being of stone. Sixtus III. gave a silver altar to S. Mary Major; Pulcheria gave a golden altar to the great church in Constantinople.

[a] Eus. V. C. ii. 24.

[b] Soc. i. 7.

Seven times in the letter he insists, with a sort of passionate emphasis, that the points at issue are minute and trivial. On all vital points, he assures them that they agree; why should they rend the Christian brotherhood about speculative opinions on which few men think alike?

Thus, in the spirit of a man of the world, for whom doctrinal truth was a mere unreality, Constantine threw aside, as absolutely unimportant, the question whether Christ was very God or no. He sent the letter by the aged confessor Hosius, bishop of Cordova. On his arrival at Alexandria, about the beginning of 325, another Council met[c]. Arius was again condemned; so were the Meletian schismatics; Colluthus submitted to the Church, and Ischyras, on whom he had laid hands, was pronounced a layman[d]. Far from accepting the Emperor's view of the controversy, the Council appears to have adopted the term *Homoousion*, in order to express the great truth that the Son was included within the very essence of the Father, without being merged in His personality[e]: that He was God of God, begotten, not made, literally, absolutely, eternally divine.

Arius sent a remonstrance to Constantine; but the Emperor was now under a different influence, as it would appear, from that which had produced his recent letter. He replied to Arius, partly by a coarse invective[f], partly by a peremptory order to recognise the Son as of one essence with the Father.

But it was now clear that neither provincial councils nor

[c] On this see Tillemont, vi. 230, on Soc. iii. 7, Philost. i. 7.

[d] Ath. Apol. c. Ari. s. 74. This of itself would dispose of the statement of the credulous Eutychius, patriarch of Alexandria in 933, that until the time of S. Alexander the patriarchs were *consecrated* by twelve presbyters. S. Jerome's statement, that until the time of Dionysius they were *chosen* and *named* by the presbyters (from their own body), is perhaps true.

[e] Sabellianism was excluded "by the ὁμοῦ, 'together,' which implied a difference as well as unity." Ath. Treatises, i. 203, note, (Lib. F.) So S. Basil, Ep. 52.

[f] He sneered at his dismal, emaciated figure, and called him "a shop of iniquity."

imperial mandates were sufficient for the need. The idea of a General Council of all bishops, such as could not have been held during the Church's season of adversity, recommended itself to Constantine. Such an assembly might also decide two other questions: 1. that of the Meletian schism in Egypt; 2. that of the time of Easter. Syria and some other districts maintained the old Quartodeciman custom, which had formerly been prevalent in proconsular Asia; while the majority of Churches made the close of the Lenten fast depend, not upon the 14th day of the month Nisan, but upon the first day of the week.

Constantine accordingly summoned the bishops of Christendom to meet at Nicæa, which was conveniently near his own residence at Nicomedia. The day of meeting was June 19, 325. The number of bishops present has been usually stated as 318[g]. Sylvester of Rome was too old for such a journey; he was represented by two of his priests. Alexander was present, attended by his deacon Athanasius. Two other faithful Alexanders were there, from Thessalonica and Byzantium. There, too, appeared Eustathius of Antioch, Macarius of Jerusalem, Leontius of Cappadocian Cæsarea, the consecrator of Gregory the "Illuminator" of Armenia; Aristaces, Gregory's son and representative; James of Nisibis; Hosius from Spain, Cæcilian from Carthage, Nicatius from Gaul, John from Persia, Theophilus "bishop of the Goths;" brave confessors, like Paul of Neocæsarea with his disabled hands, and Paphnutius from Thebais, and Potamon of Heraclea, who had each been deprived of an eye[h]; Acesius, a bishop of the Novatianist sect, who was specially invited by Constantine in his desire of unity. Among the Arianizers were the bishops of Nicomedia and Cæsarea; and the deposed Arians, Secundus and Theonas, were permitted to attend the great assembly, which was

[g] S. Ath. ad Afr. 2. Optatus, Hilary, and others, follow him. Julius of Rome says 300; Eusebius, above 250.

[h] Constantine kissed the scars of the confessors. Soc. i. 11; Theod. i. 7.

able to review all previous judgments. A large concourse of clergy and laity, present as spectators, but not as members, although some were allowed to address the Council, contributed to the grandeur of the scene. There is a question as to the bishop who presided. If Hosius did so, there is no good evidence[i] for saying that it was in the character of Sylvester's legate; and it is probable, on the whole, that he was "chief of the Council" only inasmuch as he was employed to frame the Creed; and that the actual president was Eustathius of Antioch. Before the proceedings began, a significant incident happened[k]. A pagan philosopher, who had harassed some of the bishops by his volubility, was encountered by a pious lay confessor with the simple statement of the Christian faith, and was then and there won over to accept it. Before the Emperor's arrival, the Council met in the cathedral of Nicæa. Arius was summoned and examined. He boldly declared that he held the Son to be a creature who once did not exist, who was made out of nothing by God, who might have chosen to sin against Him. A thrill of horror went through the assembly: many bishops stopped their ears[l], and said that they had heard enough; others insisted on a thorough discussion[m]. Among those who, as members of the Council or as taking part in the debates, exhibited their argumentative skill on the side of orthodoxy, Athanasius the deacon was pre-eminent.

On the 3rd of July the Council was transferred to the palace. Constantine appeared in gold and purple, but without the pomp of guards. Modest and graceful in address, he replied[n] to the loyal speech of Eustathius with an expression of his earnest wish for the unanimity of the Council. He listened to all with attentive patience, disclaiming all thought of dictation to the prelates; he was but the "fel-

---

[i] Only that of Gelasius of Cyzicus. S. Athanasius says that he *led* the synods, Apol. de Fugâ, 5. Cf. Hist. Ari. 42.

[k] Soz. i. 18.

[l] S. Ath. ad ep. Æg. i. s. 13: compare Soc. i. 9.

[m] Soz. i. 17.

[n] Eus. V. C. iii. 12; Theod. i. 7. He had already burned some memorials which bishops had given in against bishops. Soz. i. 17.

low-servant of his dear friends." Arius was heard a second time. The Eusebians, as they began to be called after the Nicomedian prelate, attempted to defend him, but were inconsistent in their statements when called on by the majority to explain themselves. The line taken by the orthodox was this[o]:—"Let us hold fast the deposit of sound doctrine; let us take the baptismal faith, received in our several Churches, as the true apostolic teaching, the true sense of Scripture, the true test of all new statements." When it appeared by this process that the very Godhead of the Redeemer was the faith which had converted the world, the bishops, willing to express the sense of Scripture in Scriptural terms, should such be found sufficient for the present emergency, proposed to declare Him to be "*of* God;" whereupon the Eusebians professed to accept this, inasmuch as "all things were of God." The orthodox went on: "He is the *Power* of God; the *Image* of the Father, and *in* Him always." The Eusebians, whispering and beckoning to each other[p], agreed to this also in their own sense: "The term, Power of God, is applied to angels, to men, even to locusts; man is God's image; in Him we have our being, and nothing shall part us from His love." Again the orthodox insisted, "He is very God." "Well," said the equivocating Eusebians, "He has been made so." The bishops then[q] quoted such texts as "the Brightness of His glory, the express Image of His substance;" "In Thy Light shall we see Light;" "I and My Father are one;" and at length, finding their opponents ready to explain away all Scriptural terms, concentrated the sense of Scripture into the phrases, "from God's essence," and "of one essence with the Father." They saw, in short, that the Homoousion was indispensable. When Eusebius of Cæsarea pre-

---

[o] See Keble's Sermons, pp. 386—414, shewing that the Nicene Creed, as expressing the true sense of the various baptismal confessions, does really give us the substance of that original "catechesis" which the apostles gave to their first converts, and which the baptismal formulas enshrined.

[p] See Ath. de Decr. Nic. s. 20, and Ad Afros, 5. [q] Ath. ad Afros, 6.

sented a creed which did not contain it, the formula was set aside as defective; when a paper by Eusebius of Nicomedia was read, which spoke of the Homoousion as plainly untenable, the "blasphemous" document was torn in pieces[r]. The term had, indeed, been given up by the Council of Antioch in the preceding century, because the heresiarch Paul of Samosata had interpreted it sophistically in a material sense[s]; but, in truth, it involved no error and no absurdity, and had been used by great writers in the sense now given to it, as expressing neither more nor less than the *essential Godhead of the Son*, or, in other words, *His very and true Sonship*.

The Council, having resolved to adopt this term, commissioned Hosius and others to frame a creed, and the result was as follows[t]:—

"We believe in one God, the Father Almighty, Maker of all things visible and invisible. And in one Lord Jesus Christ, the Son of God, begotten of the Father, Only-begotten, that is, *of the essence of the Father:* God of God, and Light of Light, very God of very God, Begotten, not made; *of one essence*[u] *with the Father;* by whom all things were made, both in heaven and in earth. Who for us men and for our salvation came down, and was incarnate, and was made Man; suffered, and rose the third day; ascended into the heavens; shall come to judge the quick and the dead. And in the Holy Ghost.

"But those who say, *Once He was not;* and, *Before He was begotten, He was not*[x]; and, *He came into existence out of*

---

[r] This is the likeliest account. Compare S. Ambr. de Fid. iii. 15; Eustathius in Theod. i. 7. [s] S. Ath. de Syn. s. 45. [t] Soc. i. 8.

[u] I venture so to render *homoousion*, because *ousia* is properly 'essence,' and *hypostasis*, in the anathemas, ought to be rendered 'substance:' see Newman's note in S. Ath. Treatises, i. 66.

[x] The Arians regarded the generation, not as an eternal *fact* in the Divine essence, but as an *event* which once occurred; before which event God had no Son. Origen had long before expressed the Catholic doctrine, ὁ Σωτὴρ ἀεὶ γεννᾶται. Ap. Routh, Rell. Sac. iv. 354. S. Athanasius says that the Arians, by their ἦν ποτε ὅτε οὐκ ἦν, rob God of His Word, and say that the Light was once without Radiance, Or. c. Ar. i. 14.

nothing; or, who say that *the Son of God is of another substance, or essence, or is created, or mutable, or changeable,* are anathematized by the Catholic and Apostolic Church."

Seventeen Arianizing bishops objected to sign the Creed. Eusebius of Cæsarea was among them; but after some consideration he gave way, on grounds which cannot be called satisfactory as regards his personal faith[y]. The phrases anathematized, he remarked, "were not in Scripture, and had caused confusion;" that was all, it appeared, that he had to say against them. Others also yielded under menace of civil penalties—for the Emperor was resolved to enforce unity; until at last only five were left, Eusebius of Nicomedia, Maris of Chalcedon, Theognis of Nicæa, Secundus, and Theonas. Maris then signed; Eusebius and Theognis[z] followed; Secundus and Theonas stood firm, and were condemned with Arius, and with two of his friends, Pistus and Euzoius. Illyria was their place of exile.

The case of the Meletians was very gently handled. "In strictness," as the bishops said, "Meletius deserved no favour;" but he was admitted to communion, and allowed to retain the title without the powers of a bishop. His clergy, after the canonical defects in their ordination were supplied, were to rank after the clergy of Alexander.

A strong feeling[a] against Judaic tendencies was exhibited in the settlement of the Paschal question. All Catholics were to keep Easter on the Sunday after the full moon following the 21st of March[b]. It was then that Constantine

---

y Soc. i. 8.

z Philostorgius, the Arian, tells us that they privately inserted an iota, so as to make Homoiousion, 'like in essence:' that Secundus afterwards said, "Eusebius, you signed to avoid exile; I am confident in God that you will be exiled within the year,"—which came to pass. This, however, looks like a story invented for the honour of a thorough-going Arian.

a Soc. i. 9.

b It seems to have been arranged that every year the bishop of Alexandria was to ascertain the right day by means of Egyptian science, and announce it to the bishop of Rome, and also to his own Church of Egypt; hence came S. Athanasius' "Festal Epistles."

asked the Novatian bishop whether he would accept the Creed and this Paschal rule. "O Emperor," replied Acesius[c], "the Council has determined nothing new. The Paschal rule and the definition of faith agree with what I have learned by tradition from the apostles." "Why, then, do you not join the Church?" Acesius answered by narrating the origin of his sect in the Decian persecution. "I must hold to the rule which denies absolution to those who sin mortally after baptism. God may forgive them, but not through the priesthood." Constantine replied, "Well, then, set up a ladder for yourself, and ascend to heaven alone."

The Niceue Council passed twenty canons, which will be found in the Appendix. A synodal letter[d] was addressed to the Egyptian and Libyan Churches, recounting what had been done, praising the venerable Alexander, and concluding thus:—"Pray for us all, that what we have thought good to determine may remain inviolate, through God Almighty, and through our Lord Jesus Christ, with the Holy Spirit, to whom be glory for evermore. Amen."

Ultimately this prayer was granted to the full: and it was the Council's loyalty to inherited faith which secured for it a position of such unrivalled majesty. When its sessions were closed on the 25th of August, individual Catholics might still have much to suffer, but the cause of the Catholic faith was won.

---

[c] Soc. i. 10.

[d] Soc. i. 9.

CHAPTER II.

From the Council of Nicæa to the Council of Sardica.

"Great Athanasius! beaten by wild breath
Of calumny, of exile, and of wrong,
Thou wert familiar grown with frowning death,
Looking him in the face all thy life long,
Till thou and he were friends, and thou wert strong."
WILLIAMS, *Cathedral.*

IT is a beautiful tradition of the Armenian Church, that on the return of Aristaces, Gregory the Illuminator received the Nicene Creed with this doxology; "Yea, we glorify Him who was before all ages, adoring the Holy Trinity, and the one only Divinity of the Father, of the Son, and of the Holy Ghost, now and ever, through ages of ages. Amen[a]."

These words might well express the joy with which the great majority of Churches would welcome the august confession when announced to them by their chief pastors. It was to them, doubtless, the full utterance of that simple faith in Christ's true Godhead, which had ever lain close to the heart of the Church — had filled her rude old hymns with majesty[b], had burst in broken words from the lips of her martyrs, had kindled her abhorrence of "a God-denying apostasy[c]," and prompted the heathen sarcasms against her worship of a crucified God. They were deeply conscious of the truth which has been admirably brought out by a living writer, that this Nicene faith "alone is an *entire* belief, of which all the elements are in unison; in which is proportion and symmetry, grandeur and simplicity; which fully realizes whatever is true in human nature, and whatever we may conceive of as proper to the Divine nature[d]." In several

[a] This is still sung after the Creed in the Armenian Liturgy. See Neale's Introd. i. 418; Chr. Rememb. xxxiii. 357.

[b] Euseb. iii. 33; v. 28.

[c] The name given to the doctrine of Theodotus, that Christ was a mere man, about A.D. 194.

[d] Restoration of Belief, p. 322.

parts of Palestine, which had been under the influence of Arianizers, the feeling would be different; and in Gaul, where the Church knew nothing of heresy, the necessity of the Creed was not felt, and for years it was very little known[e].

For the present, the Catholics appeared secure of Constantine. What he cared for, indeed, was not truth, but peace; and as he had failed to establish peace by indifferentism, he was ready now to establish it by persecution: and he made it a capital crime to retain any writing of Arius, whom he denominated a second Porphyry[f]. Some time after the Council, Eusebius of Nicomedia and Theognis were condemned and banished for communicating with heretics[g], and Constantine wrote a violent letter to the Nicomedians, denouncing Eusebius for civil as well as spiritual offences[h].

Alexander, on returning home, carried out the decree of the Council respecting Meletius, but required of him a catalogue of the bishops and clergy of his party. Meletius personally gave in a list[i], including himself with twenty-eight other bishops, and a small number of priests and deacons: and in this paper we find the title of "Archbishop." But shortly after, when on his deathbed, the incorrigible schismatic named as his successor[j] one of the bishops in his catalogue; and this John, who was surnamed Arcaph, became a second head of the schism which thus broke forth anew. The aged Alexander died within five months after the Council. It is said that in his last moments he called for Athanasius[k]. The great deacon was absent. Another Athanasius answered, "Here am I." The Archbishop, instead of addressing him, exclaimed again, "Athanasius!"

---

e S. Hil. de Syn. 63. 91.

f Soc. i. 9. Porphyry, or Malchus, was born in 233; heard Plotinus at Rome; wrote against Christianity in Sicily; and died at Rome in 304.

g See Vales. in Soz. i. 21.

h Theod. i. 20.

i S. Ath. Apol. c. Ari. 71.

j Soz. ii. 21.

k Soz. ii. 17, quoting Apollinaris.

adding at last, "You think you have escaped—but you will not escape." The words were taken for a prophecy.

This year 326 is celebrated for the proceedings of Constantine's pious mother Helena at Jerusalem. She was nearly eighty years old, and had been fifteen years a Christian, when she journeyed to the land which all Christian instincts have called holy. Guided by the local tradition to the place of Christ's burial, she ordered the mound of earth which either Hadrian [l], or some other enemy of Christianity, had raised over the sepulchral cave, to be cleared away; demolishing the temple of Venus which stood on its summit. The obstructions being removed, the "monument of the resurrection [m]" came to light. This is substantially all that Eusebius tells us. But S. Cyril of Jerusalem, writing in 347, implies [n], and in a letter to Constantius, if that be genuine, asserts, that the cross on which salvation was wrought was found at the same time with the sepulchre. S. Jerome, in 386, tells us that it was kissed by pilgrims [o]: S. Chrysostom, about 394, says that the cross had been buried, and was discovered lying between two other crosses [p]: S. Ambrose, in 395, says that Helena, finding three crosses, "adored not the wood, but the King that had hung upon it [q]." These two latter fathers tell us, that the holy cross was distinguished from the others by its title; later writers say, by its miraculous effects [r]. The silence of Eusebius is

---

[l] Hadrian is named by S. Jerome, Ep. 58. Euseb. V. C. iii. 26, says "certain godless men."

[m] Eus. V. C. iii. 28. He ascribes the work to Constantine: probably because it had his full approval.

[n] Catech. iv. 10, x. 19, xiii. 4, speaking of the wood of the cross as existing, and as having been distributed piecemeal.

[o] Ep. 46. See also Ep. 108.

[p] Hom. 85 in Joh.

[q] Orat. in ob. Theod. 43—48. He also says, as do Socrates, Sozomen, Theodoret, that two nails were found.

[r] Sulp. Sev. ii. 61, says that a corpse was revived by the touch of one of the crosses. Ruff. i. 7, Soc. i. 17, and Soz. ii. 1, that Macarius, the bishop, after prayer, caused each of the crosses to be applied to a dying woman, who was healed by the touch of the third. So Theod. i. 18, but he does not say, like the others, that the title was found lying by itself. Ruffinus

a difficulty in the way of believing that any cross whatever was found; but if, in spite of it, the evidence for the appearance of three crosses is strong enough to command our assent, it appears that we must choose between a profane imposture on the part of the local Church, and a real discovery providentially ordained.

That S. Helena's proceedings gave a great impulse to Christian belief and devotion at Jerusalem and in Palestine, cannot be reasonably doubted. The sepulchral cave was separated from the rock out of which it had been hewn[s]: it was then cased with rich marbles, and adorned with columns, so as to assume the form of a small chapel. Constantine wrote to Macarius, expressing his delight at the wonderful discovery of the sepulchre, and urging him to provide, at the public cost, all that might be needful for its due decoration[t]: and he began to erect the great Basilica of the Resurrection to the east of the sacred spot. Another church, called that of the Holy Cross, was raised in honour of the Crucifixion; and two others arose at Bethlehem and on the Mount of Olives, in honour of the Nativity and the Ascension. Under the great terebinth at Mamre, unchristian rites had been carried on; Constantine reproved the bishops for not denouncing this idolatry, and ordered the altar and the images to be superseded by a Christian church, for the worship of the Saviour who had appeared there with two angels[u]. He was active in cleansing the chief scenes of heathenish impurity[x]. Temples were razed to the ground, and their images of gold and silver melted down, by visitors armed with the imperial warrant: and while many of the pagans were thus led to embrace Christianity, others, Eusebius tells us, were at least convinced of the nothingness of idols. Churches rose by the Emperor's munificence; at Rome the

says that at the application of the third cross the woman opened her eyes and rose up.

[s] I need not refer to Williams's Holy City, ii. 76—80, &c.

[t] Eus. V. C. iii. 39; Soc. i. 9. [u] Eus. V. C. iii. 52. [x] Ibid. 54, 58.

Lateran Basilica,—converted, as the law courts easily were, into a place of Christian worship,—became the Cathedral of Our Saviour, with an adjacent baptistery dedicated to S. John. On the Vatican, where Christian piety revered the grave of the first apostle, a temple of Apollo fell, and the church of S. Peter arose[y]. Like the Lateran church, it was richly endowed with estates, both in Italy and in distant countries; and part of its Eastern property supplied the incense for its ritual. Other churches of Rome called Constantine their founder; one of these was dedicated to S. Paul, two to S. Laurence and S. Agnes; and one, which had been the Sessorian Basilica, was designated from its possession of a fragment of the Cross.

Some months after the death of S. Alexander, Athanasius was elected by a majority of the provincial bishops, in accordance with the desires of the people[z], who prayed aloud to Christ for his election, and persevered for days and nights in entreating the bishops to give them "a genuine bishop" in Athanasius, "the good, the pious, the Christian, the *ascetic*," expressing by the last term his known habits of self-denial and devotion.

The new Archbishop was about thirty years of age: the smallness of his stature seems to have been compensated by the majestic beauty of his countenance[a]. His consecration took place in the end of 326; and shortly afterwards we see him seated in council with his brethren, to hear tidings of great interest from the South. It was indeed a wonderful story of unexpected providences. The narrator was

---

y This old S. Peter's had a splendid pillared nave, with two aisles on either side. The apsidal sanctuary, screened by six columns, contained the altar surmounted by a cross.

z This is attested by the Egyptian bishops in a synodal letter, ap. Ath. Apol. c. Ar. s. 6. The Arians had a story, of which Philostorgius gives a detailed version, that Athanasius was clandestinely and irregularly elected by a small minority, — Philostorgius says, in a church at night. See Philost. ii. 16, and note in Ath. Hist. Tracts, p. 22.

a If Julian says that he was "a puny little fellow," Greg. Naz. says that he had the face of an angel. Or. xxi. 9.

Frumentius, who had been Regent of Ethiopia or Abyssinia. He told how he and his brother, Tyrians by birth, had been shipwrecked in the Red Sea, when journeying to Ethiopia with their kinsman Meropius; how the natives, then at war with Rome, put to death all on board save the two boys, whom they gave as slaves to their king; how the latter had made Frumentius his secretary, and Edesius his cupbearer; how on his death they had been made the guardians of his sons, and had administered the kingdom; how, in particular, Frumentius himself had encouraged the Christian foreigners in Abyssinia to meet for worship in a house of prayer, and had converted some of the natives. Their regency coming to an end, they had faithfully rendered up their trust, and obtained from the queen a reluctant permission to leave the country. Edesius had gone home to Tyre, Frumentius had come to tell the Archbishop of Alexandria that there were Christians in Ethiopia who greatly needed a bishop. "And who," asked Athanasius, "can be fitter than yourself for such a work?" Forthwith he consecrated Frumentius as bishop of Axum; and the newly-formed community grew up into a national Church, which honoured Frumentius as its father and apostle [b].

Three national conversions belong to the earlier portion of the fourth century, and each supplies an instance of God's "choosing the weak things of the world." In Armenia, A.D. 302, the instrument was Gregory, fourteen years a captive. In Ethiopia, it was a shipwrecked youth, raised to a position like that of Joseph: in the third case, which may here be mentioned, as occurring in the reign of Constantine, we are reminded of the maiden who waited on Naaman's wife. In Georgia, then called Iberia, we find a captive Christian woman, called Nina [c], producing a considerable impression on the natives by her devotional earnestness. She seemed to pray without ceasing, and persevered in fast,

[b] Soc. i. 19; Soz. ii. 24; Theod. i. 23.

[c] This name is not given in Soc. i. 20; Soz. ii. 7; Theod. i. 24.

and vigil, and thanksgiving, until they asked her why she followed such a rule. "This is the way of serving the Son of God!" Presently a child, grievously sick, was brought to the foreigner, in the hope that she might know of some cure. "I know this only, that Christ healed the sick;" and with these words she laid the infant on her poor bed, and prayed for its recovery. The prayer was heard. The queen herself was similarly cured of an illness; the stranger, in reply to offers of royal bounty, said that the work had been none of hers. "It is the Son of God, the Creator of all things, who has done this; if you would reward me, believe in Him!" The king,—so runs the story,—losing his way in a mist, called on the God of the foreign woman, and not in vain. His conversion carried with it his people's; Christian clergy were obtained by an application to Constantine; but Nina was reverenced as the *Illuminator* of Georgia.

Early in Athanasius' episcopate, he visited the Thebaid, which had been a stronghold of Meletians; and Pachomius, the superior of a great monastic society in the Isle of Tabenne, came forth to bid him welcome, but hid himself when he heard that Athanasius wished to ordain him presbyter.

Towards the close of 328, the Arian troubles began anew. According to one account, the arch-heretic himself and his companion Euzoius were the first of the exiles to regain Constantine's favour [d], by giving in an evasive declaration of their faith; and their recall was followed by that of Eusebius and Theognis, who presented to the principal bishops what Socrates calls a palinode, to the effect that at Nicæa they had signed the Creed without the anathemas, but that now they were ready to approve all that the Council had done. There are difficulties, however, connected with this account [e]; and another view is that they were by some means able to dupe the Emperor, and that they, in conjunction with an Arian priest, who gained a hold over

[d] Soc. i. 14; Soz. ii. 16.

[e] See Tillemont, vi. 810.

Constantine[f] by means of his sister Constantia, effected in 330 the recall of Arius and Euzoius. There is no doubt, at any rate, as to the formula which Arius gave in[g]. It marks an epoch in the history of Arianism. It avoids the out-spoken audacity which horrified the Nicene Council, and deals in phrases which might succeed in lulling suspicion, although plainly defective in a Catholic point of view. The Son of God is called "God the Word, begotten[h] of the Father before all ages:" and thus the Nicene faith was wronged by an inadequate statement, rather than by a positive denial. With equal astuteness, they contrived to combine a profession of respect for Catholic doctrine with an allusion to Constantine's former language about the undesirableness of unpractical speculations. The Emperor, at this time, was mainly interested in an event which of itself deserves a place in Church history, the dedication of his New Rome, or Constantinople, which took place on May 11, 330. It was to be a purely Christian city[i], dedicated to the God of Martyrs; and besides several other churches, three were devoted to the glory of Christ as the Wisdom, the Peace, the Strength of His people. Eusebius of Cæsarea was desired to furnish fifty copies of Holy Scripture for public reading in the churches of New Rome[k]. A cross of gold and gems was the chief ornament of the chief room of the palace, and the fountains in the forum were hallowed by the image of the Good Shepherd. It is mournful to think of the corruptions and wickednesses which almost immediately began to haunt the palace and city thus elaborately Christianized.

The Eusebian party—the chiefs of which were the Nicomedian Eusebius,—his namesake of Cæsarea,—Acacius, the pupil of the latter,—George, whom Alexander had deposed

---

[f] Soc. i. 25.

[g] Soc. i. 26; Soz. ii. 27.

[h] Γεγεννημένον, not γεγενημένον, is the reading adopted by Bingham, iii. 357, and Newman, Ath. Treat. i. 104.

[i] S. Aug. Serm. 145. c. 9.

[k] Eus. V. C. iv. 36.

from the priesthood, and who had originated the sophism about all things being from God[l],—Leontius, a smooth, cautious man who had studied in Lucian's school,—Eudoxius, afterwards notorious for his profanity,—and Valens, bishop of Mursa in Pannonia, who became equally conspicuous by shameless want of truth,—had one definite object before them, to undo the work of Nicæa. Their tactics, as now arranged, consisted of three points; 1. to maintain their hold over the Emperor; 2. to get rid of the leading Catholic bishops; 3. to propagate Arianism in forms less offensive to general Christian feeling than those which the Council had anathematized.

Their first victim was Eustathius. The patriarchal see of Antioch had suffered much in the third century by the scandal of an heretical occupant. It was now to pass through sufferings from the effect of which it never quite recovered. Eustathius was an eloquent and blameless prelate[m], who persevered in zealous defence of the truth, and would never receive the Arians into communion[n]. He had particularly expressed his distrust of the orthodoxy of Eusebius of Cæsarea and two other bishops[o]. Eusebius retorted by the charge of Sabellianism, which Arians always brought against the Catholics, and which, as we have seen, S. Alexander had to repel. On this ground, and also on the evidence of a perjured woman, suborned to blacken his spotless character[p], a synod of Arians deposed Eustathius, and Constantine banished him, as "a pollution[q]," to Illyria, in 331. Paulinus of Tyre was transferred to Antioch; and on his death shortly afterwards, Eulalius was made bishop. He soon followed Paulinus. The vacant see was offered to Eusebius of Cæsarea. He declined on canonical grounds to

---

[l] S. Ath. de Syn. s. 17.

[m] Theodoret, i. 8, cites Eustathius as explaining Proverbs viii. 22, in doing which he told how the "blasphemous writing" of Eusebius (i. e. the Nicom.) had been torn in pieces.

[n] S. Ath. Hist. Ari. s. 4.

[o] Soz. ii. 19.

[p] Theod. i. 21.

[q] Eus. V. C. iii. 60.

be translated; Constantine highly applauded his refusal[r], and thereupon, although a party in the city called for the restoration of Eustathius, the Arians placed Euphronius in the see.

Other faithful bishops were persecuted by the faction, as Eutropius of Hadrianople[s], who had warned all who visited him against the "impieties" of the Nicomedian Eusebius. The latter now wrote to Athanasius, urging him to admit Arius into communion. The answer was stern and explicit: "No communion with inventors of heresy who have been anathematized by an Œcumenical Council." Eusebius then made Constantine write in the tone of a despot to a rebellious subject: "Now that you know my will, admit into the Church all who wish to enter: if you disobey, I will send some one to expel you[t]." Athanasius wrote to impress upon Constantine, that heresy which lifted itself up against Christ had no portion in the Church Catholic. He invited the famous hermit Antony to Alexandria, who by the sanctity of his presence and his fervent exhortations did much for the Catholic cause. He told the people that, as Christian men, they could not communicate with those who made the Lord of all a creature. Meantime Eusebius, who had already secured the aid of the Meletians, devised with them a series of charges in order to ruin Athanasius.

1. The first was, that he had forced the Egyptians to contribute linen vestments for the Church services. Two of his priests, Apis and Macarion, were then actually at the court, and disproved this charge before Constantine, who condemned the accusers, and sent for Athanasius.

2. The Archbishop, on arriving, found himself accused of having sent a purse of gold to the rebel Philumenus.

---

[r] Eus. V. C. iii. 59, seq. [s] S. Ath. l. c. s. 5.

[t] S. Ath. Apol. c. Ar. s. 59. If Socrates were a mere copyist of S. Athanasius, he would hardly have said that the Emperor wrote thus from a desire of public peace and welfare; i. 27: see Chr. Remem. xl. 142.

Constantine went into this charge also, in a suburb of Nicomedia, and afterwards drove the slanderers from his presence.

3. A more elaborate calumny followed. Ischyras, as we have seen, had been pronounced by the Council of Alexandria to be a mere layman. He had, however, persisted in officiating at a little hamlet called Sacontarurum, in the Mareotis. Athanasius had heard of this when performing a visitation of his diocese, and had sent a friend, named Macarius, prohibiting Ischyras from such a procedure. The man's own relatives enforced this order, and he thereupon went over to the Meletians. A story was concocted, that while Ischyras was in church offering the oblations, Macarius came in, threw down the Holy Table, and broke the chalice [u], proceeding also to burn the church books. Constantine enquired into this case also, and the following facts were ascertained. 1. There was no church [x] in the hamlet: Ischyras had been wont to officiate in a cottage belonging to an orphan boy named Ision. 2. He was not a real priest. 3. Macarius' visit was not on a Sunday; therefore, by the Alexandrian usage, there could have been no celebration [y]. 4. There was no chalice at the place [z]. 5. Ischyras was ill in bed on the day in question [a]. 6. Ischyras had come to Athanasius after the dissemination of the story, and with tears protested that he had been compelled by violence to affirm it; this declaration he repeated in writing, and gave it to "the blessed Pope Athanasius" in the presence of thirteen clergy. "I take," he wrote, "God as my witness, that no chalice was broken, and no table overthrown, —that nothing of that which has been stated did in fact occur [b]."

These enquiries, and their results, excited the Emperor's indignation against "cabals," which he expressed in a letter

---

[u] It was sometimes pretended that Athanasius himself had broken the chalice.

[x] Ath. Apol. 85, 76.

[y] Apol. 11.

[z] Ibid.

[a] Apol. 46, 83.

[b] Ibid. 64.

to the Alexandrian Catholics; affirming also in the strongest terms his belief that Athanasius, to whom he entrusted the letter, was a sound teacher and a man of God[c].

4. The next invention was yet worse. "Athanasius has murdered Arsenius, a Meletian bishop. He has cut off the dead man's hand, and kept it for magical purposes. We can produce the hand itself." A prince of the imperial family was ordered to enquire into this matter, and sent the Archbishop notice to prepare for a trial at Antioch. At first Athanasius treated the affair with scorn. But as Constantine was disturbed by it, a deacon was sent to enquire throughout Egypt whether Arsenius were dead or alive. The messenger fell in with four persons who confessed that he was concealed at a monastery in the Thebaid. Having given this information, they lost no time in warning Pinnes, the superior of the monastery, who instantly sent Arsenius down the Nile into Lower Egypt. The deacon, reaching the monastery, found that he was too late; but took Pinnes into custody, and had him examined by the military officer in command at Alexandria. Then the truth came out; and Pinnes wrote a letter[d]—one of the most curious papers connected with the history—to John Arcaph, the head of the Meletians, who was then at Antioch. After narrating what had happened, he added: "I tell you this, my father, lest you should determine to accuse Athanasius, for I said that he was alive and had been concealed with us, and all this is become known in Egypt, and cannot any longer be kept . . . secret." In short, the conspiracy had broken down. But where was Arsenius? He had been warned to avoid Tyre. Yet, impelled, as Socrates thinks, by a special providence[e], he went to Tyre, where some friends of Athanasius, having heard that he was concealed in a house of one of the citizens, at length discovered and denounced him. The man would not confess his identity, until Paul, bishop of Tyre, made further denial useless; and then he wrote a humble

[c] Apol. 61, 62. [d] Ath. Apol. 67; Soz. ii. 23. [e] Soc. i. 29.

letter to his "dearly beloved Pope," protesting with many pious expressions that he would renounce all schism and render all due obedience to Athanasius. "I, Arsenius, pray that you may be strong in the Lord many years[f]!" John Arcaph also professed his submission to the Church: and his conduct was approved by Constantine, who also wrote a letter to Athanasius[g], which he desired him publicly to read, and in which he announced that any further plots of the Meletians should be punished by civil and not by spiritual law.

After an ineffectual attempt on the part of the Eusebians to ruin Athanasius by a council at Cæsarea, which he absolutely refused to attend[h], he was warned in the next year, 335, to attend a council at Tyre, with the threat that if he refused he should be carried thither by force. The occasion of this meeting was that a number of bishops were to attend the dedication of the church of the Resurrection at Jerusalem; Constantine desired them first to assemble at Tyre[i]. Forty-nine Egyptian bishops attended their chief[k], and protested against several of the judges as avowedly hostile to him. One of the Egyptians, Potamon, who had lost an eye in the persecution, exclaimed aloud to Eusebius of Cæsarea[l], "Do *you* sit there as a judge of the innocent Athanasius? When I was maimed in our Lord's cause, how came you to escape without betraying it?" Eusebius rose up in high wrath: "What must you be when at home in Egypt, if you can tyrannize over us here?" Paphnutius took hold of Maximus of Jerusalem, led him aside, and told him how the case really stood. Supported by the Count Dionysius, who presided over the assembly, the Arians were masters of the position; and one reckless charge followed fast upon another[m]. "Athanasius procured his election by the bad faith of a few bishops. He has scourged and im-

---

[f] Ath. Apol. 69. [g] Ibid. 68. [h] Theod. i. 28. [i] Soc. i. 28.

[k] They were introduced into the council "by a jailor, not by the deacons." Ath. Apol. 8.

[l] Epiph. Hær. 68. [m] Soz. ii. 25.

prisoned those who would not communicate with him. He has thrown down an episcopal chair. He has deposed Callinicus, bishop of Pelusium, and subjected him to military custody and tortures. He has given the see of Pelusium to a deposed presbyter. He has caused a presbyter, Ischyrion, to be imprisoned on a false charge of throwing stones at the Emperor's statues [n]." A woman was brought in to denounce him, and put to shame her employers by mistaking one of his priests for the man whom she came to accuse. Last of all, they produced "the hand of Arsenius" in a wooden box, and excited by the display of it a cry of horror. Athanasius calmly asked, "Did any of you know Arsenius?" "We knew him well." A person, muffled from head to foot, was led in: Athanasius uncovered his face, and the living Arsenius was at once recognised. But if he had not been murdered, had he been mutilated? Athanasius lifted up the long cloak first from one hand, then from the other. "Where was the third hand cut off? has God given any man more hands than two [o]?" Incredible as it may appear, the Eusebians were able to meet even this home-thrust by a cry in which the spectators joined [p],—"Away with the sorcerer!" and the authorities had to rescue Athanasius by hurrying him on board a ship. The faction resolved to revive the tale of the broken chalice, and appointed six bitter enemies of Athanasius to enquire in the Mareotis as to the facts of the case. He complained to the Count Dionysius, who exhorted the Council, in vain, to choose the commissioners fairly [q]. Remonstrances were made both to him and to the Council, by the Egyptian bishops and by the venerable Bishop Alexander of Thessalonica. It was in vain. The commissioners left the priest Macarius, the person accused by Ischyras, a prisoner at Tyre, and took Ischyras with them, "a companion in lodging, board, and wine-cup [r]." Their

---

[n] These statues were so treated in the first excitement of the controversy. [o] Soc. i. 29; Theod. i. 30. [p] Soz. ii. 25.

[q] See Ath. Apol. 77—81. This Count, however, menaced Athanasius with violence. Apol. 9. [r] Ibid. 14.

proceedings were a prolonged outrage. Philagrius, the præfect of Egypt, an apostate to heathenism, was in attendance to intimidate the witnesses[s]. In his presence, and in that of Jews and Pagans, an enquiry was carried on respecting the Eucharistic Sacrifice[t]; an enquiry from which presbyters were excluded, while catechumens, who could not have been present at the celebration, gave evidence inconsistent with the original tale. "We were present when Macarius rushed in," said some[u]; others, in still more direct contradiction, testified that the man who was alleged to be standing at the altar as a celebrant was, in point of fact, lying sick in a small cell. The report based upon this evidence was of course altogether worthless. As such, it was denounced by the Catholic clergy in addresses to Philagrius, to the Council, and to the six "conspirators[x]," with a solemn appeal to the future judgment of God. Contemptuous of these protests, Valens and Ursacius, with their four associates, completed their task by letting loose the Pagan soldiers on the helpless Catholics of Alexandria, and then proceeded to Tyre with their report.

Athanasius had not waited for their return, but, with a parting protest, set sail for Constantinople. The Council condemned him on the ground of the accusations; and Arsenius signed the sentence against his alleged murderer. The Meletians were recognised as Churchmen; and the wretched Ischyras, who had only seven adherents in Secontarurum, was actually made a bishop with that hamlet for a see[y]. The bishops then proceeded to Jerusalem, where the dedication of the great church took place on Saturday, Sept. 13, 335. Two hundred prelates attended[z]. The Basilica was in the freshness of its splendour; its roof blazed with gold, its walls were rich with coloured marble. Through

[s] Ath. Apol. 83.
[t] Julius of Rome, ibid. 31.
[u] Ibid. 83.
[x] Ibid. 73—76.
[y] A church was afterwards built for him by the Emperor's order. Ibid. 85.
[z] Maximus, then bishop of Jerusalem, was for a time beguiled by the Eusebians.

the nave with its double aisles the bishops passed into the apse, where twelve pillars, adorned with silver bowls, represented the apostles, and a gorgeous curtain hung around the altar [a]. Beyond, a cloistered court encompassed the chapel of the Holy Sepulchre. Such was the scene amid which the judgment of Nicæa was set aside, by the solemn recognition of Arius and his adherents as men who had suffered from factious jealousy, and whose creed of 330 had proved them orthodox [b].

Meantime, Athanasius had reached Constantinople. In the middle of the road, while Constantine was riding into the city [c], he was suddenly startled by encountering the Archbishop, who by sheer persistency obtained a hearing, and begged that his judges might be summoned to court. This request seemed reasonable, and Constantine wrote a peremptory letter, blaming the bishops of the Couucil of Tyre for their tumultuous violence, and commanding them iustantly to justify their sentence before him. They received this letter at Jerusalem, and Eusebian craft was equal to the emergency. They dropped the recent charges, and resolved to take the Emperor on his weak side. While, then, the majority of the bishops fled in terror to their houses, the six most active foes of Athanasius—the two Eusebii, Theognis, Patrophilus, Valens, and Ursacius—went up to court, and accused Athanasius of threatening to prevent the sailing of the corn-ships from Alexandria to Constantinople [d]. Athanasius protested that the thing was impossible for one like himself, a poor man in a private station: Eusebius of Nicomedia affirmed with an oath, that Athanasius was a rich man who could do anything; and Constantine [e], who in the hands of Eusebius was a child, turned a

---

[a] Eus. V. C. iii. 36; Theod. i. 31. [b] Ath. de Syn. 21.

[c] Ath. Apol. 86.

[d] Ibid. 9, 87. Sozomen, ii. 28, says that they revived the matter of Ischyras: Athanasius says that they durst not do so.

[e] Socrates, ii. 1, says that he had at first followed Ruffinus, who placed this persecution of S. Athanasius after the death of Constantine; but that

deaf ear to Athanasius and banished him to Treves, where the government took ample care for his maintenance, and Maximin the bishop received him with all honour, in February, 336.

The Eusebians then attacked a bishop advanced in years, who had sat in the Nicene Council, Marcellus of Ancyra. In discussion with the Arian "sophist[f]," Asterius, who had placed the Son, as a "Power of God," in the same category with the locusts, Marcellus had given some occasion for the charge of Sabellianizing. He seemed to make the Son a Power temporarily put forth by God; and although it was afterwards said that the offensive language had been used only "in the way of argument[g]," there may have been an unsoundness in his views at this period, which after-years tended to develope. The Eusebians denounced him as a heretic, and also as having shewn disrespect to the Emperor by refusing to attend the recent dedication at Jerusalem. He was deposed by a synod at Constantinople, and appealed for sympathy to the Roman Church, wherein Marcus succeeded Sylvester in January, 336. But while the Eusebians were thus far successful, Arius could make no way at Alexandria. He had been sent back thither after the condemnation of Athanasius, but Constantine found that it was expedient to recall a man whom the Alexandrians would not receive. Arius was accordingly summoned to attend the Emperor, who asked[h] if he held the orthodox faith. He answered, with a solemn oath, that he did hold it; and gave in another formula couched in Scriptural terms, professing that he did not hold the opinions imputed to him by Alexander. "If you really do hold the faith," said Constantine, "you do well to swear; but if otherwise, God will judge you for your oath." The Eusebians now resolved to bring

---

after perusing S. Athanasius's own works, he re-wrote the earlier portion of his History. But he compared S. Athanasius with a hostile writer, Sabinus; ii. 15, 17.

[f] Ath. de Syn. 18.

[g] Ath. Apol. 47.

[h] Ath. ad Ep. Æg. 18, to Serap. 2.

him publicly to Communion; and the Emperor gave them his full support.

Alexander bishop of Constantinople was now more than ninety years old. Eusebius of Nicomedia menaced him with instant deposition if he refused to receive Arius. "I cannot receive the heresiarch," was his reply. "We have brought him hither," said Eusebius, "against your will, and to-morrow, against your will, he shall come to Communion." Alexander heard this announcement on a Saturday. Attended by the Alexandrian priest Macarius[i], he betook himself to the altar of the Church of Peace, and fell on his face in an agony of prayer. "If Arius is brought to Communion to-morrow, let me Thy servant depart. But if Thou wilt spare Thy Church,—and I know Thou wilt,—then, lest heresy enter the church with him, *take away Arius*[k]."

It was late in the afternoon of Saturday. In the flush of his assured triumph over the Nicene Council, Arius walked through the city with his supporters, attracting the gaze of all the people. His high spirits were remarked, and doubtless appeared natural in one who was enjoying the discomfiture of his enemies. He seemed that day to have the world at his feet. Suddenly, as the throng approached the great porphyry pillar in the centre of the forum, he stopped short and withdrew from his friends. An internal disorder, accompanied by violent hæmorrhage, carried him in a few moments to the judgment which he had invoked. The corpse was hastily buried; men thought with horror of the Field of Blood, and the next day's Eucharist was undisturbed by heresy. The mode of his death involves no miracle; but if Arnold[l] could ascribe the ruin of the French army in Russia to "the direct and manifest interposition of God," it is no wonder that the Catholics saw in the event which

[i] See his account of it as reported by Athanasius, ad Serap. 3, who is quoted by Theodoret, i. 14. Socrates, i. 37, makes Alexander spend days and nights in prayer.

[k] Ἆρον Ἄρειον.

[l] Lect. Mod. Hist. p. 178.

"took away Arius" the terrible presence of an avenging visitation.

Alexander died in this same year 336, and Paul, whom he had recommended [m] as apt to teach, though young in years, was elected in preference to his elderly rival Macedonius, but speedily banished to Pontus by Constantine, who continued to rely on the Eusebians, and withstood the Alexandrian petitions for the recall of Athanasius. In vain did Antony write letter after letter, warning the Emperor against Meletian falsehood. Constantine replied [n] by commanding the clergy and the virgins to forbear their urgency in behalf of a turbulent man condemned by a synod. He could not believe,—so he wrote to Antony,—that so grave an assembly had been governed by personal feelings. Athanasius must assuredly be what they had pronounced him, the arrogant foe of unity and order. At the same time, Constantine was decidedly adverse to factious movements on the opposite side; and doubtless took credit for impartial justice, when he sent John Arcaph into exile, and disregarded all entreaty for his recall.

Constantine had deferred baptism,—by his own account, until he could receive it in the Jordan. Such delay had been already censured by the Council of Neocæsarea; and the Emperor's motive was, apparently, a worldly unreadiness to commit himself altogether to Christian responsibilities, masked by a lofty estimate of the effects of baptism whenever administered. Feeling that his end was near, he received the imposition of hands which made him a catechumen, the regular instructions given during the catechumenate, and then baptism from the hands of the Bishop of Nicomedia. "Now," said he, "I know I am really blessed! No one can know, as I do, the preciousness of what I have received." He died in the white robes of a neophyte, aged sixty-four, on the Whitsunday of 337. His second son, Constantius, in a partition of the empire with his brothers

[m] Soc. ii. 6.

[n] Soz. ii. 31.

Constantine and Constans, secured the dominion of the East.

Constantius was only twenty at his accession. His character was singularly repulsive. In the weakness which made him a tool of household favourites, in the despotic arrogance[o] which took the place of moral dignity, in the suspiciousness which hardened his heart and defiled his palace with kindred blood, the worst features of his father's character appear exaggerated, and unrelieved by any virtue except the avoidance of sensual sin. He fell under the influence of that priest who had swayed Constantine in favour of Arius; and Eusebius, his principal chamberlain, with whom, according to a pagan sarcasm, "he had a good deal of influence[p]," was readily converted to the laxer creed. These circumstances fixed the religious policy of his reign, and prepared a series of bitter trials for the Church.

For the present, however, there was a breathing-time. The exiled bishops were recalled in 338: Constantine II., writing on June 17 from Treves, informed the Alexandrians that he was but fulfilling his father's intentions in sending back their bishop[q]. After two interviews with Constantius, in Mœsia and in Cappadocia[r], he was welcomed at Alexandria with a burst of exulting joy. Even Arsenius begged to be restored to his communion. About the same time, Paul returned to Constantinople; but Eusebius of Nicomedia had set his heart on the see of the imperial city, and was translated thither after an Arian synod had condemned Paul. This year is also marked by the death of Eusebius the historian; Acacius, his disciple, became bishop of Cæsarea.

The party again set to work against Athanasius. "How

---

[o] We are told by Ammonius that he affected an imperturbable demeanour, which became, in fact, a dull, image-like stiffness. He used to stoop his diminutive person when passing through a high doorway. Amm. xvi. 10.

[p] Amm. xviii. 4.

[q] Ath. Apol. 87; Soc. ii. 3; Soz. iii. 2.

[r] Ath. Apol. to Const. 5.

had he dared to resume his see without the sanction of a council?" Another calumny was concocted, that he had sold the allowance of corn granted to the Alexandrian Church, and appropriated the proceeds to his own use: and Pistus, an excommunicated Arian, consecrated by the notorious Secundus, was set up as a rival bishop at Alexandria. Three clergy were sent to accuse Athanasius, on old and new charges, before Julius bishop of Rome, who had succeeded Marcus in February, 337. But a great Council of the Catholic prelates of Egypt put forth a solemn encyclic, testifying to the innocence of their chief, and denouncing the murderous animosity of his accusers [s]. He, on his part, sent messengers to Rome, who exposed the character of Pistus. Julius had been asked to recognise Pistus; he now asked the Eusebian deputies what they had to say in reply to those of Athanasius. They could say nothing; one of them, indeed, decamped by night, in spite of illness, rather than face the Alexandrian presbyters [t]; and Athanasius sent other delegates to establish his innocence before the emperors. Some sixty-three other bishops, he tells us, bore written testimony in his favour.

The Eusebians requested Julius to propose a council, and he did so, allowing Athanasius to select the place. But the Eusebians, unwilling to attend a council in the West, took occasion to hold one at the dedication of the newly-finished cathedral of Antioch, called from its splendour the Golden Church. Here, in the early part of 341, ninety-seven bishops attended, and after the solemnities of dedication, confirmed the decision of Tyre against Athanasius, by enacting, and giving retrospective force to, a canon which cut off from all hope of restoration, or even of a hearing, the bishop

---

[s] Ath. Apol. 3—19. One passage in this letter, referring to the imputation of sacrilegious violence, is remarkable: "Our sanctuaries are now, as they have always been, pure, and honoured only with the Blood of Christ and His pious worship." Athanasius says, Apol. 1, that this council consisted of nearly one hundred bishops: the Sardican fathers say eighty.

[t] Julius in Ath. Apol. 24.

or priest who should officiate after a canonical deposition. They passed twenty-four other canons[u], and three creeds. The first creed is very short, beginning, "We who are bishops have not been followers of Arius, but have examined his doctrine." It stops short of full truth, but asserts no falsehood. The second, ascribed to Lucian, and known especially as *the* Creed of the Dedication, gave very high titles to the Son, as the immutable and unvarying Image of the Father's Godhead, begotten before all times and ages. In fact, it all but called Him "Homoousion." The third was read before the assembly by Theophronius, bishop of Tyana; it was a vague, short statement, anathematizing Paul of Samosata, Sabellius, and Marcellus of Ancyra[x]. The Eusebians hoped by these formulas to persuade the Western Church of their substantial orthodoxy.

As Eusebius of Edessa, who afterwards became bishop of Emesa, declined to accept the Alexandrian bishopric, it was given by the Council to a Cappadocian called Gregory[y]. In the Lent of this year he was installed by Philagrius. Hideous outrages by pagan soldiers attended his intrusion. The Holy Table was used as an altar of pagan sacrifice; the church candles were lighted before pagan idols; the stores of the church were ransacked; Catholics, male and female, were insulted and beaten on Good-Friday and Easter-day, to the delight of the unbelievers; the old confessor Potamon was so cruelly scourged that careful nursing could only for a time restore him; and Athanasius' aunt was denied a grave. The last extremity of sacrilege was

---

[u] The first canon enforces the Nicene rule about Easter. The second is against those who will come to church for Lessons, but not for prayer and Communion. The fifth is against private conventicles. The tenth implies that chorepiscopi were real bishops. The nineteenth provides for election of a bishop by the episcopal synod. The twenty-first is against episcopal translations. The twenty-third forbids a bishop to name his successor.

[x] See the creeds of Antioch in Ath. de Syn. 22—24.

[y] Socrates, ii. 11, confounds this intrusion of Gregory with outrages of the year 356. He also supposes that Gregory was expelled by the Arians soon after his intrusion, and that George immediately succeeded him. ii. 14.

reached by casting the Holy Eucharist on the ground. This league between Pagans and Arians is significant; the former saw that in the hands of the latter Christianity lost the main part of what they abhorred.

Athanasius, acting on the command to flee from persecution [z], withdrew to Rome, after writing an encyclic to all other bishops on the infamies of Gregory's intrusion. Julius then [a] sent Elpidius and Philoxenus, two of his priests, to the Eusebians at Antioch, inviting them to a council for December, 341. Meantime Athanasius, having laid his case before the Roman Church, spent his time in frequenting its services, and took the opportunity of making the Western mind acquainted with Egyptian monasticism [b]. The Eusebians, instead of coming to the Council, detained the Roman envoys. When they did not appear, Julius and fifty bishops met in the church of the presbyter Vito, recognized Athanasius as innocent, and confirmed towards him "their fellowship and loving hospitality [c]." In January, 342, the Eusebians sent back the two envoys, the sorrowful bearers of a defiant letter, on which, at the autumnal synod of that year, Julius commented with just severity in a letter to the Eusebians [d]. He rebuked the arrogance of their tone, their subterfuges in regard to the proposed council, their detention of his envoys; dwelt on the gross unfairness of the Mareotic enquiry, the patience and nobleness of Athanasius, the orthodox statement made by Marcellus in presence of the Italian Council. He maintained that, as bishop of Rome, he had a right to be informed in case of suspicion attaching to the

---

[z] Matt. x. 23.

[a] This is according to Newman's arrangement of the order of events, (Pref. to Hist. Tr. of S. Ath.)

[b] He had with him a monk, Ammonius, who paid no attention to any building in Rome save S. Peter's. Soc. iv. 23. The letters of the Alexandrians cheered S. Athanasius. He wrote his Paschal letters as usual.

[c] Ath. Apol. 20.

[d] Ibid. 20—35. At this time, Julius says, Athanasius had been a year and a half in Rome, waiting for his accusers.

bishop of Alexandria [e]. He insisted that the churches should be relieved from outrages which provoked the mockery of the heathen, and would assuredly be visited in the day of account.

Among the bishops who had received the sympathy of the Westerns was Paul of Constantinople. In this year 342, the death of Eusebius was followed by a popular restoration of Paul. Constantius sent Hermogenes to expel him [f]. In a tumult Hermogenes was slain, and Paul was sent in chains to a castle on the Tigris; but his rival Macedonius, being implicated in the tumult, was not put in possession of the see for which the Eusebians had consecrated him.

Sapor the Long-lived, king of Persia, had been addressed by Constantine the Great in favour of the Persian Christians, whose bishop, John, had been present at Nicæa. He was now at war with Constantius, and was soon persuaded by the Magi that his Christian subjects, who would not adore the sun, were Romans at heart. He began in 343 [g] a terrific persecution. Symeon Bar-saboë, bishop of Seleucia and Ctesiphon, was cast into prison. His friend Usthazad, an old eunuch, who had apostatized through terror, saluted him as he was led away [h]. The Bishop averted his face, and Usthazad, changing his white robes for black, bewailed himself as a wretch who had denied his God, and whom his friend had disowned. His stedfastness returned, and he was beheaded on Maundy Thursday. On Good-Friday a

---

[e] He probably referred to the case of S. Dionysius of Alexandria, whose alleged errors were laid before Dionysius of Rome. Julius's own words do not bear out the statement of Soc. ii. 8, Soz. iii. 10, that according to Church law enactments made without the consent of the bishop of Rome were invalid; and see Soc. ii. 15, 17.

[f] Soc. ii. 13.

[g] That is, the 7th of Constantius, (Jerome's Chron.) Others date it in 340; others in 330. But Constantine's letter in Eus. V. C. iv. 8—13, and Eusebius's own remarks upon it, clearly imply that the persecution had not begun.

[h] See the account in Soz. ii. 9. He referred these events to the reign of Constantine.

hundred persons died for Christ, Symeon being last of all[i]. His successor, Sadoth, was also martyred. His sister Pherbutha, or Tarbula, with another Christian maiden, was denounced as having caused the Queen's illness. They were sawn asunder, and the Queen, in order to her recovery, was made to pass between their mangled remains. Although after a time the martyrdom of his favourite servant Azad induced Sapor, in his grief, to confine the persecution to the clergy, we are assured that 16,000 names of sufferers were preserved in the records of the Persian Church, and that many others perished whose names could not be known.

About this time Constantius sent an embassy to the Homerites in Arabia Felix, with a view of promoting Arian Christianity. The envoy was Theophilus, called the Indian, who had been sent as a hostage to the court of Constantine, and been ordained successively deacon and bishop. He induced the Arabian prince to build three churches; and after dedicating them, he passed over to his native island near the mouth of the Indus, and thence to parts of Hindostan, (where he taught the Christians to stand up when the Gospel was read,) and after visiting the church of Axum, returned to Constantinople.

The death of Constantine II. in 340 had left the young Constans lord of all the West. He sided with the Catholics; but the Eusebians resolved, if possible, to win him over. They accordingly sent to him, a few months after the Dedication Council, what is called the fourth of its Creeds[k]; which, like the others, was evasive and unsatisfactory. When he came to Milan in the end of 345, some bishops requested him to press his brother for a council; he did so, and then sent for Athanasius, who had been staying three

---

[i] One of his companions, Ananias, an aged man, trembled as he was made ready for death. Pusices, the master of the king's artizans, said to him, "Close thine eyes for a little space, and presently thou shalt see the light of Christ." He too was seized, confessed his faith, and suffered a cruel martyrdom.

[k] Ath. de Syn. 25.

years at Rome, and whom he received with great kindness, though they never met in a private interview[l]. Just at this time, Eudoxius and two other Eusebians came to Milan with a long formula called the *Macrostich*, which expressed the better kind of what has been termed Semi-Arianism, and blended together some Catholic aud some Arian ideas. It was very emphatic agaiust Marcellus, and his pupil Photinus[m] of Sirmium, as holding that the Word was an energy which dwelt for a time in Christ, and that on its departure His office would come to an end. This creed was intended, like its predecessor, to calm the Western mistrust. But Westerns, though unversed in theological distinctions, were ready to ask, "Where is the Homoousion?" So long as the Nicene Creed was not adopted, the most elaborate Eastern formulas profited nothing. Such was the decision of the first Council of Milan in 345.

Constans determined on another Council, which might be of sufficient dignity to restore peace to the whole Church. He told Athanasius that he had written to Constantius, who agreed to the proposal.

The place selected was Sardica, a Mœsian town on the confines of both empires, already memorable for the horrible death-scene of Galerius. About 170 bishops assembled, the Western being a small majority, in the year 347. The Easterns, about seventy-six in number, at first expected that the assembly would be like those with which they were most familiar[n], in which counts and soldiers were ready to overawe their opponents. Finding that, on the contrary, those opponents would confront and accuse them[o], they

---

[l] Ath. Apol. Const. 4. He had previously desired Athanasius to send him a volume containing the Scriptures.

[m] It called this man *Scotinus*. Such playing on words was common to the gravest ancient writers. Eus. v. 23, vi. 41, vii. 10, 31.

[n] Ep. of C. of Sard. in Ath. Apol. 48. See Ath. Hist. Ari. 15.

[o] In their subsequent Epistle they express great indignation at the fact that Athanasius and Marcellus were sitting along with the other bishops, and allowed to "join them in celebrating the Divine Mysteries." Hil. Fragm. 3. 14.

resolved, while on their journey, to take no real part in the proceedings, but simply to announce their arrival. Accordingly, on coming to Sardica they shut themselves up in the palace where they were lodged; and it was with difficulty that two of their body found their way into the church, and denounced their brethren's schemes before the Council, which was already sitting under the presidency of Hosius.

The Eusebians were repeatedly invited to attend. They sent word that they would not come until their opponents were deprived of seats in the Council. "This is a General Council," was the reply: "the whole case is to be laid before its judgment. Come and present your own statements; Athanasius and his friends are ready to meet you, and the Council is ready to hear both sides[p]." There were also present in the Council men who could shew the wounds they had suffered from Eusebian violence; and one prelate exhibited the chains which they had made him wear. There were Alexandrians who had been driven into exile; and a letter from the Alexandrian Church drew forth tears. Deputies were present from various Churches, who could tell of forged letters, of menaces from the judgment-seat, of ruffians with swords and clubs enlisted in the cause of heresy[q]. Not choosing to face these witnesses, or to meet Athanasius on equal terms, the Eusebians, including five Western bishops, withdrew from Sardica on the pretext that Constantius had sent them news of a victory over the Persians. On receiving this message, the Council rebuked their "indecent and suspicious flight," in a letter which announced that unless they returned they would be held as guilty[r]. Instead of returning, they established themselves as a Council at Philippopolis, on the eastern side of the border, re-affirmed the former sentences against Athanasius, and uttered new ones against the bishops of Rome,

[p] Hosius, and Protogenes of Sardica, were urgent that they should attend. Soc. ii. 20. Hosius even offered to hear their charges privately. Ath. Hist. Ari. 44.

[q] Ath. Apol. 45.

[r] Ibid. 36; Hist. Ari. 16.

Cordova, Treves, and Sardica. They published an encyclic, denouncing Marcellus, Paul, and the "sacrilegious" chalice-breaker, the crafty plotter of Alexandria; and they sent it to "Donatus, bishop of Carthage," as to the other prelates in their communion. Lastly, they adopted a creed[s] made up of the fourth Antiochene and the Macrostich. In all their acts they usurped the title of the "holy Council of Sardica."

The true Council, meanwhile, proceeded to examine the cases before them. They found enough in the documents to account for the secession of the Eusebians. Having regard to a long list of outrages, and, above all, to the guilt of the Eusebians as promoters of "the accursed Arian heresy," the orthodox Council of the West, acknowledging Athanasius and his brethren[t] as innocent men and true bishops, pronounced the deposition and excommunication of eleven Eusebian bishops by name. "They who separate the Son, they who alienate the Word from the Father, ought themselves to be separated from the Catholic Church, and alien from the Christian name." The solemn judgment was summed up in the words, "Let them therefore be anathema."

A Council so loyal to the faith could promulgate no formulary in place of the Nicene Creed. The bishops passed twenty-one canons, the most celebrated of which have reference to the conspicuous trustworthiness of their absent Roman brother. Hosius proposed, as he did in regard to the canons generally, that a bishop whose cause had been lost in the synod of his province might signify his wish for a new trial. His judges should then, "in honour of S. Peter's memory," write to Julius, bishop of Rome. Thereupon the bishop of Rome should commit the new trial to the bishops of the neighbouring province; and might also, if requested by the appellant, send presbyters of his

[s] Hil. de. Syn. 34; Fragm. 3.

[t] Socrates, ii. 20, names Paul of Constantinople; the Epistle of the Council in Athanasius does not.

own "to judge with the bishops." It is evident that these rules make nothing for the claim of a papal supremacy, but rather bear witness against it. It may well be that their object was a temporary one [u],—to strengthen the cause of orthodoxy by strengthening the hands of Julius. But supposing that all his successors were included in the scope of the canons, the powers described were far too small for spiritual sovereignty, and they proceeded avowedly from the Council's grant [x]. Another canon, the tenth of the series, forbade the elevation of a layman to the Episcopate until he had been tried in the offices of reader, deacon, and presbyter.

The Council wrote letters to the Emperors, to Julius, to the Church in Alexandria and in Mareotis, to the bishops of Egypt and Lybia, and to all Catholic prelates. They assured the suffering Catholics of their brotherly sympathy, dwelt on the exposure of Eusebian and Meletian calumnies, exhorted all the Alexandrians to shun "the accursed communion" of Gregory, who had never been a real bishop, and declared Marcellus innocent of having maintained that Christ's person "began to exist from S. Mary," or that His kingdom would ever have an end. Athanasius wrote personally to the faithful of Alexandria and of Mareotis [y].

The number of prelates who, either in the Council or afterwards, subscribed the decree in favour of Athanasius and against the Eusebian troublers of the Church, was 284 [z]. On this great occasion it might be truly said that the Western Churches, with many of the Eastern, stood firm on the Creed of Peter.

---

[u] See Dr. Pusey on Councils, p. 142. Yet, as Prof. Hussey remarks, (Rise of Papal Power, p. 9,) to name Julius would establish a precedent, so far as the canons were recognized.

[x] "If it seem good to your charity," or, "If it please you."

[y] Ath. Op. ii. 1047.

[z] British bishops are mentioned by Athanasius, Apol. 1, as approving the sentence; but their names are not given in his list, Apol. 50.

CHAPTER III.

From the Council of Sardica to the Retreat of S. Athanasius.

"Let us hold for certain that there is one truth which Christ has bequeathed to the world, and one Church, against which the gates of hell shall never prevail; that while error is multiform and self-destructive, this truth is essentially one."

MILL, *University Sermons.*

THE secession of the Eusebians to Philippopolis was the signal for a new persecution of the Catholics in the Eastern empire [a]. Philagrius was employed to behead at Hadrianople ten citizens who would not communicate with the seceders. This city had been determinedly orthodox. Its bishop, Eutropius, had been a confessor; Lucius, who succeeded him, had been put in bonds by the Eusebians, and was now again loaded with chains on the hands and neck, and sent to die in exile. Theodulus of Trajanople, who apparently left Sardica before the Council broke up, was put to death in his flight from Eusebian fury. Orders were sent to the authorities at Alexandria to behead Athanasius, or certain of his clergy, should they venture to return home. A reign of terror began; conveyed at the public expense, Arians passed to and fro, "seeking whom they might devour [b];" many fled at their approach into the deserts, while the dread of scourging, chains, or exile drove many to a hypocritical submission. The two bishops, Macarius and Asterius, who had withdrawn from the Eusebians at Sardica, were punished by exile in the wilds of Libya.

In the West, of course, the decrees of Sardica received the full sanction of Constans. In the latter part of 347 the second Council of Milan was held in order to carry them out. In this assembly Valens and Ursacius, finding it inconvenient to be under the ban of the West, presented a written condemnation of all who said that "once the Son

[a] Ath. Hist. Ari. 18, seq. Compare Ath. Apol. 45.

[b] Ath. Hist. Ari. 20.

was not, or that He was made out of what did not exist, or that He was not Son of God before all ages[c]." The Council also condemned Photinus of Sirmium, who carried out boldly the views which the Sardican Council had thought Marcellus clear of holding. It was of the last importance to show that the orthodox had no tenderness for a Sabellian denial of Christ's personal pre-existence. Marcellus, in fact, became gradually more and more committed to heresy, and Catholics found him to be beyond defence[d].

It was either in this year or in the following that Cyril, the chief presbyter of Jerusalem, delivered his famous Catechetical Lectures in the churches of the Holy Cross and of the Resurrection, in order to prepare candidates for baptism. More than once in this course he alluded with great severity to Marcellus[e], as one who dared to make the Word a mere effluence, and Christ's dominion temporary.

It had been resolved to apply to Constantius in behalf of the exiled bishops. Fortified by a letter from Constans, the Sardican delegates, Vincent of Capua and Euphrates of Cologne, reached Antioch about Easter, 348. The Arian patriarchs of Antioch had been five, Paulinus, Eulalius, Euphronius, Placillus, and Stephen who now held the sec. This man, who had presided at Philippopolis, undertook to ruin the character of the aged Euphrates by a flagitious conspiracy. Its detection ruined him with Constantius. He was deposed, and Leontius placed in the see. Some banished Alexandrian clergy were recalled; but Constantius would do no more, and Athanasius, invited by Constans

---

c It may be supposed that their paper given in at Milan said this, which was the language of their second paper, quoted by Athanasius and Hilary, (Fragm. 2,) for in the second they refer expressly to the first. Athanasius adds the word "God" before the "Son of God."

d Sulpicius says, ii. 64, that Arians craftily mixed up the case of Athanasius with that of Marcellus, but that at last Athanasius withdrew his communion from Marcellus as being undeniably heterodox, a sentence which Marcellus had the modesty not to question.

e See especially Cat. xv. 27, on "the new head of the dragon lately sprung up in Galatia," &c.

to Aquileia, continued to dwell there under his protection, and in friendship with Fortunatian, the metropolitan of that important see.

Gratus, the Catholic bishop of Carthage, had been present at Sardica, and had supplicated Constans in behalf of the African Church. Constans thereupon sent two envoys, Paul and Macarius, to Africa, charged with gifts from the Emperor "for all Christians." The real purpose of their mission was to win over the Donatists by an exhibition of impartial beneficence, and to use all their influence in behalf of Catholic unity. Donatus, who, as we have seen, had been recognized by the Eusebians of Philippopolis, and who, though his sect knew little of it, had Arian views, was a fitting head for the most arrogant of schisms, and a formidable adversary to any scheme of re-union. His pride, both spiritual and official, was as intense as the homage of his adherents was servile. He bore himself as if he were sovereign of Carthage. He treated his fellow-bishops as his servants; would not allow them to send him the *eulogiæ* of bread, which prelates sent to each other in token of unity; was wont to communicate in private, and then come carelessly into church. He even disliked to be addressed as "bishop[f]." His followers had an oath, "By the white head of Donatus," and used to sing to him, "Well done, good leader, noble leader!" Such was the man who, when Paul and Macarius explained their business to him, saying that they had brought the Emperor's bounty for the poor, broke forth in words altogether inconsistent with the early history of his party, "What has the Emperor to do with the Church?" adding other disloyal words about Constans. "We shall go," they replied, "throughout the provinces to distribute the Emperor's gifts." "I have written already to prevent the poor from receiving them." The wild fanaticism of the sect took fire. The rumour spread that force was to be em-

[f] See the account in Optatus, who adds that he spoke of his sect as "my party," when talking to visitors from other districts.

ployed for "the Union." It was even said that the old times of heathenish persecution, in which Donatism had been nurtured, were returning. "Paul and Macarius, those two beasts, will come and attend the Sacrifice; and when the Altar is prepared as usual, they will suddenly place an image upon it! Whoso tastes of the Sacrifice of the friends of Union is as one who eats things offered to idols[g]." It was vain to say, "No force is thought of—no one has been persecuting—not even a rod has been seen." The insane panic produced an insane fury. Another Donatus, of Bagai, called out the Circumcellions, giving them the title of "Champions of God." Their hideous violence had raged, apparently, in the days of Constantine against the Catholics' possession of the churches, and had, shortly before the period which we have reached, attained its complete organization in the old quarrel of poverty against property. Then, under Maxido and Fasir, the "leaders of the saints," they had declared war against masters and creditors[h], and spread around such terror that even their own bishops invoked the aid of the Count Taurinus, whose soldiers put many of them to the sword. Now they rushed to oppose "the Union" with the same wild craving for excitement which sometimes found vent in gross sensuality[i]: howling their war-cry of "Praises to God[k]," brandishing the huge clubs which they called *Israels*, they obliged the two envoys, in self defence, to apply to Count Silvester for a military escort. Some of these soldiers, being attacked by the fanatics, stirred up their comrades' fury. The officers could not keep them in; a battle was fought, the fanatics were worsted, Donatus of Bagai was slain, with another bishop named Musculus. These men, and two others who are said to have died in what was

---

[g] Optat. ii. [h] Compare S. Aug. Ep. 185. 15. [i] Aug. c. Ep. Parm. ii. 3.

[k] The Church's habit of perpetual thanksgiving had made "Deo Gratias" a Catholic watchword; and the Circumcellions, in altering the form to "Deo Laudes," adhered instinctively to the principle. Aug. in Ps. 132. For the clubs, Aug. in Ps. 10.

called "the Macarian persecution[l]," were revered as martyrs by the Donatists; others who were exiled for non-conformity, as was Donatus of Carthage himself, took the rank of good confessors. The Catholics afterwards used to say, "If Macarius in his zeal became cruel, we defend him not; but if you cry out against him, what shall we say of your Circumcellions[m]?"

His measures probably made few converts, but they produced much outward conformity, and a Council held at Carthage in 349 expressed by the mouth of Gratus the Church's thanks for "the end of the wicked schism." Fourteen canons were enacted. The bishops being asked whether persons who had been baptized in the faith of the Trinity should be baptized anew on joining the Church, answered unanimously, "God forbid!" True to the principles of Cæcilian, the Council forbade those who had rushed on their own death to be called martyrs. Insolent and contumacious clergy were to be censured; but clerical trials were to be very solemnly conducted, three bishops being required to judge an accused deacon. The clergy were to have no women dwelling with them, nor to undertake any secular business.

The pertinacity with which Constans insisted on the recall of the exiles placed Constantius in a difficulty, from which, in the beginning of 349, the death of Gregory relieved him. He permitted Paul to return to Constantinople, and wrote three letters to Athanasius, to the effect that he

---

[l] See Tillemont, vi. 116, on Isaac and Maximian.

[m] See Aug. Psal. c. Don., &c. Optatus says, iii. 5, that the Donatists boast of Donatus Bagaiensis and Musculus as martyrs: "quasi omnino in vindictam Dei nullus mereatur occidi!" These words Dean Milman calls "a damning passage," a proof that the Catholics "proudly vindicated *their barbarities.*" (Hist. Chr. ii. 374.) He adds, "Compare the whole chapter." The whole chapter shews that Optatus speaks of the slaughter of the two bishops as a thing done by soldiers *nobis nescientibus*. The Donatists said that they had been thrown, one from a rock, the other into a pit. S. Augustine thought it probable that they had flung themselves down, suicide being common with the men whom they had employed. Cf. c. litt. Pet. ii. 20; c. Cresc. iii. 49.

had all along sympathized with his distress, had expected him to return of his own accord, and now desired his immediate attendance. One of these letters was sent by a priest of Alexandria, another by a deacon; and six counts were employed to write encouraging letters, while Constans was informed that the Church of Alexandria would be kept vacant for its true bishop. On receiving the third letter at Aquileia, Athanasius went to Rome, to bid farewell to his friend Pope Julius, who addressed to the Alexandrians a cordial letter. Their piety—so he wrote—had awaited, and their prayers had procured, this happy end of their affliction. Their bishop and his brother,—the glorious confessor[n] who had despised death, and whose firmness in the cause of heavenly doctrine had given him a world-wide glory,—was coming home, pronounced innocent, not by Julius only, but by the whole Council. "Receive him, then, with all godly honour," ennobled the more by recent trials. "Your letters consoled him in exile[o], and now it delights me to imagine the universal joy which will hail his return, the multitudinous welcome, the glorious festivity. What a day will that be to you when my brother comes home,—what a day of perfect happiness, in which I too can join, since God has enabled me to enjoy his friendship! May God and His Son reward your noble confession with those better things to come which eye hath not seen nor ear heard." So parted the two patriarchs. Athanasius proceeded to Antioch, where Constantius received him graciously. But Athanasius did not lose the opportunity of remonstrating personally with a sovereign who had lent himself so grossly to false accusers. "Call my accusers, I beg of you; let them stand forth, and I will meet them." "No," said Constantius: "I take God to witness that I am absolutely resolved to listen to no more accusations; and

---

[n] Soc. ii. 23. These eulogistic phrases are omitted by Athanasius in his edition of the letter, Apol. 52.

[o] This is the substance of the passage.

the records of former charges shall be erased." He wrote to the præfect of Egypt, signifying that it was his pleasure to have all orders tending to the injury of the adherents of Athanasius obliterated from the order-books; and that Athanasius and his clergy were to enjoy all their former immunities. To the Egyptian bishops and clergy he wrote that "the most reverend Athanasius had not been deserted by the grace of God;" and added that to adhere to him would thenceforth be a guarantee of absolute security. He exhorted the Alexandrian laity to welcome their bishop, to make him their "pleader before God," and to be perfectly united and tranquil under his care.

Athanasius found the Catholics of Antioch divided. Some worshipped apart from Leontius, and were called "Eustathians;" others joined in the established worship, the rather that Leontius, who was a master of Arian craft, refrained from all display of his own opinions, insomuch that when some chanted "*and* to the Son," in the doxology, and others adopted the form of "*by* the Son," the cautious patriarch slurred over the critical words, and all that could be heard from him was "unto ages of ages." His policy was not to proclaim himself an Arian, but to Arianize the clergy, and thereby to work upon the Church. The two men who most stedfastly opposed him were not clergy. Flavian and Diodore, laymen who followed the monastic mode of life, gave themselves up to the work of strengthening their brethren against the insidious heresy, and called to their aid a mighty instrument[p]. By night, around the tombs of the martyrs, the stillness was broken by the psalmody of a double choir; and the antiphonal chant became the symbol and support of Catholicity. Athanasius joined the "Eustathians[q]," and contracted thereby a relation which had important results. When Constantius asked him to allow the Alexandrian Arians a single church, he asked in turn that a church might be given to the

[p] Theod. ii. 24.

[q] Soz. iii. 20.

Eustathians[r], but this the Emperor's advisers would not allow.

On his way to Jerusalem Athanasius was received at the Syrian Laodicea by Apollinaris, a young reader in that Church, highly educated, and previously, as it appears, inclined towards a kind of eclecticism, yet whose cordial kindness won the affection of his guest. At Jerusalem a council was held, which was a happy contrast to that of 335[s]. Then Arius had been treated as a much misrepresented theologian. Now all but two or three bishops embraced the communion of Athanasius, excused their former proceedings as involuntary, and congratulated the Egyptian Church on recovering its pastor. Maximus of Jerusalem had long before this repented of his share in Eusebian injustice, and was the first to sign the recognition of Athanasius, who at length could rejoice in the orthodoxy of Palestine.

Then came the holy welcome, the "glorious festivity," which Julius had anticipated for the Alexandrian Church. It was a day to make men forget the past, and to strengthen them for the future. Nor was it a mere holiday of unpractical enthusiasm. The faithful "encouraged one another in virtue." Many embraced a life of devotion, or remained single for Christ's sake; "every house seemed like a church," and the intense thankfulness found expression in works of charity[t]. Letters came flowing in from bishops who declared that their hearts had been with him while they were acting under Arian pressure. Some of these were doubtless insincere adhesions, as was the "palinode" of Valens and Ursacius. Unsought for as it was on the part of Athanasius, it was too plainly a following up of their sudden tergiversation in 347. Of their own freewill, as Hosius afterwards testified, they went to Rome, asked pardon for their offences before Julius and his clergy[u],

---

[r] Theod. ii. 12; cf. Soc. ii. 23. [s] Ath. Apol. 57. [t] Ath. Hist. Ari. 25.

[u] As Western bishops they speak with great reverence to Pope Julius, while they address Athanasius less ceremoniously. Ath. Apol. 58.

and, after receiving it, gave in a paper confessing the falsehood of their charges against Athanasius, expressing their desire to be at peace, and anathematizing Arianism "both now and for ever, as we set forth in our declaration at Milan." This letter, duly signed by both, was preserved in the Roman Church's archives [x], and a copy sent to Athanasius. They also signed letters of peace which three of his adherents presented to them; and they wrote from Aquileia with an easy confidence which real penitents would not have shewn, certifying their "lord and brother, well-beloved," that they were at peace with him, and in Catholic unity. Meantime a Council of bishops at Alexandria affirmed the decrees of the Sardican Council, and four hundred bishops throughout Christendom were now in communion with Athanasius.

Such was the triumph of 349. But on Feb. 15, 350, Athanasius lost his chief secular support. Constans, "whose kindnesses he could never forget [y]," was murdered in his flight from the rebel Magnentius. Constantius, after this tragedy, sent a gracious letter to assure Athanasius of his continued protection, concluding with, "May Providence preserve you, beloved Father, many years." On receiving this from two great officers, Athauasius proclaimed in church, "Let us pray for the good estate of the most religious Emperor Constantius Augustus," and the congregation at once responded, "O Christ, send Thy help to Constantius." The Emperor was obliged to withdraw from his campaign against Persia in order to meet the Western rebels, Magnentius and Vetranio, the latter of whom he won over. On his retiring, Sapor besieged, not for the first time, the Mesopotamian city of Nisibis, on the Roman

[x] Theod. ii. 16.

[y] The pagan Zosimus gives him an evil character. But to Athanasius, at any rate, Constans had been a steady friend; and he was a baptized Catholic, not, like Constantius, an unbaptized Arian. Athanasius testifies to his "Christian spirit." Hosius says that he never overawed a Church court, never persecuted an Arian.

frontier. James, its bishop, who had sat in the Nicene Council, encouraged the people to build up the wall which Sapor had destroyed by diverting the river, and is said also to have obtained by prayer a plague of insects which drove Sapor to retreat [z].

It was probably in this year that Maximus of Jerusalem died, and Cyril became archbishop. The story that Maximus was deposed and Cyril substituted by Acacius is inconsistent with probabilities, and with the testimony borne by the second General Council to the canonical regularity of his consecration. The other tale, which Jerome credited, that Cyril obtained the see from Acacius on condition of disclaiming the ordination which Maximus had bestowed, is utterly incredible, and probably sprang from the prejudices of a rigid party which mistrusted Cyril. His Lectures, though the "Homoousion" does not occur in them, clearly prove the soundness of his faith. Acacius did indeed take part in his election, but though excommunicated at Sardica, he was still *de facto* bishop.

Another event of this year was the final expulsion of Paul from Constantinople. Philip the prætorian præfect was appointed to decoy him to the Baths of Zeuxippus, and so convey him on board ship. He was then sent to die at Cucusus in Armenia. According to the report of Philagrius the apostate præfect of Egypt, Paul was shut up for six days without food, and ultimately strangled [a]. Macedonius now took full possession of the see, probably by means of that massacre of above 3,000 persons which is sometimes dated at an earlier period.

---

[z] Theod. ii. 30. The story makes Sapor see, on the wall of Nisibis, a radiant figure in imperial robes, which at first he took to be Constantius. It is added that S. Ephrem the Syrian, who had been baptized by James, begged him to ascend the wall and curse the Persians. His only curse was, "May they know by small insects the power of the God of Christians."

[a] Within a year Philip was disgraced, and perished miserably. Ath. Hist. Ari. 7. Socrates, ii. 16, makes Philip decoy Paul before the Council of Sardica.

Considerable excitement was produced at Antioch by the ordination of Aetius as deacon. This man, the most odious of the extreme Arians, had gone through many changes of life, as a vinedresser's slave, a goldsmith, a medical man, a guest and pupil of Arian bishops, and a professor of that disputatious logic in which the heresy was at first embodied. He was the first to affirm openly that the Son was *essentially unlike the Father*[b]. Leontius intended this diaconate to be a means of propagating Arianism. But Flavian and Diodore threatened formally to renounce his communion; and he thought it best to depose Aetius[c].

The Paschal season of 351 was marked at Jerusalem by a luminous appearance in the form of a cross, which appeared in the sky over the city. It produced a great impression; and Cyril is said to have sent an account of it to Constantius[d]. The latter was this year at Sirmium, where a council met to depose Photinus, who had been hitherto able to retain his church, in spite of former censures. The Council published a creed, which had no less than twenty-seven anathemas; some being meant to answer objections brought against Arian or Semi-Arian views,—some containing an explicit condemnation of the Photinian view, that "the Son from Mary is only a man," and that He only pre-existed in God's foreknowledge. Hilary, who had now been some two years bishop of Poitiers, and was the great support of Catholicity in Gaul, considered this creed as orthodox[e]; and the first Sirmian council is certainly the most respectable of the Eusebian assemblies, although it

---

[b] S. Basil, a. Eunom. i. 1. He was surnamed "the Godless." Ath. de Syn. 6; Soc. ii. 35.

[c] Theod. ii. 24; Ath. de Syn. 39.

[d] The genuineness of this letter, in which he mentions also the finding of the cross, has been doubted. One objection is that it contains the word "Consubstantial," which at that period Cyril would hardly have used.

[e] Hil. de Syn. 38 seq.; see the Creed also in Ath. de Syn. 27; Soc. ii. 30. Socrates is wrong about its framer. Some of its anathemas express the belief (which S. Augustine first abandoned) that in the Old Testament theophanies, God the Son Himself appeared.

cannot claim a higher place. The victory of Constantius' arms over Magnentius at Mursa, Sept. 8, 351, directly increased the influence of Valens, who persuaded the Emperor that he had received the news from an angel; and thereupon he and Ursacius proceed to recant their recantation[f]. "It was made through fear of Constans." It was, in fact, their own unforced proceeding, the evident result of a calculation of expediency.

S. Julius died April 12, 352, and his successor Liberius was soon required to attend to new charges against Athanasius, which also came before the Emperor, whom the Eusebians warned against the results of his leniency. We may take these accusations in order, with the replies[g].

1. "Athanasius influenced Constans against Constantius." He had never any wish to play such a part; and if he had wished it, he had had no opportunity.

2. "He has corresponded with Magnentius." This monstrous slander struck him mute with indignation. What should induce him to court the murderer of his friend? Could any letters from him to Magnentius be produced? Any which purported to be his, he could shew to be forgeries.

3. "He has used a church at Alexandria built by the Emperor, while yet undedicated; and this without permission." This was the great Cæsarean church. Athanasius had allowed the people to keep Easter in it, because their assembling in smaller churches had caused much inconvenience in Lent, and the people had entreated to have the use of the Cæsarean[h], in default of which, they said, they would meet in the open country.

4. "Why has he not obeyed an imperial summons to

---

[f] "To return like dogs to their vomit." S. Ath. Hist. Ari. 29.

[g] See Ath. Apol. ad Constant.

[h] He mentions other cases in which an undedicated church had been used. He had seen this done at Treves and Aquileia; and S. Alexander had so used the church of S. Theonas.

Italy?" Simply because the Emperor's letter professed to grant him *leave* to do so: which leave he had never asked —for the letter asking it was an Arian forgery.

Liberius and his council were satisfied with the statements of Egyptian bishops on behalf of Athanasius, and wrote to the Orientals accordingly[i]. But the latter had Constantius in their hands; and in the autumn of 353, the death of Magnentius by his own hand left Constantius master of the West, and at leisure to crush the man whom he had been forced to recall[k].

At this momentous crisis, what was the doctrinal aspect of the schools extraneous to Nicene orthodoxy[l]?

The Eusebians,—worldly, subtle, and unprincipled,—had for some time kept up a kind of credit by using phrases less plain-spoken than the original Arian language. The formulas connected with the Dedication Council had tended to make many persons forget the true and simple issue, Was the Son of God created, or was He not? August names were freely given to Him, and blinded many to the fact that a creature, however glorious, was, by comparison with the Creator, simply on a level with the humblest of His works. In a word, these formulas had "created a belief[m]" in minds more honest than the Eusebian leaders. Men were really holding and teaching that the Son was "Like in essence, *Homoiousion*, to the Father,"—born of His essence, before times and ages, not a creature like other creatures,—but still not essentially one with God. This was Semi-Arianism, held by many religious scholars, like Basil of Ancyra, mainly through the mistaken notion that the Homoousion implied Sabellianism. "The men were better than their creed[n]." Some of them were gradually coming to see its untenable-

---

[i] Some Arian forged a "letter of Liberius," telling the Orientals that he had excommunicated Athanasius for not coming to Rome.

[k] He was more arrogant and self-confident after 353 than before; he boasted that God was on the side of Arianism.

[l] See Newman's Arians, 169.

[m] Newman, Arians, 169.

[n] Ibid. 171.

ness. And the Eusebians, perplexed by the phenomenon which they had produced, and finding that on the West the Semi-Arian formulas had made no real impression, were disposed to adopt a more manageable principle, which Eusebius of Cæsarea had indicated, and his successor Acacius was ready to expound. Its simplicity might be more successful with the downright Westerns than the subtlety of the Homoiousion. For it threw aside all such terms as "essence," and professed to be content with the theological language of Scripture, and to know nothing beyond the "likeness" of the Son to the Father. "We have seen trouble enough arise from phrases of man's invention. Let us confess the Son to be 'altogether *Homoion*[o],' and we shall establish Christian peace." Many, doubtless, weary of the strife of tongues and the succession of formulas, listened eagerly to this teaching. Was it not sufficient to say what Scripture said? Was it not the only way to peace, and the path pointed out by religious humility? They who so reasoned saw not that when the terms of Scripture are the matter in debate, no unity can come from declining to say whether they mean one thing or another; that the true sense of Scripture *is* Scripture[p] in truth, and that a vague reply to "What think ye of Christ?" is a disloyalty fatal to hearty worship[q] and holy living.

Such was Homæan Arianism, taken up by the Eusebians when they cast off the Homoiousion, and found it necessary to provide some form of the doctrine less offensive than the *Anomoion* represented by Aetius. In that formula there was a simplicity of a certain kind; odious as it was to pious minds, it was a positive and consistent view, and its maintainers scorned all moderate Arianism as a mean thing void of courage or candour. Now, although the Eusebians

---

[o] Cyril of Jerusalem had used this formula, but in a Catholic sense. Cat. iv. 7, &c.

[p] See Waterland, on Eccl. Antiq. vii. 8.

[q] See Prof. Hussey's Acad. Serm., p. 251.

had no real and religious aversion to this extreme Arianism, yet they saw that its language was imprudently audacious; that if there were no alternative between Anomoion and Homoousion, the hope of an Arian Christendom was lost. Just now the Anomæan Aetius, as being the favourite of Gallus, the Emperor's cousin, was associated with the odium of his misgovernment at Antioch.

A new attempt to Arianize the West was now resolved upon. When Liberius sent Vincent of Capua and other deputies to Constantius, asking for a Council to be held at Aquileia, Constantius caused it to meet at Arles, where the bishop, Saturninus, was an Arian. The first thing insisted on by the Arians at the Council was, that the bishops should renounce the communion of Athanasius. The aged Vincent, who had represented Sylvester at Nicæa, unhappily conceded this point, in the vain hope that Valens and his friends would, on their side, condemn heresy. He appears to have thought it necessary to sacrifice one man, in order to secure the Creed. But Paulinus of Treves saw that in that one man the whole cause of the faith was represented. To abandon Athanasius was, in fact, to abandon Nicæa. He therefore withstood threats and persuasions, and bravely endured a painful exile.

Liberius wrote to Hosius,—"I had hoped much from Vincent. Yet he has not only gained nothing, but has himself been led into that dissimulation." There was then at Rome the chief Sardinian bishop, Lucifer of Caliaris, a man of extreme sturdiness and vehemence, who at his own request was sent with a priest and a deacon, Pancratius and Hilary, to ask the Emperor for another council which should proceed on the basis of the Nicene faith. Liberius recommended them to the good offices of one whom he knew to be "kindled with the Spirit of God," Eusebius bishop of Vercellæ, remarkable for having persuaded his clergy to adopt the monastic life.

Early in 355 the new Council met at Milan, where Dionysius the metropolitan, and his people, were earnestly Catholic.

About three hundred Western bishops were present; of Easterns, only a small number. A letter which spoke of Athanasius, not as heretical, but as sacrilegious, was sent to Eusebius to urge his attendance. He replied that he would come and do his duty. On reaching Milan he was excluded for ten days from the sittings in the cathedral. When he was admitted, the Arianizers desired him to sign a condemnation of Athanasius. With a diplomatic subtlety which marred his nobleness, Eusebius held out the Nicene Creed, saying, "First let us make sure of the faith. Some persons here are not sound. Sign *this*, and I will sign what you please." Dionysius extended his hand for the paper, but Valens snatched it forcibly away. "That has nothing to do with the present business." A great agitation followed; the people, who could hear in the nave what was passing in the sanctuary, began to murmur; and Valens, Ursacius, and their friends procured an adjournment to the palace, where Lucifer has already been temporarily detained[r].

There a new scene opened. The court influence was brought to bear on the bishops. Constantius had written, —as he pretended, in consequence of a dream,—a letter full of Arianism, which his agents attempted to pass off. While the bishops were in the presence-chamber, and Constantius, as was usual, behind a curtain which hung across the room, they were asked to adopt this paper. "The Emperor's heart is set on the peace of Christendom, and God has attested his doctrine by his success." Lucifer broke forth: "The letter is Arian—there is no true faith beside the Nicene—and all the Emperor's army would not prevent me from abhorring what is blasphemous." "Insolent men!" said Constantius; "is it their duty to school an emperor?" But in a short time he took up a different point; the rather

[r] The Bollandists (May 25) give many details, e.g. that Dionysius at another sitting did subscribe the Nicene Creed, and that the faithful obliged many Arians to leave the church, after which Dionysius celebrated the Eucharist: also, that Dionysius was left in the church when the others were summoned to the palace.

because his letter had been read in church, and indignantly rejected. He caused Valens and Ursacius to repeat the charges against Athanasius. Lucifer and Eusebius exclaimed against them as self-convicted liars: Constantius started up, saying, "It is I who am accusing Athanasius!" "You cannot," said they, "be a legitimate accuser; you do not know the facts, and the accused is not here. This is no case in which an emperor's word can suffice." The great majority, including Fortunatian of Aquileia, had no such spirit. The presence and tones of an Arian despot capable of any ferocity[s], and commanding their obedience in his own palace, fairly broke them down. They yielded, not only to sign the decree against Athanasius, but formally to profess communion with the Arians. Dionysius, in a moment of weakness, had yielded on the first point in order to secure from opponents a corresponding concession, which should leave the faith undisturbed[t]. It is said that he repented of having yielded at all, and that Eusebius "very ingeniously[u]" contrived to get his signature effaced. There is no doubt that Eusebius and Lucifer were stedfast; and when Constantius answered their appeal to canons by saying, "Let my will serve you for a canon, as it serves the Syrian bishops," they lifted up their hands, protested against his bringing "the Roman sovereignty into Church affairs," and bade him think of God and the day of judgment[x]. They were instantly condemned to exile; Dionysius, who now cast in his lot with them, shared their sentence; as did Pancratius and Hilary, the latter of whom, when cruelly beaten, found support in thinking of the scourging of Christ. A few others, apparently, stood aloof from the unhappy weakness which

[s] Ammianus says, xxi. 16, that he used sometimes to protract as far as nature would allow the agonies under which criminals expired.

[t] Sulp. Sev. ii. 66.

[u] Brev. Rom. Dec. 16. The story, as given in a sermon in the Appendix to S. Ambrose, has a doubtful aspect; and as it ascribes to Eusebius a petty stratagem, one would gladly think it false.

[x] Ath. Hist. Ari. 33, 34. Constantius, he says, drew his sword, and all but ordered them to execution.

betrayed this Council—called by Hilary of Poitiers "a synagogue of malignants [y]"—into formally undoing the work of Sardica.

Dionysius was banished into Cappadocia, from which country a man named Auxentius, ordained priest by Gregory at Alexandria, was sent for to fill the see of Milan. Maximus of Naples, though weak from illness, stood firm, and died in exile. A pious bishop, Rufinianus, was compelled by a young Arian prelate, Epictetus of Centumcellæ, to run before his chariot, until he died by bursting a blood-vessel. Lucifer was kept in a dark dungeon at Germanicia; Eusebius, at Scythopolis, the see of an old Arian, Patrophilus, was repeatedly dragged with brutal violence down a flight of stairs. Far and near, officers of the palace and of the tribunals went about threatening and denouncing all kinds of penalties to those who would not renounce Athanasius [z]. Arian clergy sharpened the zeal of the lay persecutors. To avoid scourging, chains, false charges, exile, many gave way, and some whom Constantius personally dealt with were pent up in their houses until they repeated the words, "Athanasius is out of our communion."

It is difficult to realize the misery of that time. Liberius, who sympathized heartily with the confessors [a], was now to take his turn. At first it was attempted to lure him over; Eusebius the chamberlain was sent to him with gifts [b]. "Comply with the Emperor, and accept these." Liberius replied that it could not be. He could not contravene the decrees of Rome and Sardica. If the Emperor really desired peace, let him allow a free Council to meet, *not* in his presence; to begin by securing the faith, and then take up the Athanasian question, without being swayed by the liars Valens and Ursacius. "Forgetting that he stood in a bishop's presence," Eusebius insulted Liberius with me-

---

[y] Hil. ad C. i. 8.

[z] Ath. Hist. Ari. 31.

[a] Sulpicius says that large sums were subscribed for the sufferers: and Athanasius observes that their being separated was a means of spreading the faith. Hist. Ari. 40.

[b] Ath. Hist. Ari. 35.

naces, and then presented the Emperor's gifts at S. Peter's: whereupon the Pope rebuked the keeper of the church for not casting out the unholy offering. Eusebius returned to exasperate Constantius. The Emperor determined to get rid of the man who had demanded an ecclesiastical council for the hearing of charges, and had declared war against Arianism. Rome was agitated by threats and promises employed to detach men from their bishop: the very gates and harbour were guarded against Catholics who might visit him; at length he was summoned to Milan, and personally beset by Constantius, Eusebius, and Epictetus [c]. Renounce Athanasius he would not. He insisted on justice and the Nicene Creed, representing in his own person Roman liberty and Catholic belief. He bade Constantius forbear fighting against Christ; he knew, he said, that he should be exiled, and when he was offered three days to bethink himself, answered confidently,—"Three days, or three months, will not change me; I have taken my leave of Rome!" He was banished to Berœa in Thrace, having spurned presents of money not only from Constantius, but from Eusebius, whom he scornfully bade to "go and become a Christian, before he presumed to bring alms as to a convict." Three "spies," as Athanasius calls them, "unworthy of the name of bishops," held an election at Rome, and consecrated Felix in the palace; the churches being barred against them by the laity.

The next step was to persecute the venerable Hosius. He was more than a hundred years old, and had been more than sixty years a bishop, besides his dignity as a confessor, and as eminent, to say the least, in the Nicene Council. At first he was sent for, and urged to renounce Athanasius and recognise the Arians. He replied by a severe rebuke, and returned to Spain, whither letters of

[c] Ath. Hist. Ari. 39. Theodoret, ii. 16, gives a long conversation; in which, among other things, the Ischyras affair is referred to. Eusebius says that Athanasius was proved a heretic at Nicæa! In Hist. Ari. 75, Athanasius calls Felix a man worthy of his Arian ordainers.

flattery and of menace followed him, to which he made a noble reply, preserved by Athanasius[d]. After a solemn reference to his own age and standing in the Church, he dwelt on the breaking down of the case against Athanasius, both at Sardica and elsewhere. Then he reminded the Emperor that he was a man, who must face death and judgment. "Intrude not into Church affairs, nor command us concerning them, but learn about them from us. Into your hands God gave the sovereignty; to us He entrusted the Church[e] .... This I write in my desire for your salvation. On the subject of your letter, I have made up my mind. I will not join the Arians: on the contrary, I anathematize their heresy. I will not sign the condemnation of Athanasius, whom we and the Roman Church, and the whole Synod, pronounced innocent." Constantius replied by summoning him to Sirmium.

The persecution drew from Hilary an earnest appeal to Constantius, which may have tended to produce the law published by the latter on Sept. 23, 355, that bishops should be tried by other bishops, not by the civil courts. On Nov. 6 the Emperor appointed his cousin Julian, the brother of Gallus, to command in Gaul with the authority of Cæsar.

For twenty-six months Athanasius had been left unmolested. At last, two secretaries of the Emperor, followed by Syrianus, duke of Egypt, came to Alexandria. "Now," said the Arians, "he will be obliged to leave the city." But Athanasius and his people referred Syrianus to Constantius' promises of protection: and he swore that until the Emperor's will were known he would take no step. The day before this (Jan. 17, 356) Antony had died, aged 105, calmly bequeathing "a garment and a sheepskin to the Bishop Athanasius," and entreating that his body might be

---

[d] Hist. Ari. 44.

[e] He quotes, "Render to Cæsar," &c., and says, "We have no authority to bear rule over the earth, nor have you, O Emperor, to burn incense."

buried in the monastic solitudes, and not taken into Egypt, "lest they store it up in their houses. Finally, my children, farewell: Antony is going away, and will be with you no more[f]." He died as he had lived, with a sweet bright face, the outward expression of that joyful faith[g] which had been his strength in temptation, and had prompted his own rule of monastic life: "Having begun, persevere manfully; the sufferings of this present time are not worthy to be compared with the coming glory; if we spend eighty or a hundred years in pious discipline, we shall not reign for a like number of years only, but for ages of ages[h]!" It was two years since he had told his brethren, with tears and groans, that he had seen a vision of mules kicking at "the Table of the Lord's house," and had heard a voice saying, "My Altar shall become an abomination[i]."

On Thursday night, the 8th of February, Athanasius was presiding over a vigil-service at S. Theonas' church, in preparation for a Communion on the morrow[k]. Syrianus suddenly beset the church at the head of more than five thousand armed men. Hilarius the notary, and Gorgonius, commander of the police, attended him. The Archbishop, seated on his throne within the sanctuary, calmly bade the deacon in attendance to read Psalm 136, and the people to take up the burden of each verse, *For His mercy endureth for ever*, and then all to leave the church as best they could.

---

[f] Ath. Vit. Ant. 91.

[g] Vit. Ant. 67. "His calmness of soul made his outward aspect tranquil . . . his face was never gloomy, for his mind was full of gladness. Ib. 42: "If the devils find us rejoicing in the Lord, and musing on the future bliss, and thinking how all things are in the Lord's hands . . . . they retire in confusion." He was wont to quote Rom. viii. 35, and other like texts.

[h] Vit. Ant. 16. Antony was remarkable for his love of Scripture (ib.), for his good sense (72), and for the practical simplicity of his exhortations, (20.)

[i] Vit. Ant. 82.

[k] Ath. Apol. de fugâ, 24; compare ad Const. 25, and the Protest of the Alexandrians in Ath. Hist. Ari. 81. There are some slight differences, easily reconciled, between the accounts. It may be observed that in churches where the celebration was not daily, it took place on Wednesday and Friday as well as Sunday.

The Psalm, it appears, had been finished when the doors were burst open; with a loud shout, a deadly discharge of arrows, and "swords flashing in the light of the lamps," the soldiers rushed in, killing some of the people and of the devout virgins, and trampling down others, as they pressed on to secure their main object by seizing Athanasius. He was urged, meanwhile, to escape, but answered, "Not until all the rest are safe:" then standing up, he called for prayer, and begged all preseut to leave the church. "Better my risk than your harm." He was, in fact, all but seized, and some of his friends were just in time to bear him away through the soldiers who thronged the entrance of the chancel;—safe, indeed, from their murderous grasp, but fainting from the agitation and the pressure. The invaders ran riot in the church, penetrating "where not even all Christians were allowed to enter;" the corpses of the slain were removed, but several bows, arrows, and swords remained to bear witness to the tragedy. The Catholics afterwards prevented them from being taken away, and drew up two formal protests: the second, which is extant, and is datod Feb. 12, was made after Syrianus had denied that any fatal event had accompanied the irruption, (even although the corpses were publicly exposed,) and had caused those who remonstrated to be beaten with clubs. The document, after narrating the outrage, declares that the Catholics are ready for martyrdom, but are resolved to ascertain[1] whether a persecution which has made several martyrs is sanctioned by the Emperor who had solemnly guaranteed to them the episcopate of Athanasius.

Constantius made prompt reply. He *had* willed what had been doue. Count Heraclius, the bearer of his letter, proclaimed that all the churches were to be given up to the Arians[m]. The Pagans were threatened that if they opposed

---

[1] Some of the subscribers were going to complain personally to the Emperor. They "adjure" all officers, and all whom it may concern, to let the facts be known.

[m] Ath. Hist. Ari. 54.

the mandate, they should lose their idols. The Catholics asked each other, "Has then Constantius turned heretic?" On a Wednesday, after service in the Cæsarean church, when only a few women were left who had just risen from prayer, Heraclius with a band of young Pagans and some Arians fell on them with stones and clubs, tearing off their veils, insulting them with brutal language, beating, kicking, stoning the helpless sufferers. They seized the curtains which enclosed the sanctuary, with the seats of the clergy, the episcopal throne, "and the Table, which was of wood;" some of these they burned outside the church[n]; they were only prevented by rules of heathen ritual from sacrificing a heifer in the church, and actually did sing hymns to their idols, rejoicing that "Constantius had turned Greek." Faustinus, the Receiver-general, was the ready instrument of the Arians, who roamed about the city, ransacking houses, terrifying peaceful inhabitants by their very presence[o], and searching even the tombs to discover the hiding-place of Athanasius.

Meanwhile, he whom they sought, and who had hidden himself in the wilderness "until the indignation should be overpast[p]," sent a letter to his children to comfort them with the thought that if the Arians held the churches, they held that Apostolic faith against which nothing should prevail[q]. They had need of such comfort; for the persecutors were venting their malignity on the virgins of the Church, whom they exposed to the fury of Arian women; they

---

[n] Athanasius says that one profligate youth seated himself on the throne, sang an infamous song, and then, attempting to drag the throne away, impaled himself.

[o] Men changed their residence from street to street in order to avoid their outrages. Many fled to the desert.

[p] Ath. Ap. Const. 34.

[q] Fragm. in Ath., tom. ii. 772, ed. 1857. The story that he lay hid in the house of a beautiful and pious virgin until the death of Constantius is an absurd fiction; but he may perhaps have been sheltered by her between his escape from the church and his retirement into the wilderness. Vit. S. Ath., p. cxxix.

caused Eutychius a sub-deacon to be scourged almost to death, and sent him to the worst of all the mines, which, however, he never reached, dying on his way of the wounds which had been allowed no tending. Four citizens of distinction were scourged for remonstrating, and the Arians compelled Syrianus to scourge them a second time. "We are beaten," said they, "for the truth's sake, for not communicating with heretics: beat us now as thou wilt,—God will judge thee for it." Men were persecuted for relieving the poor, for whose wants it became necessary to provide elsewhere than at the churches, the ordinary place of almsgiving. The very heathen cried shame on Arian cruelty. Monasteries were destroyed, and the inmates narrowly escaped from the fire. Clergy were banished, beaten, robbed of their stores of bread; a priest named Secundus was kicked to death, gasping out as he expired, "Let no one bring my cause before the judges—the Lord is my avenger." And now, as it would seem, a council of Arians at Antioch[r] put forth a creed to be signed by the bishops of Egypt, and sent George, a Cappadocian, to occupy the throne of Alexandria. Hereupon Athanasius wrote his "letter to the Egyptian and Lybian bishops," warning them against this new sample of Arian versatility, which professed to be a "Scriptural" confession. He had some thoughts of going at once to court, and began to draw up an "Apology" which he might then address to Constantius, and in which he meant to enter at length into the more recent charges brought against him; the tone of the paper shews that he wished to preserve as long as he could the feelings of a loyal subject[s], but the events of this year changed them into indignant abhorrence.

---

[r] See Soz. iv. 8; Tillem. vi. 394.

[s] Still, enough had happened to make eulogies on the Emperor's "piety and benignity" (Apol. Const. 32, &c.) appear unreal. Athanasius, however, never again employed such language. His writings in 357 and 358 call Constantius an Arian persecutor.

As Gregory had arrived in the Lent of 341, so George reached Alexandria in the Lent of 356. The Catholics regarded him with scorn as well as horror. He had cheated, they said, as a pork-contractor[t]; he had the reputation of being a Pagan at heart; and Athanasius declares that he was "a great proficient in plundering and killing, but wholly uninformed as to the Christian faith[u]." The man had, however, some intellectual tastes, for he collected a valuable library. As was usual with Arian intruders, he came surrounded by a military force; an imperial letter recommended him to the Alexandrians as "the most venerable George," and contrasted him with "the low-born impostor" who had become a self-condemned fugitive, and whose flatterers might "perhaps" find mercy if they forsook at last "the villain's" cause. George was attended by Aetius as his deacon, and by Eunomius, afterwards the chief of the Anomæans. His presence fanned the fire of persecution: "after Easter-week[x] virgins were imprisoned," men thrust by night out of their homes, widows and orphans plundered. Of the bishops[y] who refused to recognise the usurper, sixteen were banished, more than thirty were obliged to flee for their lives: on the whole, nearly ninety were in various ways under persecution. Many of these prelates were bowed down with age and illness; one died on his enforced journey; some were set to work in the quarries. A few were terrified into apostasy[z]; we hear of a bishop, Theodorus of Oxyrinchus, who consented tô be re-ordained by George[a]. The vacant sees were filled up by simony and other corrupt means: the new bishops were "men who prepared the way for Antichrist[b]." The Meletians, who took a purely secu-

[t] Ath. Hist. Ari. 75.

[u] Ath. ad ep. Æg. 7. Theodoret, ii. 14, says he was more savage than a wolf or a bear.

[x] Ath. Ap. de fugâ, 6. [y] Ath. Apol. Const. 27; De fugâ, 7.

[z] Some, says Athanasius, were "constrained to dissemble."

[a] His people broke off from his communion, and were for a time governed by their clergy: they afterwards procured a bishop in Heraclides.

[b] Ath. Hist. Ari. 79.

lar view of the Church, easily lent themselves to the dominant party; Apollonius, one of their bishops, joined Theodorus in persecuting the faithful [c].

During this Paschal time of 356, the Gallican Church was brought under the yoke of Arianism. Hilary of Poitiers had addressed a remonstrance [d] to Constantius after the Council of Milan, and had refused to communicate with Saturninus, Valens, and Ursacius. Julian was now ruling in Gaul. Before he went into Germany, which he did in June 356, a council was held at Beziers [e]; Hilary was not allowed to read a statement against Arianism; the "false apostles" carried matters their own way, and none stood by him but Rhodanius of Toulouse [f]. Both, by the influence of Saturninus, were banished to Phrygia, and it was when going into exile that Hilary first heard the Nicene Creed [g]: his brethren in Gaul and Britain had held, he says, the faith in its integrity without needing written formulas. But he found that heresy had created such a need; the greater portion of the ten Asiatic provinces was "really ignorant of God," i.e. overrun by pure Arianism. The church of Toulouse was, meantime, the scene of outrages such as had elsewhere marked an Arian triumph. Clergy were beaten with clubs and pieces of lead, and profane hands were laid on the Holy Sacrament [h].

We must return to Alexandria. It was the Sunday after Pentecost when the faithful assembled for prayer in a cemetery outside the city. George, indignant at their avoidance of his communion, stirred up against them the Duke Sebastian, a hard-hearted Manichean, who fell upon them with more than three thousand soldiers, and endea-

[c] Marcellinus and Faustinus, in Sirmond. Op. i. 252 seq.

[d] His "First Book to Constantius."

[e] Hil. c. Const. 2.

[f] Sulpicius says that he was sustained by Hilary's example and friendship.

[g] Hil. de Syn. 91, 63.

[h] Hil. c. Const. 11, says, "Holy persons will understand me when I say that on *Christ Himself* hands were laid."

voured to force them into conformity[i]. Virgins were held close to a fire, and wounded in the face. Some of them, with forty laymen, were scourged with thorny palm-twigs. The torturers gnashed their teeth as the victims called on Christ. Some died in a few days, and a fragment of a letter from Athanasius speaks of the Arians as sitting round the tombs to prevent their burial[k].

One misery after another had been reported to Athanasius; the persecution in the West, the persecution of his own flock by George, and now, at length, his own proscription. Constantius had ordered a strict search to be made for him, even to the southern limits of the empire; and the princes of Axum were bidden to send Frumentius, to be examined by George as to his appointment and his conduct. Then Athanasius gave up the idea of going to the Emperor. One shelter was still left him, among the monastic cells, especially those which lay to the west of Alexandria,—in Scete, near the Libyan frontier, and on the mountain of Nitria, somewhat to the north of it. Antony was gone, and Pachomius of the Thebaid, and Ammon of Nitria; but Macarius the elder, who has left Homilies, and Macarius of Alexandria were alive, and Pambo in the "wilderness of cells," who "scarcely in nineteen years" learned to practise the first verse of the 39th Psalm, and Theodore, who now presided in Tabenne, remarkable for his sweetness and sympathy; and Stephen, a friend of Antony, who while his limb was being cut off, continued his occupation of weaving palm-leaves into a basket, and reminded his brethren that "what God works must come to a good end[l]." We may think that the picture which Athanasius has given of Egyptian monasticism is more or less ideal; that many recluses, in all likelihood, fled from the world through mistaking their vocation; that the eremitic

---

[i] Ath. Apol. de Fugâ, 7; ad Const. 27; Hist. Ari. 72.
[k] Theod. ii. 14. [l] Soz. vi. 29.

life [m] was manifoldly perilous, and the cœnobitic was marred by much that was unhealthy [n]. But neither can we doubt, looking merely at the practical result of such lives on their generation, that Antony's holiness was a blessing to Egypt, and that communities which set themselves, in the face of a corrupt society, to "care for the things of the Lord," and to perpetuate in some sort the devotion of confessors, bore a witness which was not thrown away.

It was, then, to these quiet sanctuaries, which were to the eye of Athanasius as the "goodly tabernacles of Israel [o]," that he now directed his "retreat," which he justified [p] by the precept and example of Christ, and of the Saints of Scripture. The five or six years which followed it are comparatively a veiled period in his history [q]. We know that it had its days of calm, when he could compose defences, epistles, and the great Orations against Arians, and could join the monks in their Communions on Sunday and Saturday, or the twelve psalms of their nocturn office, as well as in the brief prayers "darted up" many times a-day [r]; when they could gather round him as their "father" and arbitrator, and drink in his words as oracles, and marvel at his union of contemplative with active sanctity. We know that there were times when the soldiers employed to hunt him down were so fierce in pursuit that he had to fly for his life from one monastery to another, or lurk in stifling

---

m Many hermits approximated to the cœnobitic system by living in groups of cells.

n See the case of Pior's vow, not to look upon any of his kindred, and other stories in Soz. vi. 29. The three main elements of the old monastic feeling were—1. a desire of high spirituality; 2. a wish to follow in the steps of those who in other days gave up all for Christ; 3. an intense perception of the moral evils of a society which the Church had not had time to soften or to cleanse. See S. Chrys. adv. Opp. Vit. Mon. i. 7, (tom. i. p. 55.)

o Vit. Ant. 44.

p Apol. de Fugâ. See S. Aug. Ep. 228.

q Some have thought that he found his way to Seleucia, if not to Ariminum, when councils met at those places; but this is improbable.

r The twelve psalms were a fixed number. The chanter stood in the midst, the others sitting on low stools around. For their ejaculatory prayers, see Aug. Ep. 130.

recesses[s] where a single attendant could with difficulty visit him, where he had the pain of being severed from his friends, and the worse pain of knowing that they had suffered for giving him shelter. But we know that he, if any man beside the great Apostle, knew how to be abased as well as how to abound; that in calm or in storm he was caring for his Church, guarding the simple against Arian craft, watching the progress of the controversy and the trials of foreign confessors, thinking tenderly of other men's weakness, keeping through all a patriarch's heart, and undethroned in the hearts of his people.

---

[s] Compare the story of his being hid in a dry cistern (that he was there for years is an incredible romance) with a description in his letter to Lucifer, (Ath. tom. ii. 770, ed. 1857.) "Etsi cum labore et periculo videre potui fratrem qui solet...necessaria...destinare." He says that the soldiers "go round the wildernesses, and put forth their murderous bands" against the monks. He mentions his own grief at his not being able to see the brethren, adding, "The Lord is my witness, that since the persecution began I have not been able to see my *parents*, who are alive."

CHAPTER IV.

From the Retreat of S. Athanasius to the Accession of Julian.

"Only in Athanasius there was nothing observed throughout the course of that long tragedy other than such as very well became a wise man to do and a righteous to suffer." HOOKER, E. P. v. 42. 5.

SO violent a prelate as Macedonius of Constantinople was not likely to refrain from persecuting in 356. Supported to some extent by an edict, he raged against Catholics and Novatians alike, for both parties held the Nicene Creed[a]. Agelius, the Novatian bishop, fled; banishments, confiscations, branding with hot iron, horrible tortures, forcible administration of Baptism and of the Holy Eucharist, became the familiar weapons of an aggressive heresy. Eleusius, bishop of Cyzicus, and Marathonius of Nicomedia, seconded Macedonius. Martyrius, a deacon, and Marcian, a reader, were put to death as being implicated in the tumult whereby Hermogenes had been slain. Churches were pulled down, and the Novatians, hearing that one of their own was menaced, anticipated the agents of destruction, and carried away the materials to another site, where the church was promptly rebuilt; and when an armed force was sent against the Novatians of Paphlagonia, it was repelled by a multitude armed with sickles and hatchets. In Constantinople, Macedonius resolved to remove the coffin of Constantine from the church of the Apostles, which was in a dangerous state. This excited the wrath of a large body of the people, while others supported Macedonius; a desperate conflict ensued, and the precincts of the church ran with blood. Constantius was naturally incensed against the bishop, as the cause of so much violence and scandal.

---

[a] See Soc. ii. 27, 38. He derived his information from a sufferer, the aged Novatian priest Auxano. See, too, Soz. iv. 20.

On the 28th of April, 357, Constantius visited Rome, and found the general feeling strong against Felix[b]. Some ladies of rank, at the suggestion of their husbands, petitioned him to recal Liberius. He consented (probably on the understanding that Liberius should satisfy the prelates of the court party) to restore him as joint-bishop with Felix[c]; but when his edict was read in the circus, it produced a cry of scornful indignation, "One God, one Christ, one Bishop!"

Towards the middle of this year a conference of some Arian bishops was held at Sirmium. Potamius of Lisbon—said to have sold his orthodoxy for an estate—produced a grossly heretical creed[d], which exhibited the real affinity of the adherents of Acacius to that extreme Arianism which they often found it prudent to disown. It condemned Homoousion and Homoiousion, because they were not Scriptural terms, and because the subject was out of man's reach; and while it called the Son God, and spoke of a perfect Trinity, it asserted as indubitable the superior glory of the Father[e]. In other words, the Godhead was *not* one, nor the glory equal, nor the majesty co-eternal. This is what Hilary calls the "blasphemy" of Sirmium. It had one most miserable success. Hosius had been kept a year in durance, had been repeatedly and savagely beaten, had been placed on the rack, had been made to suffer in his family affections[f], until at last, after enduring what would fix the braud of infamy on Constantius, if he had committed no other outrage, the old man consented to subscribe this creed. But whereas Vincent of Capua had given up Athanasius and clung to the faith, Hosius in surrendering the faith utterly refused to condemn Athanasius. After thus

---

[b] Theod. ii. 17. [c] Soz. iv. 11. He thinks Felix held the faith.

[d] Hil. de Syn. 11. For the Greek version, Ath. de Syn. 28; Soc. ii. 30.

[e] The Latin says, "claritate, majestate." The Greek version says "Godhead."

[f] Ath. Apol. de Fugâ, 5, speaks of the conspiracies formed against his kinsfolk. See also on his case Ath. Apol. c. Ar. 89; Hist. Ari. 45; Soc. ii. 31.

shewing that "the grey-haired saint may fail at last," Hosius was permitted to return to Spain[g]. But he never knew peace of mind; and with his last breath, two years later, he retracted his enforced concession, and anathematized the heresy. The "second creed of Sirmium" was sent to Gaul, but expressly condemned by Gallican bishops, and in particular by Phœbadius of Agen.

Liberius had spoken well in 355, but he over-estimated his own strength. After two years of banishment his intense longing for Rome threw him into a deep melancholy[h]. His deacon Urbicus was taken away from him, a privation which he felt bitterly. Demophilus, the bishop of Berœa, where he was detained, and Fortunatian of Aquileia, who himself had yielded at Milan, urged him not to sacrifice himself for a single man, so often condemned by synods; and thus he was led to renounce Athanasius, and to acquiesce in some uncatholic formula. He wrote to the Orientals, "I do not defend Athanasius,—I have been convinced that he was justly condemned;" and added that he put Athanasius out of his communion, and accepted the catholic faith of the Orientals, put forth by many bishops at Sirmium. "This I have received; this I follow; this I hold." Hilary, who transcribes this letter[i], inserts some wrathful comments of his own: "This is the perfidious Arian faith. (This is my remark, not the apostate's.) I say anathema to thee, Liberius, and thy fellows: again, and a third time, anathema to thee, thou prevaricator Liberius!" There is a question as to what creed Liberius did sign; the second creed of Sirmium, signed by Hosius, could hardly be called the creed of the Orientals; on the other hand, the first Sirmian

---

[g] The Luciferians, Marcellinus and Faustinus, have an incredible story of his persecuting Gregory, bishop of Eliberis, who stood firmly by his creed. He sat, they say, as judge, "immo super judicem," i.e. above the "Vicar" Clementius. Gregory, it is added, appealed to the judgment of Christ; Hosius tried to speak, but fell convulsed and distorted from his high throne, and was carried out as dead. Sirmond. i. 238.

[h] Ath. Apol. c. Ar. 89; Hist. Ari. 41.

[i] Hil. Fragm. 6. 6.

could hardly be thought so abominable[k] by Hilary. According to Sozomen, (who, however, places the event somewhat later,) it was a digest from the old Antiochene creed against Paul of Samosata, the Dedication Creed, and the first Sirmian. In this case, Liberius accepted Semi-Arianism; in any case, he abandoned the Nicene Creed. He wrote an abject letter[l] to Valens and his associates, asking their good offices with the Court for his immediate restoration; and to Vincent, whose fall he had once deplored, he sent an intimation that he had given up "that contest about the name of Athanasius," begging that the Campanian bishops might be informed, and that supplication might be made to the Emperor for his deliverance from his "great affliction." The letter concludes, "If you have wished me to die in exile, God will judge between me and you." Thus, in the latter part of 357, the Roman see lost its purity of faith.

This year, so memorable in Western history, was marked by the formation of a monastic system in Pontus under the superintendence of Basil. He had been, together with his friend Gregory, son of Gregory bishop of Nazianzum, a fellow-student of Julian at Athens in 355. He had afterwards visited the monks of Egypt, and those who in Palestine had embraced the monastic life under the guidance of the celebrated Hilarion. In Asia Minor Basil found that Eustathius, bishop of Sebaste, had disciples living by ascetic rules, and after attaching himself to them for a season, retired with some companions to a beautiful spot in the mountain-country of Pontus[m]. "Quiet," said he, "is the first step to sanctification:" and here he settled his com-

---

[k] Baronius thinks these expressions spurious, the invention of some pseudo-Hilary.

[l] To this letter Hilary appends, "I say anathema to the prevaricator, along with the Arians."

[m] His description of the woody mountain, the rapid river, and the secluded level ground surrounded by glens, exhibits a strong sense of natural beauty. Ep. 19.

munity, forming by degrees a rule for cœnobitic labours and devotions, which became a pattern for all subsequent monasticism in the East. They met for prayer, not only, according to the ancient Christian usage, in the night, before dawn, and at dawn, and in the evening, but at the third, sixth, and ninth hours, and at the beginning of night[n]. We cannot doubt that they used at Evensong that noble hymn which was already old in their time, and which must have had a special significance in an age when Christ's true Godhead was called in question[o]:—

"Light of gladness, Beam divine
From the glory's inmost shrine,
Where in Heaven's immortal rest
Reigns Thy Father everblest;—

"Jesus Christ, our hymn receive;
Sunset brings the lights of eve;
Day is past, and night begun;
Praise we Father, Spirit, Son.

"Night and day for Thee is meet
Holy voices' anthem sweet,
Ringing through the world abroad,—
Hail, life-giving Son of God!"

At the end of 357 or the beginning of 358 an important change took place at Jerusalem. For two years Cyril had been at strife with Acacius. He maintained for Jerusalem, as the mother-church, possessing an "Apostolic throne," and marked out for honour by the Nicene Council[p], an independence of Cæsarea which Acacius would not grant; and he was also obnoxious to Acacius on theological grounds, as holding the orthodox doctrine in fact, if not in the fulness of Nicene terminology. Acacius now summoned a small council of bishops of his own party, which Cyril

---

[n] They did not observe Prime, which was introduced afterwards at Bethlehem. They said Psalm 91 at the last office, which was the original form of the Western Compline.

[o] It is still the Vesper-hymn of the East. S. Basil quotes part of it, intimating that it had long been used by Christians, and that no one knew its author.

[p] See Appendix.

declined to attend. This was regarded as contumacy; and he was gravely accused of having committed an offence in selling some of the church ornaments to provide food for the famine-stricken poor[q]. He was condemned and expelled from Jerusalem. He appealed, with more formality, as it appears, than had been usual in such cases, to "a higher court;" proceeded to Antioch, where he found that Leontius was dead, and no one had been appointed his successor; and ultimately found a welcome at Tarsus, where Silvanus the bishop, one of the best of the Semi-Arians, received him in disregard of remonstrances from Acacius. This circumstance brought Cyril for the next few years into connection with the Semi-Arian party; and he illustrates the fact that it contained men of whom Athanasius could say, in his noble readiness to discern substantial unity under verbal difference, "We do not treat as enemies those who accept everything else that was defined at Nicæa, and scruple only about the Homoousion: for we do not attack them as raging Arians, nor as men who fight against the Fathers, but we discuss the matter with them *as brothers with brothers who mean what we mean, and differ only about the word*[r]."

The vacant throne of Antioch was filled by Eudoxius, the intriguing and thoroughly irreligious bishop of Germanicia. He gained this promotion by fraud, and the aid of court

[q] Sozomen, iv. 25, says that he sold church treasures and sacred veils. Theodoret, ii. 27, mentions a robe of cloth of gold presented by Constantine to be worn by the bishop when baptizing. Such an accusation does Cyril honour, and ranks him with other illustrious prelates, Ambrose, Augustine, Exuperius, Acacius of Amida, Deogratias of Carthage, Gregory the Great, Ethelwold of Winchester, who all in like manner sanctioned the principle that "the law of love is the highest law of all." (Trench on the Miracles, p. 313.) Observe in this case, as in that of the undedicated church, the alliance of a narrow formalism, not with orthodoxy, but with heresy.

[r] Ath. de Syn. 41. But he did not abandon the Nicene term in deference to their scruples. He simply pronounced a charitable judgment on men who had not as yet shaken off their prejudices. Time, he thought, should be allowed for a process which would one day end in their full conformity; for, as he says in the same context, since they confess so much already, "*they are not far from accepting the Homoousion too.*"

eunuchs; he openly patronized Aetius, whose views he had imbibed; he circulated an exaggerated account of Liberius' concessions, and held a synod which condemned the Homoiousion, exhibiting herein a readiness on the part of Acacius to fraternize with Anomœans as against Semi-Arians. Forthwith George of Laodicea sent a letter to Basil of Ancyra and Macedonius, to the effect that unless Aetius could be expelled, all was lost at Antioch. The letter found Basil, with others of his party, dedicating a church at Ancyra, on the 12th of April, 358. They had already heard, through Hilary, of the stedfastness of the Gallican and British Churches as against the Sirmian "blasphemy," and they now held a Council which adopted twelve anathemas in opposition to it, and asserted that the Son was *like* unto the Father not merely in power, but, "which is the chief point of our faith," in *essence* also. This Semi-Arian manifesto treated the Homoousion as implying Sabellianism, but insisted on the Homoiousion as indispensable to the real Sonship, and condemned the Homoion as effacing the distinction between "Son" and "creature." It referred to the Dedication Council, to that of Philippopolis under the name of the "Council of Sardica," and to the first Council of Sirmium. Three bishops, Basil, Eustathius, and Eleusius, with a priest, Leontius, were sent to the Emperor, who had just given to a messenger from Antioch a letter in favour of Aetius. Convinced by the deputies from Ancyra, who cancelled the anathema against the Homoousion, Constantius withdrew his letter, and wrote another which denounced Eudoxius and Aetius. The latter, with Eunomius, recently ordained a deacon, was banished into Phrygia, Eudoxius retired to Armenia, and others of the party[8] were sufferers by this Semi-Arian triumph. An Œcumenical Council was resolved upon; at first Nicæa was fixed on as the place, but its associations were not agreeable, and Nicomedia was thought of instead. But on the 24th of August—about

[8] For instance, Theophilus the Indian was exiled to Pontus.

three weeks after Liberius had entered Rome, and Felix had been driven out of it—an earthquake laid the city in ruins, and killed two bishops in its church. Consultations were then held as to the best place: and just then some change of mind induced Constantius to receive the leading Acacians into a share of his counsels. They devised the mischievous plan of breaking the single Council into two, in the hope of being able thereby to "divide and govern." Eusebius the Chamberlain advocated the change; "the bishops of the East and West might go respectively to an Eastern and to a Western Council; their journeys would be shorter, and the public expense would be so much less." Constantius agreed, and Ancyra and Ariminum were named as the two places.

While things were in this state, Hilary complied with the Gallicans' desire by giving them an account of the "Easterns' faith." The multifarious creeds which had issued from Asia perplexed the simple-minded Gallicans. Hilary, in writing this treatise, aimed at bringing about an understanding between the Gallicans and the Semi-Arians. It was highly important at this crisis to keep the Westerns from taking such a line as would exasperate the Semi-Arians of the East, when they seemed to be tending towards orthodoxy. It was equally important to assist that tendency by direct endeavours to dispel their prejudice against the Nicene formula. Hilary undertook this double task, by putting the best sense[t] which he could upon the Eastern formulas, and by exhorting the Semi-Arians to accept the Homoousion in its true sense, apart from all perversions[u], as the complement to their own Homoiousion, and as the only formula which could do justice to the

[t] As Tillemont says, viii. 445, "il excuse tout ce qui se peut excuser . . . mais il ne trouvait pas que leurs expressions, quoique bonnes, fussent suffisantes."

[u] He mentions three such perversions:—1. That Homoousion involves Sabellianism; 2. That it involves a division of the Divine essence; 3. That it presupposes a substance prior to that of the Father and of the Son. De Syn. 68.

belief in a true Son, begotten of the Father's very essence. "Such was my own previous belief, in which the Homoousion greatly confirmed me . . . Bear with me, brethren, if I say, you are not Arians; why rank yourselves with Arians by denyiug the Homoousion[x]?"

The treatise *De Synodis* was written at the end of 358. Ancyra was not thought a suitable place, and there was again an uncertainty, which led Basil to see the Emperor at Sirmium in May 359. There he met[y] Valens, George of Alexandria, and Mark of Arethusa, Germinius of Sirmium, and another bishop. They agreed that the Eastern Council should be at Seleucia in Isauria. But they also agreed, after a long discussion, which lasted till night, — the night of Whitsun-eve,—to adopt a formula of doctrine drawn up in Latin by Mark of Arethusa, who had carried the fourth Eusebian creed to Constans in 342. He himself was a Semi-Arian; but this third Sirmian creed, otherwise called the Dated Creed[z], because its heading recited the consuls of the year and the day of the month,—the eleventh of the calends of June, or May 22,—was, in fact, Acacian. It abandoned the word 'essence' as perplexing and unscriptural, and confessed the Son to be "in all things like to the Father, according to the Scriptures." It gratified the Semi-Arians by its lofty language as to the Divine Sonship[a]; but Basil evidently felt that he was inconsistent in accepting it at all, and added a note to his own subscription to the effect that he understood "in all things" to mean, "in subsistence, existence, and being." The ultra-Arian Valens, when copying it out, was dishonest enough to omit "in all things:" but Constantius compelled him to insert the words, and he was then despatched with it to Ariminum.

[x] De Syn. 88.

[y] See Hil., Fragm. 15.

[z] Ath. de Syn. 8; Soc. ii. 37. The circumstance of the date was perhaps too much insisted on by Catholic sarcasm.

[a] "Begotten before all ages, before all origin, before all conceivable time, before all comprehensible essence,—the only one from the only Father, God from God."

There the Western Council met, consisting of more than 400 bishops[b], including some from Britain[c]. About eighty were Arians, for the most part of the advanced school. Liberius was not present, nor did he send any legates. Taurus, a prætorian præfect, was charged to prevent the bishops from dispersing until they were agreed as to the faith. Constantius' letter forbade this Council to make any decree respecting the Easterns. They were to settle the question of doctrine, and send ten deputies to the court.

When the discussion began, Valens and Ursacius, supported by Auxentius and others, attempted to cut it short[d]. "Our business is simple; we are not assembled to enter on these subtleties, which will only breed discord, but to establish unity on the basis of a simple creed. Here is such a creed, expressed in clear and Scriptural language; the Emperor approves it—let the Couucil adopt it." They read the Dated Creed, whereupon many answered, "We did not come here because we wanted a creed. We have the Nicene Creed, and want no other. If you are of the same mind with us, say anathema to Arianism; or, if you will not[e], let us read the various formularies which have been issued, and measure them by the Nicene. The matter *is* indeed simple; we are not learning our faith, but have only to hold fast the faith of our fathers."

Valens and his adherents of course refused to adopt the Nicene standard. The Council proceeded to depose them as heretics of long standing who attempted to annul the only true Creed. "Let these enemies be condemned, that the Catholic faith may abide in peace." A "definition" was framed, adhering to the Nicene Creed, and declaring that "*substance*, name and thing" must be firmly retained, as established by many Scriptures. They pronounced eleven

[b] Ath. de Syn. 8.

[c] Sulp. Sev. ii. 67. He says that three of the British bishops were too poor to dispense with the State provision for their support. He thinks that this does them credit.

[d] Soz. iv. 17.

[e] Ath. ad Afr. 3.

anathemas against the Arian, Sabellian, Photinian, and other heresies: and in a letter to Constantius they narrated what they had done, and explained their principle of loyalty to Nicæa[f]. They begged him to allow no innovation, no injury to the ancient faith, observing that Arian novelties were a stumbling-block to the heathen, as well as a distress to the faithful. And they entreated permission to return to their respective churches. "Many of the bishops are worn out with age and poverty; suffer us in quietness to offer up our prayers for your good estate and for your empire, and that God may reward you with deep and lasting peace."

The Catholic deputies to Constantius were ten in number, young men[g], deficient in knowledge and judgment; the Arians were "wary and practised veterans," who found it easy to poison the Emperor's mind. Indignant at the rejection of a creed framed in his own presence, he treated the Council's deputies with coldness, and after a long delay informed them that until the Persian campaign was over he could not give his mind to their business; they must therefore await his return at Hadrianople. This resolution he announced to the Council, and received in reply[h] an assurance that the bishops would adhere to their decision, and an entreaty that they might be sent home before the winter.

So ended the first scene of the proceedings at Ariminum. The Easterns met at Seleucia on Sept. 27. The number of bishops was about 160; of these the great majority, 105, were Semi-Arians, headed by George of Laodicea, Eleusius, and Sophronius. Of the rest, some were shifty Homœans led by Acacius; a few were thorough-going Anomœans[i]; another small party, consisting of the Egyptians, George the usurper of course excluded, were loyal to the Nicene faith. Hilary, summoned as a bishop dwelling in Asia,

---

f Ath. de Syn. 10; Soz. iv. 18.
g Sulp. Sev. ii. 67; see Hooker, v. 42. 5.
h Soc. ii. 37.
i Hil. c. Const. 12.

was admitted to a seat in the Council, after declaring that his Church held that faith[k]; and he has left us some particulars of the proceedings.

Leonas, an officer of the household, was charged to attend throughout all the discussions; and after some dispute as to whether doctrine, or cases of complaint against individual bishops, e. g. Cyril and Eustathius, should be first considered, the precedence was given to doctrine. The majority were in favour of the Nicene Creed, omitting the Homoousion as obscure aud liable to suspicion; or, at any rate, of the Dedication Creed of 341[l]. The Acacians were for the Dated Creed; and their bolder Anomœan companions, as Eudoxius, uttered hideous profanities, which raised a great excitement. At last the Acacians withdrew, and the Dedication Creed was read in their absence. Next day the majority, within closed doors, adopted the Dedication Creed. The Acacians protested against this step; and when Basil and Macedonius arrived, they further protested that until those whom they had accused or condemned were excluded, they could not enter the Council. Their demand was granted, in order to leave them no excuse; and on the third day the Council again assembled.

Leonas then said, "I have a paper here, given me by Acacius; I will read it to the Council." It turned out to be a Homœan creed, avowedly of the same type as the Dated Creed[m]; it rejected both Homoousion and Homoiousion, "as foreign to the Scriptures;" but it formally anathematized the Anomoion, indicating thereby that Acacius was ready to throw over his more audacious friends. Hilary told an Acacian "who came to tempt him," that he could not understand the position thus taken up. He was answered that Christ might be called like to the Father as being the Son of His will, not the Son of His Godhead, a distinction which came strangely from the party whose watchword had been simplicity of doctrine. Sophronius, a Semi-Arian, said,

---

[k] Sulp. Sev. ii. 68. [l] Soc. ii. 39. [m] Ath. de Syn. 29; Soc. ii. 40.

after the reading of the new formula, "We shall never understand the truth, if to be constantly putting forth our private opinions be called an exposition of the faith."

On the fourth day Eleusius took high ground in behalf of the Dedication Creed as the true faith of the Fathers; Acacius urged that many creeds had been made since the Nicene. At length, after Acacius had been asked how the Son could be "altogether like," yet not "like in essence," and the disputes appeared endless, Leonas dissolved the Council. Next day he would not attend; nor would the Acacians, although summoned to appear at the enquiry into Cyril's case. The majority pronounced them contumacious. Acacius, Eudoxius, George, and six other bishops were deposed; nine other persons were excommunicated; and deputies were sent to Constantius, who were outstripped by the Acacians. Thus ended the Council of Seleucia.

Before any persons from Seleucia reached the Emperor, a conference had been held at Nicè [n] in Thrace, on Oct. 10, between the Catholic and Arian delegates from Ariminum. Constantius overawed the former. Restitutus, bishop of Carthage, their spokesman, was made to admit that Valens and Ursacius had never been heretics, and that the proceedings at Ariminum were null and void. They also signed a new edition of the Dated Creed, worse in two respects: 1. it omitted "in all things;" 2. it proscribed the word Substance (hypostasis) as well as Essence. And with this formula, which the Acacians hoped [o]—incredible as it seems—to pass off as a "Nicene" creed, the delegates returned to Ariminum. Constantius wrote to the Council, proscribing the words Essence and Homoousion, and commanded Taurus to detain the bishops until the number of those who would not sign the formula should be reduced to fifteen, who were then to be sent into exile.

The Arians at Ariminum wrote to the Easterns, i. e. the Acacians, signifying their agreement with them in faith.

---

[n] Hil. Fragm. 8.

[o] Soz. iv. 19; Soc. ii. 37.

They also wrote to the Emperor[p], expressing their joy at his prohibition of "that unscriptural name, unworthy of God, which the others were wont to apply to God and His Son." They begged that he would not detain them along with the rest, seeing that they had "subscribed the sound doctrine, and worshipped none but God the Father through Jesus Christ." The majority of the Council at first held aloof from Restitutus and his fellows, although the latter protested that they had acted under constraint. But after a time the bishops' patience gave way. They shrank from a winter on the shore of the Hadriatic; they were utterly weary of so long a sojourn at Ariminum, and this weariness disposed them to listen to any argument which might justify concession. They were told, most falsely, that the Council of Seleucia had accepted the Dated Creed. "Will you rend the West from the East?" Again, "Why will you stand out for a word? Is it Christ you worship, or is it this word Homoousion[q]?"

The resolution of the majority, thus undermined, broke down with a crash. Bishop after bishop signed the imperial creed, on the ground that the substantial doctrine of Nicæa could not depend on the word Homoousion; but about twenty still held out, headed by two Gallicans, Phœbadius and Servatius. Taurus tried both menaces and tears, urging them and imploring them to imitate, and thereby release, their brethren. Phœbadius answered, "Any suffering rather than an Arian creed." Valens, after some days had been thus spent, openly declared, as if referring to rumours about a treacherous purpose, that he was no Arian; he abhorred the Arian blasphemies. "If," he added, "you think the creed inadequate, you may affix to it what explanations you will[r]." They caught eagerly at the notion; and on a following day Muzonius, an aged African bishop[s], proposed

---

[p] Hil. Fragm. 9.
[q] Soz. iv. 19; Aug. Op. Imp. i. 76; Ruff. i. 21.
[r] Sulp. ii. 69.
[s] See Jerome, adv. Lucifer. 18. He quotes the records in the "church chests."

that the opinions popularly ascribed to Valens and his friends should be read out, and condemned by the Council. "Be it so," answered all the bishops. Claudius, an Italian bishop, was appointed to read them: Valens broke in, loudly disclaiming them, and repeating anathemas which the Council gladly echoed. "Anathema to him who denies the Son to be begotten before the ages; to be like the Father according to the Scriptures; to be co-eternal with the Father. *If any one calls the Son a creature as the other creatures are;* if any one says that He is from things non-existent, and not from God the Father; if any one says, There was a time when He was not; let him be anathema." The bishops and spectators clapped their hands and stamped with joy. Claudius added, "My lord and brother has forgotten one thing; in order to make everything clear, let us condemn this other statement: if any one says that the Son was before all ages, but not altogether before all time, implying that *something* was prior to Him; let him be anathema." Again the church rang with "Let him be anathema." Other propositions were condemned: no one now stood higher than Valens in point of orthodox reputation; all agreed in adopting the formula of Nicè in the sense of these anathemas, and Valens, Ursacius, and others of their party were sent with the news of this agreement to the Emperor.

The Council of Ariminum had thus, in the words of Sulpicius, "a good beginning and a foul conclusion." It was not until after this conclusion that all its "foulness" became apparent. There was indeed, *primâ facie*, a culpable surrender of the Nicene Creed; but the bishops thought they had kept its spirit by means of the anti-Arian statements which they had procured from Valens. And doubtless two or three of these statements were unequivocally anti-Arian. and could only be got rid of by the most absurd sophistry, But the inexperienced Westerns did not see that others were ambiguous, and that the fourth really implied Arianism. Arius himself had plainly said, in writing to S. Alexander, that the Son was "God's perfect creature, but not as one of the creatures [t]." Valens put this statement into a disguise, and the bishops accepted it as meaning that He was *not* a creature. They saw not what was implied in his phrase, "as the *other* creatures," i. e. that of all God's creatures He was the most excellent. By such miserable means, terror and detention on the one side, and shameless equivocation on the other, did Homœan Arianism, working through an ultra-Arian instrument, win its scandalous victory in the close of 359. If the event gave a severe shock to the moral authority of synods, — if it shewed that a great Council might do what the Church was called upon to repudiate,— it also exposed the untruthfulness which characterized the Arian policy [u].

We must now change the scene to Constantinople. Soon after the Conference at Nicè in October, the Acacians arrived from Seleucia [x], and prejudiced Constantius against the majority of that Council. When the deputies of the Council came, and denounced Eudoxius as the author of an Anomœan paper which they shewed to Constantius [y], Eudoxius attributed the paper to Aetius. He was summoned, and avowed that it was his. Constantius ordered him to be exiled, but did not then carry out the sentence. Eustathius proceeded. "Eudoxius agrees with Aetius. If he does not, let him condemn this paper." Eudoxius, as cowardly as he was profane, shrank from the Emperor's roused anger, and condemned the Anomoion, with other Arian terms [z]. Constantius resolved to examine Aetius, who was then brought before him and successfully encountered by Basil and Eustathius; the great Basil being in attendance on his namesake.

---

[t] Ath. do Syn. 16.

[u] Ruffinus says, i. 21, "Eâ tempestate facies ecclesiæ fœda et admodum turpis. . . . Ara nusquam, nec immolatio, nec libamina; prævaricatio tunc et lapsus erat, ac ruina multorum."

[x] Soz. iv. 23.

[y] Theod. ii. 27. This document perverted 1 Cor. viii. 6.

[z] Theodoret says that Silvanus openly avowed the Homoousion, as implied in the uncreatedness of the Word.

The Ariminian deputies now arrived, and the Seleucians in vain endeavoured to prevent them from joining Acacius and Eudoxius[a]; urging that although Aetius individually had been condemned, it was necessary to condemn his doctrine. The Ariminians at once took the side of the Acacians, and explained that their fourth anathema did in fact include Christ among the creatures. Other statements of theirs they explained away, e. g. "when we called the Son eternal, we meant in regard to future existence." "With all our hearts," said the Acacians, "do we accept the Ariminian creed;" and Constantius, after carrying on the debate through the last day and night of the year, obliged the Seleucians also to accept it.

A Council was now held (Jan. 360) at Constantinople. Some fifty bishops were present. One of them was a very eminent man, Ulphilas, successor of that Theophilus, bishop of the Goths, who had sat in the Nicene Council.

Acacius ruled the assembly. The Creed of Ariminum was adopted; but it is probable that Ulphilas and others signed it in simplicity, without any Arian meaning. Aetius was made a scape-goat by the Acacians, and deposed from the diaconate. Some few bishops declined to condemn Aetius, and were excommunicated unless in six months they should repent[b]. Having taken this line against Aetius, the Council deposed the leading Semi-Arians, but not on doctrinal grounds. Basil of Ancyra was called a hinderer of tranquillity, and accused of violent acts and neglect of all Church discipline. Eustathius had been already censured by his own father, the bishop of Cappadocian Cæsarea, and by a local Council. Macedonius had caused much bloodshed, and been lax in discipline. Cyril, Silvanus, Eleusius, and others, were similarly deposed. Banishment followed on deposition.

During the sittings of the Council, Hilary, who had followed the Seleucians to Constantinople, presented an ad-

[a] Hil. Fragm. 10.

[b] Theod. ii. 28. Letter of the Council to George of Alexandria.

dress, still extant, to Constantius[c]. He was apprehensive, he said, for the Emperor's salvation. Error was putting an unnatural sense on sacred words: the very names of Father, Son, and Spirit were being robbed of their true meaning. "There are as many faiths as fancies." In this confusion of jarring formulas, Homoiousion and Homoion were in turn asserted; nothing was sacred or inviolable: "We settle a creed a year, or a creed a month, we repent of what we have settled, defend those who repent, anathematize those whom we have defended;" "There is not a heretic who does not pretend that his teaching is Scriptural." Hilary requested leave to discuss the faith before the Emperor and Council, and concluded by referring to texts of Scripture. His request was refused; he vented his intense indignation against Constantius, as a "precursor of Antichrist," in a vehement invective which as yet he did not publish, and he was ultimately sent back to Gaul as a disturber of peace, without any remission of the sentence of exile.

The unreality of the Council's censure on Anomœanism, in the person of Aetius, was shewn by the enthronement of Eudoxius at Constantinople on Jan. 27. On Feb. 15 he dedicated the restored church of the Eternal Wisdom, for the service of which Constantius offered splendid vessels, curtains, altar-cloths, blazing with gold and jewels. In the midst of the ceremonial, Eudoxius began his sermon with these words; "The Father is irreligious, the Son religious." A commotion followed; the Bishop bade the people to calm themselves. "Surely the Father worships none, and the Son worships the Father!" A burst of laughter followed this speech, which became a good jest in the society of the capital. Eudoxius was well fitted to hand on the old tradition of Arian profanity.

In one case, however, he exhibited more reserve. Eunomius, the disciple of Aetius, was a voluble Anomœan disputant, a rationalist in principle, and very ignorant, says

[c] Hil. ad C. ii.

Socrates[d], both of the letter and the spirit of Scripture. Eudoxius appointed him bishop of Cyzicus, advising that for the present he should conceal his Anomœanism. But[e] an artifice on the part of some of his people drew from the bishop such unequivocal expressions of that heresy, that he was at once denounced before the Emperor, and Eudoxius was obliged to depose his friend; who, finding himself sacrificed, like Aetius, to the worldly policy of a man who shared his views, proceeded to form a separate sect, and became the consolidator of extreme Arianism.

The Semi-Arian bishops revoked their adhesion to the Ariminian creed, and wrote to all the Churches against Eudoxius and his party. Macedonius is said to have at this time brought forward his peculiar heresy regarding the Holy Spirit, whom he spoke of as the proper Arians had spoken of the Son. The Son was God, like in essence to the Father: the Spirit was but the minister of the Son. Athanasius, while in the desert, heard that such a theory was forming, and wrote against it to Serapion of Thmuis.

The Ariminian creed was enforced alike in East and West, and caused inconceivable perplexity and suffering. When S. Jerome says[f], "The whole world groaned, and marvelled to find itself Arian," he expresses the indignation with which the Western Church heard of the successful trickery of Valens. Liberius and Vincent refused to admit the new creed, and this firmness went far to efface the stain of former lapses. Gregory of Elvira was commended by Eusebius for refusing to communicate with "hypocrites." Lucifer wrote against Constantius in a style of rude and verbose invective, and sent his tracts both to the Emperor and to Athanasius. The latter, who had written his work on the Councils of Seleucia and Ariminum before he heard of their fatal result, acknowledged Lucifer's tracts in a letter full of sympathy; but at the same time, in a spirit unlike Lucifer's, expressed a compassionate hope for the

---

[d] Soc. iv. 7. [e] Theod. ii. 29. [f] Adv. Lucif. 7.

restoration of those who had yielded through "temporal fear." There were multitudes in the East to whom these words might apply, who had temporized or had been scared into conformity to the Ariminian creed, beside those who, like the old Bishop of Nazianzum, had accepted t because it was "Scriptural in language[g]." Of the Ariminian bishops themselves, some, in despair, adhered to the Arian communion; others, bewailing their own weakness, communicated with no bishops whatever; others wrote to the exiled Catholic bishops, professing the true faith, and imploring their communion; a few "defended their mistake as if it were a deliberate action[h]." Hilary exerted himself in Gaul to undo, as far as he could, the work of Ariminum; councils were held, at which the bishops who had yielded might recover their ground by condemning the heresy. At the Council of Paris, the prelates, replying to the Seleucians, declared that they had been deceived as to the mind of the Easterns; that they now accepted the Homoousion in its true sense; that they condemned Valens and his party; that Saturninus, who withstood all movements against Arianism, was excluded from their communion.

We find Hilary now rejoined by one who had been his disciple before his exile, and was destined to be the next great Gallican saint. This was the famous Martin. Born in Pannonia about 316, he had served in the army, and according to the beautiful legend inseparable from his name[i], had, "while yet a catechumen, bestowed the half-cloak on Christ." He had then been baptized; had obtained, some years later, his discharge from the army, and

---

[g] His son Gregory had to interpose between him and the scandalized Cappadocian monks.

[h] Jerome, adv. Lucif. 7.

[i] It is briefly this. He met a poor shivering beggar one bitter day at the gate of Amiens: having no money with him, Martin cut his military cloak in two, and gave half to the beggar. The next night, in a dream, he saw Christ clad in the half-cloak, who said to the attendant angels, "Martin, still a catechumen, hath arrayed Me in this garment."

been made an exorcist by Hilary, who would fain have made him a deacon. Visiting Illyricum, he was scourged for opposing Arianism. During Hilary's exile he led a monastic life at Milan, until he was driven away by Auxentius. He now established near Poitiers the first monastery that had been seen in Gaul[k].

The see of Antioch remained vacant until the beginning of 361, when a Council assembled which placed Meletius in the see. This excellent man had a rich persuasive eloquence, and a disposition which endeared him both to Catholics and Arians. A rumour began to spread that he was positively Catholic[l]. After some sermons of a general character[m], he was desired to take part in a series of expositions of the great controverted text, Prov. viii. 22[n]. After George of Laodicea had given a strongly Arian address,—he had now deserted the Semi-Arians,—and Acacius had read a paper which seemed to aim at a safe ambiguity, Meletius rose, and asserted in unequivocal language the essential doctrine of Nicæa. The church rang with cries of applause and wrath, proceeding from Catholics and Arians. The Arian archdeacon stopped the new patriarch's mouth with his hand; Meletius held out three fingers, then one; and when his lips were freed by the archdeacon's seizing his hands, he repeated aloud his former words, and exhorted the people to cling to the Nicene faith. This could not be borne; the Council, at another session, deposed Meletius; Constantius drove him into exile; Euzoius, the old comrade of Arius, was made bishop of Antioch; and a new creed was published[o] which affirmed the Son to be in nowise like to the Father, and to be made out of what once was not. The authors of this Anomœan formula, being asked how they

---

k If Martin died, aged more than 80, in 397 or 402, he cannot have been discharged from Julian's army at the age of 20, as the present text of Sulpicius asserts. Baronius thinks that he was baptized in 351, æt. 35, and left the army in 356.

l Soz. iv. 28. m Soc. ii. 44. n Theod. ii. 31.

o Ath. de Syn. 31; Soc. ii. 45; Soz. iv. 29.

could reconcile it with a recognition of the Son as "God of God," employed the quibble which had been originally invented by George of Laodicea, "He is of God as all things are," (1 Cor. xi. 12). But the indignation of the people compelled them to withdraw this creed, and fall back on that of Ariminum.

It may here be well to enumerate the various Arian formulas, put forth by individuals or Councils since the commencement of the controversy. 1, the letter of Arius and his friends to S. Alexander; 2, the creed of Arius and Euzoius, which beguiled Constantius; 3, a formula directed against Marcellus by a Council at Constantinople in 336; 4, 5, 6, 7, the creeds of Antioch, 341, 342; 8, the Macrostich; 9, the creed of Philippopolis; 10, first Sirmian; 11, the "letter of Constantius" proposed at Milan in 355; 12, a creed framed at Antioch, 356; 13, second Sirmian, "the blasphemy;" 14, the digest signed by Liberius, or "the perfidious faith;" 15, the formula of Ancyra; 16, third Sirmian, or Dated Creed; 17, Acacian creed proposed at Seleucia; 18, third Sirmian revised at Nicè, signed at Ariminum and Constantinople; 19, Aetius' formula, denounced by Semi-Arians; 20, Anomœan creed of Antioch. "They will never be at rest," said Athanasius[p], "until they acknowledge the Nicene Council." These tossings to and fro of Arianism, this bewildering succession of formulas, with the perpetual hurry and excitement produced by so many synods[q], were doubtless a stumbling-block to the heathen, and tended to cast a stigma on synodal action. But the list given above may shew on which side was consistency and simplicity. While heresy was thus prolific in self-contradiction, the Church stood by the one Creed of the great Council which gave the law to all her synods. Thus in 361 the downward tendencies of Acacianism were fully manifest; its natural goal was the Anomoion. And doubtless many a Semi-Arian was led by the teaching of events

---

[p] De Syn. 32.

[q] Ammian. xxi. 16.

to feel that his natural refuge against Acacians and Anomœans was that one creed which he had been taught to dread as Sabellian; that in the Ancyrene dogmatism he could find no security; in short, that he must either sink or ascend. An indication of the tendency of Arianism to breed new errors had been already given in Aerius, whose disgust at being passed over when Eustathius was made bishop of Sebaste had led him to embrace pure Arianism, and to maintain the equality of presbyters to bishops[r], —a doctrine rebuked by anticipation in the Alexandrian proceedings as to Colluthus,—to say that it was wrong to pray for the departed, and to denounce as Judaical the observance of fast-days and of Easter. We are told that his adherents mocked at the Catholic solemnities in Holy Week.

Euzoius was of course repudiated by all the orthodox in Antioch. Those of them who had up to this time remained in the established communion, broke off from it altogether, and regarded the exiled Meletius as their bishop. But those who had hitherto been known as the Eustathians, and with whom Athanasius had communicated, could not bring themselves to unite with men who recognised a bishop of Arian consecration, although he might now be of orthodox belief. This old Catholic body, therefore, continued to worship apart from their "Meletian" brethren, as well as from Euzoius and his adherents[s]. Paulinus, a priest of high character, was their head.

This year was full of agitating rumours. It had been known that the Cæsar Julian in 360 had been compelled by his soldiers to accept the imperial title, and that Constantius had spurned his proposal for a division of the empire. It was now reported that he was on his way to the East. Civil war, then, was impending. But many probably,

---

r Epiph. Hær. 75.

s The Meletians assembled in the old city on the bank of the Orontes, in what was called the Apostle church. Theod. ii. 31. Euzoius allowed Paulinus, for whom he had a great respect, to officiate in a small church in the new city, which was upon an island. Soc. iii. 9.

thought that a baptized communicant, who had been ranked among ecclesiastics as a reader, and had been friendly to Hilary on the occasion of his exile, would prove at least as good a sovereign for Christian interests as the Arian catechumen who had so long been vexing the Church. They were presently undeceived. Julian had indeed attended the Church service at Vienne on the recent feast of Epiphany[t]; but in the course of his expedition he declared himself a worshipper of the gods. Constantius, who at first talked of going to "hunt" Julian, began ere long to be haunted by superstitious presages of death; he caused Euzoius to baptize him at Antioch, and hurried westwards. At the foot of Mount Taurus he was stricken with a fever which made his flesh like fire to the touch[u]; and he expired after a prolonged death-struggle, on the 4th of November, 361.

---

[t] The Epiphany, as a distinct festival, was derived about this time by the West from the East; the Nativity (on Dec. 25) by the East from the West, about 375. See S. Chrys. in Diem Nat. J. C., c. 1.

[u] Amm. xxi. 15. Greg. Nazianzen, Orat. 21, says that with his last breath he repented of having innovated on the faith. So Theod. ii. 32.

CHAPTER V.

From the Accession of Julian to the Edict of Valens.

"I saw the unjust with towering plume,
A green tree in his native ground;
But he is gone;—behold his room:
I sought, and he no more was found."

KEBLE, *Psalter.*

THE unhappy man who was now lord of the Empire had been for some ten years a hypocrite in his Christian profession. Three causes may be assigned for his apostasy. First, there was in his nature a strong superstitious element, which craved for such excitements as he found in the Ephesian and Eleusinian mysteries. Secondly, his singularly Greek temperament invested with a false power the Paganism which had enlisted so much beauty in its service. Thirdly, Christianity itself, as represented by Constantius, his odious courtiers, his Arian disputants, had been miserably associated in Julian's mind with everything that was most worldly, base, and tyrannical. He must rank with those unbelievers to whom bad Christians have been a rock of offence. A wayward eccentricity of temper, conspicuous in his student-life at Athens [a], would dispose him to identify the system with the men; and his lack of the Roman massiveness and consistency of character will account for the strange union of opposites observable in his religion and in his conduct. The Paganism which he adopted was made up of Platonic fantasies and a petty repulsive formalism; and though he was chaste and temperate, active, and often magnanimous, his justice could be absolutely quenched by his animosities, and the philosopher could sink into a spiteful, scoffing tyrant.

One of his first cares, on entering Constantinople in the second week of December, was to clear the palace of the

[a] S. Greg. Naz. Orat. iv. 25; Soc. iii. 23.

crowd of eunuchs and other profligate courtiers, and to put to death the chamberlain Eusebius [b]. He openly professed himself the restorer of the old religion; surrounded himself with professors of a mystic Pagan "philosophy," with priests, diviners, prophets, and impostors as base as the parasites whom he had swept away [c]. Then it was that he "washed off the laver" of Baptism by a hideous self-immersion in bull's blood [d], and sought to cleanse his hands from the touch of the "Bloodless Sacrifice" by holding in them the entrails of victims [e]. He set up an image of Fortune in the great church, and while he was sacrificing there, Maris, bishop of Chalcedon, now a blind old man, was led up to him at his own request, and rebuked his impiety. "Will your Galilæan God cure your blindness?" asked Julian. "I thank my God," said Maris, "for the blindness which saves me from seeing the face of an apostate [f]." Julian heard this in scornful silence: he professed to have no intention whatever of persecuting those whom he always designated as *Galilæans*. They should not, he said, be constrained to adore the Immortals. He would make no martyrs [g]. So far from it, that he would recall those whom Constantius had banished on grounds of religion. This act of grace was really intended to produce a revival of Christian strifes, and so to weaken Christianity [h], and nothing amused him better than to assemble Christians of different parties in his palace, and set them to dispute with each other. Of course the Emperor put forth edicts for the restoration of temples, and especially commanded that Christians who had destroyed them should rebuild them at their own expense; a command which became the groundwork of many severities. It was one of his ingenious modes

---

[b] Amm. xxi. 4.
[c] S. Chrys. de S. Babylâ. 14.
[d] The Ritual of the Taurobolia, Prudent. Peristeph. 10. See Trench, Huls. Lect., p. 224.
[e] S. Greg. Naz. Orat. iii. 51.
[f] Soc. iii. 12; Soz. v. 4.
[g] S. Chrys. in Juv. et Max. 1; Greg. Naz. Orat. iii. 55.
[h] Amm. xxii. 5; Soz. v. 5.

of indirect persecution. Another was the license which he practically allowed to heathen populations[i], as those of Gaza and Ascalon, to vent their fury on defenceless Christians, who suffered death by the most hideous tortures; the Emperor coldly observing, when some such cruelties were slightly punished by the local government, that the citizens ought not to have been arrested for taking vengeance on Galilæans. A famous case of this kind was that of Mark, bishop of Arethusa, who after suffering from the Pagan citizens what none but a tragic poet, in Theodoret's opinion[k], could describe, was at length released, and converted his tormentors. Julian also, as might be expected, abolished all immunities which had been bestowed on the clergy, expelled several bishops as "leaders of sedition," let loose heathen officials against churches, confiscated Church property "in order to secure poverty of spirit," forbade Christians to be civil governors "because their law forbade them to take up the sword," or to practise as physicians or as advocates, or to teach the Greek and Roman literature[l]. "Why should they wish to teach what they do not believe? Let them expound Mark and Luke in their churches." This last prohibition, which Ammianus calls "harsh[m]," led the accomplished Apollinaris to produce Christian works on the classical model[n]. One of the professors who lost their offices by this law was Victorinus at Rome, who had been converted in old age, and after a temporary concealment of his faith, was led to profess it openly in the church, to the great delight of the Christians.

---

i S. Greg. Orat. iii. 58, 81. When heathen governors oppressed the Christians, Julian would answer their complaints with a sneer: "Bear it patiently, as your God commands you." Soc. iii. 14. Capitolinus, governor in Thrace, burnt alive Æmilius, a leading Christian. A zealous deacon at Heliopolis was killed by the people, who devoured part of his flesh. Theod. iii. 7.

k Theod. iii. 7. After many tortures he was hung up in a basket, smeared with honey, and exposed to wasps and bees. He had composed the Dated Creed in 359.

l S. Chrys. in Juv. et Max. 1. m Amm. xxv. 5. n Soz. v. 18.

Such was the petty and ungenerous policy which Julian substituted for that of open persecution. In the army he acted on a similar plan; he aimed at committing his Christian soldiers to some act which would be equivalent to idolatry[o]. Pictures of the gods were placed beside the picture of the Emperor, which was to receive an obeisance that might be construed to include them. Soldiers receiving a donative were to cast incense upon an altar. We are told that some complied unreflectingly,—that one of them soon after, when signing the cross over his cup, as was usual with Christians, was reminded of his inconsistency,—that the men forthwith rushed out, and indignantly gave back the gold, exclaiming, "We are Christians[p]."

To these varied methods of attack we must add the systematic employment of a sovereign's personal influence on all the Christians whom he thought it important to win over. They had to contend against his seductive gentleness or his sarcastic pity, which combined with the harassing discouragements above mentioned to make up what S. Jerome calls "a mild persecution, under which many Christians gave way of their own accord[q]." We can easily conceive the taunts and sneers by which the faith of Julian's Christian servants—such as was Cæsarius, the brother of Gregory of Nazianzum, who withstood all the Emperor's urgency—would be put to trial. The Galilæan religion, according to Julian[r], was a clumsy human device, the work of blunderers like Matthew, who misapplied the words of Hosea, and impostors like Paul, who contradicted the Old Testament; not to speak of "the good-natured John," who first deified *the dead Man* as an object of Christian worship.

---

[o] Soz. v. 17.

[p] Theod. iii. 17; Greg. Naz. Orat. iii. 50.

[q] Hieron. Chron. One of these men, who "had no root in themselves," was Ecebolius, a professor of rhetoric, who lived to bewail his apostasy with tears, grovelling at the church-gate and crying aloud, "Trample on me, for I am as salt that has lost its savour." Soc. iii. 13.

[r] See Lardner, iv. 332. Greg. Nazianzen, Orat. iii. 97, gives his saying about "that senseless word, Believe." See also a "malignant sneer" of his about "catching men," quoted by Dean Trench, On Mirac., p. 133.

Could sensible men, whose homage was due to the Immortals, continue in bondage to the Galilæan teachers with their ceaseless cry of "Believe, believe?" Could they fail to see the absurdity of magnifying a few cures performed in Jewish villages into an evidence of divine power in Jesus? But, scornful as Julian thus was towards Christianity, he could recommend the Pagan pontiff of Galatia to take a lesson from the rules of the Galilæan priesthood for the better government of the ministers of the gods; and could express indignation at the inhuman negligence which allowed the Gentile poor to be dependent for their bread on "the impious Galilæans[s]."

If some Christians followed the Emperor's example of apostasy under the pressure of a temptation for which they were not prepared, others exhibited an over-forward zeal which amounted to the grave mistake of courting martyrdom. Christianity had been so long dominant that the sight of a restored heathen altar was too much for their powers of self-command. And thus it was that during Julian's journey to Antioch in the early summer of 362,—while Catholic and heterodox[t] exiles were returning home on all sides, and while Gregory of Nazianzum was entering on those priestly duties which he had undertaken against his will[u],—two young men were put to death in Galatia by the Emperor's command for having overthrown the altar of Cybele. A priest named Basil, who had previously been tortured for his bold denunciations of idolatry, provoked Julian, by yet greater boldness, to give up his intention of dismissing him. To S. Basil, afterwards archbishop, Julian wrote two letters, the second of them in a tone of menace, to which Basil replied, with dauntless severity, "Demons

[s] Soz. v. 16.

[t] He recalled Aetius with special honour, as having been intimate with his brother. He praised Photinus for not holding that a woman's son could be God.

[u] He was ordained priest in the end of 361, retired into Phrygia after Epiphany, returned to Nazianzum at Easter, and afterwards wrote the noble discourse "in defence of his retirement."

have raised thee to so proud a height, that now thou liftest up thyself against God. Once we read Holy Scripture together, and nothing then escaped thee." The inhabitants of Cæsarea in Cappadocia were especially odious to Julian; for they had recently destroyed the only temple which was left standing in their city. Julian expunged Cæsarea from the catalogue of cities, imposed heavy taxes, made the clergy serve in the police force, and put to death a young man of high birth named Eupsychius, for having taken part in the demolition. Dianius, bishop of Cæsarea, died about this time, protesting on his death-bed that his signature of the Ariminian creed had not been a departure from Nicene faith. The people compelled the provincial bishops to elect in his place a man of high character, but as yet unbaptized, named Eusebius. They afterwards protested against this compulsion, and Julian's wrath against the city was increased by it. He reached Antioch about the end of June, while the Pagan women were performing the annual lamentations for Adonis.

One of his first acts at Antioch was to put to death Artemius, duke of Egypt, for having destroyed idols and lent his aid to George's violent proceedings against the temples[x]. The news of his death stirred up the Alexandrians against George, whom it was now safe to attack. He had used his great powers as bishop of Alexandria in a very oppressive fashion; had exasperated the people by claiming for Constantius a special dominion over the city; had been driven forth by a tumult, and on his return had provoked the Pagans by saying as he passed a splendid temple, "How much longer will this sepulchre stand?" It must indeed be admitted that although Pagans assisted his first intrusion, he was ultimately ruined by his open warfare against Paganism. Having found, when preparing a site for a church, that a multitude of human skulls had been buried in ground consecrated to the worship of Mithra, he exposed them to

[x] Theod. iii. 18; Amm. xxii. 11. Ammianus expressly says that George was slain after the people heard of Artemius' death.

public view as relics of victims immolated by Pagan diviners. The result was a furious outbreak, in which the Pagans, having first imprisoned George, dragged him about the city, tormented him for hours, burned his mangled corpse, and cast the ashes into the sea. Julian rebuked them in the name of their "holy god Serapis" for an outrage which had anticipated the justice of the law[y].

Athanasius had not returned to Alexandria before the death of George. After hearing of it, he emerged from his retirement, in August 362, and his people enjoyed another such "glorious festivity" as had welcomed him back in 349. All Egypt seemed to assemble in the city, which blazed with lights and rang with acclamations; the air was fragrant with incense burnt in token of joy; men formed a choir to precede the Archbishop; to hear his voice, to catch a glimpse of his face, even to see his shadow, was deemed happiness[z]. Lucius, the new Arian bishop, was obliged to give way: the churches were again occupied by the faithful, and Athanasius signalized his triumph, not by violeuce of any sort, but by impartial kindness to all, by the noble labours of a peace-maker, and the loving earnestness which could conquer hearts. Eusebius of Vercellæ and Lucifer of Caliaris were at this time returning from their exile in Upper Egypt, and a Council was resolved upon to be held in Alexandria. Lucifer was to have attended it, but he preferred to go immediately to Antioch, and Eusebius attended the Council, with two deacons to act as Lucifer's representatives. The business was of four kinds, relating to 1, the Antiochene schism; 2, the bishops who repented of accepting the creed of Ariminum; 3, a difference of doctrinal phraseology which had sprung up between two parties of the orthodox; 4, a tendency which had become apparent towards a new heresy in regard to the Incarnation.

---

y Soc. iii. 3. The popular legend of "S. George" has really nothing to do with the soldier George, who is supposed to have suffered in 303. It is an Arian allegory referring to the Alexandrian usurper.

z S. Greg. Orat. xxi. 36.

1. The Council resolved that Paulinus and his flock ought to unite with Meletius, who had now returned from exile, and his adherents. The united Church of Antioch ought to receive converts from Arianism on their confessing the Nicene Creed, and condemning Arianism, Sabellianism, and other heresies, including the new error which made the Holy Spirit a creature, and separated Him from the essence of Christ. "For there is no real avoidauce of the abominable Arian heresy, no genuine confession of Nicene faith, if one divides the Holy Trinity, and calls any member thereof a creature[a]."

2. Applying the same principle, the Council ruled that *all* who desired to return to Catholic unity should be received on these terms; and declared the creed of Philippopolis to be totally without the authority of Sardica, "for the Sardican Council declared the Nicene Creed to be sufficient."

3. There were two phrases current among Catholics as to the Holy Trinity. Some, apparently the majority, adhering to the older use of the word *Hypostasis*, as meaning *Substance*[b], asserted *One Hypostasis* of God. Others, especially those who had been connected with Semi-Arians, and were especially jealous of Sabellian tendencies, had come to use Hypostasis in the sense of *really-existing Person*, and therefore spoke of *Three Hypostases*. Mutual explanations were made. The latter party disclaimed all Tritheistic ideas, and declared that they were contending for a real Trinity of Persons, not for any division in the Godhead. The former as earnestly disclaimed all Sabellianism, and explaiued their phrase as witnessing for the undivided Godhead, without prejudice to the Personality of the Son and Holy Spirit. Both parties anathematized Arius, Sabellius, Paul of Samosata, the Gnostics, and the Mauicheans; and the Council exhorted all persons for the future to prefer the

---

[a] Ath. Tomus ad Antioch. 3.

[b] See Bishop Forbes on the Nicene Creed, p. 149.

Nicene language to either "One Hypostasis," or "Three [c]." This exhortation, however well-meant, was not, and perhaps could not be followed.

4. Explanations were made by some persons who were supposed to deny that our Lord assumed a reasonable Soul. They affirmed that they truly held it; that He could not have been really Incarnate if His Body had been without a Mind; for He was Saviour alike of soul and body, as true a Son of Man as He was Son of God; the self-same after Abraham as before him, the self-same in asking about Lazarus as in raising him up, the self-same in His Passion as in His miracles of mercy. We shall see hereafter how wonderfully these declarations anticipated the work of subsequent defenders of truth. The Council of 362 was equally illustrious for its many-sided orthodoxy, and for its wise and thoughtful moderation. The synodal letter was signed by "Pope Athanasius," Eusebius, Asterius from Arabia, and fourteen African bishops. Eusebius added to his signature the statement that "the Son of God assumed all (our nature) except sin."

Before the decree could reach Antioch, Lucifer had taken, in conjunction with two other bishops, the unhappy step of consecrating Paulinus, in order to gratify his strong sympathy with the Eustathians. "This," says Theodoret [d], "was not right; it increased the dissension," which continued, in fact, to the year 415. Eusebius, finding the wound enlarged which he had hoped the Council might heal, remonstrated with Lucifer, who broke off communion with him, with the Alexandrian Church, with all who advocated moderation, in regard to Antioch or to those who had given way in 359-360. Hence arose the sect of Luciferians, headed after Lucifer's death by that Hilary who had been a delegate of Liberius at Milan, and reproducing

---

c However, the Creed favoured the "One Hypostasis," by using the word in the sense of substance. Socrates, iii. 7, so far mistook the synodal letter as to think that it disapproved both words, Hypostasis and Ousia.

d Theod. iii. 5.

in great measure the hard austerity of the Novatians and the Donatists[e]. S. Athanasius had been too long connected with the Eustathians to disown Paulinus now that he was in fact their bishop; and Paulinus accepted the synodal letter, with a special statement penned by Athanasius[f].

The counsels of Alexandria were adopted by the vast majority of the faithful. Eusebius visited various Eastern Churches before he returned to Italy; and in Italy he found Hilary ready to co-operate with him. Ruffinus says that he played the part of a healer and of a priest, and that he and Hilary were as glorious lights irradiating Illyricum, Italy, and Gaul. Liberius, in a letter to Athanasius, made full profession of his orthodoxy as to the Trinity and the Incarnation[g]; and writing to the Catholic prelates of Italy, urged that "repentance must efface the fault of inexperience[h]," that Greece and Egypt are both of this mind, and that entire submission to the Nicene faith ought to be a passport to the Church's favour. The bishops of Italy wrote to those of Illyricum, repudiating the Ariminian, and professing the Nicene Creed, against Arius, Sabellius, and Photinus. S. Jerome[i], after saying that "Italy laid aside her mourning-weeds to welcome Eusebius," gives a vivid description of the eagerness with which those who had been ensnared by the nets of Ariminum protested, "by the Lord's Body, and by every holy thing in the Church," that they had taken the anathemas of Valens in what appeared to be their orthodox sense, without a thought of heretical

---

[e] See the memorial of Marcellinus and Faustinus in Sirmond. i. 243. "Sub vocabulo *pacis* impietas tegitur." They quote, "Not as the world giveth," &c. They disown the name of Luciferians; "Christ is our teacher." Gregory of Elvira was a Luciferian.

[f] As to 1. the reality of the Three Persons, (his own habit was to speak of One Hypostasis, but he approved the language of the Council as to this and the other phrase); 2. The rational Soul in Christ; 3. The Consubstantiality; 4. The uncreatedness of the Holy Spirit. See Epiph. Hær. 77. 20.

[g] He asserted, e.g., the true assumption of Perfect Manhood.

[h] Hil. Fragm. 12.

[i] Adv. Lucif. 19.

equivocation. Some bishops, it seems, were for deposing these repentant men; but popular feeling and Christian equity alike forbade such intemperate harshness. Spain and Gaul united with Italy and Egypt in regard to this point; and Basil, who had returned to Cæsarea before the death of Dianius, and was ordained priest soon afterwards, accepted the letter of the Alexandrian Council. The three men who were most useful at this time in carrying out the views of that letter, and securing peace to the Church, were Athanasius himself, Eusebius, and Hilary.

The Donatist exiles resolved to profit by the indulgence of the Emperor towards others who had been sufferers for their views of Christianity. They addressed Julian as a prince "in whom alone justice resided[k]," and petitioned him to recall them. His rescript, referring to this petition of "Rogatianus, Pontius, Cassianus," and others, ordered that all proceedings against them should be cancelled, "and all things return to their former state[l]." Hereupon they returned to vent their fury on the Catholics. "Subtle in seduction, pitiless in bloodshed[m]," they expelled many bishops, and renewed or exceeded their former outrages. In one place they tore off the roof of a church, showered down the tiles on the congregation, and thereby slew two deacons at the altar. Two of their bishops were forward in this sacrilege. Two others drove out a Catholic congregation at Thipasa; women were dragged along, infants were slain; a bottle of sacred chrism was flung out of a window; and the schismatics shewed yet more audaciously their disbelief in the validity of Catholic ordinances, by "casting the Eucharist to dogs." Altars were broken, scraped, carried away[n]; the timbers of which they were composed were used for

---

[k] S. Aug. in Ps. xxxvi.; c. litt. Pet. ii. 205.

[l] S. Aug. c. litt. Pet. ii. 224. [m] Opt. ii. p. 48.

[n] Opt. vi. p. 111. He adds, "What is an altar but the seat of the Body and Blood of Christ?...The Jews laid their hands on Christ upon the cross. By you He has been smitten on the altar." Compare S. Hilary's language, quoted above.

boiling water; "the chalices which bore the Blood of Christ" were melted down and sold. Baptism was iterated when Catholics joined the sect[o]; consecrated virgins were bidden to put away their purple caps[p], and receive new ones from Donatist bishops; the civil power was employed to take away from the Catholics the sacred books, the veils and the palls[q]; and the cemeteries were closed against Catholic funerals, as if to exhibit in the intensest form their abhorrence of all fellowship with the Church[r]. The most vehement zeal was shewn in making proselytes; Catholics were accosted with "Come, be Christians—redeem your souls." "Such-a-one, are you still a Pagan? How slow and sluggish you are in becoming a Christian[s]!" Those who joined them were morally deteriorated; a bitter and restless spirit seemed to possess them; they lost the very instincts of charity and humility[t]. And all this time, at Donatist altars, the Eucharistic prayer ascended in the ordinary form, "For the One Church which is spread throughout the whole world[u]!" Such were the miseries which the recall of the Donatists entailed on what soon became the Catholic minority in the province of Africa.

We must return to Julian at Antioch. The prevalence of Christianity in the city was to him a perpetual source of annoyance[x]; while the satirical humour of the people, which had never spared their monarchs, was excited by the singular aspect of "the little man with the huge beard and pompous gait," who found no pleasure in their amusements,

---

[o] Opt. v. p. 97.

[p] Mitrellæ. Opt. vi. p. 117. He adds that the mitrella is "signum, non sacramentum."

[q] The veils, apparently, for the elements; the palls for the altar. "You washed the palls, no doubt," says Optatus. "Tell us what you did with the books?" vi. p. 118.

[r] Optatus also says, iv. p. 91, that many were taught never to say "Ave" to a Catholic.

[s] Opt. iii. p. 81; vi. p. 120.

[t] Facti sunt ex patientibus rabidi, ex pacificis litigantes...ex verecundis impudentes, &c. Opt. vi. p. 120.

[u] Opt. ii. p. 45.

[x] On a high festival of Apollo he found the altar supplied with a single goose, which the priest himself had procured.

and might be seen any day amid a troop of worthless men and women, officiating in the sacrifice of multitudinous bulls [y]. "Truly he *is* a bull, running wild over the earth [z]." Julian was the more eager in procuring bulls by the hundred, and white birds at a great expense, because he was making preparations for a Persian campaign, and costly victims must win the favour of his gods. Recurring to a device of Maximin's, he cast things offered to idols into the public fountains, and caused water that had been similarly hallowed to be sprinkled on all articles of food; whereupon two young men of his body-guard, Juventinus and Maximinus, expressed their indignation, first in a private party, and then in his own presence, and were put to death by tortures, "not for their religion," it was announced, "but for disrespect to the Emperor [a]." He resolved to consult the oracle of Apollo in the grove of Daphne [b]. The response was, that the presence of dead bodies impeded the oracle. Julian found that his brother Gallus had buried within the grove, so long polluted by an impure heathenism, the body of the martyr Babylas [c]. He ordered the coffin to be removed to Antioch. Forthwith a multitude of Christians, men and women, young and old, hurried out to assist in the translation of their Saint. Daphne was six miles from Antioch; and all along the way, to Julian's inexpressible wrath, he heard a sound of triumph and defiance—the thundering chant of the Christian procession, "Confounded be all they that worship carved images, and that delight in vain gods [d]!"

---

[y] Amm. xxii. 12. 14. [z] Soc. iii. 17. [a] Theod. iii. 15.

[b] For this celebrated grove see Dean Milman's noble poem, "The Martyr of Antioch," pp. 10, 26. Sozomen, v. 19, describes the exquisite beauty of the spot, where the mass of cypresses formed a "roof" rather than a shade.

[c] Bishop of Antioch A.D. 239. S. Chrys. (Hom. de S. Bab.) says that he resisted the Emperor's entrance into his church. Eusebius, vi. 39, says that he died in prison A.D. 250; Chrysostom that he was executed.

[d] Soz. v. 19. He says that skilful chanters acted as precentors, and the rest responded in chorus. Theodoret, iii. 10, says that a car drawn by two horses conveyed the body.

Sallust, the prætorian præfect, was ordered to chastise the insolent psalm-singers. He remonstrated, but obeyed; a youth named Theodore was racked and lacerated; he calmly sang the psalm over again, and Sallust, admiring his courage, procured his release. He afterwards said that "he felt a little pain at first, but that a young man stood by wiping the sweat from his face with soft linen, so that the pain was changed into pleasure [e]." We are told of a community of religious women who provoked Julian by chanting this and similar psalms as he passed; but he contented himself with ordering the superior to receive a blow on each side of the face [f]. Another vexation befell him on the 22nd of October; the temple at Daphne, built by Antiochus Epiphanes, was destroyed by fire; he ascribed it to Christian incendiarism, the Christians to a lightning-stroke. Upon this he proceeded to severer measures, and closed the Golden Church; on which occasion Felix, his treasurer, looking at the splendid altar-plate, scoffingly observed, "See what kind of vessels are used in the service of the Son of Mary!" and was seized, says Theodoret, with a hæmorrhage that proved fatal [g]. All the priests fled from Antioch, save one named Theodore, who suffered tortures and death for not giving up the vessels in his custody [h].

In November, Julian ordered Athanasius to leave Alexandria without delay [i]. He had never, he wrote, permitted the exiles to return to their *churches*. It was absurd enough in the Christians of Alexandria to adore as God the Word a Man whom they had never seen, instead of the beneficent solar deity; but if they would do so, they might be content with other teachers of impiety. The "mean little fellow," he added,—the meddling knave, the wretch who had dared to baptize Greek ladies while Julian was emperor, should

[e] Theod. iii. 11; Soc. iii. 19; Soz. v. 20.

[f] Theod. iii. 19.

[g] Ibid. iii. 13.

[h] Soz. v. 8.

[i] Julian, says Ruffinus, i. 33, "could not keep up in regard to Athanasius the appearance of his pretended philosophic temper."

find no place in all Egypt. He even proposed, we are told, to put Athanasius to death. Pagans and Jews burned the Cæsarean church at Alexandria. The faithful, all in tears, surrounded the Archbishop, who calmly said, "Let us retire for a little while; the cloud will soon pass." He went up the Nile; being pursued, he caused the boat to turn back towards Alexandria. "Where is Athanasius?" asked the officer charged to hunt down the Archbishop. "He is near," was the reply. He returned to the city, and lay safe in concealment.

Early in 363 we hear of two officers, Bonosus and Maximilian, put to death for refusing to lay aside the Christian standard of the Labarum[k]. Count Julian, the Emperor's uncle, who had been concerned in their death and in the recent sacrilege, died by a horrible internal malady.

The last of Julian's attacks upon Christianity was his attempt to rebuild the temple of Jerusalem. He did indeed wish to aid the Jews in their desire of renewing the Levitical sacrifices, and to secure their attachment to his government in spite of its Paganism[l]; but his main object was to confound the Gospel by raising up the fabric which it had expressly doomed, and thus reviving the system of which that fabric had been the symbol and the centre. The rapturous hopes of the Jews were expressed in the scene which followed the imperial mandate, when silver spades and mattocks were employed, and earth was carried away from the excavations in the rich dresses of delicate women[m]. The faith of the Christians was expressed by Cyril's denunciations of the predestined failure. The heathen historian[n] tells us what ensued. After all possible assistance had been given by the authorities, "fearful balls of fire breaking out near the foundations with repeated attacks, scorched the workmen several times, and rendered the place inaccessible;

[k] Ruinart, p. 609. Meletius accompanied them to martyrdom. Julian had substituted for the Christian monogram the old initials (S. P. Q. R.) of the senate and people.

[l] S. Chrys. adv. Jud. v. 11; Soz. v. 22.

[m] Greg. Naz. Or. iv. 4; Theod. iii. 20; Soz. v. 22.

[n] Amm. xxiii. 1.

and in this way, after obstinate repulses by the fiery element, the undertaking was brought to a stand." Various details are added by Christian writers[o], as of an earthquake, a whirlwind, fire from heaven, a luminous cross in the air, and marks of crosses on the garments of the Jews. It may be that in these particulars there is an element of exaggeration, and that in the fiery eruption itself, as well as in attendant circumstances, natural agencies were employed. But that those agencies should manifest themselves at that particular crisis will appear accidental, as men speak, to those only who do not estimate the exceeding awfulness of the occasion,—the unparalleled historical position of Julian, the mystery of iniquity in his general policy, and the specially Antichristian malignity of this attempt at a confutation of Christ's words[p].

"His shafts, not at the Church, but at her Lord addrest[q],"

might well be cast back upon himself by a manifestation of "the finger of God," as real and awe-inspiring as any of those *per se* natural phenomena, the presence of which under particular circumstances made them a sign of judgment against Pharaoh.

Julian had but "a short time." Early in March he set forth on his Persian expedition. On June 26, 363, he received his death-wound in the course of a painful retreat. That it wrung from him the cry of "Thou hast conquered, Galilæan!" may be only a Christian "rumour[r]," growing out of the intense conviction that He *had* conquered. It is quite as awful, if we rightly consider it, that the man who had thus conspicuously lifted himself up against the Son of God should have expired with the tranquil self-satisfaction of a philosophic unbeliever[s]. We are told of several in-

---

[o] e.g. Soc. iii. 20; Soz. v. 22; Theod. iii. 20; Greg. Or. iv.; Chrys. adv. Jud. v. 11, vi. 2.

[p] Those words undoubtedly included in their scope the whole Judaic system. And to this system Julian undertook to give once more a visible establishment.

[q] Lyra Apostolica, p. 212.

[r] See Theod. iii. 25.

[s] Amm. xxv. 3.

stances in which a knowledge of the event appeared to have been mysteriously communicated at the very time of its occurrence. The most famous is that of the Christian grammarian at Antioch, who, when the great sophist Libanius asked him with an exulting sneer, "What is the Carpenter's Son doing now?" answered, "He is preparing a coffin[t]." Theodore of Tabenne, and Pammon, were in a boat on the Nile with Athanasius, who, speaking of the Church's misery, declared that he had a more cheerful heart in persecution than in peace, whereupon his two friends smiled at each other, and Theodore said, "This very hour Julian has been slain[u]." We read also of the illustrious Alexandrian scholar Didymus, hearing in a dream that day that Julian was dead, and that he might send word to Athanasius[x]; of Sabas, a pious monk, who suddenly dried his tears, and told his friends that the wild boar was lying dead[y]; of an officer sleeping in a church while on his way to the army, and seeing an assembly of saints, two of whom went out, and in next night's dream returned, having executed their commission of judgment[z]. Whatever account is to be made of these anecdotes, they at any rate shew what the Church felt in being delivered from the Apostate; and his career might be described by that other story of his proceedings at Cæsarea Philippi. In the place of a famous statue of the Saviour, Julian sets up an image of himself: but lightning hurls it to the ground, and it lies a shattered and blackened mass[a].

Jovian, the first of the body-guards, who had confessed Christianity before Julian[b], was hastily chosen Emperor. The Christian ensign was again displayed; the army was ready again to declare itself Christian as soon as the artificial support given by Julian to an effete idolatry was withdrawn. Imperial edicts went forth, undoing the Anti-

---

[t] Theod. iii. 23. [u] Ath. Op. ii. 695. [x] Soz. vi. 2.
[y] Theod. iii. 24. [z] Soz. vi. 2.
[a] Ibid. v. 21. He says, "From that day, even until now, it is there in this condition." [b] Soc. iii. 13.

christian work of the Apostate; and Jovian, a frank, straightforward soldier, adopted a religious policy, not only Christian, but unequivocally Catholic, and having thus taken his side, exhibited some impatience of any attempt to alter his resolution. He wrote to Athanasius, praising his loyalty to Christ and his contempt for all perils in the cause of orthodoxy. "Our Majesty, therefore, recalls thee. .... Return to the holy churches, and be the pastor of God's people, and send forth with them prayers in behalf of our Clemency [c]." He also requested from him a statement of the true faith as distinct from the manifold sectarian opinions [d]. Athanasius, who had already returned to Alexandria before Jovian's letter of recall arrived, assembled a Council, which put forth an important doctrinal epistle [e], referring the "religious Emperor" to the Nicene Creed. "The true and pious faith in our Lord," the bishops proceed to say, "is manifest to all men, being known and read out of the Divine Scriptures [f]. In this faith were the Saints made perfect and martyred; and now have they departed and are in the Lord. And this faith would have remained unscathed for ever, had not the wickedness of some heretics ventured to counterfeit it." They go on to describe Arianism, and (as in the synodal letter of 362) to expose the Arian principle in its recent Macedonian form, without naming Macedonius. They claim, as adhering to the Nicene faith, the majority of the Eastern Churches, and the Churches in Spain, Britain, Gaul, Italy, Dalmatia, Dacia, Mysia, Macedonia, all Greece, all Africa, Sardinia, Cyprus, Crete, Pamphylia, Lycia, Isauria, Pontus, Cappadocia, Libya, Egypt, and the neighbouring countries. Then, after reciting the Creed,—including, of course, the anathemas,—they add, "To this faith, O Augustus, it is needful for all men to adhere, as being divine and apostolic." They depre-

---

[c] Ath., tom. ii. 622. [d] Greg. Or. xxi. 43. [e] Ath., tom. ii. 622.

[f] A passage most characteristic of S. Athanasius. See de Incarn. Verb. 56; c. Gent. 1; ad Ep. Æg. 4; de Dec. Nic. 32.

cate the "plausible arguments and logomachies" of Arianism, and observe that the Nicene fathers were not content to say, "The Son is *like* the Father;" for He is not simply *like*, but is very God of God; "but they used the word *Homoousios*, as expressing the property of a genuine and true Son, truly and by nature Son of the Father. Neither did they make the Holy Spirit foreign to the Father and the Son, but rather glorified Him with the Father and the Son in the one faith of the Holy Trinity, because in the Holy Trinity there is one Godhead."

Athanasius brought this letter to Jovian at Antioch, according to a gracious invitation. He was treated with distinguished honour, while Lucius and other Arians received four times a repulse from Jovian, who displayed on these occasions a mixture of shrewdness, humour, and not unnatural irritability. They met him at first as he was riding out of the city. "We pray your Majesty and Piety to hear us." "Who and whence are ye?" "Christians, my Lord, from Alexandria." "What do you want?" "We pray you, give us a bishop." "I have bidden your former bishop Athanasius to be enthroned." "So please you, he has been many years under accusation and in exile." A Catholic soldier interrupted them: "May it please your Majesty, inquire about these men; they are the leavings of the vile Cappadocian George, who have laid waste the city and the world." Jovian spurred his horse, and rode into the country. Again they presented themselves before him, and talked of the accusations which had sent Athanasius into exile. Jovian threw aside these accusations as of too remote a date, and said, "Do not talk to me about Athanasius: I know of what he was accused, and how he was exiled." "But we have other charges to bring forward." "You will never make good your case by a tumult of voices; I cannot talk to each of you,—choose two of yourselves, and two of the people, to speak for the rest." "So please you," they persisted, "give us any one but Athanasius." Jovian's patience here gave way: "I have made up my mind about Athanasius;" then in Latin, "Strike them, strike them." The Arians urged what was, even for them, a daring falsehood, that nobody would join Athanasius in prayer. "I know by careful inquiry that he is right-minded and orthodox." "He speaks well enough," said the Arians, incautiously; "but his meaning is insincere." "Enough!" said Jovian, "you attest the orthodoxy of his words: his meaning is beyond man's scrutiny." "Allow us to hold assemblies." "Who prevents you?" "May it please you, *he* denounces us as heretics." "That is his duty, and the duty of all sound teachers!" "Sire, we cannot endure this man, and he has taken away the ground belonging to the churches[g]." "Aha! it was a matter of property, then, and not of faith, that brought you hither? Begone to church, you have a celebration[h] to-morrow; and after the dismissal you can each of you write down the facts as you believe them to be. Athanasius is here also. He that knows not the doctrine of the faith, let him learn from Athanasius! You have to-morrow and next day." When some of the Antiochenes caught Lucius, and presented him to Jovian, saying, "May it please you to see this man whom they want to establish as bishop," Jovian asked, "How came you hither, by sea or land?" "By sea, so please you." Jovian uttered a jocose but irreverent imprecation against the sailors for not throwing him into the sea; and caused some of the court-eunuchs to be tortured for espousing his cause against Athanasius.

But Jovian was not only the first decidedly Catholic emperor; he was the first consistently tolerant one. He gave the Pagans full liberty of worship, and rebuffed the Semi-Arians, in his blunt emphatic mode of speech, when they begged him to banish the Anomœans. Meletius seems to have received with unpromising coldness the attempts of Athanasius to mediate between him and Paulinus; and in a Council at Antioch he allowed the slippery Acacians to

---

[g] τὰ τεμένη τῶν ἐκκλησιῶν. [h] σύναξις.

accept the Homoousion[i] in this sense, that the Son "was begotten of the Father's essence, and was like to Him in essence;" an explanation characteristically evasive, for it reduced the great testing phrase to the measure, 1. of a less distinct phrase which preceded it in the Creed; 2. of the Semi-Arian formula. They also joined in the Council's denunciation of the Anomœans; who, doubtless indignant at these compliances, proceeded to consolidate their body by the consecration of new bishops.

Jovian died, aged 33, on Feb. 17, 364; and Valentinian, who is said to have struck a Pagan priest for sprinkling lustral water upon him, while he was attending Julian to the gate of a temple, was chosen Emperor. He was in several respects a great prince, who "always seemed above his present fortune[k];" his main fault, which in fact proved fatal to him, was a relentless ferocity of temper. In about a month after his election he gave the sovereignty of the East to his younger brother Valens, a feeble prince capable of becoming a cruel one.

In the course of this year Valentinian came to Milan. Hilary and Eusebius were still there, upholding the Catholic cause against Auxentius, and keeping the faithful apart from his communion. The Emperor, who was a Catholic, was also naturally impatient of religious dissensions, and did not choose to worship in a conventicle while the actual bishop professed himself really orthodox. He therefore put forth an edict that no one should disturb the Church of Milan. This, as Hilary said, was indeed to disturb it; and he denounced Auxentius as in fact an Arian. Valentinian ordered a trial: Auxentius professed his belief in Christ's true consubstantial Godhead. Being ordered to make a written statement, he obeyed, and insisted on the authority of Ariminum, accused Hilary and Eusebius as contentious

---

[i] Cassian, de Incarn. vi. 3, (Bibl. Patr., tom. 5. par. 2, p. 77,) refers to the "Antiochene Creed," i. e. an altered form of the Nicene, containing the Homoousion. "It speaks," he says, "the faith of all Churches." It must have been adopted by this synod. [k] Soc. iv. 1.

men who had been deposed, and spoke of the Son in words which might either mean that He was "a true Son" or "a true God." Valentinian was satisfied: Hilary protested that Auxentius was a trickster; but the Emperor, weary of the controversy, ordered him to leave Milan. He did so, and then addressed a letter to "all adherents of the inherited faith[l]," beginning, "Fair is the name of peace, but who can doubt that no peace but that of Christ is the peace of the Church or of the Gospels?" He warned his readers against making the Church depend on secular protection; denounced those who in the Church's name had recourse to sentences of exile and imprisonment; inveighed against Auxentius as a treacherous Antichrist; and insisted that walls did not make a church, that mountains and forests were now safer than the basilicas of Milan.

The Semi-Arians now determined to hold another Council. They sent the Bishop of Heraclea to ask Valentinian's leave. He answered, "My place is among the laity; I have no right to interfere in such matters. Let the bishops[m] assemble where they will." They met accordingly at Lampsacus in 365. The assembly was of the same character as the Councils of Ancyra and Seleucia: it asserted the Homoiousion, condemned the creed of Ariminum, confirmed that of the Dedication. It declared itself against Eudoxius, the chief of the Anomœans in ecclesiastical dignity, and against Acacius, whose acceptance of the Homoousion had been as short-lived as it was evasive. The Eudoxians were summoned to repent, and pronounced, after a time, contumacious; but Valens inclined to their side, and exiled the deputies of the Lampsacene Council. Eleusius, who appears to have regained Cyzicus after the deposition of Eunomius, was terrified by Valens into conformity to the opinions of Eudoxius, but returned home and made con-

[l] Hil. c. Aux.

[m] Ἱερεῖς. Here, as in so many other places, the highest order of the priesthood is meant. Soz. vi. 7. Socrates, iv. 2, makes them apply to Valens.

fession of his weakness in full church[n]. The Emperor had a design on the Church of Cæsarea, which was weakened by the absence of Basil, whom Eusebius' jealousy had driven back to his retirement. But hearing of his Church's peril, he returned to Cæsarea, was reconciled to Eusebius, and baffled Valens. Meantime the more thorough-going Anomœans, who had not forgiven Eudoxius for his abandonment of Aetius and Eunomius, showed their abhorrence of his dissimulation by rebaptizing even Arian proselytes.

In their distress and peril, the Semi-Arians bethought themselves of the orthodox West and its emperor. They sent to Liberius three deputies, Eustathius, Silvanus, and Theophilus, with instructions to enter into his communion and profess the Nicene Creed. We need not attempt to analyze their motives, nor inquire how far their comfortless position as subjects of Valens assisted them in seeing their untenable position between the pure Arians and the orthodox. Liberius at first looked coldly on the delegates. They assured him that they had come to see the true meaning of Homoousion; it meant nothing more than was held by those who had stood out for Homoiousion. Such an explanation could hardly be satisfactory. Would they, Liberius asked, state their faith in writing? They complied. Their paper, in the form of a letter to their "lord, brother, and fellow-minister Liberius[o]," began by asserting the orthodoxy of the Council of Lampsacus, and of other recent assemblies of that kind, and their own commission to represent them. They professed that they had held, did hold, and would hold to the end, the Creed of the 318 at Nicæa, in which the Homoousion was holily and piously employed. They anathematized all heresies opposed to that holy Creed, and especially the Ariminian creed, accepted at Constantinople through the craft of perjured men who passed it off

[n] Soc. iv. 6. He inserts after this event the episcopate of Eunomius.

[o] It is obvious that on the Papal theory such expressions, coming from bishops who were professedly desiring the favour of Rome, would be grossly deficient in humility. See the letter in Soc. iv. 12.

as "Nicene[p]." After setting forth the Nicene Creed in full, they declared themselves ready to have their orthodoxy tried, if it ever should be needful, "before such orthodox bishops as your Holiness[q] may approve." Liberius, on receiving this paper, wrote to sixty-four Eastern bishops by name, and to all their orthodox brethren, expressing his satisfaction at the Catholic statement of their representatives; a copy of which, to prevent all misapprehensions, he appended to his letter, retaining the original at Rome. He repeatedly dwelt on their full acceptance of the Nicene Creed, "which contains the perfect truth," and "being contained in *Hypostasis* and the word *Homoousion*, repels like a strong fortress all the assaults of Arian perversity." He explicitly described the Ariminian creed as procured by Arian craft, which beguiled even those whom he was addressing. Now, having ascertained their return to sanity, he recognized them as in union with the orthodox Church. Neither in the paper of the three delegates nor in the profession of faith which they made soon afterwards in Sicily, was there any assertion of the identity of Homoousion with Homoiousion; so that when Liberius' eventful life was closing in September, 366, he had the comfort of thinking that, after his melancholy lapse in former days, he had been instrumental in receiving the submission of a great body of Easterns to the Creed which he had once cast away. He had succeeded not only to the "Chair of Peter," but to the blessing which followed on his repentance; he had been converted, and had strengthened his brethren.

It is painful to speak of the next scene in Roman Church history. Damasus, a man of sixty, priest of the church of S. Laurence, was elected bishop. "But after a short time Ursinus was consecrated by certain bishops, and invaded the Sicinine (church), with his supporters, whither the people of Damasus' party rushing together, persons of

---

[p] Granting that some Westerns may have been deceived by the similarity of Nicæa and Nicè, is it credible that Easterns could be so?

[q] A title then given to all bishops.

both sexes were most barbarously slaughtered." Such is the account given by Jerome[r]. We are told also that Ursinus, indignant at the election of Damasus, gathered together a band of his friends, and caused Paul bishop of Tibur to consecrate him in the Sicinine or Liberian basilica; after which, on Oct. 25, a month after Liberius' death, the party of Damasus besieged the church, burst open the doors, and attacked their opponents. On that one day the pavement of the basilica was covered with 137 slain persons. The adherents of Ursinus maintained[s] that he had been duly elected by the old supporters of Liberius; that Damasus broke into the Julian church with adherents of the baser sort, who committed a massacre; that he was afterwards simoniacally elected and consecrated in the Lateran; that in order to regain possession of seven priests adhering to Ursinus, whom he had seized and their friends had rescued, he attacked the Liberian church and left there a multitude of corpses. In this case there is first the question, which of the two was legitimately elected? And we may most reasonably think that the right lay with Damasus, in whose favour we have the recorded opinion not of his friend Jerome only, but of Ambrose, who tells us that "holy Damasus was chosen by the judgment of God[t]:" not to speak of the high

[r] See his Chronicle. Ruffinus, ii. 10, says that Ursinus, infuriated at being postponed to Damasus, collected a band of turbulent men, and secured the aid of a simple rustic bishop, &c.

[s] See the memorial addressed to Theodosius by Marcellinus and Faustinus, two Luciferian priests who joined the Ursinian party because Damasus "tried to persecute" Ephesius, the Luciferian bishop at Rome, while the clergy of Damasus broke in upon Macarius, a Luciferian priest, and dragged him over flints until he received a mortal wound. The preface to this memorial in Sirmond. i. 227, says that Damasus perjured himself by owning Felix as bishop; that in the sedition he was supported by charioteers, gladiators, and labourers; that not one of those slain in the Liberian church belonged to his party; that three days later the faithful (Ursinians) recited "against him" Ps. lxxix. 2; that Ursinus was expelled, recalled, again sent into exile, his rival having bribed the court; that Damasus committed a third massacre at the cemetery of S. Agnes, where the faithful had assembled for prayer; that bishops, invited to the anniversary of his consecration, declined to condemn Ursinus.

[t] Ep. 17.

place which he filled for many years in the estimation of the orthodox[u]. A conscious intruder could hardly have become that Damasus whom the Church and the Catholic sovereigns held in such honour, and who was the prominent encourager of works of piety and charity among his people. Still there is the fact that he was to some extent connected with miserable deeds of violence done in his cause; and if we suppose that what he did on Oct. 25 was to authorize the forcible ejection of an usurper from a church, we cannot think him clear of responsibility for the inevitable results of such a command, however far they may have been from his contemplation. Ammianus takes for granted that both he and Ursinus were fired with ambition to gain that proudest of episcopal seats, and enjoy "the rich offerings of matrons[x]," the splendour of garb, the chariot, the more than royal banquets, which were adjuncts to the bishopric of "the City[y]." He could not, of course, know much of Damasus' character; but it cannot be forgotten that a taste for state and display formed part of it, that he was by nature inclined to value a position of great dignity, and that Prætextatus, the Pagan præfect who was more successful than his predecessor in quelling the sedition, was wont to say to Damasus, "Make me bishop of Rome, and I will at once turn Christian[z]!"

Ursinus was expelled from the city; but his partisans continued to disturb it by their clamorous accusations against Damasus.

Germinius bishop of Sirmium had been one of those who proposed the third Sirmian creed for acceptance at Ariminum. He now[a] took up a phraseology so reverential in re-

---

[u] Theodoret, v. 2, speaks highly of his sanctity and zeal. Ruffinus says that the carnage was turned to the prejudice "boni et innocentis sacerdotis," of whose "innocence God became the vindicator."

[x] Marcellinus and Faustinus call Damasus "matronarum auriscalpius."

[y] Amm. xxvii. 3. He adds that Roman bishops would be truly happy if they lived in the simple style of some provincial prelates, "pure and modest in the sight of the eternal Deity and His true worshippers."

[z] Jerome, c. Joan. 8.

[a] Hil. Fragm. 13.

gard to Christ's dignity as to give much disquiet to his old friends Valens and Ursacius. While sitting in council with other bishops, they wrote to him, Dec. 18, 366, asking him to disclaim the phrase, "Like to the Father in all things, excepting that He is not unborn," and to adhere rigidly to the Ariminian language, "Like to the Father according to the Scriptures." Germinius, addressing the other bishops assembled, peremptorily replied that he did hold what had been complained of, and maintained it to be Scriptural, and conformable to the original draft of the third Sirmian creed.

In the beginning of 367 we find the Eastern delegates, well supplied with letters of peace from Western Churches, appearing before an orthodox Council at Tyana [b]. Eusebius of Cappadocian Cæsarea was president. The delegates were recognized as true Catholics, and letters were written exhorting all the Eastern bishops to meet in Council at Tarsus before the summer heats set in, and consolidate the union which had been effected. It seemed as if the breach would at length be healed, and the Apostle's birthplace give a new triumph to Apostolic Christianity. But some thirty-four bishops met in Caria, and declared that, with every wish for unity, they could not admit the Homoousion nor abandon the Dedication Creed. And Valens, who had already begun to persecute the Novatians for their orthodoxy, and had banished their aged and pious bishop Agelius, was just at this time urged by his Arian wife to receive baptism from Eudoxius on the eve of his Gothic war [c]. Thus committed to Arianism, the Eastern Emperor forbade the meeting at Tarsus [d], and put forth an edict fruitful of suffering for the East, that all bishops expelled by Constantius and recalled by Julian should be again expelled from their cities [e].

---

[b] Soz. vi. 12. [c] Theod. iv. 12. [d] Soc. iv. 12.

[e] Soz. vi. 12. Marcellinus and Faustinus say that the guilty weakness of many Catholic bishops under Constantius proved a stumbling-block to Valens. The Arians could say, "These men once held our faith;" and Catholicism could thus be associated with inconsistency. "Hæc, hæc res decepit Valentem!" Sirm. i. 245.

Such was the disappointment of hopes, and the fulfilment of fears, in 367. There was to be once more an Arian persecution; and all the Semi-Arians could not be won over to the Church. Those who stood aloof from the Nicene faith were from this time known as Macedonians; "Semi-Arianism" disappears from history.

CHAPTER VI.

From the Edict of Valens to the Death of S. Basil.

"Oh by Thine own sad burthen, borne
So meekly up the hill of scorn,
Teach Thou Thy priests their daily cross
To bear as Thine, nor count it loss!"
Christian Year.

THE edict of banishment came to Alexandria; and the præfect of Egypt prepared to expel Athanasius. The Catholics remonstrated; "The edict refers to those whom Julian recalled, whereas Athanasius was the bishop whom Julian specially persecuted." Fearing a tumult, the præfect allowed Athanasius to remain until he could hear again from Valens; but one evening Athanasius secretly left his house, which was a part of the cathedral buildings, and a few hours afterwards the præfect came with an armed force, hoping to seize him without exciting observation. They searched the house in vain, from the uppermost rooms to the basement. It is said that he concealed himself in his father's tomb for four months; at last the Emperor found it best to quiet the agitation of Alexandria, and prevent any difficulties which might arise from his elder brother's stedfast orthodoxy, by terminating this fifth and last dispossession of Athanasius[a]. At first the persecution was not of a very bitter kind. No attack was made on the Church of Cæsarea, where Basil was now at work in cordial union with the Archbishop, doing his utmost to please and serve the man from whose unfriendliness he had formerly so much to suffer[b]. Eusebius found in him an affectionate and invaluable assistant, energetic in organizing the faithful against the Eunomians, supporting the weakness of some, piercing the consciences of others, healing divisions, uniting the Cappadocian Church in "loyal devotion to the Trinity." No

[a] Soz. vi. 12; Soc. iv. 13.

[b] Greg. Orat. xx. 58.

wonder that although second in dignity, he was the real ruler of the Church.

On Sept. 15, 367, Ursinus returned to Rome, but was again banished by Valentinian on Nov. 16, with seven of his adherents: but the position of Damasus was not made secure without fresh severities against the Ursinian party. Valentinian ordered that all cases in which bishops were involved should be tried not by secular judges, but by the Roman bishop and his colleagues.

We may notice here a famous Eastern Council, which was probably held *about* this time[c], although the precise date does not appear ascertainable,—that of Laodicea in Phrygia. It consisted of thirty-two bishops, and its sixty canons were received into the code of the Universal Church. Some relate to discipline, e. g. to the cases of penitents and of the twice-married, and to the reception, by anointing, of converts from certain sects. Others, to Church administration: e. g. bishops are to elect a bishop—the people are not to elect a priest—bishops are not to be appointed for villages—neophytes are not to be made bishops. But the majority relate to matters connected with Christian worship. None but the regular chanters are to sing in church. No psalms by private individuals are to be sung. A lesson is to be inserted after each psalm. The prayers said at None are to be repeated at Vespers. The Gospel is not to be omitted in the Saturday Celebration. After sermon are to follow prayers for catechumens and penitents, then the prayers of the faithful, then the Holy Offering, (i. e. the most solemn part of the service, beginning with "Lift up your hearts.") None but priests are to communicate within the sanctuary. No clerks below the diaconate are to handle the sacred vessels, or administer the Holy Sacrament. "Bread must not be offered in Lent on any day but Sunday and Saturday[d]."

[c] Fleury dates it in 367; Pagi in 363; Beveridge in 365. Others have placed it as far back as 320.

[d] That is, on all other days Communion is to take place by means of the reserved or "presanctified" Sacrament, as now in the Roman Church on

There must be no Oblation in private houses. No love-feasts may be held in churches. No candidate for Baptism may be received after the second week in Lent. Those who are being "illuminated" are to learn the Creed, and to say it to the bishop or priest on Thursday before Easter; after Baptism they are to receive the "heavenly chrism" (in Confirmation). Throughout Lent there must be fasting on dry food. The fast must not be broken on Thursday before Easter. Martyrs' days are not to be kept in Lent; the martyrs to be commemorated on the Sundays and Saturdays. No marriages, nor birthday feasts, in Lent. Anathema to those who Judaically abstain from work on Saturdays. On Sundays, if possible, men are to abstain. Men are not to join in Pagan entertainments, nor to receive unleavened bread from Jews, nor to cast out devils without authority, nor to forsake God's Church in order to hold conventicles for angel-worship [e]; anathema to those who practise this secret idolatry. Magic, astrology, and the amulets called phylacteries, are forbidden. Only the Canonical Scriptures must be read in church. To this last decree is usually appended a catalogue of the Scriptures which may be read; Baruch being included in the Old Testament, the Apocalypse excluded from the New. But there seems at least good reason for questioning the authenticity of this catalogue as a "part of the original conciliar text [f]."

On the 13th of January, 368, S. Hilary died at Poitiers. Damasus, as soon as the abatement of the Ursinian tumults gave him leisure, held a Council against Arianism, in which Valens and Ursacius were again excommunicated,—in 368 or 369. Athanasius thereupon held a Council of ninety Egyptian bishops, and wrote in their name to thank Damasus for this act, but to recommend that Auxentius should be the object of a similar censure. Another letter

---

Good Friday. The Council in Trullo, A.D. 691, ordered the Liturgy of the Presanctified to be celebrated on all days in Lent except Sundays, Saturdays, and the Feast of the Annunciation.

[e] See Col. ii. 18. [f] See Westcott on the N. T. Canon, 500—508.

was sent by the Council to all the African bishops, insisting on the authority of the Nicene Council, as "an inscription on a pillar" confounding all heresies without exception; the special purpose of the letter being to give a death-blow to all pleas in behalf of the creed of Ariminum [g]. It applied to the series of uncatholic creeds the doom against every plant which the Father had not planted: and it re-affirmed the sense of Hypostasis as meaning Substance in Heb. i. 3. The concluding words have a grand simple solemnity. "No Christian can have any doubt in his mind about the fact that our faith is not in a creature—but in one God the Father Almighty, ... and in one Lord Jesus Christ,—and in one Holy Spirit; one God, who is acknowledged in the holy and perfect Trinity, into which also we being baptized, and joined in the same to the Godhead, believe that we shall inherit the kingdom of heaven in Christ Jesus our Lord. Amen."

Towards the middle of the year 370 two very different prelates died, Eudoxius of Constantinople and Eusebius of Cappadocian Cæsarea. The latter died in the arms of Basil, who had nobly played the part of a good shepherd in the famine which had recently visited Cæsarea [h],—selling his inheritance to feed the sufferers, and including Jews as well as Christians in his bounty. There was, however, a party, chiefly among the upper classes, obstinate in dislike of Basil. They felt, no doubt, that he was too lofty in his single-mindedness to serve their purposes; and now, when the great see of Cæsarea was vacant, they opposed his election to the utmost, alleging, apparently, his weak health as a paramount objection. The opposition was happily overcome by the two Gregories, father and son,—the latter of whom advised Basil to withdraw from Cæsarea until the election should be over,—and Eusebius, bishop of Samosata, who had won the admiration even of Constantius by his firmness in refusing to surrender the election-deed of Mele-

---

[g] Ath. ad Afros.

[h] Basil. Hom. in Fam. et Sicc.

tius which had been placed in his keeping[i]. The aged bishop of Nazianzum came to Cæsarea in a litter, to assist in the consecration of the new archbishop. Weak and worn as he was, he took a prominent part in the solemn ritual,—the imposition of hands, the unction, the enthronement. And thus, in June 370, Basil began his nine years of episcopal trials, anxieties, and disappointments, all to be endured under a continual pressure of bad health. The episcopate was to him a burden indeed. Yet Gregory of Nazianzum could truly say that "what he did with one hand was worth more than what another man did with the labour of both." As primate of Pontus, or as bishop of Cæsarea, he was unwearied in his apostolic labours; seeking out fit persons for holy orders, busying himself in the improvement of divine service and in the rekindling of devotional zeal, framing, in substance at least, the Liturgy which bears his name, and is still used by the Greek Church on ten days in the year; diligent as a preacher, constant in visiting the sick, the founder of a hospital which resembled a town, guarding Church discipline[j], rebuking clerical misconduct, winning over by a noble frankness and gentleness the bishops who had resisted his election. Such were some of his works in his own more immediate sphere of duty; but his anxiety to fulfil his ministry kept him watchful for the welfare of the whole Church.

About this time we may place the controversy between Parmenian, the Donatist bishop of Carthage, and Optatus, the Catholic bishop of Milevis, to which we are indebted for much of our knowledge of Donatism.

On July 29, 370, Valentinian published a law which shows the extent to which secularity had taken hold of the

---

[i] Theod. ii. 32.

[j] See Epp. 53, 54: he tells his chorepiscopi that some of them are accused of simony in the matter of ordination; and rebukes them for ordaining without first laying before him the names of candidates. In Ep. 55 he rebukes a priest for transgressing the Nicene canon which forbade women, except relations, &c., to be inmates of the houses of clergy, (*synacti* or *subintroductæ*).

Roman Church. He forbade clergy and monks to haunt the houses of widows or orphans; and annulled every bequest by a woman to her spiritual guide [k].

Some months after the death of Eudoxius, the Catholics of Constantinople, who had but a single small church in the city, chose Evagrius for their bishop. He was banished into Thrace: the Arians chose Demophilus of Berœa, who had been the tempter of Liberius [l]. The dominant Arians tyrannized over Catholics at their will; and eighty clergy who went to remonstrate with Valens at Nicomedia were, by his order to Modestus the præfect, put on board ship as if to go into exile. When the vessel was entering the Propontis the crew set her on fire, took to the barge, and left the prisoners to their doom [m]. Meletius was banished to Armenia, and Flavian and Diodore, now no longer laics, were again called upon to sustain the faith in Antioch. They assembled the faithful in caverns, by the river-side, and in the open country. Paulinus, who, as we have seen, had so won the respect of the Arian bishop as to be allowed the use of a church within the city [n], was now permitted by the Arian monarch, "on account of his exceeding piety [o]," to remain undisturbed.

Basil had much to bear at home from painful misunderstandings with a kinsman, his uncle Gregory; with his yet unconciliated suffragans; with Catholics who suspected him for his Semi-Arian connections, or who discerned treason to the faith in the cautious language which he employed as to the Divinity of the Holy Spirit, whom on one occasion, with a view to some weak brethren, he designated rather as uncreate than as consubstantial [p]. Looking abroad, he saw an

---

[k] Jerome says, "I do not complain of the law, but I grieve that we should have deserved it. Yet even this provident severity was insufficient as a check to avarice." Ep. 52 ad Nep.

[l] Basil says, Ep. 48, that "Demophilus has a show of sanctity."

[m] Soc. iv. 16; Soz. vi. 14. [n] Soz. v. 13. [o] Soc. iv. 2.

[p] They scrupled about applying this term to the Holy Spirit, and urged that he was not called God in Scripture. Basil meant gradually to lead

Arian prince making war upon Catholicism; the worst form of Arianism overrunning the East; the general schism which was to have been healed at Tarsus still dividing brother from brother; the special schism between Paulinus and Meletius extended into a dissension between the West and the East. The miseries of the time weighed down his soul. To whom under Heaven could he turn for aid and sympathy? There was yet living one man, one "great and apostolic soul[q]," the natural centre of unity for all the faithful, honoured both by East and West, able, if any one was, to draw them both together. Whether in regard to particular or general difficulties, it was natural to turn to Athanasius.

Very beautiful and touching is the relation now formed between these two saints. Basil receives an intimation that Athanasius has excommunicated a wicked governor of Libya, and forthwith proclaims the sentence in his own church[r]. He begs Athanasius to use his influence with the Westerns for the recognition of Meletius, to *manage* Paulinus, to stir up the Eastern orthodox by his letters, and to plead like Samuel for the churches. He calls him the "head" of Christendom, and expresses his ardent desire to see his face[s]. Athanasius sends one of his priests to visit Basil, and on hearing of the suspicions entertained as to his orthodoxy in regard to Macedonianism, exhorts the doubters to put away their fears, and be thankful for so "glorious" a bishop[t]. To Damasus Basil also wrote, entreating on behalf of the suffering Easterns that far-reaching and generous kindness for which the Roman bishops had been celebrated[u]. Athanasius about this time gave a new proof of his superiority to narrow formalism. The people of Palæbisca and Hydrax, two towns in the diocese of Erythrum, persuaded the aged Bishop Orion to

---

them to the full truth, by showing them that He had all the Divine attributes.

[q] Basil, Ep. 80.

[r] Bas. Ep. 60.

[s] Epp. 66, 67, 69, 80.

[t] Ath. ad Pall., tom. ii. 763, 764.

[u] Ep. 70. Dionysius of Rome, Basil observes, had sent agents to redeem the Cæsarean Christians from captivity.

let them have a prelate of their own. He deputed Philo to consecrate the man of their choice, a young layman of practical ability named Siderius. This consecration, performed by a single bishop, and without any sanction from the throne of Alexandria, was doubly irregular in a canonical point of view. But the great Patriarch allowed it to stand, and even promoted Siderius to the more important see of Ptolemais [x].

The request which Athanasius had made to Rome for a special condemnation of Auxentius was complied with by Damasus in a large Council of Italian and Gallican bishops, probably held in 371. The inviolable character of the Nicene Creed was again enforced. We have the synodal letter as it was sent to Illyricum, and also as it was sent to the Easterns, authenticated by the signature of a Milanese deacon [y]. Basil wished for a deputation of Westerns, to aid in resisting the Eastern heretics and in reuniting the orthodox; but he trusted that this might come in time. He had an interview with Modestus in the autumn of 371, when he amazed the præfect by his boldness [z]. He would never "adore a creature," i. e. the Son as conceived of by the Arians. "Do you not fear what I can make you suffer?" asked Modestus. "Tell me what it is," said Basil. "Confiscation, exile, tortures, death." "Find out some more potent menace," was the calm reply. "Nobody ever spoke so boldly to Modestus," said the præfect, bewildered by the Archbishop's lofty scorn. The significant answer was, "Perhaps you never before fell in with a bishop!" Modestus, utterly foiled, called Valens himself to aid in conquering Basil. It was Epiphany in 372 when the Emperor attended service in the cathedral of Cæsarea [a]. He found the church thronged with "a sea" of people. The

---

[x] Synesius, Ep. 67.

[y] In the letter to Illyricum as given by Theod. ii. 22, but not as in Soz. vi. 23, occurs a statement that "bishops" were sent from Rome to Nicæa. Valesius would read ἐπίλεκτοι, "chosen men." For the letter as sent to the Easterns, which contains a like statement, cf. Mansi, iii. 459.

[z] S. Greg. Orat. xx. 73.

[a] S. Greg. l. c. 76.

chant of the Psalms pealed forth like thunder. The archbishop stood, as was then usual, behind the altar[b], which was between him and the people; but although his face was turned towards them, he seemed rapt and absorbed in the service. Around him stood the attendant ministers, and throughout the church all was reverence, solemnity, and order. The unearthly majesty of the scene struck Valens with awe. His nerves gave way when he advanced to present his offering, and no hand was extended to receive the gift of a heretic: he would even have fallen, but for the support of one of the clergy. On another occasion the effect was deepened by a conversation which he held with Basil; but no such impressions could be lasting on such a mind, and when he arrived at Antioch the persecution of Catholics became a fiery trial indeed. Basil's letters describe the state of the East, the expulsion of faithful pastors, the promotion of daring Anomœans, the contempt of Church laws, of theology, of piety; the hard worldliness of the prevailing tone, the bewilderment of the simple, the triumph of unbelievers. "Old men lament when they think of old times; the young are worse off, for they have known nothing better." The faithful avoid the established "teachers of blasphemy," and meet for prayer in the wilderness[c]. At Edessa the Catholics were deprived of their bishop[d], and forbidden to meet in the cathedral. Instead of obeying, they crowded thither. Modestus encountered a woman on her way to church, leading a little child. She answered his inquiries by saying that she meant the child to share in the crown of martyrdom with herself. Upon this, Modestus gave up his attempt on such a people, but he exiled some eighty of their clergy on their refusal to hold communion with the Emperor.

---

[b] His throne was at the eastern extremity of the sanctuary, and he would advance from it towards the altar, which stood nearer to the "holy doors."

[c] Epp. 90, 92; "to the Western bishops," and "to the Italian and Catholic bishops."

[d] Theod. iv. 16; Soc. iv. 18; Soz. vi. 18.

Soon after the Roman Council had condemned Auxentius, Athanasius was obliged to take more formal notice of the error respecting our Lord's true Manhood which had been condemned in the Council of 362. It was about 369 that this error assumed a more definite form, though even then it was not known as the theory of Apollinaris. It started from the idea of the true Divinity of Christ; and professing exceeding reverence for Him, argued that if He had had a human mind, or "reasonable Soul," He must have had sinful instincts, and further that the one Christ would have been, in fact, two. The conclusion was, that the Word supplied the place of a mind in Christ[e]. This proposition denied the truth of the Incarnation, by denying that Christ assumed the whole of that Manhood which He came to redeem. And the downward impulse of heretical thought led the followers of Apollinaris, the real propagator of the doctrine, to maintain that "Incarnation" meant only a converse of God with man, and that Christ's Body was not really born of Mary, but was a portion of the Godhead converted into flesh. These opinions, and others akin to them, were now gaining a hold on Corinth. Their show of piety made them powerful with minds which would have resisted errors of a different type; and the temper which shrank back from such an awful nearness of God to man as was implied in a perfect Incarnation, disguised itself in the garb of jealousy for God's honour. Athanasius, being applied to by Epictetus, bishop of Corinth, wrote a tract against the monstrous notion of a body consubstantial with Godhead, whereby the truth of Christ's birth from Mary, the truth of His Sacrifice, the truth of His Manhood, were annulled. He also wrote two books against the heresy, but without naming Apollinaris, who was his old friend, and whom, perhaps, he believed to be not committed to it. Another former friend, twenty years older than himself, whose errors

[e] Equivocation was sometimes resorted to on this point. It was said, "Christ has really a mind;" meaning, that the Word was to Him instead of it. Epiph. Hær. 77. 23.

he had been obliged to acknowledge as undeniable, and as the source of great scandal to the Catholic cause, Marcellus of Ancyra, whom Basil had recently again denounced[f], sent his deacon Eugenius to Alexandria, with a statement of belief which might be called half satisfactory. It anathematized the "insanity" of Photinus, and distinctly asserted the Word's personality; but it omitted to affirm the perpetuity of Christ's Manhood and kingdom. Athanasius' suffragans accepted this declaration; his own signature is absent,—perhaps has been lost accidentally.

The year 372 was distinguished by the martyrdom of S. Sabas, a Christian Goth, for refusing to eat things offered to idols; and by three important episcopal consecrations. Gregory, Basil's brother, became bishop of Nyssa. Gregory of Nazianzum was fixed upon by Basil to occupy a new see which he was determined to found at Sasima, in order to strengthen the see of Cæsarea against the aggression of Anthimus, bishop of Tyana, who claimed to be a metropolitan, because his city had just been made the head of a division of Cappadocia. Sasima was a comfortless, unhealthy town, full of noise and dust, and inhabited by an unsatisfactory set of people; of all places the least fitted to be a home for the shrinking and sensitive Gregory. Regardless of Gregory's objections, Basil compelled him to receive consecration; he attempted to settle at Sasima, but was driven away by the violent Anthimus, who had on one occasion stopped Basil's way home by a band of freebooters.

Gregory took up his abode at Nazianzum as his father's coadjutor; and the unhappy result of the matter was that he never again felt thoroughly at home with Basil, and one

---

[f] Ep. 69. Basil urges that the Westerns should condemn Marcellus. The Benedictine biographer of S. Basil thinks that the mission of Eugenius took place soon after 363, and that afterwards Athanasius found it necessary to withdraw his communion from Marcellus. There is a curious anecdote in Epiph. Hær. 72. 4, that when Epiphanius asked S. Athanasius what he thought of Marcellus, Athanasius signified by a smile that Marcellus had just managed to clear himself.

of the most beautiful of Christian friendships was permanently marred by a strong will and a lack of sympathy. In July S. Martin was chosen bishop of Tours by the unanimous desire of the whole district.

S. Athanasius could not do all that Basil had hoped. Although Meletius, at Basil's recommendation [g], had shown his wish to be in communion with Alexandria, the old ties between Athanasius and the Eustathians could not be broken; and the schism remained unhealed. Athanasius' work was now done. He had sat on the throne of S. Mark for forty-six years, and was past seventy, when he ended his life and labours on Thursday, May 2, 373 [h].

His glorious career illustrates "the incredible power of an orthodox faith, held with inflexible earnestness, especially when its champion is an able and energetic man [i]." One is struck with the variety of gifts and the unity of aim which it exhibits. The infidel historian deemed him fit to rule an empire, and obviously he had to the fullest extent the power of dealing with men; yet he was publicly called for as "the ascetic" at his election, and in exile he was a model of monastic piety. If he is great as a theologian, and intensely given to Scripture and sacred studies, he is "pre-eminently quick in seeing the right course, and full of practical energy in pursuing it [j]." He is as kindly in his judgments of Liberius, and Hosius, and the Council of Ariminum, as if he were not the bravest of confessors. He can make allowance for the difficulties of Semi-Arians, and recognize their real "brotherhood" with himself. "Out of the strong comes forth sweetness." It is this union of inflexibility and dis-

---

g In Ep. 89 Basil tells Meletius that nothing can be done unless he will write first to Athanasius, who was grieved by the previous failure of his efforts to be in communion with Meletius.

h "Post multos agones, multasque patientiæ coronas." Ruff. ii. 3. "Quem hæreticæ persecutionis procella non contrivit, sed probavit." Cassian de Inc. Dom. vii. 29. The date 373 seems better supported than 371; it has the authority of S. Proterius of Alexandria, the Chron. Orient., and S. Jerome; Socrates would give 371.

i Ranke, Popes, ii. 222.

j S. Basil, Ep. 152.

cretion, of firmness and charity, this manysidedness as a pattern for imitation[k], which makes him emphatically Athanasius *the Great*. And wherever we find him,—confronting opponents, baffling conspirators, biding his time in Gaul or Italy, turning his hour of triumph to good account for his flock, calling on them in the hour of deadliest peril to praise the Everlasting Mercies, burying himself in cells and dens of the earth, bearing honour and dishonour with the same kingliness of soul, uniting the freshness of early enthusiasm with the settled strength of heroic manhood, writing, preaching, praying, suffering,—he is enkindled and sustained throughout by one clear purpose. What lay closest to his heart was no formula, however authoritative—no Council, however œcumenic. His zeal for the Consubstantiality had its root in his loyalty to the CONSUBSTANTIAL[l]. He felt that in the Nicene dogma were involved the worship of Christ and the life of Christianity. The inestimable Creed which he was said to have composed in a cave at Treves, is his only in this sense, that, on the whole, it sums up his teaching; but its hymn-like form may remind us that his maintenance of dogma was a life-long act of devotion. The union of these two elements is the lesson of his life, as it was the secret of his power; and by virtue of it, as has been well said[m], although "again and again it is *Athanasius contra mundum*[n], yet Athanasius is

---

k S. Greg. Orat. xxi. 9. He was, in the words of the Parisian Hymn for the Common of Bishops,—

"The lame man's staff, the blind man's sight,
The sinner's guiding light;
A father, prompt to hear each call,
And all things made to all."

l "Athanase etait enflammé, dès sa jeunesse, de la passion qui fait les Saints, l'amour de J. C. Le jour ou il crut voir dans les discours d'Arius une atteinte portée à l'honneur de ce Dieu chéri, il bondit d'indignation, et . . . consacra désormais sans relâche à la défense du Verbe Incarné, toutes les ressources d'une science immense et d'une dialectique invincible, dirigées par un grand bon sens et par une volonté de fer." De Broglie, *L'Eglise et l'Empire*, i. 372.

m Chr. Remembr. xxxvi. 206.

n When he stood up *contra mundum*, it was *propter Ecclesiam*. His

in truth *the immortal*, and ever in the end prevails." "Hæc est victoria quæ vincit mundum, Fides nostra."

He had been asked to recommend a successor. He named his old friend Peter, who was elected and enthroned[o]. But the præfect Palladius, with a band of soldiers and other unbelievers, attacked the church of S. Theonas, and re-enacted the horrors of 356. Pagan hymns and foul words resounded through the church; a youth in woman's attire danced upon the altar where, says Peter[p], "we invoke the Holy Spirit;" a shameless wretch, seating himself upon the throne, delivered a discourse in favour of immorality; virgins were insulted, and some of them even killed with clubs. Peter escaped; by one account, he was for a time imprisoned. Euzoius of Antioch, and Magnus the imperial treasurer, were sent by Valens with a great force to install the Arian Lucius. "No monks, chanting hymns from Scripture, preceded" the new bishop; a far different sound hailed his arrival. "Welcome," cried the Pagans, "thou bishop that deniest the Son,—thou whom Serapis loves and has brought hither!" Lucius openly denied that Christ was truly God, and Peter denounces him as an idolater, who worshipped a being whom he declared to be not from all eternity. Magnus arrested nineteen clergy, commanded them to embrace the Emperor's faith, assured them that even were it not the truth, a compulsory conformity would involve them in no sin, and that their choice lay between wealth and exile. They answered, "It is no new thing for us to serve God. We never will believe that the Son is finite and created; if the Son were not eternal, God was not always Father. The Homoousion is based on Scripture." They were imprisoned, tortured, put on board a vessel bound for Phœnicia, though a storm was raging at the time. A Roman deacon bearing letters from Damasus

strength, under God, lay simply in the fact that he was witnessing for the immemorial faith, which had been affirmed as Catholic at Nicæa.

o Soc. iv. 20.

p See his Epistle in Theod. iv. 22.

was barbarously beaten [q], and sent by sea to perish in the mines. Citizens, and even their children, were put to the torture; monks were seized and hurried into exile, bishops [r] dragged before the tribunal and banished to a place inhabited by Jews. Some of the faithful were slain, and their corpses, as formerly, kept unburied. Well might S. Basil write to the Alexandrians, "Is not this the great apostasy [s]?" Peter had escaped to Rome, and was kiudly received by Damasus. The horror with which Lucius was regarded appears in the story of Moses, who was named bishop of the "Saracens" to the east of Palestiue, at the request of their queen Mavia, but refused to be consecrated by Lucius. "I know that you cannot confer the Holy Spirit." "How," asked Lucius, "do you conjecture this?" "I do not conjecture, I know it. Your words are blasphemy, your acts are barbarous and impious." He received consecration from exiled Catholic bishops.

S. Martin, as soon as he became bishop, had begun that course of evangelic labours which won him the title of the Apostle of Gaul. He went about the country, opposing heathenism in its strongholds; on one occasion, it is said [t], he accepted a challenge made by the Pagan priests to stand bouud beneath a sacred pine-tree which they offered to cut down. The tree yielded to their blows, and was on the point of falling upon the bishop: he made the sign of the cross; it swayed to the other side, and fell harmlessly: multitudes were won over to the faith. Miraculous powers, indeed, are said to have frequently accompanied Martin's preaching, and although there may be great exaggerations on the subject, we may well suppose that the work which he had to do in Gaul would be attested by some such divine tokens. He went in the summer of this year to Milan,

---

[q] "On entering the vessel he made the sign of the cross."

[r] One bishop, named Melas, was found by the soldiers trimming his church lamps. He waited on them at table. Stories are told of miracles wrought by the confessors. See Soz. vi. 20; Theod. iv. 21.

[s] Ep. 139.

[t] Sulp. Vit. Mart. 10.

where Valentinian, though prejudiced against him by an Arian wife, was induced at last to receive him graciously.

One of Basil's greatest troubles began about this time, in the rupture between him and Eustathius of Sebaste. This prelate, whom Basil had for years looked upon with respect for his strictness of life, and whose laxity of doctrinal principle he had not suspected, was, as we have seen, one of the Eastern deputation to Liberius, and appeared on the whole to have detached himself from his old Arian connections [u]. In 373, as it appears, Basil, hearing that Eustathius was regarded as really unsound, although the Catholic Council of Tyana had restored him to his bishopric, requested him to sign a long confession of faith, which concluded by affirming in strong terms the Divinity of the Holy Spirit, and distinguishing Him from all "ministering spirits." Eustathius accepted it in precise terms. "I, Eustathius, bishop, having read the above-written to you, Basil, acknowledge and approve it, and subscribe it in the presence of my brethren." But after promising to attend a council which Basil proposed to call for the establishment of a complete understanding between him and those who had deemed him heterodox, he never appeared, and went so far as to hold assemblies in which he denounced Basil, and even to break off all communion with him, on the ground that he had written a letter to Apollinaris. Basil then found, as he expressed it, that "the Ethiopian could not change his skin;" that the effects of a heretical training were, in this case at least, not to be got rid of. Eustathius continued to calumniate and revile Basil as an Apollinarian, a "Consubstantialist," an "innovator" on the old doctrine as to the Holy Spirit. When Basil proposed that he should declare unequivocally against Macedonianism, Eustathius took refuge in verbose evasions, and Basil saw that peace was out of the question. He was afflicted about

[u] He had been a pupil of Arius, and had afterwards cleared himself of suspicion by presenting a sound confession to Hermogenes, bishop of Cæsarea.

this time with repeated attacks of illness; and had the annoyance of finding that Evagrius, a messenger from the West, who intimated that some letters from the East had not given satisfaction, refused to communicate with the Meletians. He wrote to Evagrius that he was eager for peace, but could not act without Meletius.

Early in 374 he was greatly comforted by the accession of Amphilochius, the friend of Gregory, to the see of Iconium, and exhorted him to "be strong and of a good courage, to remember Who would aid him to bear his burden, and to 'cast his care upon the Lord.'" But this year was saddened by the exile of his friend S. Eusebius of Samosata. An officer came to send Eusebius into banishment: the bishop quietly bade him conceal his errand, "lest the people in their zeal should drown you[x]." He then said the evening service, took one domestic with him, and crossed the Euphrates at night. Some of his flock overtook him; he recited to them the texts about obedience to rulers, accepted a few gifts from his dearest friends, prayed for them all, exhorted them to be stedfast in the faith, and went his way. His people would not speak to or visit the Arian who was appointed his successor. After he had been at the public bath, they let out the water as impure. The new bishop, a gentle-spirited man, could not bear to be under the ban of his nominal flock, and resigned the see. The next Arian bishop was of sterner stuff, aud punished abhorrence with sentences of exile.

On July 12, 374, a Gallican Council was held at Valence[y], for the restoration of discipline. S. Phœbadius appears to have presided. The canons relate to cases of bigamy, of the marriage of widows, of dedicated virgins who enter upon "earthly nuptials," of men falling back after baptism into idolatry, or reiterating their baptism[z], or falsely accusing themselves in order to avoid ordination.

---

[x] Theod. iv. 14. [y] Mansi, Concil. iii. 492.

[z] This is called "polluting themselves by an unholy washing."

Towards the end of this year Auxentius of Milan died. Valentinian desired the people to choose a successor. The governor of Liguria, named Ambrose[a], was in the act of exhorting the people to observe order, when a child suddenly uttered the words, "*Ambrose Bishop*." The people took up the cry; it was deemed a special case, in which divine intervention pointed out the predestined bishop. It mattered not, in their view, that Ambrose was not yet baptized. The principle embodied in a Sardican canon, which required a time of probation before the episcopate, was held not to apply to an occasion so extraordinary. Ambrose tried various means of escaping from a burden which he unfeignedly dreaded. He attempted to destroy the high opinion which had been formed of him, somewhat after the manner which had just been censured at Valence. He attempted flight, and did actually hide himself for a time, but was given up by the owner of his place of refuge to the authorities who were busy in searching for him. Finding resistance hopeless, he asked that none but a Catholic bishop might baptize him. This was readily granted. Seven days after his baptism he was consecrated, Dec. 7, 374, being thirty-four years old. Whether the form of the Sardican canon was to some extent complied with by conferring on him, during that week, the inferior orders, has been doubted. From the Greek historians[b] we should infer the negative: but Paulinus, his secretary and biographer, is a much higher authority, and his words are, "It is said that after his baptism he discharged all ecclesiastical offices" before his consecration[c]. In any case Ambrose might well say of himself, that he was "snatched from the tribunals to the epi-

---

[a] He had been an advocate, and Anicius Probus, prætorian præfect of Italy, a noble and generous Christian magistrate, gave him the governorship with words which were afterwards deemed prophetic. "Vade, age non ut judex, sed ut episcopus." Paul. Vit. S. Ambr. 8.

[b] Soc. iv. 30; Soz. vi. 24.

[c] Paul. Vit. S. Amb. 9. Bingham seems to have misapprehended this passage. (Book ii. 10. 7.) The Roman Breviary, Dec. 7, and Martene, de Rit. Eccl. ii. 22, say that he passed through all the orders.

scopate, and had to begin to teach before he had begun to learn." He set himself to study theology under Simplicianus, a Roman priest.

The ecclesiastical history of these years, so far as the East is concerned, might be described as a history of the sufferings of S. Basil. Seldom has any man of his personal and official eminence in the Church been so heavily burdened by the trial of opposition, misrepresentation, isolation, and seeming failure. The bishops of the coast of Pontus listened to his enemies, and shrank from his fellowship. There is a mournful pathos in the great Basil's letter to these hard-judging brethren [d]. He disclaimed all notion of being above criticism; he was willing to humble himself for any fault that could be proved against him [e]; but he entreated them for the sake of the "One Lord, the one faith, the one hope," to meet him in any place that they might think best, and give him an opportunity of removing their suspicions. In this, apparently, he succeeded. He had more difficulty with the Neocæsareans [f], who had, to say the least, Sabellian tendencies, and could not endure the emphasis with which he was wont to speak of the Three Persons. They also disliked his encouragement of monasticism, and the vigil-services which he had introduced. It appears that the people, under Basil's auspices, assembled in church before day-break, and after a solemn confession of sins, proceeded to chant the Psalms, sometimes antiphonally, sometimes under the leadership of a precentor; prayers were inserted between the psalms; and at dawn the congregation united in the *Miserere*. It also appears that the Neocæsareans, who objected to the vigils as having been unknown in the days of their apostle, S. Gregory the Wonder-worker, (A.D. 240,) had no scruple about perform-

---

[d] Ep. 203.

[e] His reserved manner was sometimes attributed to pride: but he did not shrink from kissing a leper, and in Ep. 56 he owns that he is apt to be forgetful. In Ep. 262 he assures a monk that he need not apologize for writing to him.

[f] Epp. 204, 207, 210.

ing "litanies" or processional devotions, which were equally devoid of his authority.

The year 375 witnessed some exhibitions of Western sympathy for the Eastern orthodox. An Illyrian Council[g] wrote to the bishops of Asia Minor, strongly affirming the doctrine of the Three Consubstantial Persons; and Valentinian added a rebuke to those Eastern bishops who were abusing the imperial authority to the overthrow of the Catholic faith. He denounced those who rendered to Cæsar the things that were God's, and set forth a doctrinal statement, condemning those who explained away Homoousion as a mere synonym of Homoion, and declaring Christ to be not a God-bearing man, but an Incarnate God. He died in November, 375, and his son Gratian, a boy of seventeen, who had been eight years associated with him in the empire, became sole master of the West. Soon afterwards, in 376, Gratian ordained that ecclesiastical cases arising from dissensions or slight offences should be locally tried by the synods; while cases arising from criminal action should be tried by judges ordinary or extraordinary, or by the chief civil magistrate of the district.

Basil had some reason for quoting the fable of the wolf and the lamb[h] in regard to the reckless accusations showered upon him. He was called a Sabellian, an Apollinarian, a Tritheist, a Macedonian. On the latter point, we have already seen him defended by S. Athanasius. But the charge was revived, on the ground that he had used a suspicious form of the doxology; "Glory be to the Father, *through* the Son, *in* the Holy Spirit." Finding it necessary to defend himself, Basil prayed[i] that he might for ever be abandoned by the Holy Spirit if he did not adore Him together with the Father and the Son: and he composed a treatise "Concerning the Holy Spirit," which he dedicated to his friend S. Amphilochius[j], to whom he had recently

---

[g] Some date this earlier. The letter is in Theod. iv. 9.

[h] Ep. 189.

[i] S. Greg. Orat. xx. 100.

[j] Amphilochius is the author of a remarkable passage on the relation of

addressed three epistles on points of discipline, which became part of the Eastern canon law. Eustathius persevered in his calumnies against Basil, and at last, in order, as Basil says, to win the favour of Euzoius, signed at Cyzicus a formally Macedonian creed. Basil thereupon broke the silence which for three years he had observed towards his adversary, and wrote him a formal letter of remonstrance[k].

Heresy in various forms appeared now to be triumphant in the East. It is supposed that Ulphilas, bishop of the Goths, although he had signed the creed of Ariminum, had not consciously abandoned the Catholic faith[l]. He had led a body of his countrymen over the Danube, and was regarded by them as their Moses and their apostle. He "had undergone many perils for the sake of Christianity," and had given to his flock an alphabet and a version of the Scriptures, from which he thought good to omit the four books of Kings lest they should increase his disciples' passion for war. He was about this time sent to implore aid from Valens against the heathen Goth, Athanaric, and was induced[m] to adopt the Emperor's religion. Strong in his ascendancy over the Christian Goths, he unhappily succeeded in bringing them over to Arianism, by the assurance that the difference between it and Catholicism was only superficial. Thus did Constantine's old fallacy revive, after fifty years, to present the heresy to simple-minded barbarians, who having once thoroughly grasped it, for ages would not let it go.

The extreme Arians, or Eunomians, although separate from the established Arianism, were powerful enemies of the suffering Church. They used to profess a perfect comprehension of the Divine Nature, and to ask the Catholics, "Do you worship what you know, or what you know not?" Basil

---

the Father to the Son. "The Father is greater and equal; greater than He who slept in the stern, equal to Him who rebuked the sea . . . greater than He who received vinegar to drink, equal to Him who poureth out as wine His own proper Blood."

[k] Ep. 223. See Epp. 226, 244.

[l] Soz. vi. 37.

[m] Theod. iv. 37.

taught his brethren to answer, "The word *know* is ambiguous; we can know God's goodness, and His majesty; *we cannot know His very essence*[n]." He had written, several years before, five books against Eunomius. He was vigilant in opposing Apollinarianism, which he considered to be a revival of the old Valentinian heresy[o], inasmuch as it denied our Lord's Body to be truly of the Virgin's substance. All our interest in the Incarnation, he contended, must depend on the real union of our flesh to Godhead[p]. Apollinarian tracts were widely disseminated, in which the subject was discussed on grounds of *à priori* reasoning; and this unscripturalness of the heresy[q],—a point which it had in common with Arianism,—was combined with a strange Judaism which looked for a restoration of the ritual of the Law[r]. And as Apollinaris had denied the Blessed Virgin to be the real Mother of the Word Incarnate, some were led on to a denial of her perpetual Virginity, and others, by re-action, made her the object of an idolatrous homage. First in Thrace, and then among the women in Arabia, there grew up a custom of placing cakes (*collyrides*) on a stool covered with linen, offering them up to S. Mary, and then eating them as sacrificial food. Epiphanius, bishop of Salamis in Cyprus, who about this time began his great work against heresies, severely condemned these two extremes. He denounced those who denied Christ's Mother to be Ever-virgin as "Antidicomarians," adversaries of Mary, who deprived her of "honour" due; but he insisted that according to the essential principles of Christianity, "worship" was due to the Trinity alone[s].

Meantime the Eastern Catholics, who were stedfast in worshipping the Trinity, were often obliged to pay that

---

[n] Ep. 233. [o] Ep. 261. [p] Ep. 262. [q] Ep. 263.

[r] "Again a typical pontiff after the True Pontiff, and sin-offerings after the Lamb of God . . . and divers washings after One Baptism, and the ashes of a heifer, . . . and the shewbread after the Bread from Heaven," &c. Ep. 265.

[s] "Let Mary be had in honour; but let the Father, Son, and Holy Spirit, be worshipped: let no one worship Mary." Hær. 79. 7.

worship in the open country, and under the open sky. The aged and the sick, women and children, formed part of these faithful congregations. Cold and heat, winds and storms, were preferable to sanctuaries which had become the scene of Arian "polytheism," and the "worship of the image." Festivals were changed into days of mourning: the preacher's voice, the nightly chant, were silenced; the altars were bereft of "the spiritual service," and "the holy exultation" of a Communion-day was become a thing of the past[t]. And the Westerns, Basil complained, had no pity for these sorrows. Damasus was, in his view, a cold and haughty prelate, who would not stoop from his pride of place to hear the truth from men who stood below[u]; from "that Western superciliousness," he bitterly said, no relief could be hoped for[x]. Two priests, Dorotheus and Sanctissimus, were sent to Rome as envoys from the East, first in 376[y], and afterwards in 377. Kind words were the result of the first mission; but on the second occasion Dorotheus, in a conversation with Damasus and Peter, heard Meletius and Eusebius spoken of as Arians[z]. In truth, it was not simply a question between the Westerns as supporters of one bishop at Antioch, and the majority of the Easterns as recognizing another. Paulinus and the Westerns adhered to the old phrase, "One Hypostasis," meaning one Divine Essence, and suspected Meletius and the Easterns of Arianism on account of their assertion of "Three Hypostases." The latter replied by imputations of Sabellianism, and complained that the disciples of Marcellus were indulgently regarded by Paulinus[a]. All the charitable pains taken by the Council of Alexandria appeared to have been thrown away: and it is amid these unhappy complications that the great name of Jerome becomes important in Church history. Eusebius Hieronymus,

---

[t] Bas. Epp. 242, 843. [u] Ep. 215. [x] Ep. 239, A.D. 376.

[y] So the Benedictines. Tillemont places their first mission in 374.

[z] Ep. 266. Dorotheus made an angry reply to Peter, which Basil accounts for by "the difficulty of the times." [a] Bas. Ep. 263.

a Dalmatian by birth, who had in early life been an advocate at Rome, had been baptized, and had spent some time at Treves and Aquileia [b], was now living as a monk in Syria, with two companions. The Syrian monks importuned him to confess the Three Hypostases. He answered that he fully believed in the Three Persons, but could not take Hypostasis to mean anything but Essence [c]. They insisted that he should accept the phrase as well as the doctrine. In his perplexity he applied to Damasus. It was natural that he should do so. Rome was associated with many solemn moments of his undisciplined youth [d], and with his subsequent baptism; and her bishops had been conspicuously true to the faith, except in the one sad instance for which Liberius had lived to atone. Their "primacy of honour," on the whole, had been adorned by a faithfulness which accounts for Jerome's fervid language: "While foxes were in the vineyard, and the seamless coat was rent, he felt moved to seek food for his soul where the heritage had been kept from corruption." The kindness of Damasus invited him, although his grandeur was overawing. Following "Christ only as Chief," Jerome professed to be in communion with the See of Peter. "On 'this rock,' I know, the Church is built; whoso eats the Lamb outside that house is profane. I know not Vitalis"—whom Apollinaris had recently made bishop of his sect at Antioch—"I disown Meletius, I know not Paulinus. Whoso gathers not with thee, scatters; that is, whoso is not of Christ is of Antichrist." He begs Damasus, "by the crucified Salvation of the world," to signify whether the belief in Three Persons may be expressed by "Three Hypostases;" intimating at

---

[b] At Treves he copied out S. Hilary's work on Synods; at Aquileia he found that the evil done by Fortunatian's lapse had been repaired by his successor Valerian.

[c] S. Basil was just as positive that Hypostasis could *not* be identified with Ousia. See Ep. 236.

[d] He used to go with other boys on Sundays to visit the tombs of the apostles and martyrs, and descend into the awful gloom of the catacombs. In Ezech. lib. xii. c. 40.

the same time his own opinion, that no explanations can clear the phrase from the "poison" of Tritheism [e].

This appeal, which meant, in fact, "Rome has been, and is, the stronghold of S. Peter's faith, and I am safest in following her guidance," was made about the beginning of 377; and in the following year the claim of Apollinaris to be in communion with Damasus was refuted by his condemnation at the Council of Rome [f]. Damasus wrote a synodal epistle, which pronounced twenty-two anathematisms, e. g. against those who said that the Spirit was made by the Son; that the Word was in place of a rational soul to Christ; that the Word would come to an end; that the Son was not omniscient and coequal; that He was not in heaven even while on earth; that His Divinity suffered; that He did not suffer in flesh, or was not in flesh at God's right hand, or would not return in flesh at the judgment; that the Spirit was not Very God, even as Father and Son, with the same divinity, majesty, glory, will, coequal, co-eternal, and co-adorable; that the Three are three Gods, not one God. "For," says Damasus, "we are baptized in the Name of the Father, Son, and Spirit, not (as Jews and Heathen think) in the names of angels and archangels." This "Tome of the Westerns [g]" was sent in the first instance to Paulinus.

But the year 378 was chiefly marked by the recall of the Catholic exiles and the close of the Arian ascendancy. Valens put an end to the persecution when he was on the eve of his last campaign against the Goths. Gratian, who

---

[e] Ep. 15, al. 57. See the following Ep. 16, in which he says, "I cry aloud in the meantime, Whosoever is in communion with the chair of Peter is my friend."

[f] Ruffinus says that the Council decreed "that whosoever should deny the perfection, either of the Humanity or of the Divinity of the Son, who was both God and Man, should be deemed an alien from the Church; which judgment was confirmed by a synodal decree, both at Alexandria and at Constantinople, and thenceforward the Apollinarians seceded from the Church," &c.

[g] It is probably the document afterwards so described by a Council at Constantinople.

was preparing to support his uncle, deemed it right to acquaint himself more fully with the Catholic doctrine before encountering the perils of war; he accordingly applied to S. Ambrose, who sent him the first part of a treatise in five books, *De Fide*[h].

Valens perished in the battle of Hadrianople, August 9, 378; and it was amid the successful ravages of the Goths that S. Ambrose, in order to ransom captives, caused[i] the unconsecrated vessels of the church to be broken and melted down. In reply to Arian cavils, he said that souls were more precious than gold in the sight of God. He was actively fulfilling his ministry according to the exhortations of Basil, who had congratulated him on his accession to "the apostolic prelacy," and encouraged him to "fight the good fight, and renew the footprints of the Fathers[k]."

One of Gratian's first acts as sovereign of the whole empire was to grant the request of a Roman council for a civil sanction to its decisions against the partisans of Ursinus. Another was to proclaim toleration to all sects, except Manicheans, Photinians, and Eunomians. Peter now returned to Alexandria; Meletius returned to Antioch, and proposed to Paulinus[l] that they should unite their flocks, and place the Holy Gospels on the episcopal chair, and that the survivor of them should tend the church alone. Paulinus declined to consent[m]; and Sapor, a military officer, was ordered to put Meletius in possession of the cathedral, which had been in the hands of Euzoius. Eusebius of Samosata went about various cities, establishing Catholic bishops. He lost his life in this pious labour. In a little city of Syria, an Arian woman flung down a tile from the roof of her house on the head of Eu-

---

[h] "Tu vincere paras, qui Christum adoras...qui fidem vindicas, cujus a me libellum petisti." De Fide, i. prol. [i] Ambr. Off. ii. c. 28. [k] Ep. 197.

[l] Theod. v. 3. The book of the Gospels, in the ancient Church, was considered a kind of symbol of Christ Himself.

[m] So Theodoret. "Paulinus said that canons forbade him to take as a colleague one who had been ordained by Arians." Soc. v. 5.

sebius, who died shortly afterwards, and was honoured as a martyr [n].

His friend Basil did not enjoy more than a few months of the Church's renewed peace. He died, an old man before his time, on the 1st of January, 379, saying, "Into Thy hands I commend my spirit." His funeral was attended by multitudes, who thronged to touch the bier, or the fringe of his funeral garments; even Jews and Pagans joined in the mourning [o]. It was felt that "a prince and a great man" had been taken away; and there were probably those who believed that the noble life then closed at the age of fifty had been shortened, not only by frequent illnesses, but by the hard pressure of his brethren's injustice, and the breaking down of plans for the Church's welfare. "I seem for my sins," so he had written in 377 to Peter of Alexandria, "to be unsuccessful in everything [p]." Yet doubtless he, whose correspondence is so rich in words of comfort for his afflicted friends, whose sympathy was so ready for those whose portion was the dreariest [q], was enabled to look beyond temporary failure, to be "blest in disappointment," and to know that his labour should bear fruit in God's own time.

---

[n] Theod. v. 4. Eusebius made his friends promise never to search for the woman. On the death of Eusebius see Greg. Naz. Or. xxv. 21.

[o] Greg. Naz. Or. xx. 105. [p] Ep. 266. [q] Epp. 107, 269.

CHAPTER VII.

From the Death of S. Basil to the Conversion of S. Augustine.

"Peace-loving man, of humble heart and true!
What dost thou here?
Fierce is the city's crowd; the lordly few
Are dull of ear!
Sore pain it was to thee, till thou didst quit
Thy patriarch-throne at length, as though for power unfit."
Lyra Apostolica.

EIGHTEEN days after S. Basil's death, Gratian made Theodosius, the son of a general who had reconquered Britain, emperor of the East. Theodosius was now thirty-two. The Eastern capital had been for nearly as many years — reckoning from the final expulsion of Paul — a domain of Arianism. It was resolved to reclaim it by the ministry of Gregory of Nazianzum, who had for some time been a recluse at Seleucia; and he consented, although with reluctance, to devote himself to this great work, "since in God's providence he was absolutely compelled to be a sufferer [a]." He went accordingly to Constantinople, and lodged in a kinsman's house. He was welcomed by the suffering remnant that still clung to the faith of Alexander and of Paul. The congregation was formed early in 379, and the house dedicated as "the Anastasia," the place where the Catholic faith was to rise again. There Gregory exhibited, before a population corrupted by heresy and irreverence, the living energy of the Church as a spiritual body. Daily services were accompanied by eloquent preaching. "The worship of the Trinity" was the missionary's watchword. After earnestly warning his hearers against the miserable levity which, in conformity with the spirit of Arianism, was filling every place, from the forum to the supper-room [b], with fearless disputation on the most awful

---

[a] Ep. 14.   [b] Or. xxxiii. 7.

topics, he delivered the four great discourses on the Nicene faith[c] which secured to him the title of *Theologus*, the maintainer, that is, of the Divinity of the Word[d]. On the Divinity of the Holy Spirit he spoke, as he had always done, without any such reserve as had brought trouble on S. Basil. But while proclaiming the Trinity, he was careful to guard the Unity; he set forth the Catholic doctrine as the middle way between Sabellian confusion and Tritheistic severance[e]. Yet the Arians denounced him as a Tritheist, stirred up mobs to pelt him in the street, and a base crowd of women, monks, and beggars to profane the Anastasia by their wanton insolence[f]. He was content to be a mark for public scorn. "They had the churches and the people, he had God and the angels! They had wealth, he had the faith; they menaced, he prayed; his was but a little flock, but it was screened from the wolves, and some of the wolves might become sheep[g]." Many such conversions took place; the charm of Gregory's eloquence, the spiritual beauty of his character[h], the winning sweetness which was combined with his zeal for orthodoxy, the conspicuous unworldliness which contrasted with Arian self-seeking, could not be unimpressive even in Constantinople. Jerome, who had quitted his retirement, and been ordained priest by Paulinus without being bound to a particular cure, came to Constantinople, listened with delight to Gregory's sermons, and conversed with him on passages of Scripture. Peter of Alexandria approved of his work, and united with others in the desire to see him regularly established in the see of Constantinople; but ere long, unhappily, he lent himself to the nefarious schemes of an unprincipled and plausible adventurer named Maximus, who retained the long hair, the staff, and the white dress of a

[c] Or. xxxiv.—xxxvii.

[d] In Or. xxxv. 15, he speaks of the Blessed Virgin as *Theotocos*, 'Mother of God.'

[e] Ib. xxiii. 30; xxiv. 13; xxxii. 53.

[f] Ib. xlviii. Ep. 81. They broke into the sanctuary, set their leader on the throne, and proceeded to hold a drinking bout.

[g] Ib. xxv. 41.

[h] Prolog. Ruffini.

Cynic philosopher, while professing to be a zealous Christian. This man, who came to Constantinople with an intention of securing the bishopric, found it easy to win the confidence of one so childlike as Gregory, and was actually panegyrized by him in open church[i], as having suffered for true religion. Certain Egyptian bishops, sent by Peter to consecrate Maximus, succeeded in enthroning him by night while Gregory was ill, were driven out of the church next morning by an indignant multitude, and completed the ceremonial in a flute-player's house, cutting off at the same time "the Cynic's" long hair. He and they were obliged to leave Constantinople; Theodosius would not take up his cause; and after insolently threatening the Archbishop of Alexandria that he should be ejected if he did not stir in his behalf, Maximus was himself expelled from Alexandria.

Towards the end of 379 a Council at Antioch under Meletius accepted the synodal letter from Rome. And we may probably assign to this year a celebrated Council of which the date has been disputed. Fifteen bishops met at Gangra in Paphlagonia, and condemned a certain Eustathius with his followers. If this man is to be identified with the Eustathius of Sebaste[k], the Council can hardly be prior to the 263rd Epistle of S. Basil, which never mentions it while describing his enemy's career, and which was written in 377. The bishops, it appears, had to deal with a self-righteous and heretical form of asceticism. Eustathius had declaimed against marriage, held aloof from married persons, contemned the Church fasts, denounced the eating of flesh-meat, set up conventicles of his own, and encouraged slaves to run away on grounds of religion. Such is the statement of the synodal letter to the Armenian bishops. It is followed by twenty-one canons in the form of anathematisms, against those who imitate these mal-

---

[i] Or. xxiii., which now bears the name of Heron instead of Maximus.

[k] See Soc. ii. 43. Baronius and Tillemont think that it was a different Eustathius.

practices; in particular, who refuse to communicate with a married priest, who insult the married, who observe celibacy, not because of the holiness of a virgin life, but from a detestation of matrimony[l]; who despise the Church services, the fasts, the commemorations of martyrs, and the love-feasts; who hold meetings for worship without ecclesiastical sanction; who slight Episcopal authority; who fast on Sundays; who on pretence of ascetic strictness wear a peculiar garb, neglect to educate their children, forsake their parents, or, if women, cut off their hair. The bishops expressly distinguished between a due regard for the virginal and devotional life, and superstitious extravagances which neither Scripture nor the Church had sanctioned. They were clearly determined to crush any growth of Encratism, which might introduce a Gnostic abhorrence of the Creator's gifts[m] under the guise of Christian self-denial; or any such spiritualism as, in the Montanistic movement, had trampled on Church order and cast off Christian humility. Early in 380, Theodosius, having fallen ill at Thessalonica, received baptism from its bishop, Ascholius, whose orthodoxy he had ascertained; and he then addressed, on Feb. 28, an edict to the people of Constantinople, commanding all his subjects to observe the faith which S. Peter delivered to the Romans, and which Damasus and Peter of Alexandria then professed; that faith which alone deserved the name of Catholic, and which recognized the one Godhead of Father, Son, and Spirit, of coequal majesty in the Holy Trinity. He knew not that Peter had died on Feb. 14, and had been succeeded by his brother Timothy.

The Catholic bishop in Constantinople—he was not as yet bishop *of* Constantinople—was subjected to "the scornful reproof of the wealthy." There was nothing in him, they thought, save the preaching faculty; he was quite a poor man, low-born, country-bred, with no dignity of

---

l Can. 9.

m See 1 Tim. iv. 1—5.

manner and no power of conversation. He was out of his element in high society, seldom appeared in public, could not make himself agreeable, nor take his proper place among the citizens[n]. His gentleness, after all, was nothing but feebleness. To this latter taunt Gregory replied[o], that at any rate he had not been guilty of such outrages as had made up the vigorous administration of Arian bishops; he had never profaned sacred vessels, brought in Pagans to insult the Christian altar, mingled the Sacramental Blood with the blood of Catholic victims, or denied their corpses the shelter of a grave. Yet he felt that his temperament and habits were to some extent a disqualification for so trying a post; and was only dissuaded from resigning it by the passionate entreaties of his flock, including mothers and children, that he would not forsake them. After a day had been spent in contending against their loving urgency, Gregory yielded to the solemn remonstrance, "If you depart, the faith departs with you[p]." He consented to remain until a fitter man could be appointed.

We hear about this time of the rise of the Priscillianist heresy. Priscillian, a well-born and eloquent Spaniard[q], had adopted a strange compound of various errors originally brought into Spain from Egypt. Its chief elements were the following[r]: 1. Pantheism,—the essential divinity of the human soul; 2. Sabellianism; 3. The Son only a power; 4. Docetism; hence a fast was kept on Sunday; 5. Fatalism; 6. Astrology; 7. Pre-existence of souls; their previous sins punished by their detention in bodies; 8. Man's body the devil's work; 9. Marriage condemned; 10. No resurrection; 11. Freedom taken in adulteration of Scrip-

---

[n] See Or. xxv. 28; xxxii. 74. [o] Ib. xxv.

[p] Carm. de Vitâ suâ, 76.

[q] Sulpicius, Hist. ii. 72, says that Priscillian had many gifts both of mind and body, but was vain, restless, and inquisitive. He learned his heresy from a lady and a rhetorician.

[r] S. Leo, Ep. 15. Sulpicius calls the Priscillianists *Gnostics*.

ture; 12. Falsehood allowed as to personal belief[s]; 13. Reliance on magic.

The principal maintainer of this system was of strict life, capable of long fasts and vigils, careless about wealth, apparently devout and humble, and fascinating in address. He "led captive silly women," and won over two bishops, Salvian and Instantius. Idacius, bishop of Merida, went to work against the new heresy with a violence which tended to "feed the flame." On Oct. 4, 380, a Council at Saragossa[t] condemned Priscillian and his followers, and passed canons against their practices. A perpetual anathema was denounced as the penalty of "receiving the Sacrament in church, but not partaking of it;" the heretics had been wont to take it into their hands, but to refrain from eating. Another canon forbade men to absent themselves from church and walk barefoot at Christmas-tide. Another condemned the assembling during Lent in secret chambers or mountain recesses. Others refer to secession from the clerical to the monastic life, and to the age for taking the veil.

On the 24th of November, Theodosius came to Constantinople, and proposed to Demophilus, the Arian bishop, that he should "subscribe the Nicene Creed, and thereby reunite the people[u]." He declined to abandon his belief, and was at once commanded to surrender the churches. He summoned his people, reminded them of the text which prescribed flight from persecution[x], (Matt. x. 23,) and transferred their worship to ground outside the city. Lucius, who had fled to Constantinople from Alexandria, accompanied Demophilus. The Emperor warmly embraced Gre-

---

[s] They had a watchword, "Jura, perjura, secretum prodere noli." This indifference to truth was a feature in the Basilidian, Manichean, and Paulician heresies. Akin to it were the equivocations in which Arians, Apollinarians, Pelagians, &c., indulged.

[t] Mansi, iii. 633.

[u] Soc. v. 7.

[x] Socrates spiritualizes this text: S. Athanasius, as we have seen, took it literally.

gory, saying, "God by my hands gives the church to you and to your labours[y];" and in spite of the clamours of an Arian populace, he proceeded to put Gregory in possession of S. Sophia. For this, however, an armed force was necessary. The black clouds that overhung the city as the procession moved along, were chased by a sudden burst of sunshine, while the Catholic bishop, worn with sickness, but stedfastly looking upward, passed, amid loud thanksgivings and demonstrations of rapturous delight, within the gates of the chancel. But his nerves were so shaken by the excitement, and by having seen one man draw a sword against him, that he was obliged to depute a priest to address the people, who were calling on Theodosius to enthrone him forthwith. "For the present our duty is to thank God; other matters may be reserved for another time." The words were received with the clapping of hands so common in that state of society, when the lively Greek temperament was too strong for Christian reverence. Gregory seldom visited the palace, and never exerted himself, after the manner of Arian prelates, to win the favour of courtiers and chamberlains; he was even blamed by his own people for remissness in using his influence on their behalf. He went on in his own way, as a meek, unworldly pastor, preaching, praying, visiting the sick, never enriching himself, winning hearts by single-minded charity. One day his sick-chamber was thronged by affectionate adherents, who after thanking God that they had lived to see his episcopate, withdrew. A young man, pale and haggard, remained at the foot of the bed, in mournful silence, and in a suppliant attitude. "Who are you, and what do you want?" asked Gregory. The youth groaned bitterly, and wrung his hands. Gregory was moved to tears, and on learning from another person that this was the man who had sought his life, said to the weeping penitent, "God be gracious to you; all I ask is, that henceforth you give up yourself to Him[z]!"

[y] De Vitâ, 95. [z] Ib. 107.

On Jan. 10, 381, Theodosius by a second edict forbade heretics, especially Arians, Photinians, and Eunomians, to hold assemblies within towns; gave back all churches to Catholic bishops; assigned the Catholic name to all believers in the undivided Essence of the Trinity, and especially denounced those who did despite to the Holy Spirit, "by Whom we receive what we hope for."

About this time Meletius of Antioch conferred the diaconate on John, whom we know best by the appellation of Chrysostom. He was the son of Secundus, a military officer; born about 347 at Antioch; and on his father's death, soon afterwards, he became indebted for a careful and Christian training to his pious mother Anthusa. He studied rhetoric under the accomplished Pagan teacher Libanius, who afterwards, on being asked to name his own successor, replied, "John would be the fittest, if the Christians had not stolen him[a]." He was baptized by Meletius; his chief friend was named Basil, and Anthusa's earnest pleadings were required to counteract Basil's proposal that they should both retire into monastic life. Chrysostom, as we may most conveniently call him, could not resist his mother's appeal; he continued to live at home, but in the practice of monastic asceticism and the diligent reading of Scripture. He studied theology under Diodore, the companion of Flavian, and Carterius; and among his fellow pupils in the rhetorical school whom he drew over to a higher learning was Theodore, afterwards bishop of Mopsuestia. From Diodore he learned to prefer the literal interpretation of Scripture to the allegorical. It was probably about 372—374 that he and Basil were spoken of as likely to be made bishops; and Chrysostom, by a singular artifice, procured Basil's consecration while evading the burden for himself[b]. For several years he carried out the plan which during his mother's lifetime he had abandoned, living first in cœnobitic "taber-

---

[a] Soc. vi. 3; Soz. viii. 2.

[b] The justification of this stratagem is the least pleasing portion of his far-famed treatise "On the Priesthood."

nacles," and afterwards as a hermit in a cave, until his health gave way under repeated fasts, and he was obliged to return to Antioch, where he entered the ministry.

Theodosius now resolved to assemble a Council in order to settle the affairs of Constantinople and Antioch, and to crush the Macedonian heresy[c]. The bishops, 150 in number, met at Constantinople on May 2, 381, exactly eight years after the death of S. Athanasius. No bishop from the Western empire attended; and Meletius, although disowned by the West and Egypt, was appointed to preside. Theodosius greeted him with the reverence of a son. There were many illustrious Eastern bishops present, as Gregory of Nyssa, Cyril of Jerusalem, Amphilochius of Iconium. Thirty-six Macedonian prelates were summoned, but it was found impossible to reconcile them to the Church; they refused to accept the Homoousion, and utterly ignored their promises to Liberius.

In regard to Constantinople, the Council pronounced that Maximus the Cynic had never been a true bishop; and ignoring the cavil that Gregory had been bishop of Sasima or of Nazianzum, and that therefore he ought not to be translated, they established him as bishop of the imperial city. He hoped that this position might enable him to reconcile the East and West. Meletius, whose name, as Gregory said, expressed the sweetness of his character, who had recently shown his unselfish meekness by proposing to share the bishopric with his rival, and who had made himself so dear to the Antiochenes, that they engraved his likeness[d] on their rings, their cups, and the walls of their bed-rooms, was now attacked by an illness which proved fatal. He exhorted the bishops to peaceful courses, and died while the Council was sitting, a saint outside the communion of Rome. His funeral was magnificent[e]; lights were

[c] Soc. v. 8. [d] S. Chrys. Hom. de S. Mel. i. tom. ii. 519.

[e] "Where now," asked S. Gregory of Nyssa in his funeral sermon, "is that sweet calm look, that radiant smile, that kind hand which was wont to second the kind voice?"

borne before the embalmed corpse, and psalms sung in divers languages[f]; honours repeated in all the cities through which it passed until it rested beside the grave of S. Babylas at Antioch.

And now Gregory entreated his brethren to recognize Paulinus. He was an aged man, and could not hold the see long; let him for the rest of his days be acknowledged by all Christendom as bishop of Antioch. This was clearly the right course; but the party-feeling of the younger bishops prevailed. They could not bring themselves to give a triumph to the Westerns, and elected Flavian[g] to succeed Meletius, thus ensuring the continuance of the schism. Gregory was bitterly disappointed; and the revival of the absurd claim of Maximus by Timothy and the Egyptian bishops, when they arrived at Constantinople, increased his vexation and despondency. Weary of heing made perforce "a man of strife and of contention," conscious of being disliked by several of his brethren, oppressed with a sense of failure, and exhausted by the labours of the last two years, he resolved to resign the bishopric. "I have been far enough from raising this storm; but make a Jonah of me, if you will." He applied to Theodosius, "not for wealth, nor splendid church ornaments, nor preferment for relations, but for leave to yield to the envious and narrow-minded[h]." It had been against his own wish that he accepted the throne of Constantinople; he was now most willing to leave it. Theodosius reluctantly consented, and Gregory delivered in the Council his celebrated Farewell[i]. He gave an account of his mission, and glorified God for the success which had attended it. Had not the little wrath been followed by the great mercy? Had not stumbling-blocks been removed from the path? Constantinople was now an "em-

---

[f] Soz. vii. 10. It was usual at that time to sing on such occasions, "Turn again then unto thy rest, O my soul."

[g] Socrates, v. 5, says that Flavian was one of six clergy who had engaged to recognize the survivor of the two rival bishops.

[h] De Vitâ, 757.

[i] Orat. xxxii.

porium" of the faith. It had a living and working Catholic Church, a venerable presbytery, deacons and readers well ordered, a docile, zealous, and true-hearted people, who were ready to die for the worship of the Trinity. Something, at least, he had done "towards the weaving of this crown of glory:" and he could appeal, like Samuel, to their knowledge of his unselfishness. But he was growing old and weak; he could not wrestle with adversaries who ought to have been friends; he knew not that he had been expected to emulate the stateliness of consuls and præfects, and he begged, as a worn-out soldier, to receive the warrant of his discharge. Then, in a tone more loving and more pathetic, he bade farewell to the Anastasia, to the cathedral, to the other churches, to the sacred relics, to the episcopal throne, to the bishops and clergy who "ministered at the holy Table, approaching the approaching God;" to the "Nazarites," the psalmody, the nocturnal offices, the virgins, matrons, widows, orphans, and poor; the hospitals, the crowds which had attended his preaching, the Emperor and the Court, the city, the East and West. "They lose not God, who abandon their thrones; rather, they win a throne above. Little children, keep the deposit; remember how I was stoned. The grace of our Lord Jesus Christ be with you all!"

The vacant throne was filled by the election of a man who, like S. Ambrose, was unbaptized and in high secular office at his election. In no other respect, however, did the prætor Nectarius resemble him whose anomalous elevation to an archbishopric had already been so amply justified. The people of Constantinople, by choosing Nectarius, showed why they had been to a great extent dissatisfied with Gregory [k]. They did not want a bishop of genius or saintliness, but a well-born, dignified, and courteous gentleman. Nectarius appears to have been this, and little more. He was

---

[k] Sozomen, vii. 8, says that Theodosius, in spite of the opposition of Flavian and other bishops, persisted in thinking Nectarius the best man.

forthwith baptized, and consecrated while he wore the white garments of a neophyte.

The Council made certain alterations in the Nicene Creed, in order to meet the errors of the time. Amphilochius had indeed said that the Creed as settled at Nicæa was sufficient to overthrow Macedonianism; but it had been thought expedient by Eastern bishops, for several years past, to supplement it by clauses more or less derived from the ancient formulas of the East; and the Creed thus augmented had been presented in two forms, a shorter and a longer, by Epiphanius in his treatise called *Ancoratus*. The shorter of these forms[1] supplied the Council with all the additions which they thought fit to adopt, as follows: "*before all ages*[m]—*from heaven*—*of the Holy Ghost and the Virgin Mary*[n]—*and was crucified for us under Pontius Pilate*—*and was buried*—*and sitteth on the right hand of the Father*—*again, with glory*—*whose kingdom shall have no end*[o]," (a clause which pointedly rebuked the Marcellian notion of His temporary reign,) and all the words after "Holy Spirit," except the *Filioque* clause, which was added by a Council at Toledo, probably that which made Catholicism the established religion of Spain in 589[p]. Manifestly the assertion of the Holy Spirit's essential difference, as the adorable *Lord and Life-giver*, from all created and ministering spirits, had been intended when first introduced by Eastern bishops, and was now intended by the Council, to erect a barrier against the Macedonian development of Arianism. The clause, "Who spake by the prophets," had been in the creed of Jerusalem. The Church had in the Nicene anathematism been called "Catholic and Apostolic;" the creed of Jerusalem and that which Arius gave in to Con-

---

[1] Epiph. Ancor. 120. [m] Ap. Constit. Jerusalem.

[n] Ancient Roman. [o] Jerusalem, (see S. Cyril's Cat. Lectures.)

[p] The Council of Toledo in 447 has been cited as professing the *Filioque*. But see Waterland on Ath. Cr. ch. 1, (vol. iii. p. 109). The great Toledan Council in 589, in the third chapter of its confession of faith, anathematized all who denied that the Holy Spirit proceeded "à Patre et Filio."

stantine had affirmed its unity; its sanctity had been proclaimed in the oldest formulas of the West[q]. The omission of "holy" in our version of the Constantinopolitan Creed is unaccountable. The memorable confession of "*one Baptism for the remission of sins*," which had stood exactly thus in the shorter of the Epiphanian creeds, and at Jerusalem had included the words "of repentance," distinctly makes Baptism the means of conveying such remission; and the emphatic *one* appears to have been simply an echo of S. Paul's "one Baptism," Eph. iv. 5, without any reference to the controversy between those who baptized converts from heresy and those who recognized their previous Baptism[r]. The Council inserted "heaven and earth" into the first clause of the Creed, and omitted "in heaven and earth" in the clause "by whom all things were made[s]." The words, "that is, of the Father's essence," and the clause "God of God," were omitted as unnecessary[t]; the latter has been restored by the Western Church. The anathematism was omitted[u]; but it is still retained in the Armenian Liturgy.

The Council of 381 passed four canons. The first pronounced the Creed inviolable, and anathematized all heresies, naming seven[x]. To understand the second, which guarded the bounds of territorial jurisdictions, we must observe that the ecclesiastical divisions of the empire were for the most part conformed to the civil. The "Diocese," or aggregate of provinces, was in things civil governed by a Præfect or Vicar; in things spiritual, by an Archbishop or

---

[q] S. Cypr. Ep. 69. 7. "Dost thou believe the remission of sins and life everlasting through the Holy Church?"

[r] See Bishop Phillpotts' "Letter to his Clergy," 1851.

[s] The shorter Epiphanian had the phrase in both clauses.

[t] The shorter Epiphanian had the former, but omitted the latter. *Deum de Deo* is not in the Gelasian Sacramentary, Murat. Lit. Rom. i. 540. It was confessed by the great Toledan Council of 589.

[u] The shorter Epiphanian had it, and the longer made it refer to the Macedonians as well as the Arians.

[x] The Eunomian or Anomœan, Arian or Eudoxian, Semi-Arian or Pneumatomachist, Sabellian, Marcellian, Photinian, Apollinarian.

Exarch,—the name of Patriarch being not as yet a technical title[y]. Similarly, the "Province" had its civil head in the President or Proconsul, its spiritual in the Metropolitan. There were six "Dioceses[z]" in the West, beside the Roman præfecture; accordingly, the Western Church was divided into seven great portions. The "Suburbicarian Churches," or those of the ten provinces governed by the Vicarius Urbis, comprehending Italy south of the province of Milan, Sicily, Sardinia, and Corsica, formed, with Rome and its vicinity, the proper patriarchate of the bishop of Rome, who had besides a recognized Primacy of honour throughout the whole Church[a]. The other six Western dioceses were those of "Italy" (under Milan), Western Illyricum (under Sirmium), Africa (under Carthage), Spain, Gaul, and Britain. The seven Eastern dioceses were those of "the East," properly so called, Egypt, Asia, Pontus, Thrace, Macedonia, Dacia, respectively subject for Church purposes to the bishops of Antioch, Alexandria, Ephesus, Cæsarea, Heraclea, Thessalonica, Sardica[b]. Beneath the fourteen great bishops who were by this scheme in the first rank of the hierarchy, stood the Metropolitans, or heads of provincial Churches, themselves the superiors of the ordinary bishops[c]. The canon of Constantinople provided that the affairs of each

---

[y] Gregory Nazianzen, Or. xxxii. 79, applies it to bishops personally venerable, such as Eusebius of Samosata, whom he also calls an "Abraham-like" old man.

[z] *Diocese*, as used by the Council of Arles, which addressed Sylvester as holding "the greater dioceses," bore, according to Bingham (b. ix. 1. 12, and 2. 2), its modern sense. A *Parish*, in the ancient Church, meant a city and its vicinity, subject to a bishop.

[a] The Roman prelate was, 1. bishop of Rome; 2. patriarch, and for the most part metropolitan also, of the suburbicarian churches; 3. the only Western bishop who had an apostolic see; 4. the first in dignity among all bishops.

[b] Macedonia and Dacia had been separated from the Western empire in 379. But Damasus, desiring to retain them in the Western Church, made the bishop of Thessalonica his vicar.

[c] The archbishop of Alexandria had a special power over his suffragans, in that he was the sole metropolitan, as well as the head of the Egyptian patriarchate.

diocese and province should be settled by local authority. It was followed by the famous third canon, which, without freeing the see of Constantinople from the authority of the exarch of Heraclea, gave "a primacy of honour to the bishop of Constantinople next after the bishop of Rome[d], *because Constantinople was New Rome.*" It is certain, however, that the bishop of Rome enjoyed this pre-eminence, not simply because his city was Rome, but also because he "held the chair of Peter[e]." The fourth canon was against Maximus[f]. The bishops, after passing these canons, informed Theodosius that they had "restored unanimity," settled Church doctrine, and legislated for Church order; they therefore requested a civil sanction for their decrees. The Emperor granted it, and ordained on July 30 that all churches should belong to bishops who confessed the Trinity. He also named eleven prelates, Gregory of Nyssa being one, as necessary centres of communion for the dioceses of the East.

The Council of 381 is called Œcumenical, but it owes this title to the general acceptance of its Creed. It was by no means a representative of the Universal Church, and its third canon was disowned by Rome until the popedom of Innocent III.[g]

We must now turn to the West. Palladius, an Arian bishop, had requested Gratian to summon a Council, and expected that it would be general, not simply Western. But Ambrose, who about this time was writing for Gratian his

---

[d] This was equivalent to a degradation of the thrones of Alexandria and Antioch.

[e] On the "eminency" of S. Peter, as we understand it, see Moberly's Gr. Forty Days, p. 189.

[f] The 5th and 6th canons, so-called, are considered to belong to the Council of 382; the 7th is inadequately supported by external evidence, and is a statement, not an enactment, as to the reception of converts. Beveridge (vol. xii. p. 92, A.-C. L.) considers it to be a shortened form of a letter written from Constantinople to the patriarch of Antioch after 455. See Routh, Scr. Op. i. 422.

[g] For the argument from this Council against modern Papal claims, see Meyrick's Papal Supremacy, p. 15.

work "on the Holy Spirit," persuaded him that as the Easterns had met at Constantinople, it would suffice to hold a Western Council at Aquileia. This advice prevailed; a small Council of some thirty bishops met on Sept. 1, under the presidency of Valerian of Aquileia; and Palladius repeatedly protested that he had expected "a full Council." The bishops called on Palladius to condemn the statements in Arius' letter to S. Alexander. Like the Eusebians at Nicæa, he had recourse to pitiable evasions; he would call Christ "Very Son," "good and powerful," but would not say whether He were created or uncreate. When asked, "Is Christ Very God?" he answered, "He is the power of our God." He adduced the texts John xvii. 3, 1 Tim. vi. 15, John xiv. 28[h]. As he would not condemn Arius, he was deposed; he sneered at the proceedings,—"Have you begun to play? play on." His companion Secundianus, who rejected as unscriptural the proposition "The Son is Very God," was condemned with him. The debate lasted from daybreak to 1 p.m. The bishops wrote to Gratian, and his brother Valentinian II., describing what had been done, and complaining of Ursinus as a confederate of Arians and a troubler of the principal Church in the Roman empire. To Theodosius they wrote in favour of Paulinus, and requested another Council at Alexandria. They also expressed themselves[i] in favour of the claims of Maximus as having the support of Alexandria, and against the proceedings of the Constantinopolitan synod. If Nectarius were upheld against Maximus, they saw not how the East and West could continue in communion. Rome, Italy, and all the West might fairly claim to be consulted on such a matter.

Theodosius replied by a letter which to some extent satisfied the Westerns[k]; but they asked for an explicit

---

[h] The bishops explained this latter text in the manner usual with Westerns, "greater in regard to the Manhood."

[i] This letter, Ambr. Ep. 13, is from Ambrose and the other bishops of the Italian diocese.

[k] S. Ambr. Ep. 14.

condemnation of Apollinaris in a full Council. A second Council met at Constantinople in 382. Gregory, who was now at Nazianzum, declined to attend. He had never, so he wrote[l], seen a Council end well. These assemblies, what with ambition, and what with disputatiousness, tended rather to increase the evils of the time. For his part, he thought seclusion the only safety. Now we cannot explain away this censure as pointed at Arianizing synods; Gregory was plainly referring to party struggles within the Church. But while we admit that Catholic Councils had suffered from evils produced by the Arian controversy, we cannot ignore the writer's temperament, which expresses itself in this very context by despair about all co-operative action.

The bishops of Constantinople, invited to a Council at Rome, wrote to Damasus, Ambrose, and the other bishops there assembled, declining, though in kind language, to attend. They described the sufferings from which the Eastern orthodox were slowly recovering; set forth the Catholic doctrine as neither confounding the Persons nor dividing the Substance, and as recognising a perfect Humanity assumed by the all-perfect Word; and vindicated, as canonically unquestionable, the episcopal character of Cyril, Flavian, and Nectarius. The Westerns, however, continued faithful to Paulinus, who came to Rome this year with Epiphanius and Jerome. The latter became secretary to Damasus, who consulted him on Scriptural points[m]. He wrote a tract against Helvidius, who maintained the view of the Antidicomarians; and he began to acquire an influence over pious Roman ladies, as the widowed Paula, Fabiola, and Marcella, Blesilla the widowed, and Eustochium the virgin daughter of Paula. He supported the principle of monasticism with all his energies, at a time when the Pagan interest in Rome was bestirring itself

[l] S. Greg. Ep. 130.

[m] Such as the word Hosanna, the vengeance for Cain, clean and unclean beasts, the time of the Exodus, the parable of the prodigal.

against what it deemed a Christian aggression. In the senate-house there stood an altar of Victory, which Constantius had removed when he visited Rome, and Julian had restored. Gratian, who showed his Christian zeal by refusing the robe of the Pontifex Maximus, which emperors had usually worn, again removed the altar. The "great city," which had been "drunken with the blood of the saints," contained at this time a multitude of Pagan sanctuaries, and was still, in spite of the energy and stateliness of its Church, a stronghold of idolatry. Among its Pagan nobles were Prætextatus, famous for his sarcasm about the Roman episcopate; Flavian, one of the prætorian præfects; and Symmachus, the great orator of the party, who now went to plead for the restoration of the altar. But Damasus sent a memorial from Christian senators, repudiating all share in the Pagan petition, and declaring that they would not come into the senate-house if it were granted[n]. Ambrose took charge of this memorial; Gratian refused to admit Symmachus into his presence, forbade by edict all legacies to temples, and took away privileges from Pagan priests.

Meantime Gregory, hearing that Apollinarians were invading Nazianzum in his absence, wrote to the priest Cledonius a memorable letter,—one of those documents of the fourth century which refuted beforehand the heresies of the fifth. He affirmed true Godhead and perfect Manhood to be combined in the One Person of the Crucified, who was the adorable Son, whose Mother was "Mother of God[o]," and who assumed, in order to redeem it, the whole of the nature that fell in Adam.

A third Council met at Constantinople in 383, in order to attempt a reconciliation between the Church and the sects. Theodosius produced a confusion of tongues[p] by asking the

---

[n] S. Ambr. Ep. 17.

[o] "If any one believe not S. Mary to be Theotocos, he has no part in God...If any one rely on a Man who has no mind (νοῦς), he is unworthy of perfect salvation."

[p] Soc. v. 10.

non-Catholics, "Do you accept the doctors who lived *before* your respective schisms?" He afterwards called upon five representatives of the Catholic, Novatian, Arian, Eunomian, and Macedonian communions to state their tenets in writing; and all statements which denied the Homoousion he tore in pieces. The Novatians, who accepted it, were favoured by Theodosius, who on July 25, 383, went so far as to forbid all meetings of heretics, even in private houses. No Catholic adviser seems to have warned him against such methods of defending the Kingdom of Christ; but his penal enactments were not always carried into execution[q].

And now Maximus, the rebel general of the army in Britain, having crossed over into Gaul, made war on Gratian, who was deserted by his soldiers, and treacherously[r] murdered at Lyons, Aug. 25, in his twenty-fourth year. Tidings of the tragedy came to Milan; Ambrose mourned for the young sovereign who had been to him as a son, and had called upon his name in the moment of death[s]. Justina, the Arian widow of Valentinian I., placed the young Valentinian II. in the arms of the Catholic archbishop, who at her request visited Treves, and procured terms of peace from the invader. Maximus contented himself with the sovereignty of Gaul, Spain, and Britain.

There was now in Rome a professor of rhetoric, about thirty years of age, named Augustine[t]. He was born in a city of Numidia in 354, and was formally made a catechumen in his infancy, but not baptized. His boyhood was wild and vicious.

At nineteen he was ensnared by the Manichean heresy. That wonderful misbelief, then about a century old, but

---

[q] Soz. vii. 12.

[r] Andragathius swore on the Gospels that his life should be safe, and having thus lured him to a feast, slew him and kept his corpse unburied. S. Ambr. in Ps. lxi. c. 23—25.

[s] De ob. Val. 80, "Doleo in te, fili Gratiane, suavis mihi valde," &c.

[t] His full name was Aurelius Augustinus.

destined to defy the Church for ages, to be a power in mediæval France, and to exert an influence even over modern scepticism, has been described[u] as "the attempt to array a philosophy of nature in a Christian language, to empty Christian truths of all their ethical worth, and then to use them as a gorgeous symbolic garb for clothing a system different to its very core." Its founder, Manes, had been a man of various gifts; full of ardour and imagination, scientific and accomplished, proclaiming himself an inspired teacher who could exhibit the essential ideas of Christianity set free from all Judaic elements, and promising his votaries an absolute knowledge which should supersede the necessity of walking by faith. Augustine was impressed by the importance which Manicheism appeared to assign to "Christ" and "the Holy Spirit," not seeing that these sacred names were applied to beings of its own invention[x]; and he was fascinated by the lure of intellectual freedom[y], by the Pantheistic derivation of man's soul from the "lucid mass" of the Divine essence[z], and by the assurance that sin was the outcoming of a dark

---

[u] Dean Trench's Huls. Lect., p. 25, ed. 1854. Manes began to promulgate his views about A.D. 270. He was professedly a Christian, perhaps a priest. He was excommunicated when he became an heresiarch; driven away by the Magi, patronized by one Persian king, but put to a cruel death under another in March, 277. His system was strictly dualistic. There was, he said, an original, eternal division between the kingdoms of light and of darkness. The Good Being, "the Father," who reigned over the former, seeing the dark powers of the latter on the point of invading His bright realm, sent forth a being called the Mother of Life *from His own essence*, to guard its frontier. She made the first man; the dark powers swallowed up a part of his essence, i. e. a part of God's. Thus were particles of light imprisoned in matter; the evil one concentrated them in Adam, in whom also there was an evil element.

[x] Confessions, iii. 10. "Christ" meant the unimprisoned part of First Man. The imprisoned part was "Jesus patibilis."

[y] De Util. Cr. 2. The story of Genesis was inverted. It was *God* who persuaded Adam to taste of the tree of knowledge.

[z] Conf. iv. 26, 31. To a Manichean, the great fact to be considered in all mundane things was the struggle of divine particles to escape from material bondage.

element separate from his personality[a]. For nine years his pious mother Monica persevered in prayer for his conversion[b]. In his twenty-ninth year he discovered by conversing with Faustus, a Manichean bishop, of whom he had heard great things, the hollowness of Manichean professions of universal knowledge[c]. Difficulties which had occurred to his mind were not removed by Faustus. The hunger of his nature for real and satisfying truth was not to be appeased by "the husks" of a theory alike pretentious and unspiritual. In this state of mind, the prospect of employment as a teacher of literature drew him, against his mother's wish, to Rome, where, after recovering from a dangerous fever, he still associated with the ascetic class[d] of Manicheans, but not with his former confidence in the system. This was a crisis in his spiritual history. He could not thoroughly accept Manicheism; he thought Catholicism carnal[e] and untenable; he was half disposed to embrace the Academic scepticism. His pupils were in their own way as unsatisfactory as those whom he had left at Carthage; and he was glad to accept a professorship at Milan, the appointment to which had been placed in the hands of Symmachus. Thus the gifted Pagan zealot became the means of bringing him into contact with Ambrose, who received him with paternal kindness, but whose teaching appeared to him rather eloquent than true.

Symmachus himself, now præfect of Rome, made a second

---

[a] Confessions, v. 18. This may be connected with his fondness for astrology, ibid. iv. 4.

[b] Ibid. iii. 19, 20; v. 15, 17. A Catholic bishop comforted her by saying, "The son of those tears cannot perish," iii. 21.

[c] Ibid. v. 3—10. The hierarchy of Manicheism consisted of a supreme chief, twelve "masters," seventy-two bishops, with priests, deacons, and missionaries. The ritual was remarkable for its simplicity, as had been the case with the Marcionite heretics.

[d] The "Elect," as distinguished from the "Hearers," who had to support and serve the Elect, and were less rigidly bound by rules.

[e] The Incarnation was a difficulty; he thought it must involve a debasement of the Godhead. Manicheism had utterly denied that its Christ had a real body; his sufferings were only a semblance, representing the sufferings of "Jesus patibilis" in corporeal bondage.

application in behalf of the altar of Victory. He pleaded "with bated breath" for the toleration of a worship which Rome was too old to abandon, and which might be considered as virtually akin to the Christian—another mode of serving the same God[f]. Ambrose reminded Valentinian that no Pagan was obliged by a Christian sovereign to join in Christian worship, and that his boyish years would not excuse a weak betrayal of Christianity; acknowledged the "glowing colours" of the Pagan plea, but pronounced its splendour to be illusory. "They talk of a God; they worship a statue!" He dwelt on the moral deadness and impotence of Paganism; contrasting the six or seven women whom purple attire and rich endowments could induce to become vestals with the multitude of Christian virgins, and the wealth of Pagan priests spent on themselves with the Church's wealth which fed the poor. Valentinian refused to restore the altar. The high tone taken by Christians as against Pagans at this period stirred up Libanius to denounce "the men in black," i. e. the monks, as greedy and violent; and Jerome himself denounces some monastic hypocrites who made up for their fasts by midnight revelry[g]. Severe fasting, in this year 384, cut short the life of Blesilla. Paula fainted with grief amid the funeral solemnities; the people "muttered" indignantly[h], "We said it would come to this; she has killed her daughter with fasting, and now grieves that she died in widowhood. Those vile monks! when will they be driven from the city,

---

[f] Relatio Symm. ap. Ambr. It is remarkable to find Paganism thus entreating Christianity to recognize that view of the religions of the world against which martyrdom had been a protest. Symmachus' words remind us of Pope's "Universal Prayer." "Æquum est quicquid omnes colunt, unum putari......Quid interest quâ quisque prudentiâ verum requirat? *Uno itinere non potest perveniri ad tam grande secretum.*" Æmilian the præfect had said to S. Dionysius of Alexandria, "Why cannot you worship your God *along with those* who are gods by nature?" Eus. vii. 11.

[g] Ep. 22, c. 28.

[h] Ep. 39 (25.) S. Chrysostom says that idle people were heard to boast of having beaten and incarcerated this or that monk. Adv. Opp. Vit. Mon. i. 2.

—nay, rather, stoned or drowned?" But while the harsher side of monasticism confirmed many Pagans in their hatred of the Church, we must in simple justice remember how many were won to Christ by the power of monastic faith and self-devotion [i].

After the Council of Saragossa, the two Priscillianist bishops had made Priscillian bishop of Avila. Idacius, and another prelate named Ithacius, who is described as having "nothing of holiness" about him [k], as hating Priscillian chiefly on account of his fasts, procured the exile of the heretics. They vainly sought a hearing from Damasus and Ambrose, but persuaded Gratian to allow of their return. Ithacius denounced them to Maximus, who referred the case to a Council at Bordeaux. Priscillian was there permitted to appeal to Maximus. At the court of Treves, the accused and accusers found Martin with the Emperor, who treated him with great reverence as a saint [l]. Martin rebuked Ithacius, begged Maximus to "spare the unhappy men," and protested against "the hearing of a Church cause by a secular judge." He even obtained from Maximus a promise to shed no blood, and, relying on this, quitted Treves. Torture wrung from Priscillian a confession (probably false) of impure practices; and on this ground he, with six others, was beheaded. It was the first infliction of death for heresy; but, in this case, for heresy alleged to endanger public morals.

The aged Damasus died on Dec. 11, 384, after a long pontificate, in which he had exhibited great activity and vigour. He had also been a poet and a church-builder; and under him the crowded churches and the thundering Amens [m] gave evidence of his people's hearty devotion. He was succeeded by Siricius, one of whose first acts (Feb. 11,

---

[i] Soz. vi. 34.

[k] Sulp. Hist. ii. 73.

[l] It was then that Martin passed the wine-cup to his chaplain before the Emperor; an act which Maximus himself admired. The Empress waited on the Bishop at table. Sulp. Vit. B. Mart. 23; Dial. ii. 7.

[m] Jerome, in Gal. lib. ii. præf.

385) was to write the first of the "decretal epistles," in reply to some questions which Himerius, bishop of Tarragona, had addressed to Damasus. The most important point in this letter is the assertion that priests and deacons were bound, as a matter of Christian duty, in consequence of their daily Eucharistic ministrations, to observe perpetual continence[n]. Siricius also orders converts from Arianism to be received by confirmation only; adults, except in case of urgent need, to be baptized in the Paschal season only; candidates for ordination to pass regularly through the degrees of reader, acolyte, subdeacon, deacon, to the priesthood. Certain penitents are allowed, as a favour, "to attend the celebration of the Mysteries," but are forbidden to join in "the feast of the Lord's Table[o]."

The Empress Justina was ungrateful to S. Ambrose. In Lent, this year, she demanded in her son's name, for Arian worship, first the Portian basilica outside the walls of Milan, and then in its stead the new and larger church of the Apostles within the city[p]. Officers of state came to Ambrose on Friday before Palm Sunday; he answered, "The Priest cannot give up the temple." On Saturday the præfect in vain endeavoured to obtain at any rate the Portian church. On Palm Sunday Ambrose was in the baptistery, explaining the Creed, as was usual on that day, to the *competentes*, or candidates for the Easter baptism; the ordinary catechumens[q] having left the church. A message informed him that curtains were being put up in the Portian,—the ordinary sign of the Emperor's claiming any place[r]. "How-

[n] The Nicene Council had expressly declined to impose this rule. Soc. i. 11. The Eastern Church in the Quinisext Council in Trullo, can. 13, rejected the Roman practice, but did so on the implied ground that celebration was not a daily duty. It was not so regarded in the days of S. Athanasius, nor by S. Basil.

[o] Persons in this position were called *Consistentes*.

[p] Ambr. Ep. 20.

[q] The three classes of catechumens were hearers, kneelers, and "competents."

[r] A "veil" was always hung before the entrance of the Emperor's presence-chamber.

ever," Ambrose wrote to his sister, "I remained at my duty, and began to perform Mass[s]." While he was "making the oblation," he heard with grief that Castulus, an Arian priest, was in the grasp of the Catholic population, and forthwith sent clergy to his rescue. During Holy Week the Catholic tradesmen were fined and imprisoned; Ambrose was urged by counts and tribunes to submit. "If," he firmly answered, "I were asked to yield what was mine, I would not refuse, although what is mine belongs to the poor. But what is God's I cannot surrender." The next scene is laid in the Portian, on the Wednesday. During the Lessons from Job, the soldiers who had surrounded the church began to enter, for the purpose, as they said, of prayer. Ambrose began to preach on Job's trials, and reiterated his principle, "The Emperor has no sovereignty over the things of God. Palaces belong to the Emperor, churches to the Priest." Meanwhile the attempt which had that day been made to seize the new church was abandoned. The congregation requested their bishop's presence, but he sent some priests thither instead. A court-secretary came to rebuke his "domineering." "Yes," he replied, "the priest has his dominion—it is in his weakness: 'when I am weak, then I am strong.'" He stayed all night at the Portian, which was watched by soldiers. On Thursday,—the solemn day for absolving penitents[t],—while Ambrose was preaching on the lesson, which consisted of the book of Jonah,

---

[s] "Missam facere cœpi." The earliest instance, apparently, of this term (derived from the dismissal, 1. of the catechumens, 2, of the faithful,) being used for the Eucharistic service. The "great oblation," as performed by S. Ambrose, probably ran thus: "Being mindful of His most glorious Passion, and Resurrection from the dead, and Ascension into heaven, we offer unto Thee this immaculate Sacrifice (*hostiam*), reasonable Sacrifice, bloodless Sacrifice, this holy Bread, and Chalice of life eternal." See the writer De Sacram. iv. 27.

[t] About a century later, the Roman rite for this "reconciliation" prescribed that the penitent should be presented by the deacon in an address to the bishop, beginning, "Venerable pontiff, the accepted time is come, the day of God's propitiation and man's salvation." The penitent was then absolved by collects said over him. Gelas. Sacr. Murat. i. 549.

word came that the soldiers were recalled from their post, and the tradesmen's money had been restored. A scene of impetuous joy followed; the people clapped their hands, the soldiers rushed in and kissed the altar. So ended the first struggle of the Arian court with Ambrose.

Timothy of Alexandria died on July 20, 385. He was the author of an epistle on Penance, in which he spoke of "the spiritual Sacrifice" as offered up on Sundays and Saturdays [u], but of Communion as a daily occurrence. To understand this, we must observe that, as we learn from S. Basil [x], the Egyptian Catholics were allowed to take home the Eucharist administered in church [y], and daily to eat a portion. This practice had existed from the second century [z], and was prevalent at Rome [a], but was obviously liable to great abuses. Timothy was succeeded by Theophilus.

Jerome had at first been greatly esteemed by the Roman Christians. But the roughness and bitterness of his nature, his open scorn for the fopperies and meannesses of some of the clergy [b], and his success in drawing Roman ladies to the monastic life, had involved him in such odium, that even his outward aspect, his "walk and smile," furnished occasion

---

[u] In the West, as we have seen, daily celebration was common. S. Monica "never on any day omitted to attend the Oblation." S. Aug. Conf. v. 17.

[x] Ep. 93. He himself was wont to communicate on Sundays, Wednesdays, Fridays, Saturdays, and on Saints' days.

[y] In S. Cyprian's time persons used to keep the "Sanctum Domini" at home in a box, (*arca*). De Laps. 16.

[z] Tertullian, De Orat. 19, advises persons on a fast-day to attend the celebration, to "take the Lord's Body," and to "reserve" it instead of communicating. And see his Ad Uxor. ii. 5.

[a] Jerome, Ep. 48. c. 15: "I neither blame nor approve the custom."

[b] See the sarcastic description in Ep. 22. c. 28, of clergy dressed in the extreme of fashion, dainty and elegant as bridegrooms, and wheedling ladies out of articles that suited their taste. He had probably also come into collision with the seven Roman deacons, who bore themselves with a haughtiness which he traces to their small number. He had seen them at private parties "benedictiones presbyteris dare." See his indignant words, Ep. 146, against the insolent manner of the "servant of tables towards those *ad quorum preces Christi Corpus Sanguisque conficitur*."

for gross calumny. Disgusted by obloquy which doubtless broke forth unrestrained after the death of his patron Damasus, Jerome quitted Rome in a mood which had little of self-mistrust or meekness, calling himself "a fool for wishing to sing the Lord's song in a strange land," and telling his female friends that "at Christ's tribunal the character of every man's life would appear[c]." He set sail for Antioch, where he visited Paulinus.

Meantime, Augustine at Milan was working his way towards Catholic belief. Gradually he came to feel that there was truth as well as beauty in the sermons of Ambrose, but did not venture to take up his time in priva e and doubted whether a life like his could be happy[d]. Monica joined her son at Milan, and told him that she felt certain of living to see him a Catholic[e]. He took his place for the present among the Church catechumens; but worldly passions, and difficulties raised by Manicheism, destroyed his peace of mind, and made him fearful of "dying before he had found the truth[f]." His friends Alypius and Nebridius were partners in his search for it[g]. He discovered the falsehood of the Manichean taunt, that Scripture debased the Deity by human limitations; but Manicheism had its own material conceptions of Deity, from which Augustine found it hard to emerge[h]. His perplexities, however, steadily diminished. Firmly believing in God's providence, looking for a judgment to come[i], and seeking for help in his sore need, he began to see that freewill was a reality, that the principle of faith was reasonable[k], that the true God was in truth a Spirit[l], that those Scriptures which heresy had disdained, but which a Christendom had attested, gave that answer to his deepest cravings which the noblest heathen books could never supply[m]. The doctrine of Christ's Divinity was for some time

---

[c] Ep. 45, (99).
[d] Conf. v. 24; vi. 3.
[e] Ibid. vi. I.
[f] Ibid. vi. 10; vii. 7.
[g] Ibid. vi. II.
[h] Ibid. vi. 4; v. 25; vii. I.
[i] Ibid. vi. 26; vii. II.
[k] Ibid. vii. 5; vi. 7.
[l] Ibid. vii. 16.
[m] Ibid. iii. 9; vi. 8; vii. 13, 14, 27.

foreign to his thoughts; and he tells us that Alypius imagined the Church to be committed to the untenable Apollinarian theory [n].

Jerome quitted Antioch for Jerusalem towards the end of 385; thence proceeded to Alexandria and to the monasteries of Egypt, and ultimately settled at Bethlehem. Paula followed him thither, visiting the sacred places of Palestine on her way. It is evident from the account of her pilgrimage [o] that enthusiasm or inventiveness had already fixed upon certain buildings as veritable monuments of the Gospel history.

On Jan. 23, 386, an edict in Valentinian's name ensured freedom of worship both to Arians and Catholics, but expressly menaced the latter with death if they should cause any disturbance. His mother resolved to attack Ambrose again. An Arian bishop who took the name of Auxentius claimed the throne of Milan. Ambrose was called on to plead against him in the imperial consistory. He gave in a written refusal to admit the principle of lay judges in matters of faith, and cited the words of Valentinian I., "It is not for me to judge between bishops." The present sovereign, he boldly observed, was young and unbaptized; one day he would see the absurdity of asking a bishop to "place his rights at the feet of laymen [p]."

He took up his abode within the church, which was again filled with a zealous congregation,—including Monica,—and guarded, as before, by soldiers who prevented all egress. To calm agitation and enkindle courage, he set the people to sing hymns which he had written [q], full of terse and condensed energy, and to chant the Psalms antiphonally, "after the manner of the East." He knew "how mighty a strain" was the doxology to Father, Son, and Spirit, which "made

---

[n] Conf. vii. 25. [o] Jerome, Ep. 108, (27.) [p] Ambr. Ep. 21.

[q] Twelve hymns, supposed to be really his, are extant. The second concludes with words which might have suited this occasion; "Christum rogemus et Patrem, Christi Patrisque Spiritum, Unum, potens, per omnia Fove precantes, Trinitas."

all who sang it teachers[r]." After some days had been thus spent, Ambrose preached, apparently on Palm Sunday, assuring his flock that he would never abandon them; referring to Elisha in Dothan and Peter in prison[s]; denouncing "Auxentius" as writing and dictating cruel orders. The lessons of the day,—Naboth's history and the entry into Jerusalem,—supplied him with illustrations. He quoted the passage about "tribute to Cæsar," and said that in the Church there was but one Image, Christ the Image of the Father. There was no question about paying taxes; they were levied, as of course, on Church lands. That the Church had gold to bestow, he denied not; *Christ's poor* were her stipendiaries. He summed up his principle in the words, "The Emperor is *within* the Church, but not *above* it[t]."

It appears that the soldiers were withdrawn, and that Ambrose was left free to dedicate a church, the Ambrosian; after which the people asked him to place some relics of martyrs in the new church, according to custom. "I will," he said, "if I can find any:" and he bade them dig in the earth before the chancel screen of S. Felix and S. Nabor. Two skeletons with a quantity of blood,—so he writes to his sister[u],—were found, carried to S. Fausta's, watched there all night, and taken up next day for transfer to the Ambrosian, as the bodies of S. Gervase and S. Protase, of whose martyrdom some old men had heard. As the procession moved along, a blind man named Severus, who had been a butcher, touched the hem of the pall, cried out that he had received sight, and called on those who knew him to test his words. Other wondrous cures were spoken of in a sermon preached that day by Ambrose; but this was the

---

[r] Serm. c. Aux. 34. See. Aug. Conf. ix. 15.

[s] He adds the story of S. Peter fleeing from Rome, and meeting Christ at the gate. "Lord, whither goest Thou?" "I come to be crucified again." Peter "understood that He was to be crucified again in His servant." Serm. 13.

[t] Compare the letter of Hosius to Constantius.

[u] Ep. 22.

chief case. The Arians denounced it as a fraud, but did not disprove it; and the account given by Ambrose is supported by the distiuct attestations of Augustine[x], and by Paulinus, who wrote his life of Ambrose while Severus was still living, aud serving in the Ambrosian church. Ambrose caused the relics to be buried on the right of the altar, "where," said he, "Christ is the Sacrifice." That the event called forth a burst of devotion to Christ, and stopped Justina's persecution of Ambrose, cannot be thought unnatural.

In the ensuing summer, Augustine, who had been deeply moved by an account of the life of S. Antony, and of "the sweet ways" of Egyptian monks, passed through a hard struggle with his lower impulses, which held him back longer than any remnants of Manicheism from a thorough self-surrender to the faith. At length, as he lay under a fig-tree, weeping aud longing for deliverance, he heard a child's voice in the next house say repeatedly, "Take up and read." Remembering that Antony's career had been determined by his coming into church while the words were read, "Sell all that thou hast aud give to the poor," he returned to his lodging, where he had left Alypius, opened a copy of the Epistles, and read the first words that he saw[y]: "Not in rioting and drunkenness, not in chambering aud wantonness, not in strife and envying; but put ye on the Lord Jesus Christ, and make not provision for the flesh." "No further," says he, "would I read—nor needed I." The darkness was past, and the true light shone; he and Alypius went at once to Monica, and declared themselves converts to the Catholic faith. "With exulting joy she blessed Thee, who art able to do above that which we ask or think." Au-

---

[x] Conf. ix. 16. Serm. 286; "I was there, I was at Milan, I know that miracles occurred," &c. De Civ. Dei, xxii. 8. S. Augustine speaks of S. Ambrose as knowing by a dream where the relics lay. Ambrose only says he had "cujusdam ardor præsagii." And Augustine speaks of the bodies as uncorrupt; Ambrose speaks of skeletons. But on the main points they agree.

[y] Rom. xiii. 13; Conf. viii. 29.

gustine resigned his professorship, for which, indeed, weak lungs had begun to disqualify him; and retired with his friends to a country house, where he "reposed from the fever of the world[z]," and began to prepare for baptism at the ensuing Easter. Ambrose recommended him to study Isaiah, but he found the opening passages difficult; the Psalms, especially the fourth, entered deeply into a heart which after so many restless fever-fits had "found rest in Him for whom it was made[a]."

---

[z] Conf. ix. 5.

[a] Ibid. i. 1.

CHAPTER VIII.

From the Conversion of S. Augustine to the Death of S. Ambrose.

"Posterity has applauded the virtuous firmness of the archbishop; and the example of Theodosius may prove the beneficial influence of those principles which could force a monarch, exalted above the apprehension of human punishment, to respect the laws and ministers of an invisible Judge."

GIBBON, ch. xxvii.

THE execution of Priscillian was designed by Ithacius and his party to be merely the beginning of a fierce onslaught upon heretics. They obtained from Maximus an order, to be carried out by imperial officers, for the seizure and execution of all the Priscillianists in Spain; and they were disposed to regard a pale face or a peculiar dress as sufficient evidence of Priscillianism[a]. They were now assembled at Treves for the consecration of a bishop. S. Martin, they knew, was coming to Treves; they knew also what he would think of their doings; and they caused messengers from the Emperor to forbid his approach unless he came peaceably disposed towards the Council. "I shall come," answered Martin, "with *Christ's* peace." He arrived by night, went to pray in the cathedral, and next day entreated Maximus to spare the lives of two high officers who had been faithful to Gratian, and "not to send tribunes with the power of the sword into Spain." Maximus deferred his answer; while Martin held aloof from the Ithacians, and supported one bishop who had condemned their conduct. They fell prostrate before Maximus; "If Martin," they said, "is allowed to be the avenger of Priscillian, all is undone; the truth is, Martin himself is a heretic." The Emperor tried to win over Martin, but failing in this, commanded the two officers to be executed. Martin heard of this late at night, and instantly demanded access to the Emperor. "If you will

[a] Sulp. Dial. iii. 15.

spare those men, and recall the tribunes, I will communicate with the bishops." The terms were at once accepted; Martin performed his promise, but would not record the act by his signature. Next day he quitted Treves, mourning over what he deemed his weakness in condoning one deed of blood for the sake of preventing others. His biographer says that after this compliance his powers of exorcism were lessened, and that he never attended another synod. This scene at Treves illustrates the tender-heartedness of the aged saint, who had seen life in such various forms, and preserved through all the sweet compassion which had flowed forth at sight of the Amiens beggar[b]. We need not suspect exaggeration when we read that as a bishop he never punished injuries to himself; that "no one ever saw him angry or troubled;" that his face was "ever bright with heavenly cheerfulness;" that Christ's name was ever on his lips, peace and kindness ever in his heart[c].

Early in 387 an increase of taxes provoked the people of Antioch to sedition. They threw down the brazen statues of Theodosius and of his deceased wife, the pious and charitable Flaccilla[d]; dragged them about with ropes, and broke them in pieces. Such an outrage in those days was regarded as an offence against the Emperor's person[e]; and Theodosius' one great fault was a wrathfulness which nearly resembled Valentinian's. Flavian set forth, a little before Lent, to appease him[f]; and met Hellebicus and Cæsarius, two great officers of the Empire, sent from court to avenge

---

[b] At the gate of Paris he kissed and blessed a leper, who, it is said, was straightway healed. Sulp. Vit. Mart. 19.

[c] Sulp. Vit. 26. This picture resembles Adamnan's account of S. Columba, "Omnibus carus, hilarem semper faciem ostendens." Vit. S. Col. Præf.

[d] She used to visit the sick at their houses, and serve up their food in hospitals, "*because* God had made her an empress." Theod. v. 19.

[e] Constantine had thought otherwise. Hearing that stones had been flung at his statue, he stroked his face and said with a smile, "No wound here."

[f] S. Chrys. Hom. 21 ad Pop. Ant., tom. ii. p. 215. The old man had the pain of leaving his sister apparently at the point of death.

the insult. His absence was well supplied by Chrysostom, who had recently received priest's orders, and who began to turn this trouble to good account by a course of "Sermons on the Statues," as they are called. In these he endeavoured to allay the people's terror, and to convince them of their besetting sins,—of which swearing was the chief,—and so far succeeded that the churches were thronged all day. Hellebicus and Cæsarius arrived, erected their tribunal, and went to work by prosecutions, scourging, torture, and imprisonment—their own hearts suffering from the pain they reluctantly inflicted[g]. The cheerful animation of Antioch was exchanged for blank despair; the forum became a scene of arrests; the daily question was, "Who has been seized to-day,—who has been punished, and how?" Two ladies of rank, the mother and sister of one of the prisoners, were seen crouching with veiled faces at the door of the judgment-hall, and listening to the cries of anguish from within[h]. Pious monks from the hill-country availed themselves of the freedom of speech which was generally permitted to their order, and told the judges that they would undertake to move the Emperor's pity if they might go as envoys to him. An old hermit named Macedonius bade them tell the Emperor, "It is easy to set up new brazen images, but if you kill men who are made in God's image, you cannot undo your work[i]." Flavian, on reaching Constantinople, shed tears when Theodosius asked, "Did I deserve this outrage? or if I did, could they not have spared the effigy of her that is gone[k]?" The aged bishop reminded him that by pardoning instead of punishing he would win the richest of all diadems, and raise new statues in a people's heart. The

---

g Hom. 13. 1.

h Chrysostom was led by this spectacle into a train of thought like the "Quem patronum rogaturus" of the *Dies Iræ*. Hom. 13. 2.

i Hom. 17. 1; Theod. v. 20.

k Hom. 21. 2. This dialogue says nothing about the murder of Antiochene magistrates, which Theod., v. 20, asserts the rioters to have committed.

Emperor's kind and noble heart had prompted him to liberate all prisoners at the preceding Easter, with an expressed wish that he could also restore the dead. Here, then, was an opportunity: Antioch was even now at the gates of Hades. A word from him could raise it up—and what a glory would the Christian name derive from such an act of mercy! How would the Gentiles say, "The Christians' God is great indeed, if an old man bearing His priesthood can move an emperor to forego so just a revenge." Flavian then solemnly reminded Theodosius of the condition attached to God's forgiveness, and of the day of reckoning in store for all. Theodosius was moved, and said, "It is no great thing for men to pardon their fellow-men, since the Lord of the world became a servant for our sakes, and was crucified by those whom He had blessed, and prayed, 'Father, forgive them!'" He bade Flavian convey his pardon to Antioch, and sent on a more expeditious messenger to announce it. The city was joyously illuminated; Flavian arrived in time for Easter, and declared that God alone had softened Theodosius. The narrative shews on what terms men held life and liberty under the Cæsarean system, even when its head was a Theodosius; and it is significant that after all the misery which Antioch, for "the crime of a few," had suffered, the resolution to inflict no more was magnified as an act of superhuman benignity. S. Ambrose would probably have spoken out for justice, where Flavian was fain to weep and implore.

On the eve of that Easter festival, April 25, 387, the baptistery at Milan witnessed a memorable sight. After the series of lessons usual on Holy Saturday, Augustine and his son Adeodatus[1], with Alypius, were led to the font, where a priest and a deacon attended on S. Ambrose. With faces turned westward, they renounced "the devil

---

[1] A promising boy of fifteen; born to Augustine in the days when he used to pray, "Give me chastity, but not yet." Adeodatus "in ability surpassed many learned men." Conf. ix. 14; see viii. 17.

and his works, the world, its luxury, its pleasures," and then turned eastward in recognition of Christ. Ambrose performed the solemn benediction of the font; each candidate descended into it, was asked, "Dost thou believe in God the Father Almighty?" answered, "I believe," and was immersed in the water; professed in like manner his faith "in our Lord Jesus Christ and His Cross," and "in the Holy Spirit," and was immersed a second and third time [m]. Ambrose then anointed the head of each, with a prayer that it might be "unto life eternal." Their feet were washed, (according to a Milanese usage which was not Roman,) they put on their white vestments, received "the spiritual seal" whereby "Christ *confirmed*" them [n], and were led in procession up the church, chanting the 43rd Psalm, while Augustine's happiness overflowed in tears [o]. They saw the altar in its fair array [p], decked for the Easter Communion; and were at once admitted to the highest privileges of the Church [q].

They resolved to return to Africa, and there to form a religious household. S. Monica, in the fulness of her joy, acted both as mother and as servant to them all [r]. She went with them to Ostia, where they prepared for the homeward voyage. One day she and Augustine were leaning against a window of the house where they lodged, and talking of the future blessedness, "what it must be to enter into God's very presence after the resurrection." Suddenly she told him that as all her hopes for this world were fulfilled, she desired to live no longer. In a few days she was seized with a fatal illness, and calmly expired about

---

[m] S. Amb. de Myst. 28, (the book was probably written about this time), and the treatise de Sacram. ii. 20, which Dr. Pusey attributes to a disciple of S. Ambrose, (Doctr. R. Pres. p. 467.)

[n] De Myst. 42. Chrism is not mentioned, but was probably applied to the forehead; the former unction being a distinct rite.

[o] Conf. ix. 14.

[p] De Myst. 43.

[q] The "Chronicle" of Dacius, bishop of Milan, which spoke of SS. Ambrose and Augustine as composing the *Te Deum* on this occasion, is spurious.

[r] Conf. ix. 22.

a week afterwards. Her grandson's loud weeping was hushed by a scruple on Augustine's part against any such display of sorrow; they chanted the 101st Psalm, performed the burial, and attended the celebration of the Eucharist[s], with the same painful constraint of natural feeling; at length Augustine found relief in tears, though not without an apprehension that men, if they knew it, would judge him hardly[t]. He deferred his voyage for the present, and settled at Rome.

Justina, having failed to crush S. Ambrose, employed him again in her service. He visited Treves to ask Maximus for a ratification of the peace, and for the delivery of the remains of Gratian[u]. Maximus treated the Archbishop with disrespect, by refusing to see him except in public audience; and Ambrose, on entering the consistory, declined the proffered kiss of peace, on the ground of this affront to his dignity. After some conversation, Maximus promised to consider Valentinian's request. Ambrose held aloof from the communion of the prince who had slain his master, and of bishops whose hands were stained with blood, though it were the blood of heretics. In consequence of this, Maximus bade him leave the city. His chief regret was that an old and dying bishop, Hyginus, was ruthlessly hurried into exile. "When I begged that the old man might not be thrust forth without a cloak and a feather-cushion, I was thrust forth myself[x]." Fearing an invasion at their own doors, Justina and her son took refuge at Thessalonica. Maximus became lord of all

---

[s] "The Sacrifice of our ransom was offered for her." Conf. ix. 32.

[t] Conf. ix. 33.

[u] Ep. 24.

[x] Tenderness was one of his main characteristics. Paulinus dwells on his power of rejoicing with them that rejoiced, and weeping with them that wept, and on his solicitude for the poor and for prisoners. Vit. 39. See his beautiful books on the death of his brother Satyrus, A. D. 379. "Lacrymavi ergo, fateor, etiam ego—sed lacrymavit et Dominus!" i. 10. "O infelicia illa, sed tamen dulcia suprema osculorum pignora!" 19. "Toto te animo ac mente complector—nec mihi te aut mors aut tempus avellet." 72, 74.

Italy; but Valentinian, by intercourse with Theodosius, was brought over to the Catholic faith.

In a zeal for this faith, which was altogether genuine, if "not according to knowledge," Theodosius, on March 10, 388, forbade heretics (especially naming Apollinarians) to inhabit cities, to ordain clergy, to hold assemblies, or to appear before the Emperor. He now made war on Maximus, who was defeated in Pannonia, and put to death at Aquileia in the summer of 388. Theodosius remained at Milan several months. It was probably in the early part of his stay [y] that, after approaching the altar to present his offering, he did not return, like other laymen, to the nave, but continued standing in the sanctuary. Ambrose asked what he wanted; he replied that he intended to communicate. Ambrose, by his archdeacon, bade the Emperor withdraw from a place which was reserved for the clergy. Theodosius at once acquiesced, explaining that he had been accustomed at Constantinople to remain in the sanctuary, but thanking Ambrose for giving him better instruction. In another case, the prelate's admonition was less reasonable and less readily obeyed. The Christians of Callinicus had burned a synagogue; Theodosius ordered their bishop to rebuild it. Some monks of the same place, having been insulted by a party of Valentinian heretics, had burned the "temple" of the latter. Theodosius ordered them to be punished. Ambrose could not look upon this as a matter of social order. In a long letter, more impassioned than logical [z], he contended that Theodosius was making himself a champion of Judaism, and went so far as to represent Christ as warning him not to give a triumph to His foes. He followed up this letter by a sermon, at the end of which Theodosius said, "You have been

[y] Theodoret, v. 18, puts it after his penance; but surely he would not have been so long at Milan without making an offering at the altar.

[z] Ep. 40. He actually argued that since Julian had not punished heathens for outraging churches, Theodosius ought not to punish Christians for lawless violence done to a synagogue.

preaching at me." Ambrose did not deny it. "Well," said the Emperor, "I certainly did give rather a severe order, but I have softened it. Those monks commit many outrages!" Ambrose flatly refused to proceed with the Eucharistic service until the Emperor promised to cancel the obnoxious orders. Theodosius at last gave way. Ambrose pertinaciously repeated, "I depend upon you—I depend upon you." "Yes, depend upon me." Then Ambrose went up to the altar. "I would not have done so," he triumphantly adds, "if he had not given me a full promise."

A third application in behalf of the altar of Victory was not so promptly refused by Theodosius as Ambrose probably expected; but after some days, his bold and faithful exhortations had their effect [a]. Theodosius and Valentinian visited Rome on June 13, 389; Augustine having probably quitted it for Africa before their arrival. The presence of two Christian emperors induced many Roman nobles to profess conversion from idolatry; and the Lateran cathedral was thronged by applicants for "the sacred sign and the chrism of spiritual kingship [b]." Numbers visited the "Confession of S. Peter" at the Vatican, the veneration of which had become, in many instances, the "superstitious adoration of a sepulchre [c]." Theodosius planned a stately basilica, without the walls of Rome, in honour of the other great Apostle, whose grave, says a writer of the second century [d], was pointed out in the Ostian Road, and whose name has always been associated with S. Peter's in the foundation of the Roman See.

At the instance of Siricius [e], Theodosius made a law of civil disfranchisement against the Manicheans, whose lead-

[a] Ep. 57. [b] Prud. c. Symm. i. 587.

[c] See S. Aug. de Mor. Eccl. i. 75.

[d] Caius, priest of Rome, in Euseb. ii. 25.

[e] He had already taken precautions against the reception of "the Lord's Body by the impure lips" of Manicheans, and ordered that even converts from Manicheism should only receive it by way of *viaticum* on their deathbeds.

ing men, "the Elect," had given great scandal in Rome by their hypocrisy and immorality, resisting the efforts of an honest-minded "Hearer," or ordinary Manichean, for the establishment of a community of "Elect" under his own roof, to live by a rule derived from the "epistle of Manes[f]." Jerome had, some years before, spoken of the name of "Manichean" as opprobriously applied by self-indulgent Roman ladies to those whose faces were "pale or sad[g]."

Jerome was now, "in sheltered nooks of Palestine," combining monastic devotion with intense study. By this time Paula had built several monasteries at Bethlehem, in one of which Jerome apparently lived, but without discharging priestly functions[h]. Others were occupied by women divided into three companies[i]; the offices were, matins, terce, sext, none, vespers, midnight; every sister was obliged to know the Psalms; and the love of psalmody became so common at Bethlehem, that the ploughman was heard to sing Alleluia, and the reaper and the vinedresser to cheer their toil with "something of David[k]." It was only on Sunday that the sisters went to the adjacent church at the cave of the Nativity. Jerome's chief occupation at this time was the carrying out of an undertaking begun six years before. In 383, at the request of Damasus, he had corrected, by the Greek Testament and Septuagint, the existing Latin version of the Gospels and Psalms, which was in a very corrupt state. He now went through the whole of the Old Testament in that version, (which was called the Old Italic,) so as to bring it into conformity with that edition of the Septuagint which he found in Origen's *Hexapla*. The Psalter as edited by Jerome in 383 became known as the Roman, and was long used by the Roman Church, which still retains in her daily office its version of Psalm 95; the whole "Roman Psalter" is now confined to S. Peter's, and a few churches in Spain. The more

---

[f] S. Aug. de Mor. Man. ii. 74. This man Constantius became a Catholic, c. Faust. v. 5. [g] Ep. 22. 13.

[h] Epiphan. in Hieron. Ep. 51. 1. [i] Ep. 108. 19. [k] Ep. 46. 11.

correct Psalter included in Jerome's larger work, usually dated in 389, became prevalent in Gaul about the end of the sixth century, and hence acquired the name of Gallican. It gradually won its way to general acceptance.

The Italian Church was at this time troubled by the teaching of Jovinian, who had passed from ascetic to luxurious habits,—from fasting, as Jerome expresses it, to dainty meals, from coarse black to silk and white linen. His propositions were, 1. That virginity was not a higher state than marriage, and that Christ was not literally the Virgin-born[l]. 2. That the true baptism was a purely inward process, which ensured perseverance and salvation; so that any Christian who fell away showed thereby that he had never been regenerate[m]. 3. That fasting was not better than eating with thankfulness. 4. That there would be no difference of degree in the rewards or punishments of the next world. Jovinian drew away many persons from the monastic life. Siricius assembled his presbyters, and excommunicated Jovinian with four others; they went from Rome to Milan, but Siricius wrote a letter "to the Milanese Church" denouncing their unheard-of doctrine[n], and carefully distinguishing between the special honour paid by the Church to virginal devotedness, and any disparagement of matrimony[o]. Ambrose and other bishops then at Milan wrote to thank Siricius. "Good is marriage," they said, "but better is virginity;" and they insisted on the miracle of the Nativity in all its fulness. It appears that this same Council of Milan confirmed the excommunication of Ithacius, which had been recently pronounced by Ambrose.

While the Council was sitting, terrible news came from

---

[l] His view was different from that of the Antidicomarians.

[m] Compare the Calvinistic theory.

[n] "Never did any such dogs as these bark at the Church's sacred truth."

[o] "We assist at marriages," says Siricius, "with the veil," i. e. the yellow bridal-veil which the priest appears to have blessed. "Marriage," says S. Ambrose, Ep. 19, "ought to be sanctified, *velamine sacerdotali et benedictione.*"

Thessalonica. The people of that city had quarrelled, in a disgraceful cause, with Botheric, the commander-in-chief of the forces in Illyricum; and having risen in tumult, had murdered him and several other officers. At first, Theodosius had been kindled into fury; Ambrose, apparently, had calmed him; but the high officials of his court, particularly Ruffinus, his chancellor, or "master of the offices," had persuaded him to order that seven thousand persons, neither more nor less, should be put to death by soldiers in the circus of Thessalonica. An attempt on Theodosius' part to recall this order came too late. The massacre lasted three hours; the most piteous case[p] was that of a father, who offered himself as a substitute for his sons; the soldiers answered that they could only spare one of the youths, because they had to make up their tale of victims. The unhappy man, gazing on both, could not make up his mind to choose one before the other; and the impatient soldiers cut down both. Such was the tragedy of which Ambrose now heard[q]. Wishing to give Theodosius time to bethink himself, he withdrew for a while from Milan, and wrote to the Emperor. He observed that "he alone of the court" had been kept in ignorance of the recent mandate; were he now to be silent, he would incur the doom of the unfaithful watchman[r]. The Emperor's virtues were marred by an impetuous temper which his courtiers were too apt to stimulate. The deed which had been done had no parallel. The Emperor must repent like David. "You are a man, and temptation has come upon you; conquer it. Only penitence can take away sin. No angel nor archangel can do it; even the Lord Himself forgives no sinners, save those who repent. I would persuade you, I entreat, exhort, admonish." The devil, he proceeded, had been envious of that kindness of heart, which was the

[p] Soz. vii. 25. [q] Ep. 51.

[r] Ezek. iii. 19. Paulinus says that he wept over those who confessed their sins to him, and so drew forth their tears. "He considered himself as fallen with the fallen." Vit. 39.

crowning grace of the Emperor's character. For his own part, he could not offer the Sacrifice in the presence of one stained with the blood of many innocents. Theodosius might offer an acceptable sacrifice[s] after he had become truly penitent. "I am attached to you, I love you, I pray for you; but I love God better."

Theodosius attempted to enter the church as usual; but Ambrose, who had returned to Milan, met him at the gate, took hold of his purple robe[t], and asked, according to Theodoret, "How can you presume to receive the most holy Body of the Lord, and to carry His precious Blood to lips which ordered so much bloodshed[u]?" "David himself committed crimes," said Theodosius. The answer was ready: "You followed him in sin, follow him also in amendment." The Emperor was formally excluded from Church-communion; and thus did Ambrose, "in the name of justice and of humanity[x]," and, in truth, of Christ and the Gospel, "rebuke the greatest sovereign of the age." It was probably in allusion to this memorable deed that Chrysostom said, addressing the clergy, "If the unworthy person who comes to Communion be a general or a præfect, or even he that wears the diadem, debar him; your commission is greater than his. But if you are afraid, refer him to me: I will shed my own blood, sooner than administer Blood so awful, contrary to what is meet[y]."

On June 16, 390, a Council met at Carthage. Its chief enactments were, an enforcement of Siricius' rule as to

[s] A remarkable passage, as indicating the part borne by the people in the sacrifice of the Eucharist. So the very old Roman Canon, "Qui Tibi offerunt hoc sacrificium laudis."

[t] Soz. vii. 25.

[u] Theod. v. 18. Compare the language of S. Cyprian, de Lapsis, 14. "Quod non statim—ore polluto Domini Sanguinem bibat,—irascitur."

[x] Milman, Lat. Chr. i. 79. Compare the story told by Eusebius, vi. 34, of the Emperor Philip called the Arabian, that he professed Christianity, but was compelled by the bishop on Easter-eve to take his place among the penitents, on account of his crimes. S. Athanasins, as we have seen, excommunicated the governor of Libya.

[y] In Matth. Hom. 82. 6.

priests and deacons, and a prohibition of the unnecessary multiplication of episcopal sees.

We may probably place in this year a scandal in which a deacon of Constantinople was implicated, and on the ground of which Nectarius, by the advice of an Egyptian priest named Eudæmon, abolished the office of the Penitentiary priest, which had been instituted after the Novatian schism. While this office lasted, it had been incumbent on those who wished for direction as to whether their sins required public or private penance, to consult the Penitentiary. They were now left free, as before the institution of the office, to choose their own spiritual physician, or simply to use their own discretion as to approaching the holy Mysteries[z]. This relaxation diminished the number of those who practised confession, either in public or in private; while at Rome, where stricter views of penitential duty were prevalent, every Lent saw the "godly discipline" carried out as a working system, with prostrations and bitter weeping, expulsion of penitents from the church, and their solemn re-admission on Maundy Thursday[a]. But it must be observed that open penance was reserved for the heavier offences; and that nowhere in the ancient Church was confession of all sins to a priest made compulsory[b].

Sozomen considers that this event preceded a law made by Theodosius, June 21, 390, that no woman under sixty should be admitted deaconess. This office was sometimes held by virgins, but Theodosius required them to be widows with children, according to the custom of Tertullian's time. Their duty was to assist at the baptism of women, to instruct female catechumens in private, and to assist in works of charity. Another law, dated Sept. 3, 390, condemned the disorderly conduct of certain monks, who caused disturbance in cities by interfering with the process of justice on grounds less reasonable than the sufferings of Antioch had supplied.

---

[z] Soc. v. 19.
[a] Soz. vii. 16.
[b] See Tertullian, Lib. Fath., pp. 379—408.

According to the strict law of the Church, a deed of blood must be followed by years of penance. Eight months intervened between the exclusion of Theodosius from the church and the feast of Christmas, 390. On that "most venerable of all festivals, the mother and fountain of them all[c]," Theodosius wept bitterly because he was excluded from the Presence which was open to slaves and beggars[d]. Ruffinus, the adviser of the massacre, whose cruel and treacherous nature was not understood by the frank-hearted Theodosius, induced him to seek an interview with Ambrose in the episcopal house. Ambrose rebuked him for attempting to break through the rules of the Church. He replied that he respected them,—that he only came to sue for absolution. Ambrose asked what repentance he had manifested. He replied that he would obey whatever was enjoined. Ambrose then required him to make a public acknowledgment of his crime, and to enact that none should be executed until thirty days after the sentence. Theodosius at once consented, and was permitted to enter the church. He threw himself on the pavement[e], repeating, "My soul cleaveth to the dust, quicken Thou me according to Thy Word;" and the sight of their emperor stripped of his purple, and imploring with tears the Divine forgiveness, drew forth the pitying sympathy of the people who had formerly dreaded his bursts of wrath[f].

Very soon afterwards, in the beginning of 391, Augustine was, against his will, ordained priest by Valerius bishop of Hippo, who authorized him to preach in his presence—a privilege unheard of in Africa. It was then that Augustine, when asking for some time to prepare himself, observed that "nothing was more comfortable than the ministerial office discharged in a perfunctory and men-pleasing

---

[c] S. Chrys. de Philogon. 3, tom. i. 497.

[d] Theod. v. 18. His account seems too rhetorical to be altogether trustworthy.

[e] Ruffinus, ii. 18, says, "he did public penance in the face of the whole Church."

[f] S. Aug. de Civ. Dei, v. 26.

temper, but nothing in the sight of God more wretched, woeful, damnable[g]."

The warfare of Christianity against Paganism now took in great measure the form of a direct onslaught on the temples. Theodosius had prohibited divinations by an edict of May, 385, and had ordered Cynegius, the præfect of the East, to close the Egyptian temples. Enthusiastic monks begau to destroy temples as the natural homes of idolatrous divination; Marcellus, bishop of Apamea, lost his life in a conflict with Pagans, who had armed in defence of a temple in his district. Theophilus of Alexandria was a prelate whose zeal was more likely to take this form than to promote Christ's cause by "weapons not carnal." He was engaged in converting a temple of Bacchus, given him by the Emperor, into a church; and his exposure of the symbols of an impure worship provoked the Pagans to rise in sedition. They seized some Christians and dragged them within the vast enclosure of the Serapeum, or temple of Serapis, a deity brought into Egypt by Ptolemy I. and identified with Bacchus[h]. The temple stood on an artificial height, and was the centre of a quadrangle, which was itself encompassed by halls and chambers. Within the sanctuary was seated the vast image, in the form of a long-haired personage, bearing a bushel on his head, and touching both sides of the temple with his arms. Such was the stronghold of idolatry, in which the Christian prisoners were cruelly martyred. An accomplished and enthusiastic Pagan philosopher, named Olympius, took the command of the Pagans who garrisoned the Serapeum. While the military authorities wrote for instructions to Theodosius, Olympius assured his adherents that the worship of the gods did not depend on images which might be broken[i]. Theodosius'

---

[g] Ep. 21.

[h] The Romans had adopted his worship. There was at York a temple "Deo sancto Serapi." Ruffinus, ii. 23, says that some identified him with Jupiter, some with the Nile, and others thought him a representation of Joseph, &c.

[i] Soz. vii. 15. See Hooker, b. v. 65. 15.

letter commanded the destruction of all the temples in Alexandria. The Pagans were reduced to despair. Olympius fled by night from the Serapeum; the Christians believed that amid the dead stillness he had heard a voice within the closed and guarded fane, as of a person chanting *Alleluia*[k]. The temple was abandoned to the Christians. In defiance of the rumour that if the image of Serapis were approached, heaven and earth would come together, Theophilus gazed scornfully on the enormous figure, and commanded a soldier to smite it with an axe[l]. Many Pagans shrieked in horror; but Serapis could not "judge his own cause, nor redress a wrong[m]." Blow upon blow shattered the idol; a swarm of rats leaped forth from its head, and it was dragged through the streets and burned piecemeal. Thus in one triumphant day was the pride of Alexandrian Heathenism laid low for ever. The work of destruction went on throughout Egypt; hideous secrets came to light, revealing the lust and cruelty of the Pagan priesthood; and one image was preserved for a perpetual record, that Pagans might never deny that they had worshipped an ape. Many conversions followed these events, the date of which is variously given as 389 or 391. Edicts dated in February and June 391 forbade all religious use of temples, and imposed penalties on magistrates who should violate the prohibition. Care was taken to raise churches on the site of the Serapeum and other temples.

The Eustathian communion at Antioch had now a new head in Evagrius, whom Paulinus had consecrated to be his successor, and whom S. Ambrose with all the West acknowledged. A council at Capua proposed that Theophilus should arbitrate. Flavian was employed about this time in detecting the heresy of the Massalians or Euchites, a body of fanatics[n] who had existed for many years in the East,

---

[k] Sozomen says he was "informed of this." The story, at any rate, is grandly symbolical.

[l] Theod. v. 22.

[m] Baruch vi. 54.

[n] See S. Aug. de Hæres. 57. As to their "doing nothing else but pray,"

and whose theory was a fanatical spiritualism which called the Sacraments ineffective, laid exclusive stress on prayer poured forth under violent agitation, pretended to sensible perceptions of God's presence, and approximated to Pantheism in the assertion of man's perfectibility. The horror which such views excited in the minds of Churchmen was natural; yet they took possession of many minds which in the monastic life had become unhealthy. As they were combined with a total contempt of truthfulness, it was difficult to convict a Massalian, who would disown or anathematize the opinions imputed to him; and this difficulty led Flavian to an unworthy adoption of their own craft. He pretended that he wished to learn from the aged Adelphius[o]; and having thus obtained his confidence, turned upon him as a heretic self-convicted. The Massalians were condemned both in Syria and Pamphylia. Bonosus, bishop of Sardica, had lately given scandal by asserting that S. Mary had other sons than Christ. The Italian bishops insisted that those of Macedonia should act as his judges, instead of referring the case to them. He was tried accordingly, and suspended.

Jerome's labours on the text of Scripture were carried on in 391 by his memorable translation of the Old Testament directly from the Hebrew, which became known in after-days as the Vulgate.

On Theodosius' return to Antioch towards the end of 391, he wished to terminate the schism by referring Flavian's claim to the judgment of the West. Flavian, an adept in diplomacy, managed to gain time, and afterwards secured Theodosius' favour by a speech congenial to his generous heart. "I am ready to stand a trial as to my personal faith and conduct. But I have no mind for a contest about the primacy of Antioch; I had rather resign it,

---

see a sarcastic retort of Hooker's, b. v. 74. 1. Epiphanius, Hær. 80, says that if one mentioned Christ to a Massalian, he would answer, "I, too, am Christ."

[o] Theod. iv. 11.

and I will do so." Theodosius bade him retain his throne and govern his flock [p].

A fourth application about the altar of Victory took place in the beginning of 392. The deputation could wring nothing from Valentinian [q], who gave his answer without any communication with S. Ambrose. The young Western Emperor was now in Gaul. He gave promise of a noble reign, being just and equitable, tender-hearted [r], pure in life, and sedulous in imperial duties. He was but twenty years old. The chief danger that he had to dread was the domineering insolence of the Frank, Arbogastes, who had been active in the overthrow of Maximus. Valentinian resolved to return to Italy: but as yet he was unbaptized, and his affection for the bishop whom he had once been taught to oppress made him wish to be baptized by none but Ambrose. He sent a messenger summoning Ambrose to Vienne, and eagerly awaited his return. "Think you that I shall see my father?" Three days afterwards, on Saturday afternoon, May 15, 392, Arbogastes caused him to be strangled in his palace. It was Whitsun-eve, one of the two solemn days on which baptism was generally administered. When Ambrose presided over the rites with which Valentinian was buried beside his brother at Milan, he poured forth his grief and love in a discourse, the most famous passage of which speaks of the murdered prince as having longed for baptism, and *therefore* received its benefits [s]. Otherwise, reasoned the loving saint, catechumens dying for Christ could be no true martyrs; "but if they were baptized in their own blood [t], Valentinian was baptized by his piety and desire." One of the most touching features in the theology of the Church is

---

[p] Theod. v. 23. [q] S. Ambr. Ep. 57. [r] S. Ambr. de Ob. Val. 36.

[s] De Ob. Val. 51. Further on, 75: "*He* baptized thee, because human offices were wanting."

[t] Saturus, a catechumen, a companion of S. Perpetua, was bathed in blood by the first bite of a leopard; the people, in scornful allusion to the Christian belief as to this "baptism of blood," cried out, "Salvum lotum, salvum lotum!" See also S. Cypr. Ep. 73, c. 19. Ven. Bede, Hist. Eccl. i. 7, uses the phrase.

thus associated with the tragedy of Vienne, and with the affectionate faith of Ambrose[u]. Arbogastes set up, as a nominal emperor, the rhetorician Eugenius, who was, at least inclined to Heathenism.

On August 27, 392, Augustine held a disputation with the Manichean priest Fortunatus. It turned on the questions, whether the soul had a divine substance, as the Manicheans asserted; and whether man had free-will, which they denied. At last, Fortunatus could not explain why, on the Manichean hypothesis, God sent the soul, a part of Himself, to suffer misery and defilement amid "the nation of darkness." The conference came to an end; and Fortunatus quitted Hippo, but never embraced the faith.

On the 8th of November, 392, Theodosius struck a blow at Heathenism more downright and sweeping than any which it had yet sustained from a Christian emperor. "Let no man of whatsoever rank, order, or quality,—whether honourable by birth or office, or of mean condition,—presume in any place or any city to offer sacrifice to senseless images, or to worship household gods with fumes and smoke." Those who offered sacrifice or used divination were to be punished as traitors. A variety of acts less formally idolatrous, such as the erecting of a turf altar to be garlanded with flowers, were specifically forbidden under definite penalties; and Theodosius, when he set his hand to this law, doubtless felt that at last he had raised a rampart which no heathenish ingenuity could undermine.

The writings of Jovinian were sent to Jerome by some members of the Roman Church, and he wrote two books in reply, characterized by a painful vehemence and exaggeration. Although he disclaimed the Encratite view, which denied marriage to be God's ordinance, he used language

---

[u] He proceeds, in words which allude to Virgil's lament for Marcellus, to speak of offering the Eucharist for Valentinian's soul. "Give the holy Mysteries to my hands...give the heavenly Sacraments....Not with flowers will I strew his tomb, but will bedew his spirit with the odour of Christ!" c. 56.

which seemed to imply that it was but a tolerated evil: and the coarse abusiveness in which he indulged must have seemed excessive, even in an age which was over-tolerant of such personalities in a grave discussion.

Eugenius allowed the restoration of the altar of Victory; and sacrifices and divinations were performed at Rome on his behalf. Ambrose wrote to him as to a Christian who was trifling with the Searcher of hearts.

A schism now broke out within the Donatist body. Primian became the Donatist bishop of Carthage in 392. He excommunicated, on some grounds which cannot be ascertained, a deacon named Maximian, who formed a party which treated Primian just as Cæcilian was treated by the early Donatists[x]. One charge against Primian was, that "he had mingled the wicked with the communion of the saints;" another, that he had assaulted clergy[y], and led on mobs against "the houses of Christians." Twelve bishops consecrated Maximian; more than a hundred condemned Primian in a Council held on June 24, 393. Augustine began this year to write against the Donatists; his first production being a curious "psalm," or ballad, intended to convey the Church's case to simple minds. Its burden was, "All ye who rejoice over peace, now judge truly." The history of Donatism was reviewed, and the evils of separation set forth on Scriptural grounds. The net was to retain good and bad fish until it was landed on the eternal shore. The tares were to grow up with the good seed. Under the old covenant, those who sighed over the abominations of Jerusalem[z] did not abandon the temple and altar. The Lord bore with Judas, giving him a share in "that first Sacrament of the Supper." The Donatists

---

[x] "See how God rendered to them what they had said of Cæcilian." S. Aug. in Ps. 37. s. 2. His thought was, "The wheel is come full circle."

[y] He was said to have thrown a priest into a sewer. The Donatists repeated a saying of his about the Catholics; "They carry many an imperial letter; we present the Gospels only." S. Aug. post coll. 53.

[z] Ezek. ix. 4.

could not, any more than the Catholics, secure their community from the presence of bad members; so that they had not, on their own showing, gained anything by deserting their Mother, who "cast out the wicked when she could, and was obliged to bear with those whom she could not expel, until they should either be healed, or severed from her in the end." On Oct. 8, 393, a Catholic "Council of Africa" was held, in presence of which Augustine delivered a discourse on Faith and the Creed. It passed forty-one canons, and relaxed to some extent the severity of former canons, as to the position of Donatist clergy after their submission to the Church.

Jerome's expressions about marriage had caused much scandal, which he endeavoured to remove towards the end of 393, by a "Defence" addressed to Pammachius[a]. He repeated that he was wholly free from Encratism and Manicheism; he urged that his treatise had acknowledged marriage to be honourable, although inferior to virginity, and that he had not condemned second or third marriages.

His most intimate friend was Ruffinus of Aquileia, now living as a priest under John, bishop of Jerusalem, who had succeeded Cyril in 386. Ruffinus was a great admirer of the writings of Origen[b]; and Jerome, nine years before, had told Paula that the charge of heresy brought against them was got up by the jealousy of inferior minds[c]. Such rude injustice to the convictions of so many Churches, which profoundly distrusted Origen's spiritualism, as tending to the abatement of the positive, historic, and dogmatic element in religion, for the sake of conciliating an external philosophy, did not betoken a calm or steady persuasion as to the safety of the great Alexandrian's line of thought. Accordingly, when in 393 a pilgrim from the West, named

---

[a] Ep. 48 (50).

[b] Born A.D. 186; died 250. See the admirable Life of Origen in Archdeacon Evans' "Biography of the Early Church."

[c] In his peculiar style, he says that the impugners of Origen's orthodoxy are "mad dogs." Ep. 33.

Aterbius, denounced Ruffinus and Jerome as Origenists, Jerome at once disclaimed all sympathy with Origen, while Ruffinus kept within doors in order to avoid the sight of his denouncer. John of Jerusalem was inclined to Origenism; Epiphanius, who regarded it with horror, visited Jerusalem in the Lent of 394. John received the old prelate into his house, and invited him to preach in the church of the Resurrection. Epiphanius denounced Origenists, in such a way as to show what he thought of his host[d], the archbishop then present, who exhibited his impatience and contempt by signs equally unmistakeable, and sent the archdeacon to bid him be silent. As they passed to the church of the Holy Cross, the people thronged round Epiphanius to kiss his feet and touch his mantle[e]. John preached in his turn, and reprobated the "Anthropomorphists," who took literally the texts which ascribed to God "a body, parts, and passions[f]." While he spoke, he looked hard at Epiphanius, who afterwards quietly rose and said, "I too condemn the Anthropomorphists,—but we must also condemn Origenism." A shout of laughter showed the congregation's enjoyment of this retort. On another occasion, when on his way to celebrate service with John at Bethel, Epiphanius found on a village church-door a curtain on which was painted a figure of Christ, or of a Saint. The sight offended his rigid scruples[g]; and being wont to take his own course, with small regard for circum-

---

[d] Jerome admits this, c. Joan. 11. "You and your company," he adds, "sneered, rubbed your heads, and nodded to each other, as much as to say, 'The old man is in his dotage.'"

[e] Sozomen, vi. 32, says that he was a man of wide-spread fame.

[f] These persons, that is, held what Augustine, while a Manichean, imputed to the whole Catholic body.

[g] See his letter (Hieron. Ep. 51. c. 9) to John of Jerusalem. His feeling was that of the austere Spanish Council of Eliberis, or Elvira, in the beginning of the fourth century. Since that time pictures had been more frequently used, and sometimes abused. S. Aug. de Mor. Eccl. Cath. i. 34; the passage implies that the pictures, which some persons "adored," were set up in sacred places. But they did not become common in churches until a somewhat later period.

stances, he forthwith tore the curtain, and advised that it should be used as a shroud for the poor. The keepers of the church naturally observed, "If he *will* tear our curtain, he ought to give us another." "So I will," said Epiphanius; and he did, in fact, send them the best he could procure. Finding John estranged from him, he withdrew to Bethlehem, where he received a cordial welcome. One of the monks of Bethlehem was Jerome's brother Paulinianus, who was always afraid of being forcibly ordained, according to a strange practice not uncommon[h] in days when many good men through diffidence avoided the priesthood. The monastery needed a priest, for Jerome's morbid humility would not allow him to officiate; and Epiphanius contrived to seize Paulinianus, and confer holy orders on him, "stopping his mouth lest he should protest in the name of Christ." This violent act was certain to anger John, as being an infraction of his diocesan authority; and he bitterly inveighed against Epiphanius[i], who wrote a letter in which he endeavoured to defend the ordination, and stated withal eight heads of Origenism which he imputed to the bishop of Jerusalem. Of these the chief were, that the Son could not behold the Father, nor the Holy Spirit the Son; that souls had existed and sinned before they came into bodies; that Satan would return to his heavenly estate. In the strife between John and Epiphanius, Ruffinus and Jerome naturally took opposite sides.

On April 24, 394, a council of 310 Donatist bishops met at Bagai, and upheld the cause of Primian, denouncing

---

[h] See Bingham, b. iv. 7. 1. S. Augustine wept while he was being presented for ordination.

[i] Epiphanius imagined that the ordination of a Bethlehemite monk at Eleutheropolis, which was not within the diocese of Jerusalem, was not an interference with John's authority. But the person ordained belonged to John's diocese; and Epiphanius was in truth copying the conduct of those bishops of Palestine who ordained Origen at Cæsarea without any authority from his own bishop Demetrius. Euseb. vi. 23. The letter of Epiphanius was translated by Jerome; the original is not extant. Jerome did not intend the translation to be publicly circulated. Ruffinus impugned its accuracy. Ep. 57 (101).

Maximian as a minister of Korah and a corrupter of the truth.

Ambrose had warned Eugenius that if he continued to favour heathenism, the Church would not receive his offerings. This in fact took place; Eugenius was shunned at Milan as an apostate. When he set forth to meet Theodosius, who reached Italy in the summer of 394, Arbogastes and Flavian the prætorian præfect vowed that they would turn the cathedral of Milan into a stable[k] if victory declared for Eugenius. In the first encounter Eugenius was successful. The generals of Theodosius spoke of deferring the campaign until the next year; but he declared that the Cross should never retire before the image of Hercules on the standard of the enemy. Again he bade his soldiers advance, and prayed that if he had come thither in a cause approved by God, He would stretch forth His hand. Then, it is said, a wind sprang up[l] which drove back the enemy's arrows, blinded them with dust, and threw them into hopeless confusion. Such was the victory at Aquileia, Sept. 6, 394, which caused even the unbelieving Claudian[m] to write of Theodosius,—

> "O nimium dilecte Deo—cui militat æther[n]!"

Eugenius and Arbogastes were put to death. Theodosius shewed a princely kindness to the children of the chief rebels; they had sought shelter in a church, and he gave them a Christian education. He wrote to Ambrose, requesting him to give thanks for the victory. "I took your letter with me to the altar," wrote Ambrose in reply[o]; "I placed it on the altar, and held it up in my hand while I was offering the Sacrifice." The Emperor scrupled for some time as to approaching the Holy Communion, on the ground that so much blood had been shed, although in a fair field and in a good cause. "The Penance" had sunk into his mind. He is said by the Pagan historian Zosimus[p]

---

k Paulin. Vit. S. Ambr. 31. l Ruff. ii. 33. m S. Aug. Civ. Dei, v. 26.
n De tert. cons. Hon. 96. o Ep. 61. p Zos. iv. 59.

to have at this time made a vain attempt to detach the Roman senate from the religion of their fathers.

Towards the end of this September a Council was held at Constantinople, attended by Nectarius, Theophilus, Flavian, Gregory of Nyssa, Amphilochius, and Theodore of Mopsuestia, a bishop who afterwards became the head of a rationalizing school of theology. In this assembly Nectarius referred to "the Apostolic canons." The series of canons now known by that name is considered to be a collection, undigested and imperfect, of rules and decrees which obtained in the Eastern Church before the Nicene Council.

Alypius, Augustine's friend, was now bishop of Thagaste. He sent some writings of Augustine against the Manicheans —doubtless including his treatise "On the Usefulness of Believing[q]," written soon after his ordination—to a man of noble birth, great literary culture, and fervent devotion, named Paulinus, whom he had known at Milan. This produced a friendship between S. Augustine and Paulinus. The latter had been recently ordained priest at Barcelona; he sold his large estates, and gave their proceeds to the poor[r]; and then, passing into Italy, settled at Nola, devoting much of his time and thoughts to the honour of a local saint, Felix. Jerome became acquainted with him, and in reply to his congratulations on the advantage of living in Palestine, sent him a remarkable letter[s], in which he warned him

[q] In this work he refers to the Manichean promise, "We will give you truth, not by exacting obedience to authority, but by pure and simple reasoning." He deals with Manichean cavils against the Old Testament, and insists that all its contents are "noble, divine, and absolutely true;" c. 13. Heretics themselves, he says, do in fact require faith; and the Catholic Church has a prior claim on our confidence; c. 30, 31.

[r] Hence S. Martin proposed him to Sulpicius as a model Christian. Vit. B. Mart. 26.

[s] Ep. 58 (13). S. Gregory of Nyssa also had said, "I believed in the Incarnation before I saw Bethlehem....It is not by change of place that we draw nigh to God!" Orat. de Euntibus Hierosolyma. He contends against the idea that pilgrimage is a part of Christian perfection, declaring that vice and bloodshed prevail in Jerusalem, and that a man may stand on Golgotha with a heart full of evil.

"not to think that anything was lacking to his faith because he had not seen Jerusalem," a city in which, side by side with the holiest places, were haunts of worldly and sensual corruption. He also drew a clear distinction between the clerical life, instituted by the Apostles, and the monastic, which imitated that of Elijah and Elisha[t], the sons of the prophets, and the Rechabites. On the clerical duties he wrote about this time a remarkable letter to the young priest Nepotian[u], exhorting him to avoid whatever might raise suspicion as to the probity of his ministerial life[x], to be constant in the study of Scripture, to take heed that his conduct "did not shame his teaching," to obey his "High-priest[y]," to avoid empty declamations; not to seek for the applause of his audience, nor to court great men even on the pretext of "interceding for the unhappy;" not to impose on himself excessive fasting, nor while abstaining from oil to indulge in other dainties; to eschew all Pharisaic demonstrations, and through good and evil report to march on steadily as Christ's soldier.

On Jan. 17, 395, the great Theodosius died at Milan, aged sixty. His last advice to his sons Arcadius and Honorius, who were respectively to govern the East and West, was to consider true religion as the safeguard of the peace of the empire. "I loved the man," said S. Ambrose in his funeral oration, "who thought better of a reprover than of a flatterer,—who inquired for me with his last breath[z]." Arca-

---

[t] It is simply wonderful that he should have adduced Elisha as a prototype of men whose aim was individual sanctification to be secured by retirement.

[u] Ep. 52 (2).

[x] He refers to "frequent gifts," as handkerchiefs, and "sweet little notes" from ladies; and mentions the law of Valentinian I. against legacies to monks and clergy.

[y] This letter, which asserts a parallelism between the Jewish and Christian hierarchies, (see S. Clement of Rome, ad Cor. c. 40,) shows how little right Presbyterians have to claim S. Jerome. Like other Church-writers of his time, he calls the bishop *Pontifex*, and says, "We know the bishop and the presbyters to be what Aaron and his sons were." See the conclusion of his famous Ep. 146 (85), ad Evangelum, where the parallelism is fully drawn out. See also c. Joan. 37.

[z] De Ob. Theod. 34, 35. He added that Theodosius thought more of the

dius was about eighteen, Honorius eleven; the former[a] was governed by Ruffinus, the latter by Stilicho, who, however, put his rival to death within the year. The two princes had been under the tuition of Arsenius, who having provoked the boyish malice of Arcadius by chastising him, hid himself among the monks of Egypt. On coming to the throne Arcadius learned the place of his retreat, implored his pardon, and offered him a vast sum of money for the monks and the poor. Arsenius sent him a message, "God forgive us all! but I am dead to the world, and cannot become an almoner." He became famous among the "abbats" of his time for humility and self-denial; and he received the will of a kinsman, which conveyed to him an estate, with the laconic expression, "I died before he did." About this time Cassian, probably of Thracian birth, who was an inmate of a monastery near Bethlehem, visited the monastic cells of Egypt, where he spent some years.

This year S. Augustine struggled to carry out an ordinance of the recent African Council against the unseemly revels called "Rejoicings," held within churches in honour of the Saints. A mild form of this abuse had been habitual with such pious persons as S. Monica; but when at Milan she had visited the churches with small baskets of food and wine, she had learned that the practice was forbidden by S. Ambrose[b]. Her son's earnestness at length succeeded in substituting for these "rejoicings" additional reading and psalmody, which occupied the people until the time of evening prayer. The seriousness of the evil is shown by his solemn adjurations: "Think of your own peril, and of ours who have to give an account for your souls. I conjure you by *His* humiliation, by the blows and spitting on His

---

state of the Church than of his own sufferings as a dying man. He prayed, "Give perfect rest, O Lord, to Thy servant Theodosius!" c. 36; and presently added, "Theodosius abides in light, and glories in the companies of Saints;" c. 39.

[a] Philostorgius mentions his half-shut eyes which indicated his languid character; xi. 3.

[b] Conf. vi. 2.

face, by the buffets, the crown of thorns, the Cross, the Blood[c]!" One who could so plead and so prevail was naturally marked out by his pastoral success, as well as by his theological reputation, for the highest functions of the ministry; and shortly before Christmas, 395, being then forty-one, he was consecrated as coadjutor to Valerius of Hippo. That the appointment of a coadjutor bishop was inconsistent with the literal sense of the eighth Nicene canon, neither he nor Valerius were then aware[d]. His deep sense of Episcopal responsibilities is expressed by repeated references to the "burden" laid upon him, and by entreaties for the prayers as well as the obedience of his flock[e].

Freed from the fear of Theodosius, a multitude of barbaric tribes invaded the Eastern empire. Bishops and clergy were murdered, horses were tethered to the altars, and the remains of martyrs dug up. "It is our sins," wrote S. Jerome[f], "that have made the barbarians strong, and overthrown the Roman forces."

S. Ambrose was employed during the year 396 in abating the dissensions of the Church of Vercellæ, which kept that see long vacant. He wrote a long letter on the subject[g], exhorting the people of Vercellæ to proceed in a right spirit to the election of a bishop. He referred to S. Eusebius of Vercellæ, as the first Western prelate who had combined the clerical with the monastic life, and as having "preferred exile to ease," and "raised the standard of confession." He also warned them against two monks who had quitted the monastery near Milan[h], and were propagating Jovinian's

---

[c] Ep. 29. See Serm. 46: "If we were to say to you, 'Go, celebrate these feasts of rejoicing,—crown yourselves with roses before they be withered,—banquet when you please in the house of your God,'—perhaps we should gather larger congregations."

[d] Ep. 213.

[e] Serm. 339, 340, &c.; Ep. 231.

[f] Ep. 60.

[g] Ep. 63. He begins, "Ambrose, a servant of Christ, called a bishop."

[h] S. Augustine speaks of this monastery as full of good brethren, and fostered by Ambrose. Conf. viii. 15.

views. Afterwards he himself visited Vercellæ, and procured the election of the pious Honoratus.

His own noble life was drawing to a close. Stilicho, on hearing that he was taken ill, begged him, by messengers of high rank, to pray that he might yet live for Italy. Ambrose made the memorable reply; "I have not so lived among you as that I should be ashamed to live; yet I fear not to die, for we have a good Lord[i]." From 5 p.m. on Good Friday until shortly after midnight his lips incessantly moved in silent prayer; and after receiving from Honoratus "the Lord's Body as a good *viaticum*," he breathed his last on the 4th of April, 397.

[i] Paul. Vit. 45.

CHAPTER IX.

From the Death of S. Ambrose to the Death of S. Chrysostom.

"And thus for thee, O glorious man, on whom
Love well-deserved, and honour waited long,
In thy last years, in place of timely ease,
There did remain another loftier doom,
Pain, travail, exile, peril, scorn and wrong—
Glorious before, but glorified through these."

TRENCH'S *Poems.*

THE feud between Jerome and the "Origenists" had been kept up with considerable acrimony. The bishop of Jerusalem had appealed to Theophilus of Alexandria [a], who agreed with him in opinion, and whose envoy, the priest Isidore, on coming to the scene of the controversy, took open part against Jerome. For some time Theophilus took no notice of Jerome's letters. Vigilantius, a priest of Barcelona sent to Jerome by Paulinus, had spoken of him as an Origenist, and drawn forth a letter in which Jerome declared that he had read Origen only as he had read other authors who in certain points were disapproved by the Church [b], and that he did not deny him to be heretical and worthy of anathema in his views "on the resurrection, on the state of souls, on the devil's repentance," above all, in that he had asserted the Son and Holy Spirit to be the Seraphim. But, added Jerome, it was quite consistent with this persuasion to translate and recommend what was good in Origen's work [c]. In 397 Ruffinus resolved to return to the

[a] His letter began, "As a man of God, and adorned with apostolic grace, you undertake the care of all the Churches, especially of that which is in Jerusalem," (Jerome, c. Joan. 37). This hyperbole illustrates the important fact, that sonorous titles given in those days to powerful bishops, by those who sought their favour, must not be taken too literally.

[b] Ep. 61 (75).

[c] He adduces the case of S. Eusebius of Vercellæ, who had translated all that was sound in the Commentary on the Psalms by a heretic, (Eusebius of Cæsarea).

West; but before doing so, he succeeded in effecting a reconciliation between himself and Jerome. They met and joined hands at the celebration of the Eucharist[d] in the church of the Resurrection.

We may with some probability assign to this year, 397, the mission of S. Ninian, the apostle of South Scotland. He was the son of a British prince, apparently in Cumberland. He had travelled to Rome for the purpose of sacred study[e], in the pontificate of Damasus, from whom and from Siricius he received many kindnesses. Siricius, hearing that in the north-west of Britain there were tribes that knew not the name of Christ, consecrated Ninian as a missionary bishop, and sent him back to Britain. On his way he visited S. Martin, whose holiness made a deep impression on his mind, and from whom he procured workmen skilled in church-building, that in his barbarous diocese he might have a church which should recall in some sort to his mind, and secure to his flock, the architecture of Christian Italy, which for so many years had been associated with all his notions of Church life. After labouring for a while in Cumberland, he fixed his seat north of the Solway, on the promontory where stood the chief settlement of the Novantes, which appears to have even then borne the name of Leucoikidia[f], (White houses,) the oldest form, in that case, of Whithern. S. Ninian's main field was the province of Valentia, as the father of Theodosius the Great had styled it,—including all Scotland south of the wall of Antonine, which ran between the Friths of Forth and Clyde. This region might be divided into three parts,—Lothian, soon afterwards, it seems, invaded by the Vecturiones, or Southern Picts[g], (who have left their name on the Pentland

[d] "Immolato Agno." c. Ruff. iii. 33.

[e] Bede says, iii. 4, that he was "regularly instructed at Rome in the faith and mysteries of truth."

[f] Supposed to be the true reading of Leucopibia. See Lives of the English Saints, Life of S. N., p. 90.

[g] "The Southern Picts received the word of truth by the preaching of Ninias, a most reverend bishop and a most holy man." Bede, iii. 4.

hills); the northern part of Strath-clyde, inhabited by the Britons, whose capital was Alclyd, or Dunbarton, (the castle of the Britons); and Galloway, to some extent inhabited by Scots, who had made several immigrations from Ireland, and in conjunction with the Picts had, thirty years before, made their way as far south as London. Ninian may have extended his care to the southern part of Strath-clyde, and also to the territory lying north of Antonine's wall; but Valentia, with its ceaseless storms of warfare, would call out all the energies of one who bore the Gospel of peace.

On Sept. 1, 397, a Council, called the third of Carthage, enacted fifty canons for the African Church. Some of them related to the Eucharistic service; nothing was to be offered therein but bread, and wine mixed with water[h]; the priest standing at the altar was to address prayer to the Father only[i]; the celebrant must be fasting, save on "the anniversary of the Lord's Supper," i. e. at the evening celebration peculiar to Maundy Thursday[k]. No prayers were to be used in church, until they had been sanctioned by well-instructed brethren[l]. Baptism and the Eucharist must not be given to the dead[m]. In Easter-tide catechumens must not be admitted to any "sacrament" save "the usual salt[n]." None were to be ordained until they had made their families Catholic. Priests must not ordinarily reconcile penitents, nor without the bishop's knowledge consecrate virgins, nor make the chrism in any case. Translations of bishops were forbidden. Congregations belonging

---

[h] It need hardly be said that the Mixture is mentioned by S. Justin Martyr, Apol. i. 65; S. Iren. v. 2; S. Cypr. Ep. 63, &c.

[i] See Keble on Euch. Ador., p. 113.

[k] S. Aug. Ep. 54. 9. See Owen on Dogm. Theol., p. 403, that this observance was a shadow of the Agape. It was forbidden by canon 29 of Council in Trullo, A.D. 691. The Gelas. Sacr. had a Vesper-mass for this day.

[l] See Bingham, b. xiii. 5. 7.

[m] Bingham, b. xi. 4. 3; b. xv. 4. 19.

[n] S. Augustine says that as a child he was made a catechumen, and received this salt. Conf. i. 17.

to a diocese[o] were not to set up bishops of their own without the diocesan's leave. The Council made a list of "canonical Scriptures," i. e. those which might be read in church[p], which included Tobit, Judith, Wisdom, Ecclesiasticus, Maccabees.

The 11th of November, 397, is usually assigned[q] as the date of S. Martin's death. He foretold his approaching end, and on perceiving the sorrow which the announcement caused, uttered the often-quoted prayer, "Lord, if I be yet necessary for Thy people, I shrink not from the labour: Thy will be done!" Though wasted by fever, he did not intermit "the work of God," the daily and nightly prayers. He would not allow himself to be placed on a couch of straw. "My sons, a Christian's death-bed should be ashes." On ashes he lay, with eyes and hands raised upwards; and his last words were a defiance of the arch-enemy[r]. The natural grief of his people was modified by the thought of his entry into blessedness; they deemed it a duty "both to rejoice for Martin and to weep for Martin;" and no lament could be more touching than that of the faithful biographer, who during the Saint's lifetime had stirred the heart of multitudes by the published memoir of a character so gentle and so great. S. Ninian, on hearing of his death, dedicated

---

o *Diocese* was used by the Africans in its present sense; see the acts of the Conference of Carthage, i. c. 116, &c.

p See note in Oxford edition of Fleury, vol. ii. p. 123.

q On the authority of Gregory of Tours. Sulpicius' account would give 402, i. e. sixteen years after the Council at Treves in 386; but corruption seems to have been at work on his text, in regard to chronology.

r "Quid hic adstas, cruenta bestia? nihil in me, funeste, reperies." Sulp. Ep. 3. One of the most striking passages in Sulpicius is that (Vit. 25) in which he describes Martin as seeing a form arrayed in glory, with diadem and purple, and serene in aspect. "Acknowledge, Martin, him whom thou seest. I am Christ;—why doubtest thou?" Martin answered, "I will not believe that he is Christ who cannot show the marks of the Passion." On this narration, which Sulpicius heard "from Martin himself," see "Church of the Fathers," p. 414. "Many spirits are abroad, more are issuing from the pit. The credentials which they display are the precious gifts of mind, beauty, richness, depth, originality. Christian! look hard at them with Martin in silence, and then ask for the print of the nails."

in his honour the first stone church ever seen in Britain, which he reared as the cathedral of Valentia, and the aspect of which[s], coinciding with the old name of "White-houses," perpetuated it under the form of "Candida Casa." He organized there a monastic society, a school for boys, and a seminary of future priests. In many a rough wild heart, the sight of that fair church, conspicuous on its promontory, may have produced the first perceptions of the beauty and stability of the new faith, brought by a British prince from a city heretofore associated with legions, ramparts, and iron-handed repression.

The see of Constantinople was now vacant. Nectarius had died in the end of September, after an episcopate which had relaxed the general tone of his clergy. "Then," says the biographer of S. Chrysostom, "there came together some who were not wanted—presbyters in dignity, but unworthy of the priesthood[t],—besetting the palace gates, resorting to bribery, falling on their knees even before the people." Disgusted by this scandalous eagerness for an office which saints were wont to dread, the faithful entreated Arcadius to look out for one who could administer it worthily. Eutropius, the Emperor's chamberlain, who had succeeded to the ascendancy and to the vices[u] of Ruffinus, had learned by visiting Antioch to admire the character of Chrysostom. He made Arcadius write to Asterius, the "count," or military commander, at Antioch, desiring him to send the priest John to Constantinople, without causing any public excitement. Asterius sent a message to Chrysostom, asking him to meet him "at the churches of Martyrs near the Roman gate." Chrysostom complied; was placed in a public conveyance, and hurried away from the scene of his early life and priestly labours. Several bishops were summoned for the consecration. The-

[s] Bede, iii. 4, derives Candida Casa purely from the White Church. Still, a coincidence is not improbable.

[t] Palladius' words are, *πρεσβύτεροι μὲν τὴν ἀξίαν, ἀνάξιοι δὲ τῆς ἱερωσύνης.* Chrys. Op. xiii. p. 17.

[u] See Gibbon, ch. xxxii.

ophilus of Alexandria, who had wished for the appointment of his priest Isidore [x], was the more reluctant, after reading Chrysostom's character in his face, to officiate in the ceremony. Eutropius showed him some papers, saying, "Choose between consecrating John, and undergoing a trial on the charges made against you in these documents [y]." Theophilus could make but one reply. He consecrated Chrysostom on Feb. 26, 398, but he never forgave him for having been the cause of this severe mortification.

Chrysostom set to work as a reformer of abuses [z], perhaps with somewhat more of impetuosity and less of considerateness than was expedient in a position of so much difficulty. He found the clergy tainted by luxurious and covetous habits, and commanded them not to frequent the tables of great men. He struggled against the practice of entertaining "spiritual sisters;" in fact, says Palladius, against the unseemly and evil life which was the accompaniment of these "syneisacti [a]." Several clergy were deprived; Chrysostom drew upon himself the bitter dislike of many members of their body. He examined the accounts of the Church-steward, cut off superfluous expenses, and ordered the sum thus saved to be applied to the maintenance of hospitals. He scrutinized the lives of the widows; he earnestly besought contributions to a fund for the poor [b]; he exhorted the faithful to attend the nocturnal services, but to leave their wives at home with the children [c]. He rebuked the rich for their pride and selfishness. So great was the charm of his "golden-tongued" eloquence [d], and of the unmistakeable nobleness

---

[x] He had sent Isidore in 388 to Rome, with orders to congratulate either Theodosius or Maximus, according to the event of the war.

[y] Soc. vi. 2.

[z] Pall. Vit. S. Chrys. c. 5. p. 18. In considering the work which he got through, we must remember that he knew not what good health was.

[a] On the Syneisacti, or Subintroductæ, see the third Nicene canon, and S. Chrys. de Sacerd. iii. 17. For his discourse on the subject, see tom. i. p. 228.

[b] In Act. hom. 11. c. 3.

[c] See in Act. hom. 26. c. 3.

[d] He disapproved of the practice of applauding a sermon. In Act. hom.

of his character, that "the city put on a new aspect of piety;" the worship[e] of Church-people became more real, their lives more earnest and pure.

Jerome had been reconciled to Ruffinus, but was again at strife with Bishop John. The latter had circulated a "Defence" in reply to Epiphanius, but, as Jerome contended, had not really met his accusations by a distinct disclaimer of Origenism[f]. Before Easter-tide, an eclipse of the sun had scared many persons by the expectation of coming judgment; forty converts had given in their names for baptism to the monks of Bethlehem, but although there were five priests in the monastery, it had been thought best to refer them to the clergy who had charge of Bethlehem, and they, under orders from their bishop, refused to receive the "competents." John had also excluded the inmates of the monastery from the sacred cave of the Nativity; they "saw heretics freely entering, and stood sighing at a distance[g]." Jerome wrote a treatise addressed to Pammachius, in which he reiterated the eight points of false doctrine which had been imputed by Epiphanius to John, and generally set forth his grounds of complaint against the bishop. Ruffinus, at Rome, employed himself, at the request of a certain Macarius, on a task which was certain to rekindle the stifled feud—the translation of Origen's book "on Principles." He ingeniously referred to Jerome as having made many people desirous of reading Origen, by his own translation of one of Origen's homilies, executed at Rome in the time of Damasus. Ruffinus himself took extraordinary liberties with his text, by suppressing every passage which he thought unsound, a procedure which he justified on the ground that heretics had been busy in

---

30. c. 4. He preached from the lectern, not from the sanctuary, in order to be better heard, Soz. viii. 5.

[e] The Liturgy of S. Chrysostom, which is derived from that of S. Basil, was probably arranged by S. Chrysostom as to its "main substance and order." See Palmer's Orig. Lit. i. 79; Neale's Introd. i. 317, 319.

[f] c. Joan. 5.

[g] Ibid. 42.

tampering with Origen's works[h]. This translation produced a great excitement; a zealous Roman lady named Marcella (whom Ruffinus designated as Jezebel) put herself forward in oppositiou to "Origenism;" and Ruffinus thought it best to procure a commendatory letter from Siricius, and to withdraw to Aquileia.

This year, 398, was a time of suffering to the Church of Africa. The rebellion of Gildo gave occasion to his Donatist supporters[i] to make attacks upon the Church, which apparently called forth a law of Honorius against those who did violence to the clergy or the Catholic places of worship; persons convicted of such offences were to be punished capitally[k]. S. Augustine held a discussion with a Donatist bishop named Fortunius[l]; preached against the custom of attending idolatrous feasts for the sake of pleasing great men[m]; and answered questions put to him on the degree in which any contact with Heathenism was allowable[n]. The 8th of Nov., 398, is the date usually assigned for the Council called the fourth of Carthage. But there is considerable uncertainty as to this Council, the enactments of which have not been included in the oldest collections of synodal decrees. It may be, indeed, that they were considered as forming a distinct code, and were therefore not embodied in the collection of Dionysius Exiguus[o]; or it may be that they were the work of various African Church authorities, and that the assembly called

---

[h] Yet he adjured all copyists of his "translation," in presence of the Holy Trinity, by the resurrection and by hell-fire, to add nothing, omit nothing, alter nothing. Jerome, Ep. 80 (Ruffinus' Preface).

[i] The chief of these was a bishop named Optatus. Africa groaned under this satellite of Gildo, S. Aug. c. ep. Parm. ii. 8. He oppressed the Church ten years, c. litt. Pet. i. 24; was a robber, an oppressor of widows and orphans, a breaker-up of marriages, ib. ii. 82; died in prison, ib. ii. 209.

[k] The bishop's complaint was not to be waited for.

[l] Ep. 44.

[m] Serm. 62. Pagans, he says, are led to ask, "why should we forsake the gods whom the Christians join with us in serving?"

[n] Ep. 46, 47. The questions were such as these; "May one buy fruit from a pagan priest's garden, or bathe in a bath used by pagans at their festivals?"

[o] See Tillemont, xiii. 983.

the fourth Council of Carthage must be considered unhistoric, although the decrees assigned to it belong, in fact, to this period[p]. Certainty on this point is probably unattainable; but there is no doubt that these "canons," or, as they are also called, "statutes of the Church," were "highly esteemed by the ancients[q]," and represent to us a mass of ritual and other law which deserves to be carefully studied. They begin with the examination of a bishop-elect, who is to profess his faith, among other points, in the baptismal remission of all sins both original and actual[r]. At his consecration, the book of the Gospels is to be held open on his shoulders[s]; the principal consecrator is to pronounce the blessing, the other bishops are to touch the head with their hands. The ordination of a priest is to be performed in the manner still retained by the Church of England; while the bishop blesses the new priest with imposition of hands, the priests present are also to lay their hands on his head[t]. But the bishop alone is to lay his hand on the deacon, who is "consecrated not for priesthood, but for ministering[u]." Rules are given for the bestowal of the inferior orders of subdeacon, acolyth, exorcist, reader, ostiary, and chanter,—the last being conferred by the priest alone[x]. Rules for clerical conduct follow; the bishop

---

[p] Cave says, Hist. Lit. i. 369, "mihi ipsi in hac re satisfacere haud possum."

[q] Fleury, b. xx. c. 33. He ignores the question of the reality of this Council.

[r] This canon certainly looks like a product of the subsequent Pelagian controversy.

[s] So in the Apost. Constit. viii. 4. The Gelasian Sacramentary embodies these African rules for consecration, &c. Murat. i. 619.

[t] This custom, apparently based on 1 Tim. iv. 14, has never been received by the Eastern Church, which interprets "the presbytery" as meaning "bishops."

[u] In a larger sense, the word *sacerdotium* was used to include the diaconate, Optat. i. p. 39.

[x] The Roman Church has suppressed the office of chanter, which was recognized by the Laodicene Council. Innocent III. could not persuade the Greeks to recognize acolyths, exorcists, or ostiaries (door-keepers). The Greek Church reckons five orders; bishop, priest, deacon, subdeacon,

is to avoid secular business, to administer ecclesiastical law in the presence of his clergy, and to recognise the priests as his colleagues except in church, where only he is to sit higher than they. The deacon is to serve the priest, to wear an albe during the oblation, not to administer "the Eucharist of Christ's Body" in the priest's presence, except by his order. Laymen are not to preach before clergy, except at their bidding. Clergy who can work are to earn their bread by trade or tillage [y]. Women are not to preach nor baptize. No one is to be hindered from entering the church until after the dismissal of catechumens. Penitents must kneel even on festal days. The offerings of the contentious must be refused; care must be taken of those who suffer for Catholicism.

The disorderly conduct of monks who abused their privilege of interceding for criminals was again condemned, by a law of Arcadius in July, 388. And there is undeniable evidence for the prevalence of gross abuses, in the form of lawless idleness and hypocrisy, among the monks of this time [z].

One of S. Chrysostom's earliest successes appears to have been the reconciliation of Rome and Alexandria to Flavian of Antioch. Siricius died on the 26th of November, 398, and Anastasius succeeded him.

Among those of the higher classes in Constantinople who

---

reader. The Roman now merges the episcopate, as an order, in the priesthood; but the two were distinguished by Egbert, archbishop of York, A.D. 734.

[y] Sordid occupations were forbidden to clergy. But Epiphanius, Hær. 80, speaks of priests who pursued some honest handicraft; and Sozomen, vii. 28, tells us of an aged bishop, Zeno, who was constant at daily matins and vespers, yet wrought as a linen-weaver.

[z] Jerome, Ep. 22, on the Sarabaites, or vagabond monks, whom he calls "Remoboth." See also S. Augustine, de Opere Monachorum, wherein he speaks of impostors who sell "limbs of martyrs, if indeed they are of martyrs." Jerome also, in Ep. 125, speaks of monks who are worldly in all but dress and profession; who live luxuriously, who are as haughty as præfects. He also admits that damp cells, excessive fasting and study, the tedium of solitude, &c., have driven some monks into disease of mind.

were offended by the uncompromising character of their new archbishop, was Eutropius, who had raised him to the see. The Church, under Chrysostom's government, was becoming, in his view, unmanageable; and he procured a law to annul the right of asylum in churches, which had been growing up during this century. But he was soon driven by a revolution in the Emperor's counsels to clasp the altar as the safeguard of his life. Chrysostom violated the new law in defence of its author; and while Eutropius lay cowering in the sanctuary, bade the people take home this new lesson on the "vanity of vanities[a]." "The altar is more awful than ever, now that it holds the lion chained." He called on his hearers to beg the Emperor's mercy, or rather, to ask the God of mercy to "save Eutropius from threatened death, and enable him to put away his crimes." He withstood the indignation of the Court in the cause of Christian humanity; but Eutropius himself quitted the church, and was condemned to exile, Jan. 17, 399.

S. Chrysostom was not only active in building up the Church at home, but zealous in extending it abroad. He sent missionaries to preach to the wild nomads on the banks of the Danube[b]; consecrated Unilas bishop of the Goths[c]; appointed clergy to reclaim the Scythians resident at Constantinople from Arianism; and procured an imperial order for the destruction of temples in Phœnicia. Honorius in the preceding year had ordered the destruction of all traces of idolatry; but in January, 399, he forbade the Christians to disturb those statues which were ornamental to public places. At Easter the Christians made a general attack on the temples of Carthage, by way of exhibiting the falsification of the prophecy with which the Pagans had consoled themselves, that Christianity would perish after lasting for 365 years. The great temple of "the Queen of heaven," which had long been closed and deserted, was re-opened, cleansed, and dedicated as a church by the

---

[a] Hom. in Eutrop., tom. iii. p. 381. [b] Theod. v. 31. [c] Ep. 14.

bishop Aurelius, who erected within it his episcopal chair [d]. To prevent further danger from the tumults which such proceedings might excite, Honorius prohibited all destruction of temples, as distinct from idols; his brother in the East, by a law of July 13, commanded the rural temples to be *quietly* destroyed.

Pammachius and Oceanus, Jerome's friends at Rome, requested Jerome to put forth a faithful translation of Origen's treatise [e]. He complied, assuring them [f] that his eulogies on Origen had referred "to the commentator, not to the dogmatic theologian,—to his ability, not to his faith;" that even supposing he had, as a young man, thought too well of statements which were heterodox, that was no reason for binding him to such errors in old age. He regarded Ruffinus as in heart a thorough Origenist, and was eager in protesting that he himself had never been one at all.

Theophilus, as we have seen, had been favourable to Origenism. But he had been brought into collision with the gross anthropomorphism of the majority of Egyptian monks. One of the most venerable was Serapion. When assured by a Cappadocian deacon that the Eastern Churches understood the Divine "image and likeness" in a spiritual sense, Serapion threw himself on the ground, and cried out with tears, "You have taken away my God, and I know not whom to worship." Others reviled Theophilus, who deceived them by talking about "the face of God [g]." "Will you not, then, anathematize Origen?" "Yes, I will." He called a synod, and fulfilled his promise. Anastasius, on his part, cited Ruffinus to appear before him. Ruffinus declined, on the ground that he could not, after thirty years' absence from his relations, leave home again at that time. After stating his faith in orthodox language, he made a solemn declaration: "Beside this faith, which our

---

[d] S. Aug. Civ. Dei, xviii. 54.
[e] Ep. 83 (64).
[f] Ibid. 84.
[g] Soz. viii. 11.

Church of Aquileia holds with the Churches of Rome and Alexandria, I never held, nor—in Christ's name I say it—shall hold any other. They who raise dissension and scandal from motives of mere envy shall give an account of their doings [h]." Anastasius, who frankly said in a subsequent letter [i] that previously he "did not know who Origen was, or what language he had used," condemned Ruffinus in spite of these assurances, and pronounced—as he wrote to Simplicianus of Milan—that every heterodox position of Origen's was condemned by the Roman Church [k].

Two Councils in the West distinguish this year 400. The first was held at Carthage, May 27. Some care was taken to prevent the frauds practised in regard to relics of Saints; and it was resolved to apply to the government for the destruction of the remnants of idolatry even in woods and trees [l].

The first of the memorable series of Councils of Toledo was held in September 400. It dealt with the case of Priscillianists converted to the Church; denounced the Priscillianist practice of receiving the Sacrament without communicating [m]; spoke of a "daily Sacrifice," and of the warning needful for habitual non-communicants; spoke of the Roman bishop simply as "the *Pope* that now is;" and describes a "penitent" as one who, after doing public penance under sackcloth for a *crime*, was restored to God's altar.

S. Augustine at this time was taking in hand several works; e. g. "On Faith in Things Unseen"—"On Catechizing the Simple"—"On the Agreement of the Evangelists:" he began his great book on the Trinity, and the

---

[h] Ruff. Ep. ad Anast.

[i] To John of Jerusalem. In this he says of Ruffinus, "What he is doing, or where he is, I have no wish to know."

[k] Ep. 95.

[l] See the story of S. Martin and the pine-tree. S. Benedict cut down the grove of Apollo at Monte Cassino. Among the heathenish practices forbidden by Edgar and Canute was worship paid to certain trees. Johnson's Engl. Canons, i. 415, 513.

[m] See the Council of Saragossa.

elaborate work against Faustus, the Manichean bishop whom in his Confessions [n]—the matchless autobiography composed about 397—he characterized as that "great snare of the devil" whose knowledge he had found so shallow. He opposed the Donatist principle,—that since "God heareth not sinners," the wickedness of the minister hindered the effect of the ordinances,—in his replies to the letters of Parmenian (a former Donatist bishop) and Petilian, and in his treatise on Baptism. His position was, that the Church was not deprived of spiritual privileges by the presence within her of sinners whom she could not expel without peril of schism; seeing that the presence of the One all-holy Mediator [o] secured for His Church a perpetual acceptance, and to His ordinances a perpetual vitality. He also wrote about this time his answers to the queries of Januarius, in regard to Church usages. In the first of these two letters [p] he speaks of Baptism and the Eucharist, and other ordinances prescribed in canonical Scripture, as the Christian Sacraments; attributes traditional customs of the whole Church to Apostolic authority or to general Councils; notices several customs, both general and particular, as fasting before Communion [q], more or less frequent Communion, and the mode of keeping Saturday [r]. The second letter, which is much longer, contains that passage on burdensome observances [s] which is referred to in the introduction to the Prayer-Book.

S. Chrysostom, this year, showed his firmness in resisting

---

[n] Conf. v. 3.

[o] C. Ep. Parm. ii. c. 8. See de Bapt. iii. 15. "If the light of the sun or of a lamp contracts no impurity from being diffused through places full of dirt, surely no man's crimes can defile Christ's baptism."

[p] Ep. 54: compare de Doctr. Chr. iii. 13.

[q] A general custom; "placuit Spiritui Sancto, ut in honorem tanti Sacramenti in os Christiani prius Dominicum Corpus intraret, quam cæteri cibi." He also mentions the exception to this rule in regard to the *second* celebration on Maundy Thursday.

[r] Monica had wondered to find the Saturday fast (which was observed at Rome) unknown at Milan. It was unknown in the East.

[s] He is speaking of *præsumptiones*, petty *unauthorized* practices, (e. g. of keeping the bare foot from touching the ground during the week after baptism,) not of practices ordained by "councils or church-custom."

the claim of the Arian Gainas, the Gothic commander-in-chief of the East, to the possession of a church in Constantinople. He was holding a Council with some other bishops, when a Lydian prelate named Eusebius accused Antoninus, the exarch of Ephesus, of simony and other offences. The charge was not at that time made good; but in a few months Antoninus died, and his clergy induced S. Chrysostom to visit the church [t] in January 401. He held a Council of seventy bishops at Ephesus; the enquiry proved that six bishops had bought consecration from Antoninus. They were deposed; and at the same time Chrysostom deprived Geroutius, bishop of Nicomedia, who had gained and kept the see in defiance of a censure pronounced on him by S. Ambrose, under whom he had served as deacon. He also procured for Porphyrius, bishop of Gaza, at Easter, 401, an imperial decree against idolatry as practised at Gaza. He found that Severian, bishop of Gabala, had been caballing at Constantinople, and quarrelling with the irritable archdeacon Serapion [u]: he espoused the latter's view of the case, and was only reconciled to Severian by the interference of the empress Eudoxia. She was at this time on excellent terms with the Archbishop. The Arians were wont to spend great part of the night in the porticos, chanting antiphonally [x] their Arian hymns, as, "Where now are they that make Three One?" before issuing from the city to perform their Sunday and Saturday services outside the walls. Chrysostom procured from the bounty of the empress the means for organizing a statelier procession. Bearing silver crosses

---

[t] "We beg your Reverence to come down and reform according to God's will the Ephesian Church, which has been long afflicted, partly by Arians, partly by selfish and ambitious Churchmen." Pall. Vit., c. 14. This visit to Ephesus was a great extension of the power of Constantinople; for, strictly speaking, the "diocese of Asia" under the exarch of Ephesus was altogether independent of the Thracian diocese, and the latter was still nominally under Heraclea.

[u] Soc. vi. 11; Soz. viii. 10.

[x] Soc. vi. 8; Soz. viii. 8. Socrates says that S. Ignatius introduced chanting, after he had seen a vision of angels singing responsive praises to God.

to which waxen torches were attached, the Catholics went about the city with a full display of their superior numbers, chanting the nocturnal hymns of the Church. Public peace was incompatible with such open rivalry; a tumult ensued, and the Arians were prohibited from singing hymns except in private.

Meantime, Theophilus had begun to denounce Origenism in his Paschal letters. In that for 401, he set down as Origenistic errors, 1, the view of Marcellus as to Christ's kingdom having an end; 2, Universalism; 3, annihilation of the body; 4. the disallowing of prayer to the Son [y]. He quarrelled with the old priest Isidore, who fled to Nitria. This mountain, with its five hundred cells [z], was the stronghold of Origenism in Egypt; the other monastic settlements having been possessed by the opposite error. The chief Nitrian monks were Dioscorus, bishop of Nitria, Ammonius, Eusebius, and Euthymius; they were known as the *Tall Brothers.* Theophilus ordered them to be expelled; when they came to remonstrate, his eyes flashed [a],—his face became livid,—he threw his episcopal pall round the neck of Ammonius, struck him on the face with open palm and clenched fist, and cried, "Heretic, anathematize Origen!" They returned to Nitria; the patriarch, in a council, condemned them unheard, and proceeded by night to attack their monasteries, at the head of a drunken band. Dioscorus was dragged from his throne; the cells of the other three were burned, together with copies of both Testaments, and even the reserved portions of the Holy Eucharist. It was said that a boy perished in the flames. The Brothers, with many of their companions, fled to Scythopolis in Palestine, hoping to support themselves in a place famous for palms, by their occupation of weaving palm-baskets. The enmity of Theophilus hunted them out of this refuge; they reached Constantinople, and fell at Chrysostom's feet.

---

[y] Jerome, Ep. 96. He translated these letters. [z] Soz. vi. 61.

[a] Pallad. Vit., c. 6. Theophilus here showed the proverbial bitterness of the renegade.

"Who is it," asked he with tears, "that has injured you?" They answered, "Pope Theophilus; prevail upon him, father, to let us live in Egypt, for we have never done aught against him or against our Saviour's law." He lodged them in the church called Anastasia; allowed them to attend the service, but in order to avoid, if possible, a breach with their persecutor, debarred them from receiving the Communion. He wrote to Theophilus in the tone of a "son and brother," praying him to be reconciled to the fugitives; but Theophilus, who disclaimed his right to interfere, defamed them as sorcerers and heretics, and called in Epiphanius as his ally, who held a synod against Origenism, and exhorted Chrysostom to do the like.

Jerome supported Theophilus unreservedly. He was now in the full tide of controversy with Ruffinus. One angry tract called forth another[b], until Jerome himself became sensible of the wretchedness of such a quarrel, and Augustine entreated him to close a scene which chilled and saddened every true friendship.

Innocent the First, one of the greatest of the ancient Roman bishops, began his pontificate in May 402.

S. Chrysostom had too much respect for the rights of the see of Alexandria to interfere very vigorously on behalf of the Tall Brothers[c]. They therefore appealed to the Emperor and Empress, who ordered Theophilus to be summoned, and the accusations against the Brothers made on his part to be examined. The accusers had no case, and were thrown into prison. Theophilus delayed to obey the summons. He persuaded Epiphanius to visit Constantinople in order to carry on the war against Origenism. The old man, on this occasion, exhibited more plainly than ever the faults of character which had marred his usefulness. One of his first acts after landing was to ordain a deacon[d]. He spurned Chrysostom's offers of hospitality, refused to

---

[b] Ruffinus' "Invectives" in 401: two books of Jerome's in the end of the year; a rejoinder from Ruffinus; a last reply from Jerome in 402.

[c] Pall., c. 8.

[d] Soc. vi. 12.

eat or to pray with him, and endeavoured to procure from the bishops then at Constantinople an assent to the decree of his own synod against Origenism [c]. At Eudoxia's desire, the Brothers paid him a visit: "Who are ye?" "Father, we are the Tall Brothers. What do you know of our disciples or of our writings?" "Nothing." "Why then," asked Ammonius, "have you condemned us as heretics unheard?" All that the hasty old man could say was—"You were reported to be so." They shamed him by replying, "We treated you far otherwise, when we defended your books against a like imputation [f]." Soon afterwards, in May, 403, he quitted Constantinople, and died on his homeward voyage [g].

Theophilus, who openly said he was "going to Court in order to depose John," arrived in June, with a "load" of gifts from Egypt and India. He at once assumed a tone of contumelious hostility towards S. Chrysostom. He would not visit or speak to him; he abstained from entering the church. While Chrysostom declined to hear judicially the complaints of the Tall Brothers, Theophilus was concocting a scheme for his deposition. There were many bishops and clerg who desired it, whose tempers rebelled against godly discipline, or who deemed themselves slighted by the Archbishop's blunt uncourtliness [h]. Eudoxia, who had heard of a sermon in which he lashed the pride of women [i], took the side of his enemies, who determined to hold a Council at a suburb of Chalcedon called "the Oak." The bishops who attended were thirty-six. John, the successor of Serapion as archdeacon, appeared as chief accuser. Twenty-

---

[c] Theotimus, bishop of Scythia, withstood him upon this point, and declared that he knew of no false doctrine in Origen. [f] Soz. viii. 15.

[g] Socrates, vi. 14, Sozomen, viii. 15, mention, as a report, that Epiphanius said to Chrysostom, "I hope you will not die a bishop," and that Chrysostom replied, "I hope you will not reach Cyprus." But this story was probably invented after the death of S. Chrysostom.

[h] Acacius, bishop of Berrhœa, had been disgusted with the lodging provided for him by Chrysostom, and had vented his spleen in the curious menace, "I will cook a dish for him!" Pall. c. 6. [i] Soc. vi. 15.

nine charges were advanced. Some were of open violence; that he had beaten and chained a monk, had struck a man in church so as to draw blood, and then had offered the Sacrifice. Others were of evil speaking: he had written slanders against the clergy; he had called them "not worth three obols;" he had slandered them in a treatise[k]; he had accused three deacons of having stolen his pall; he would not speak to Acacius; he had stirred up the church servants against Severian; he had called Epiphanius by abusive names. He was also charged with misconduct[l] in his office; he had sold church furniture, had been careless in conferring orders, had hired bishops to abet his persecution of clergy; he was as unsocial as a Cyclops[m]; he saw women in private; he had behaved irreverently in church; he ate wafers while sitting on his throne[n]. Some of these charges were gross exaggerations of that plain-spoken severity which knew no respect of persons, and which occasionally, no doubt, went beyond the bounds of prudence. Others were inventions more or less malignant. One of the basest was the charge about disposing of church ornaments; like other saints[o], he had done so for the sake of the suffering poor. While these charges were being read at the Oak, he sat in his palace with forty bishops, and consoled them by quoting texts of Scripture. "I am now ready to be offered. Do not weep and break my heart! To me to live is Christ, and to die is gain." "Remember," he added, "that life is but a journey. Are we better than patriarchs, prophets, apostles?"

Now entered two young bishops from "the holy Council

---

[k] Probably this referred to his treatise against the *Syneisacti*.

[l] A charge of immorality was not spared.

[m] Like S. Gregory Nazianzen, he could not play the host as an archbishop of Constantinople was expected to do. He had a weak stomach and a constant headache, and therefore dined alone. Pall., p. 41.

[n] He had advised people to eat wafers soaked in water after receiving the Holy Sacrament.

[o] S. Cyril of Jerusalem, S. Ambrose, &c. S. Jerome mentions S. Exuperius of Toulouse, a contemporary, as "carrying the Lord's Body in a wicker basket, His Blood in a glass," Ep. 125. c. 20.

at the Oak," citing "John" to appear, with other clergy. The forty bishops sent a deputation to remonstrate with Theophilus. Chrysostom, for himself, sent word that he objected to Theophilus and three others as disqualified, by avowed hostility, to be his judges. Another deputation came from the Oak; another went thither in return, and was treated with gross violence. A bishop named Isaac produced a new list of charges, three of which were remarkable. Chrysostom had used strong language about the fervour of rapturous devotion, which was brought up against him as unseemly. He had been emphatic in his assurances of Divine long-suffering[p]; "If you sin again, repent again!" This was denounced as an encouragement of sinners in their sin. "He had eaten before administering baptism, and given the Eucharist to persons who were not fasting;" two charges which he denied with remarkable vehemence[q]. Witnesses were heard as to the alienation of church furniture. The Council pronounced him contumacious, and deposed him, requesting Arcadius also to punish him for insolence towards Eudoxia. Appealing in vain to a more just tribunal, he was dragged from his church, and hurried by night into Bithynia. That night an earthquake shook the palace; Eudoxia wrote to the exile, entreating him to return. He was escorted to the city by a joyous multitude, bearing tapers and chanting psalms, who forced him, in spite of the irregularity of such a proceeding, to ascend his throne before the sentence of the Council could be annulled[r]. This was, however, speedily done by a synod of sixty bishops; the hostile assembly could not stand its

---

[p] This was a common topic with him; but he was careful to warn men against presuming on God's goodness: e.g. in Matt. hom. 61. c. 1; in 1 Cor. hom. 23. c. 5. For a noble passage on "the abyss of God's benignity," see de Sacerd. iii. 15.

[q] Ep. 125; "If I have done this, may my name be effaced from the roll of bishops," &c. Serm. ant. iret in exsil. 4; "They say, You baptized after you had eaten. If I did this, let me be anathema," &c. He is referring to the Paschal baptisms, which were immediately followed by the celebration.

[r] He delivered a sermon, which is in tom. iii. 427.

ground, and Theophilus, after meanly forcing the two surviving Brothers[s], on the ground of their monastic obedience, to ask his pardon, consulted his safety by flight to Alexandria.

New troubles soon began. In September a silver statue of Eudoxia was erected near the cathedral, and the Manichean governor of the city encouraged wild and heathenish dancing in its honour, which interrupted the Church service. Chrysostom spoke strongly on the subject, and was said to have begun a sermon with the words, "Again Herodias rages, again she demands the head of John[t]." The foes of the archbishop seized their opportunity; Theophilus sent three bishops to Constantinople, and Arcadius declined to communicate with Chrysostom on Christmas day. Several hostile prelates held a council, and accused the archbishop of violating the canons of the Dedication Council[u], by resuming his throne before he had been canonically restored to it. His friends replied, "Will you then commit yourselves to a Council which condemned Athanasius, and to a canon repudiated at Sardica[x]?"

On Jan. 26, 404, Paula died at Bethlehem. Her daughter Eustochium attended the deathbed, occasionally withdrawing to pray in the cave of the Nativity[y]. Paula's last breath was spent in murmuring such texts as the first verse of Psalm lxxxiv., and in faintly assuring Jerome that all was well with her. When her voice became inaudible, she continued to sign the cross on her lips. Her funeral rites were performed by bishops, who lent their hands to the bier, or carried lamps and tapers before it, or led the choirs which chanted psalms in Syriac, Greek, and Latin. Monks,

---

[s] Ammonius and Dioscorus were dead. Sozomen, viii. 17, says that the other two were terrified into saying, as monks were wont to do, even if unjustly treated, "Forgive us."

[t] The homily which begins thus is considered spurious. Tom. viii. p. 609.

[u] Can. 4.

[x] It was also observed that the Council which, *after* S. Chrysostom's return, restored him, was larger than that of the Oak.

[y] Hier. Ep. 108.

virgins, inhabitants of all the cities of Palestine, thronged to the church of the Nativity, where her grave was prepared; "it was deemed a sacrilege to be absent when the last offices were being rendered to such a woman."

The disputes at Constantinople came to a head before Easter. The feeble Arcadius was persuaded to order that Chrysostom should leave the church. He replied that he would never, of his own free-will, abandon the charge he had received from the Saviour[z]. Easter-eve came, April 16. Arcadius said to the chief adversaries of Chrysostom, Acacius and Antiochus, "See to it that you are not giving me wrong counsel." "On our heads," they answered, "be the deposition of John!" One of the forty faithful bishops bade Eudoxia fear God, and have pity on her own children. The solemn services of the day were held in the Baths of Constantine. Thither the people thronged, abandoning the churches. It was resolved to break up this assembly; Lucius, captain of a band of soldiers, was sent with four hundred barbarian recruits to clear the Baths about 9 p.m. They pressed onwards to the font, dispersed the catechumens, struck the priests on the head until their blood was mingled with the baptismal water, rushed up to the altar prepared as usual for the Communion of the new-baptized, and overthrew the sacred chalice[a]. Thus were the Arian horrors renewed. On Easter-day, Arcadius, riding out of the city, saw some 3,000 neophytes in their white robes. "Who are those persons?" he asked. "They are heterodox people," was the answer; and a new onslaught was made upon them. During the Paschal season, those who would not disown S. Chrysostom were cast into the prisons, where they sang hymns and celebrated the Eucharist. Within the churches, instead of joyful worship were

---

[z] Pall., c. 9.

[a] This apparently is what Palladius means by—"overthrew the symbols." S. Chrysostom, writing to Pope Innocent, not to the uninitiated, says, "The most holy Blood of Christ, as might be expected in so great a tumult, was spilled on the clothes of the soldiers." Tom. iii. 519.

heard the sounds of torture, and the terrible oaths by which men were commanded to anathematize the Archbishop. His life was twice attempted: his people guarded his house; he wrote an account of what had happened to the bishops of Rome, Milan, and Aquileia[b]. Innocent, who had already heard Theophilus' version of the story, continued his communion for the present to both parties, but summoned Theophilus to attend a Council in which Nicene canons only should be recognized. Towards the end of Whitsun-week, Arcadius was prevailed upon to send another mandate to Chrysostom. "Commend your affairs to God, and depart." Chrysostom was persuaded to depart secretly; he called his friends to prayer, kissed them, bade farewell in the baptistery to the deaconesses, and desired them to submit to a new bishop, if he were ordained without having solicited the see. "The Church cannot be without a bishop." While the people waited for him to mount his horse at the great western door, he went out at the eastern; remembering[c], in regard to the prospect of exile, that "the earth was the Lord's, and the fulness thereof;" recalling the trials of the prophets, the three holy Confessors, S. John Baptist, and S. Stephen; and repeating to himself the words of Job, "Naked came I out of my mother's womb, and naked I return thither!" This was his final expulsion, June 20, 404; he crossed over to Bithynia, while a fire broke out which consumed the cathedral, (except the sacristy,) and also the palace of the senate. Some ascribed it to incendiaries; others called it a sign of divine wrath. Several of Chrysostom's friends, the "Joannites" as they were called, were cruelly treated, as if guilty of the fire; Eutropius, a pious young reader[d], was torn with iron hooks, and died in prison. Arcacius, an old priest, who had been made to swear that he would never accept a bishopric, was consecrated for the see;

---

[b] The bishop of Aquileia was S. Chromatius, who had begged Jerome to write no more against Ruffinus.

[c] S. Chrys. Ep. 125 to Cyriacus.

[d] Sozomen, viii. 24.

Olympias, Chrysostom's chief female friend, a high-born, wealthy, and noble-hearted widow, was mulcted for not acknowledging the new bishop. Other pious women were harassed for their loyalty to Chrysostom. The place of his exile was Cucusus, in Armenia; and there, after a journey the pain of which was only alleviated by marks of sympathy and revereuce[e], he arrived in the middle of September. The bishop of Cucusus offered to resign the see in his favour; and Dioscorus, a man of rank, entreated him as a favour to occupy his own house, which he fitted up for the exile's conveuience, with "a liberality and beneficence," against which, Chrysostom writes, "I am continually exclaiming[f]." Very soon after he reached Cucusus the Empress Eudoxia bore a dead child, aud expired.

Flaviau died about this time, "without having consented to John's deposition[g];" Constantius, a friend of the Saint's, was the fittest person to succeed, but a priest of infamous character named Porphyrius procured the see for himself, and compelled the majority of the people to hold external communion with him. Others refused, at all hazards, to profess adhesion to a man whom all abhorred. On Nov. 18 a law was made against all who should hold off from the communion of Arsacius, Theophilus, and Porphyrius. Among those who were in consequence expelled was Cyriacus, bishop of Synnada. He came, with others, among whom was Cassian, now a deacon of Constantinople ordained by S. Chrysostom, to inform Pope Innocent of the state of affairs. Innocent therefore wrote to Chrysostom, exhorting him to patience by Scriptural examples: "A good man can be exercised, but he cannot be overcome, while the divine Scriptures fortify his mind. Venerable brother, let your conscience comfort you." He also wrote to the clergy and laity of Constantinople, declaring against the authority of

---

[e] Yet this was not invariably the case. Pharetrius, bishop of Cæsarea, showed him no sort of kindness; and monks of that city threatened to burn the house over his head. All this time he was suffering from fever. Ep. 14, ad Olymp.

[f] Ep. 13.

[g] Soz. viii. 24.

the Antiochene canons, and adding that he was considering the best plan for a General Council.

In December, 404, S. Augustine held a discussion with Felix the Manichean, who avowed that the chief attraction of Manicheism in his own case was its promise of gratifying curiosity about the material world[h]. One main point raised in this debate was whether the soul were part of the Divine essence, and required to be freed from contact with "the nation of darkness," by such means as Manichean fancy represented. Felix, like Fortunatus, was silenced; but, unlike him, had the candour to embrace Catholicism.

This year is marked by the self-sacrifice of Telemachus, a monk who was visiting Rome when Honorius, after the deliverance of Italy from Gothic invasion, celebrated his triumph by public games. Telemachus attempted to separate the gladiators, and was stoned to death by the people; but those hideous contests were immediately abolished by law.

During this winter the Donatists were unusually violent. Circumcellions fell upon Maximian, the Catholic bishop of Bagai, beat him savagely with the timbers of his own altar[i], wounded him with swords[k], left him for dead, seized him again and flung him from a tower. The care of a peasant and his wife enabled Maximian to travel to Italy, where he showed his ghastly scars to Honorius. The result was a decree, afterwards called the "Law concerning Union," Feb. 12, 405, which imposed penalties of various kinds, short of death, on "rebaptizers." In defiance of this edict, the Circumcellions fell upon Catholic clergy, and poured a mixture of lime and vinegar into their eyes[l].

There had now been for several years at Rome a British[m]

---

[h] S. Aug. de Act. cum Fel. i. 9.

[i] S. Aug. c. Cresc. iii. 47. Compare the wooden altar at Alexandria, burned in 356.

[k] Formerly they had confined themselves to the clubs called *Israels*. S. Aug. c. Ep. Parm. i. 17.

[l] S. Aug. Ep. 88.

[m] Ep. 186. 1. Prosper calls him *coluber Britannus*.

monk named Pelagius. He was a friend of Paulinus of Nola; and Augustine had heard him mentioned "with high praise as a man of right faith," and had "loved" him accordingly [n]. He had written a treatise on the doctrine of the Trinity. Strict and earnest in practical religion, he heard with indignation the feeble self-excusing to which indolent Christians had recourse. His feeling was, "You deceive yourselves by talking thus about your weakness. You *can* serve God, if you have the will." A bishop one day quoted to him Augustine's prayer, recorded in his "Confessions," and already, it seems, proverbial; "Give what Thou commandest, and then command what Thou wilt [o]." Pelagius could not endure such language [p]. It seemed to him to cut at the root of all personal exertion, and to encourage listlessness under the garb of piety. And thus, about 405, he was led on, by a defect of humility in his moral nature, and by an intellectual tendency to exaggeration and one-sidedness [q], into a view of human capabilities which left no place for supernatural help, and narrowed the gulf between Christianity and Heathenism. He began, as Augustine heard [r], to "dispute against the grace of God;" but not so as to cause any public agitation. His view was, in few words, "We need *no inward grace*, for we have *no inborn sin*." How far he was indebted for it to "a Syrian named Ruffinus," himself the pupil of Theodore of Mopsuestia [s], or, as Jerome said, to Ruffinus of Aquileia, must be left uncertain; but it seems that he embodied its essence, with considerable caution and reserve, in a tract on practical duties, and a commentary on S. Paul [t].

---

[n] De Gest. Pel. 46; Ep. 186. 1.

[o] Conf. x. 40. "*Da quod jubes, et jube quod vis.*" He adds, "Imperas nobis continentiam." See ib. 45, 60.

[p] De Dono Persev. 53.

[q] See Guizot, Civilis. in France, lect. 5.

[r] De Gest. Pel. 46; see de Pecc. Orig. 24.

[s] Marius Mercator, Commonitory, in Aug., tom. x. 1681.

[t] The tract was known by the names of *Testimonia* and *Capitula*. On this work, and on the Commentary, see De Gest. Pel. 2, 5, 7, 39; De Pecc. Orig. 24.

Meantime the saintly exile at Cucusus, while suffering from illness and intense cold[u], and in constant peril from freebooters, continued to discharge the office of a good shepherd. He wrote letter after letter to Olympias, exhorting her to remember that the only trial really terrible was sin[x], and that exile and proscription were as nothing compared with the ineffable blessedness in store[y]. He lamented that faithful bishops were suffering for adherence to his communion; he exhorted them and their clergy to be of good courage, and to keep the text, Rom. viii. 18, constantly in their minds[z]. His pastoral thoughtfulness extended far beyond a merely general care for his brethren's welfare. We find him rebuking two priests of Constantinople, one of whom had only preached five times between his expulsion and October, while the other had not preached once[a]; setting on foot a mission to the Pagans of Phœnicia[b]; anxious to have a good bishop consecrated for the Goths, and to extricate Maruthas, bishop of Martyropolis in Mesopotamia, who had preached in Persia, from his connection with the party of Theophilus[c]; drawing closer the old ties which bound him to the clergy of Antioch[d]; and employing part of his friends' contributions in the redemption of captives and the relief of the poor[e].

Innocent boldly espoused his cause as that of a confessor for righteousness' sake. He assembled a synod, and persuaded Honorius, who had already remonstrated with Arcadius, to write in a more peremptory tone, demanding a council at Thessalonica, and pointing out Theophilus as

---

[u] Ep. 6. ad Ol. He passed sleepless nights; no amount of clothing or fire could keep him warm. [x] Ep. i. ad Ol.

[y] Ep. 16. He alludes to her sufferings as well as to his own.

[z] Tom. iii. 527.

[a] Ep. 203. He adds, "This is more painful to me than my solitude here." See too Ep. 119.

[b] See Ep. 126. He will do all he can to provide the missionary with what is required, even if he has to write a thousand times to Constantinople on the subject. See Epp. 53, 54, 123.

[c] Ep. 14. [d] Ep. 130. [e] Soz. viii. 27; Pall., c. 11.

the reputed author of present evils[f]. One of the Western bishops sent by Honorius and the Roman synod to the East was Gaudentius, whom S. Ambrose had consecrated to the see of Brescia, and who is known by his Paschal sermons to the new-baptized.

In this year, 405, a correspondence of considerable interest came to an end[g]. Augustine and Jerome had for years been discussing whether the Septuagint could claim an absolute authority, and whether S. Peter's weakness and S. Paul's rebuke at Antioch were simulated or real. Each party at length gave up an untenable position. Augustine came to see the value of an independent translation from the Hebrew text; and Jerome, apparently, learned the more important lesson that Scripture could authorize no pious frauds[h].

Towards the end of the year the furious incursions of Isaurian robbers, filling the country with rapine and bloodshed, compelled S. Chrysostom to take shelter in the castle of Arabissus[i]. The winter was again a time of discomfort; he could not obtain a sufficiency of medicines; and the snow-drifts prevented him from receiving his friends' letters[k]. Arsacius, who died in November, was succeeded in March by Atticus[l], a man of learning, practical ability, and open-handed benevolence, but a declared foe of Chrysostom. About this time the Western delegates, with four Eastern bishops, were

---

[f] Pall., c. 3.

[g] See Aug. Epp. 28, 39, 40, 67, 68, 71, 72, 73, 75, 81, 82. (Jerome had been vexed to find that a letter of Augustine's, instead of being transmitted to himself, had been circulated in Italy. Augustine explains that this was by no fault of his; and so comes to use the words in Ep. 82. 33, about "the episcopate being greater than the priesthood, *according to the honorary titles used by the Church*," i. e. "I cannot address you as you address me, by the name of *blessed pope*.")

[h] Adv. Pel. 22. A low standard of social fairness, in the decaying empire, had its influence, as we have seen, on some eminent Churchmen. Experience of Manichean delusions prepared S. Augustine to insist with special energy on the duty of *truthfulness in the cause of Truth*.

[i] Ep. 69. He had already been obliged to hide himself in glens and woods.

[k] Epp. 15, 127.

[l] Soc. vi. 20; vii. 2, 25.

intercepted in their way to Constantinople, and confined in a Thracian fortress[m]; their credentials were violently wrung from them, and instead of being allowed to see Arcadius, the Westerns were sent back to Italy, the Easterns banished to the frontiers of the empire[n]. On their way they were cruelly harassed, robbed of their money, wearied by prolonged days' journeys, compelled to lodge in synagogues or in the lowest haunts of profligacy. One of them consoled his brethren by observing that their presence recalled the wretched women to thoughts of God, which might result in their salvation and His glory. S. Chrysostom's biographer mentions, in connection with these confessors, the tortures and exile endured by Serapion, whom Chrysostom had made exarch of Heraclea, and by Stephen, a monk who had carried letters to Innocent: also the sufferings of other "Joannites," two of whom hid themselves for three years in an upper chamber. That the persecution was in great measure a systematic revenge on Chrysostom as the representative of clerical strictness, is evidenced by such a fact as that a venerable man named Hilary was scourged, "not by a judge, but by the clergy." Chrysostom wrote to thank his Western friends[o] for their sympathy, and sent a second letter to Innocent, assuring him that "in this third year of exile, amid famine, pestilence, war, sieges, indescribable solitude, and daily peril from Isaurian swords, he was greatly consoled and delighted by Innocent's genuine, stedfast, and abundant charity."

It was apparently in 406 that Jerome saw a treatise, by Vigilantius of Barcelona, in which the honours paid to the memory of Martyrs were attacked with indiscriminating impetuosity. There was doubtless a dangerous element already at work in these observances, which S. Augustine had not failed to notice[p]. A thoughtful and temperate warning against superstitious abuses would have been a

---

[m] Pall., c. 4. [n] Ibid., c. 20. [o] Epp. 182, 155, 184, &c.

[p] De Mor. Eccl. Cath. i. 75, above referred to. But it must be observed that S. Augustine thought it lawful to ask the prayers of the Saints.

well-timed service to religion. But Vigilantius denounced all reverence for the remains of martyrs as "the worship of a little dust wrapt in a rich cloth;" and gave a shock to Christian instincts by denying that the Church at rest could intercede for the Church militant[q]. He did not impugn the reality of the miracles which his contemporaries believed to be performed at the tombs of Saints; but he denied that they were of profit to any except unbelievers. He censured those who sold their property for purposes of almsgiving; desired the abolition of all vigils save that of Easter[r], on the ground that they led to disorders; condemned the monastic life, and recommended that celibacy should be considered as absolutely disqualifying a man for ordination. In a single night,—for the messenger was in haste to leave Palestine,—Jerome penned a tract against Vigilantius, in which he exhibited all the violence which makes his controversial style so painful. He defended (among other points) the veneration of saintly relics, but asked the "madman" Vigilantius, "Who ever worshipped martyrs?" He denied that tapers were burned during the day-time in their honour, but affirmed that throughout the East the lighting up of tapers in broad day-light was a mode of welcoming the reading of the Gospel.

Three years had passed away since Alaric and his Goths had been defeated at Pollentia; and Italy was now thrown into new agitation by the descent of a motley host of Northern barbarians, under the leadership of Rhadagaisus. This was a worse terror to the Christians, inasmuch as Rhadagaisus was not a Christian like Alaric, but professed a bloody idolatry. Yet the Roman Pagans expected no

q See Bp. Pearson's Minor Works, ii. 54.

r The Council of Eliberis, a century earlier, had forbidden women to keep vigil in churches. Bishop Sparrow questions whether any canon ever abolished the actual watchings; Rationale, p. 103. As he observes, the Council of Auxerre in 578 did not abolish, but only regulated them. Vigilantius desired to have *Alleluia* confined to the Easter-services, in opposition to the usage of Spain and Palestine, but in accordance, if Sozomen, vii. 19, is correct, with that of Rome.

favour from a Northern heathen, and filled the city with wild outcries[s] against Christianity as the cause of all their perils. The cloud dispersed on the overthrow of the invading forces by Stilicho; but the remnant of them entered Gaul, Dec. 31, 406, and the western bank of the Rhine became a scene of misery and bloodshed. Mentz was taken, and thousands were butchered in its church[t]. At Rheims the archbishop and others were put to death at the church-door; at Auxerre the bishop became a martyr on the very day of his consecration. The ravaged towns were polluted by ghastly corpses, lying unburied and tainting the air[u].

The winter of 406-7 was severe, but Chrysostom preserved his health by never stirring out of a close and well-warmed chamber[x]. In the summer, his enemies, dreading his influence on the Antiochenes, who went to visit him[y], procured an order for his removal to Pityus on the shores of the Euxine sea. His guards were ordered to exhaust him by long journeys. Through scorching heat and drenching rains he was hurried on, and never allowed the refreshment of the bath; one only of the guards being disposed to shew him furtive kindnesses. For three months this painful journey lasted; at length they halted at the church of S. Basiliscus, a short distance from Comana in Pontus. That night the sufferer had a foreboding that his release was at hand[z]. In the morning, Sept. 14, 407, he begged

---

[s] "Fervent tota urbe blasphemiæ." Orosius, vii. 37. See S. Aug. Serm. 105, De Civ. Dei, v. 23.

[t] See Jerome, Ep. 123. 16.

[u] Salvian, de Gubern. Dei, vi. He regards these horrors as a scourge for Christian unfaithfulness. Men had indulged in heathenish amusements; in particular, they had even left the churches during a festival service, ("Christum in altario dimittimus,") in order to see the public games.

[x] Ep. 4.

[y] Pall., p. 39. He says that these brutal conductors (compare the "leopards" of S. Ignatius, ad Rom. 5,) were delighted when the burning sun beat cruelly on "the saint's head, which was bald like Elisha's."

[z] Palladius says he had a vision of S. Basiliscus, (who had suffered under Maximin,) who said to him, "Courage, brother John, to-morrow we shall be together."

to be allowed to stay in the church until eleven a.m. It could not be; he was forced to proceed, but after travelling about four miles he was so evidently dying that they returned to the church. There he asked for white garments, and exchanged for them those which he wore. He was still fasting; he received the Holy Communion, doubtless from the priest of the church, offered up his last prayer, added his usual thanksgiving, "*Glory to God for all things*," and "sealed it with a final *Amen*." "Then he stretched out his feet, which had run beauteously for the salvation of the penitent and the rebuke of habitual sinners [a]," and calmly expired in about the sixtieth year of his age, and in the tenth of his episcopate. He was buried beside the martyr Basiliscus, the funeral being attended by a throng of monks and virgins from Syria, Cilicia, Pontus, and Armenia. No comment on his glorious life could be so expressive as the doxology with which it closed [b], and which, gathering into one view all its contrasts, recognized not only in success and honour, but in cruel outrage and hopeless desolation, the gracious presence of a never-changing Love.

---

[a] Palladius is thinking of the charge of over-indulgence in regard to penitential rules, which was brought against him, and which Socrates endorses from his quasi-Novatianist point of view, vi. 21. But, as Tillemont says, xi. 136, S. Chrysostom was simply proclaiming God's readiness to forgive all sinners on their repentance. "John of Repentance" was a name given to him.

[b] Thankfulness "for veiled benefits as well as apparent ones" was the habit of his life. See, especially, in Eph. Hom. 19, c. 2: "Utter nothing before this, 'I thank Thee, Lord!'" See also his references to Job i. 21, e.g. in Rom. Hom. 2. 1; ad Pop. Ant. Hom. i. 10.

CHAPTER X.

From the Death of S. Chrysostom to the Death of Pope Innocent.

"Thou, grieving that the ancient curse
Should doom to death an universe,
Hast found the medicine, full of grace,
To save and heal a ruined race."

Conditor alme siderum, NEALE'S Version.

THE wrongs of S. Chrysostom had divided the East and West. Innocent and the Westerns would have no fellowship with those who adhered to Theophilus and Atticus; and for some time the condition of communion with Rome was the insertion of the name of "John, bishop of Constantinople," on the *diptychs* [a], or folded tablets which recorded those who were to be mentioned at the Eucharist.

Arcadius, whose feebleness had led him into tyranny, did not long survive his victim. He died on May 1, 408, leaving the throne to his son Theodosius II., a boy of eight, whose education was in the hands of his sister Pulcheria, a young princess of thoroughly noble character. His temper was sweet and docile, and she could easily train him in devotional habits; but she could not supply the natural defects, which appeared in feeble prejudice and morbid scrupulosity [b]. On August 23 an intrigue of the court of Honorius destroyed Stilicho, the "Deliverer of Italy." In the extremity of his peril he took sanctuary in the cathedral of Ravenna. His enemy, the base Olympius, who had supplanted him in ascendancy over Honorius,

---

[a] These were plates of wood, ivory, gold, or silver, on which were inscribed the names usually recited at the Eucharist. They were the names, 1. of the Apostles and other chief saints; 2. of eminent persons who had died in Catholic communion; 3. of those living persons whom the Church thought good to honour. In the East, Spain, and Gaul, they were read before consecration; at Rome, partly before and partly after.

[b] Soc. vii. 22; Soz. ix. 1; Theod. v. 36, 37.

swore to the bishop that Stilicho's life would be spared. He came forth, and was led to execution [c].

In the autumn of 408 Alaric besieged Rome for the first time [d]. Terror and wrath, in the minds of the Romans, were soon absorbed in the agonies of famine. The heathen historian tells us that the præfect of the city, hearing that some Etruscan diviners professed to be able to launch thunderbolts against the enemy, procured from Innocent, as the most important personage in the city, a secret permission for the exercise of their rites; but that they further insisted on the official presence of the senate, which being refused, they went their way [e]. It does not seem likely that the Pope should grant a licence which the senate withheld; and Innocent, with his high spirit and stedfast conscientiousness, was by no means the man to be scared into concessions which would make him partaker in "the sin of witchcraft [f]." And the story is yet further discountenanced by Innocent's presence, as an envoy, at the court of Ravenna, in January, 409, when Honorius made a severe law against all diviners.

It appears to have been during the year 408 that Augustine's mind underwent a change as to the duty of a government towards the enemies of the Church. He had once thought "that no one ought to be forced into Christian

---

[c] Zosim. v. 34. S. Augustine mistook Olympius for a pious Christian, Ep. 96. He professed a great zeal for the faith.

[d] Socrates, vii. 10, says that a good monk remonstrated with Alaric as he was hastening to Rome, and that Alaric replied, "I am not acting of myself, but there is one who is ceaselessly urging and commanding me to lay Rome waste." So Soz. ix. 6.

[e] Zosim. v. 41. Sozomen, ix. 6, does not "assert," as Dean Milman (Lat. Chr. i. 99) says, and hardly "insinuates," as Gibbon says, that the divinations were performed. "They undertook to drive away the barbarians...... ἀλλὰ τούτων μὲν οὐδὲν ὄφελος ἔσεσθαι τῇ πόλει, ἡ ἀπόβασις ἔδειξε. For the right-minded saw full well that it was God's wrath which brought this upon Rome," &c.

[f] For the horror with which the Church regarded divination, see Ancyran canon 24, Laodicean 36. S. Augustine, Serm. 9. 3, calls the consulting of aruspices "spiritual fornication." See his Ep. 55. 12, 13.

unity[g];" but the working of penal laws appeared to him so effective in producing an external conformity, that he became a convert to the coercive principle, and defended it in an elaborate letter[h], with strange confusions between moral and physical "compulsion," and between providential and human modes of government. However, painful as his argument is, we must in fairness remember that he had seen the Church attacked, not simply by an opposing sect, but by a sect whose weapon was murderous brutality; and that when, towards the end of 408, it became a capital offence to disturb the Church's worship, Augustine entreated the proconsul of Africa to "forget that he had this power of inflicting death[i]." In the course of 409, Honorius, apparently in order to secure the support of all classes, put forth a short-lived edict of toleration.

Pelagius had continued in Rome, and had been joined by an Irishman[k] named Cœlestius, remarkable for his outspoken boldness, and his dialectical ability; and the two friends appear to have left Rome in 409, and settled for a short time in Sicily.

Cassian took up his abode at Marseilles in the same year, and began to establish in Provence the monastic system which he had so much admired in Egypt.

Early in 410, two remarkable men were raised to the episcopate. Paulinus had become distinguished among

---

g Compare S. Chrys. de Sacerd. ii. 4.

h Ep. 93. He quotes Luke xiv. 23 and John vi. 44, where the *drawing*, he says, is by "fear of Divine wrath." Persecution, he contends, may sometimes be righteous. From the fact that God's sterner providences lead men to "serve Him in fear," he infers the rightfulness of coercive laws against schismatics. Contrast the lessons which another Augustine gave to Ethelbert; Bede, i. 26.

i Ep. 100; S. Augustine was adverse to capital punishment in any case, as depriving a man of time for amendment, Ep. 153.

k So at least it has been supposed; Jerome speaks of Pelagius as a huge fat dog of Albion, "habet progeniem Scoticæ gentis." This expression has been variously understood as, "derives his lineage from the Scottish (Irish) race," (Benedictine editors of S. Aug.), and "has an offspring of Scottish blood," (Noris' Hist. Pelag., p. 24.) In another of his prefaces to Jeremiah, Jerome speaks of an "ignorant calumniator, *Scotorum pultibus prægravatus*."

the devout clergy of his time; he had done much for Christiau art and sacred poetry, especially by building a new church near the tomb of S. Felix, adorning it with pictures and mosaics, and explaining the latter by inscriptions in verse. In one of these representations, Christ was depicted as a lamb, the Holy Spirit by a dove, while the Father was indicated by words issuing from a cloud; twelve doves signified the Apostles, and four streams issuing from a rock on which the Lamb stood were apt symbols of the four Evangelists [l]. Other paintings were direct representations of Old Testament subjects, intended to instruct and edify [m] the country people who came to keep the festival of the Saint. It cannot be denied that his enthusiasm for S. Felix, as expressed in the poems which he wrote on every return of the festival, was carried to an excess for which there was no precedent, and became a precedent for "later corruptions [n]." He also paid great honour to S. Martin, and visited Rome annually on the feast of S. Peter and S. Paul [o]. When the bishop of Nola died, Paulinus was naturally chosen to succeed him, and justified the choice by an administration full of genuine pastoral love.

The other appointment was of a very different kind. The metropolitan see of Ptolemais was vacant; and Theophilus was bent on placing in it a philosopher named Synesius, who was, and felt himself to be, unfitted on various grounds for such a charge. He had been an enthusiastic attendant on the lectures of Hypatia [p], the gifted female teacher of Neo-platonism; and the pantheistic spirit of that system, originally constructed by Ammonius Saccas [q] in the end of the second century, in order to eclipse

---

[l] See Trench, Huls. Lect., p. 49.

[m] Paul. Natal. 9.

[n] Robertson's Ch. Hist. i. 331.

[o] Ep. 2 to Delphinus. On one of these occasions, he says, Anastasius received him with great kindness.

[p] See his Ep. 16; he calls her his mother, &c.; in Ep. 10 he addresses her as having a divine soul; in Ep. 153 he requests her judgment on his works.

[q] See Newman's Arians, p. 60; Robertson, Ch. Hist. i. 88. Plotinus

Christianity by a grand aggregate of the highest results of natural speculation, had left its impress on his thoughts and language[r], although he was a professed believer in Christ. It was natural for Christians whose minds were at all influenced by Neo-platonism to affix an esoteric sense to Christian dogmas, since the philosophers had borrowed several Christian phrases[s] for their own convenience; and Synesius explicitly declared that he could not accept the doctrine of the Resurrection of the Body, in the sense ordinarily received[t]. Other difficulties he had, and frankly owned them; he had always been fond of amusements, especially hunting[u], and he had always, on principle, avoided business and responsibility. He tells us[x] that he begged of God "on his knees, at various times and places," to give him "death rather than the priesthood;" and he called God and man to witness that he made an open avowal of those opiuions which "philosophic demonstrations" had rooted in his mind. Yet after all this, Theophilus persisted in making him a bishop. Sensitiveness about doctrinal soundness could hardly, indeed, be expected from a man who had passed, to serve a purpose, from Origenism to the persecution of Origenists, and then, the purpose being served, had shamelessly resumed his old habits of Origenistic study[y]. But while Theophilus was blameworthy in bearing down with a high hand the scru-

---

began to lecture in 244, died at Rome 270. Porphyry was born 233, died 304. Jamblichus died under Constantine.

[r] As in his first hymn, l. 81—94, and his language on the Trinity in hymn 3 is coloured by Platonic mysticism. He also speaks of spirits as "gods," hymn 3, l. 168, which was in accordance with the language of this Alexandrian philosophy.

[s] Neo-platonism had a "Trinity" consisting of "The One,"—Reason,—and Soul.

[t] Ep. 105. He also said he could not believe that the world would be destroyed.

[u] "How can I bear to see my dear dogs deprived of their hunting?"

[x] Ep. 57.

[y] Being asked to account for this tergiversation, he calmly replied that Origen's books were like a meadow full of flowers; that he culled the fairest, and avoided the thorny ones. Soc. vi. 17.

ples of Synesius, the appointment turned out better than he had any right to expect. The truthfulness, humility, and religious temper of the philosopher-bishop bore fruit not only in a faithful and vigorous episcopate, but apparently in the removal of his objections to the common creed[z].

The second siege of Rome in 409 had ended in the temporary setting-up of Attalus by Alaric, as the rival of Honorius: the third ended in the taking of Rome, August 24, 410. The Gothic king, in the hour of his triumph[a], ensured the lives of all who should take refuge in the churches of S. Peter and S. Paul. Marcella, after being severely beaten by Goths in search of booty, was conveyed with her daughter Principia to the latter basilica, the architectural glory of Honorius' reign. An aged Christian virgin, being required by her captor to surrender the gold and silver which was in her keeping, produced an array of splendid vessels which filled him with amazement. "These are the sacred property of the Apostle Peter: lay hands on them if you dare." The Goth, overawed, sent to know the pleasure of Alaric, who ordered the vessels to be borne in safety to S. Peter's. The house where they were found was a long way distant from the Vatican; and as all Christians were allowed to take part in the removal, the band of those who bore the glittering treasures on their heads, guarded by Gothic swords, became ere long a vast procession, sweeping on with solemn chant. The sound echoed afar through the city, and was caught up as an assurance of safety by many who were cowering in hiding-places. They started up, and followed the choral train, which thus preserved the lives of many Pagans who took sanctuary in its favoured ranks[b]. This was indeed the dying day of Paganism; and when Innocent, who was then at Ravenna, returned home, he must have felt, as Jerome did on hearing of that tremendous hu-

---

[z] See Tillemont, xii. 529.

[a] Orosius, vii. 39.

[b] Augustine complains that such persons afterwards reviled the Christian name, which had that day been their safeguard: De Civ. Dei, i. 1.

miliation, that a "day of the Lord" had come on the harlot-city of the Apocalypse [c]. Terrible as were the sufferings of the proud Roman nobility, many of whom were carried into slavery, or had to beg their bread in foreign lands, it could not but occur to a Christian that the "eternal city" had been the Church's great antagonist, and that its abasement removed the main hindrance in her path to full supremacy.

Ruffinus was now in Sicily, on his way to Palestine. One of the last sights that he beheld was the fire which marked the track of Alaric along the shores of Southern Italy. He died in the end of 410, and Jerome had no other language for such an event than a declaration that "the scorpion was buried, and the many-headed hydra had ceased to hiss [d]."

Synesius had, at the beginning of his episcopate, warned his clergy to disperse the conventicles of the Eunomians [e]. He now, in 311, came forward against the detestable cruelties of a professed Catholic, Andronicus, governor of Ptolemais. This man revelled in the invention of new tortures [f], and in the agonies which they produced. Synesius' remonstrances were treated with scorn and anger; the forum continued to ring with shrieks [g], and the tyrant affixed a public notice to the church doors, forbidding the priests, with brutal menaces, to shelter any fugitive at the altars. A man of rank had offended Andronicus, and was barbarously tortured at an hour when the heat of the day kept most persons from visiting the judgment hall. Synesius heard of it, and came at once to show his sympathy with the sufferer. Andronicus was exasperated, and said, three times over, to his victim, "It is vain to trust in the Church; —no one shall deliver you from the hands of Andronicus, no, not if you were to clasp the feet of Christ!" The bishop forthwith convoked his clergy, and pronounced this sentence; "The Church of Ptolemais gives this admonition to

---

[c] Ep. 46. c. 11. [d] In Ezech. prol. [e] Ep. 5.

[f] Ep. 58; six instruments are named, as a thumb-screw, a lip-screw, a feet-twister, a squeezing-engine, &c. [g] Ep. 57.

all her sister Churches throughout the world: To Andronicus and his associates let no church-ground be open. Let every sacred place, whether church or precinct, be closed against them. I command all private persons, and all magistrates, never to be under the same roof or at the same board with him: and the priests are especially warned never to address those men while living, nor to attend their funeral when dead. Whosoever shall contemn this Church as belonging to a small city, and receive those who are under its ban, let him know that he has divided that Church which Christ ordained to be one. Be he Levite [h], Priest, or Bishop, we will treat him as Andronicus, never join hands with him, never eat at the same table, much less partake with him of the Mystic Service." The excommunication was suspended, against the bishop's own judgment [i], when Andronicus made professions of repentance; he renewed his crimes, and the sentence was carried out. But ere long he himself became a sufferer from injustice, and the noble-hearted bishop, by importunate entreaties, "delivered him from the doom of death [k]," and endeavoured to interest Theophilus in his favour.

In the summer of 411, the Catholic bishops of Western Africa held a conference with the Donatists at Carthage. They had requested Honorius to summon the Donatists for such a meeting, and he ordered Marcellinus, one of his secretaries, to preside [l]. Marcellinus promised to those Donatist bishops who should attend, exemption from recent penalties, and solemnly promised, by the Holy Trinity, the Incarnation, the Emperor's salvation, and the day of judgment, to act with entire impartiality. His proclamation came forth in February: in May, 270 Donatist prelates entered Carthage with considerable pomp. The Catholic

---

[h] The analogy recognized between the Jewish and Christian hierarchies made it natural to call deacons *Levites*. [i] Ep. 72. [k] Ep. 89.

[l] Aug., tom. ix. 816. When a conference was first proposed, Primian answered, "The sons of the martyrs ought not to meet the offspring of traditors." Breviculus Collat. iii. 4.

prelates were 286 in number. Eighteen on each side were to hold the conference; and the Catholics assured Marcellinus [m] that if they should convince the Donatists that the Church Universal could not have been destroyed by the alleged sins of a few men, then they would admit the Donatists to an equal share in episcopal honours, so that a Catholic and an ex-Donatist bishop should sit together in church, each in turn occupying the higher seat. Or if the people would not endure to have two bishops in one city, then both should resign and a new bishop be elected [n]. This noble offer was followed by exhortations from Augustine, urging the Catholic laity to avoid all strife and excitement, and to make the Ember fast an occasion for earnest prayer [o]. The Conference was opened on the 1st of June in a large hall [p]. All the Donatists were present, but only the eighteen delegates on the Catholic side. After the imperial rescript, the commissioner's letters of summons, and some other documents had been read, the Donatists endeavoured to stifle the discussion by quibbles which, Augustine says, would have been intolerable even in a secular court [q]. Long disputes were raised about the instruments of delegation, and the Catholic bishops who had signed them were called in, and "recognized" by their Donatist neighbours. The Donatists were invited by Marcellinus to sit down, but they declined to do so, saying "much in praise of themselves, much in praise of the commissioner [r]," and afterwards alleging, as their reason, the text "I will not sit among the

[m] S. Aug. Ep. 128. This proposal had been previously discussed in full council, and only two had objected. One of these, an old man, spoke against it; the other "showed his feeling by his looks." But both yielded to the decided opinion of their brethren. De Gest. cum Emerito, 6.

[n] "Did our Redeemer descend from heaven to make us His members, and do we shrink from descending from our chairs, to save His members from cruel rent?"

[o] Serm. 357.

[p] Augustine calls it spacious, cool, and cheerful. Post Coll. 58.

[q] Brev. Coll. i. 8; Ep. 141. 3. Their chief speakers were Emeritus and Petilian. See Coll. i. 22; comp. Coll. iii. 142.

[r] Brev. i. 13. See Petilian's speech, Coll. i. 145. He spoke of his brethren as aged confessors, of Marcellinus as just, benignant, respectful.

ungodly[s]." Their object was to weary out their adversaries, and avoid coming to the merits of the case. At length, on the third day[t], the Donatists' proposal that the old documents of the case should be read before the later ones, proved fatal to their evasive policy. "So be it," said Augustine. "Then we ought to begin with those acts which prove that your predecessors appealed to Constantine about the case of Cæcilian[u]." These records the Donatists were particularly anxious to keep in the background; and Petilian imprudently exclaimed[v], "We are being gradually led on into the heart of the matter." The Catholics naturally said, "If you wish to discuss the question, which party can claim to be the Church, we will meet you on purely Scriptural grounds; but if you mean to go into the cases of individuals, of course we must refer to the public records[x]." Marcellinus interposed by saying, "Let the Acts be read[y]." And thus, says Augustine, "the business did at last fairly begin[z];" yet interruptions of the most frivolous kind ensued[a], and a discussion respecting a recent Donatist paper brought up the question of doctrine. Was not the "field" in the parable declared to mean the *world*[b]? ought the *Church* to endure the presence of bad members? The Catholics, speaking by Augustine, answered that the world, in that passage, meant the world evangelized[c]; that the kingdom of heaven was also described as a net and a threshing-floor, in which good and evil were for the present

---

[s] Coll. ii. 4; Brev. ii. 1. Marcellinus, upon this, had his own seat taken away, and the Catholic delegates stood up.

[t] Not, however, until after long debates as to the Catholics' having petitioned for this conference, and as to the meaning of the word "Catholic." S. Augustine interpreted it as "extended through the world:" Gaudentius the Donatist as "Sacramentis plenum, perfectum, immaculatum." Coll. iii. 101, 102. [u] Coll. iii. 141—144. [v] Post Collat. 43; Coll. iii. 151.

[x] Coll. iii. 187. [y] Ibid. 216. [z] Brev. iii. 7.

[a] The Donatists asked the Catholics whether Cæcilian were their "father" or "mother." Coll. iii. 231. Augustine answered, "He is our brother; *habeo caput, sed Christus est.*" [b] Matt. xiii. 38.

[c] Coll. iii. 265. He quoted texts in which "the world" was used in a good sense, John iii. 17, xvii. 21.

commingled; that the Church believed discipline to be most needful[d], and that the exemption of some offenders from its operation was only in order to secure the great blessing of unbroken unity, and was by no means an obstacle to that genuine separation from the wicked, which shewed itself in avoidance of their sin. The Donatists charged the Catholics with believing in two Churches. They answered, "The Church is holy and is one; but here it exists under one form, and in the next world it will exist under another."

They then resumed the question of fact, not without some tedious digressions about the "persecutions" which the sect had sustained, and about the conduct of Mensurius, Cæcilian's predecessor. The real issue was, whether Cæcilian's adherents, or his enemies, deserved in their own time the name of Catholic? The old controversies about the Council of Carthage which had condemned him, and the Council of Cirta which destroyed the credit of his judges[e], were mingled with a reference to the Maximianist schism which had reduced the Donatists' case to an absurdity. The Donatist leaders appear by this time to have become reckless; they declared that Pope Melchiades was a traditor, and produced documents which raised a long dispute as to whether he had been cognizant of the guilt of a certain Strato, whom the Donatists alleged to have been his deacon. This may serve as a sample of the irrelevancies to which they had recourse; nor is it surprising to find that these men actually referred to Optatus as proving that Constantine had condemned Cæcilian. Optatus had said that Constantine, for peace' sake, detained Cæcilian at Brescia. "Here is nothing," said the Catholics, "about his condemning Cæcilian." "Read the

[d] Here the original records break off, Coll. iii. 281, leaving a gap once filled by 303 chapters which have perished. The sentence, forming c. 585, is extant.

[e] There was a very long discussion as to the historical reality of this council. One point was, whether twelve bishops could have met to hold a council during persecution? The Catholics triumphantly adduced the acts of martyrs, which recorded their avowal of having held assemblies for service, (*collectæ*).

whole passage," said Marcellinus, "that we may judge of the author's meaning." It was read, and proved that Cæcilian had been "pronounced innocent." The audience could not restrain their laughter; the Donatists with great simplicity observed, "We did not ask to have *that* read!' suggested that Optatus had concealed the facts, and proceeded yet further in self-contradiction, by adducing their predecessors' address to Constantine against "*his* worthless bishop," and the letter of recall from exile in which the Emperor had stigmatized their proceedings. The proceedings closed[f] with the reading of the "vindication of Felix." Marcellinus, having ascertained that the Donatists had no more evidence to produce, desired both parties to withdraw, and drew up a sentence[g] in which the main element[h] was a decision of the question of fact, in favour of the innocence of Cæcilian, and, as consequent on that decision, an order for the suppression of Donatist conventicles, and the restoration of churches which "his benevolence, without any imperial precept," had allowed to be occupied by Donatists. This judgment was confirmed by Honorius on Jan. 30, 412[i]; he abrogated all laws made in favour of the Donatists; imposed fines on all of them, from the "Illustres[k]" to the Circumcellions; banished their clergy, and ordered the country labourers to be reclaimed by "frequent strokes of the lash." The Donatists loudly declared that Marcellinus had been bribed; and Augustine denounced the profligate audacity

[f] Some notion of the extent to which the Donatists had protracted them may be gathered from the fact that the records of the first day's hearing occupied 224 chapters; those of the second, 83; those of the third, 585. S. Augustine might well draw up an "Abridgment of the Conference."

[g] Aug., tom. ix. 840.

[h] He does, indeed, enter on theological ground so far as to say that according to Holy Scripture a charge made against Cæcilian could not, were it proved, affect the position of the Church.

[i] Aug. ix. 841.

[k] This title was given to the highest classes of magistrates. "Spectabiles" and "clarissimi" were inferior titles. Honorius includes the "domûs nostræ homines" in this penal law. In 414 he deprived the Donatists of civil rights, and "loaded them with perpetual infamy."

of a party whose slanders had been so often put to shame[l]. The patience and fairness of Marcellinus are evident from the records.

Spain was at this time suffering from the Vandals, the Suevi, and the Alani. We read of a council being held in 411 at Braga, in S. Mary's church, where Pancratius, the bishop, described the miseries and sacrileges of the time. "The barbarians are laying Spain desolate, destroying churches, putting Christ's servants to the sword, profaning the shrines of the Saints. Let us provide a remedy for souls, lest our people be drawn by their sufferings into apostasy. Some of the invaders are barbarians, some profess the Arian heresy. Let us, for the confirmation of faith, pronounce against such-like errors." He repeated a confession of faith which to some extent resembles the *Quicunque*[m], and which speaks of the Holy Spirit as "proceeding from the Father *and the Word;*" but this latter phrase is doubtless a spurious addition. He also consulted his brethren as to the best mode of preserving the relics of the saints. Elipandus of Coimbra, observing that the barbarians were pressing the siege of Lisbon, advised that the bodies of saints should be decently hidden in caves, and a memorandum in each case sent to Braga. Soon after, one of the bishops wrote to the archdeacon of Braga that Lisbon had bought off the barbarians, but that Coimbra was taken and Elipandus carried into captivity.

Many of the Donatists, we are told, joined the Church after the Conference[n]. But many others declared that no evidence in the world should detach them from their party[o]; and some of their clergy and Circumcellions murdered one priest, and barbarously maimed another[p]. Marcellinus drew forth a confession of their guilt, "not by the tortures of fire

---

[l] Post Coll. 15, 57.

[m] "Credo quod in hac Trinitate non sit majus aut minus, prius aut posterius."

[n] Possidius, Vit. Aug., c. 13. [o] S. Aug. Ep. 139. [p] Ep. 133.

and iron hooks," but simply by scourging [q]; and Augustine entreated, in letters to him and to his brother the proconsul, that "the sufferings of God's servants might not be avenged" by any extreme punishment, but that the government would act in the merciful spirit of the Church whose cause it took in hand.

But now the Donatist controversy recedes from the foreground, and a conflict with actual heresy takes its place.

While S. Augustine was absorbed by the business of the Conference, he once or twice [r] saw Pelagius at Carthage. Something also he heard, in casual conversation, of a theory which supposed the Church to baptize infants, "not for remission of sin, but for their sanctification in Christ [s]." He was startled, but thought little more about it; there was then no opportunity for pursuing the subject,—the speakers were persons of no weight,—and the matter was soon forgotten. Pelagius departed to Palestine. But Cœlestius remained at Carthage, and endeavoured to obtain the priesthood [t]; a design which was frustrated by his own boldness of speech. Paulinus, a Milanese deacon, who was then at Carthage, engaged in writing the life of S. Ambrose [u], accused Cœlestius, before Aurelius bishop of Carthage, of publicly avowing and widely disseminating [x] the following propositions:—

1. Adam was created mortal.

---

q Ep. 134. He says in Ep. 133 that bishops frequently employed scourging in their own courts.

r De Gest. Pel. 46. s De Pecc. Mer. iii. 12. t Ep. 157. 22.

u He addressed it to his "venerable father Augustine."

x Mar. Merc. in Aug., tom. ix. 1681, 1686; S. Aug. de Gest. Pel. 23. In one of Mercator's tracts he copies from the records the propositions as given above; the 7th has been omitted from this text, but is implied by his mentioning "seven." S. Augustine's order is—1, 2, 5, 6, 3, 4. He places 7, with two others, in a class apart, as connected with Pelagius. Mercator, in another tract, sets down 1, 2, 3, 4, 7: then adds, "These five articles produce one most impious and wicked proposition; he went on, 'Man can live without sin, and easily keep God's commandments; for men existed without sin before Christ's coming, and the Law conveys men to heaven just as the Gospel does.'"

2. Adam's sin harmed himself only.

3. Infants are born in Adam's unfallen state.

4. Mankind did not die in Adam, nor rise in Christ.

5. The Law conveyed men to heaven, just as the Gospel does.

6. There were sinless men before Christ came.

7. Infants, though unbaptized, have life eternal.

On being questioned by a Council, at which Augustine was not present, Cœlestius answered, "What I said was, that I doubted about the transmission of sin, but still that I would accept the judgment of any one to whom God had given the grace of knowledge. I have heard different language held by presbyters in the Catholic Church[y]." "Tell us their names," said Paulinus. "I have heard," said Cœlestius, "the holy presbyter Ruffinus, who abode at Rome with the holy Pammachius[z], deny any transmission of sin." "Any others?" "Yes, several." "Name them." Cœlestius evaded the point, asking, "Is not one priest (*sacerdos*) enough for you?" As to the third proposition, he was at first disposed to be evasive, and then said that the question of original sin was an open one among Catholics; adding, "I have always said that children need baptism, and ought to be baptized; what do you want more?" The Council, of course, wanted a true statement as to the ground of such need; and not obtaining it, pronounced Cœlestius excommunicate[a]. He spoke of appealing to Rome, but instead of doing so, took up his abode at Ephesus.

On comparing these propositions of the disciple with the earlier working of the master's mind, we see that Pelagianism is reducible to two principles—the denial of Supernatural Grace, and the denial of Original Sin; and that the former of these denials, though logically based upon the latter, was in fact the original element of the system. In

---

[y] S. Aug. de Pecc. Orig. 3.

[z] This does not suit Ruffinus of Aquileia. Præf. ad Aug., tom. x. 15.

[a] "Auditum, convictum, confessum, detestatumque ab Ecclesiâ, ex Africâ profugisse." Orosius, Apol. in Aug., tom. x. 1698.

other words, the spiritual sufficiency of nature was enforced and accounted for by the non-existence of the Fall. Augustine's bitter remembrances of Manicheism would make him specially abhorrent of a theory which lessened men's dread of sin, fostered a heathenish self-reliance, and nullified the mystery of the New Creation. He felt the greatness of the crisis; he saw that as by former heresies which affected religion on the side that looked to God, so by this which was conversant with its aspect towards man, a blow was struck at the very essence of Apostolic Christianity; and he attacked the new doctrine both in sermons [b] and in treatises [c], "which set forth the doctrine of the Church as to the first and Second Adam, the need of a Saviour for infants [d], the difference between original sin and "the following of Adam [e]," between regeneration and the imitation of Christ. He quoted the Punic Christians' language, which spoke of Baptism by the name of *Salvation* [f]; assumed infant baptism as a principle, and argued back from it to an inherited sinfulness [g]; refuted the fallacious distinction drawn by Pelagians, between "life eternal" for which baptism was not requisite, and a "kingdom of heaven" to which it admitted [h]; denounced the Pelagian system as a novelty [i]; and insisted on the need of *real* "grace," not given in consequence of pre-existing merits, but given to originate true goodness, such as could not be produced by the old Law, which supplied no spirit of help, awoke no filial devotion [j], and was in fact the "littera occidens."

In the East, this year, we find Maruthas, who had already done good service in Persia, but had unhappily taken part

---

[b] Serm. 169, 174, 176.

[c] De Pecc. Meritis; De Spiritu et litterâ; Ep. 140.

[d] Serm. 174. 7. "Christ," he says, "must be recognized as *a Jesus* for baptized infants."

[e] De Pecc. Mer. i. 9.

[f] Ibid. i. 34. They also called the Holy Eucharist *Life*.

[g] Ibid. i. 39, 63.

[h] Ibid. i. 58.

[i] Ibid. iii. 12.

[j] De Sp. et Litt. 4, 11, 16, 20, 22 (in this section he repeats his *Da quod jubes*), 26, 32, 42, 45, &c. In this invaluable treatise on Justification S. Augustine strongly asserts free-will.

with S. Chrysostom's enemies, again sent as an embassy to Persia, and convincing the king, Isdigerdes, of the impostures of the Magian priesthood[k]. On October 15, Chrysostom's worst enemy, Theophilus, closed his episcopate of twenty-seven years: a melancholy instance of great powers rendered baneful to the Church by a worldly spirit and a violent temper. He was succeeded by his nephew Cyril.

In the next year, 413, the Burgundians, settled on the Rhone, chose "the God of the Romans" for their protector against the Huns, and put themselves under the care of a Gallican bishop, who instructed them for a week, baptized them, and thus secured a large body of barbarians to Catholicism[l]. The miseries which the Roman empire was suffering from Northern invaders were laid by the Pagans, as usual, at the door of Christianity; and Augustine was led by his "zeal for God's house against the Gentiles' blasphemies" to begin his great work, *De Civitate Dei.* He was also employed about this time in refuting a species of Antinomianism, which regarded orthodoxy without obedience as sufficient for salvation[m]. Pelagius was corresponding with the noble Roman virgin Demetrias, and insinuating his heresy by telling her that she inherited earthly honours, but could of herself acquire spiritual[n]. Augustine, in June 413, preached in the great church of Carthage on the true grounds of Infant Baptism, quoting S. Cyprian's lucid statement of the truth[o].

Eighty-five years had passed away in 414 since the exile of S. Eustathius. Instead of the profligate Porphyrius, a truly pious prelate named Alexander now sat on the throne of Antioch. His gentle and earnest character prevailed with the Eustathian remnant, and effected the close of the

[k] Soc. vii. 8.

[l] Soc. vii. 30.

[m] In his De Fide et Operibus. These persons against whom he wrote might be called Solifidians.

[n] S. Aug., tom. ii. 1107; Ep. Pel., c. 11. "Spirituales divitias nullus tibi præter te conferre potest. In his ergo jure laudanda—quæ nisi *ex te* et in te esse non possunt."

[o] Serm. 294. Cyp. Ep. 64.

long schism. He visited their church at the head of his own clergy and laity; the two bodies celebrated their reunion by psalmody, and proceeded together in one majestic stream[p] to the new cathedral. Thus, at last, the Church of Antioch attained that blessing of peace, which the Alexandrian synod of 362 had desired for it in vain. The good patriarch also gave token of his spirit by placing S. Chrysostom's name in the diptychs; whereupon he received the brotherly communion of Innocent, who took pleasure in supporting the claim of "S. Peter's Eastern see" to jurisdiction over Cyprus, and to a control over episcopal consecrations throughout the Eastern "diocese."

The power of the see of Alexandria, within its own jurisdiction, was very great[q]. Theophilus had stretched it to the uttermost; and Cyril, on first attaining the lofty seat of S. Athanasius, appears to have suffered morally by the elevation. Like his uncle, he was hostile to S. Chrysostom's memory, and, in consequence, was out of communion with the West. The evil of his uncle's example hung about him for some time, obscuring the nobleness which was to shine out afterwards. He desired above all things the ascendancy of the Church; as to the means of obtaining it, he had fewer scruples than became a minister of Him who rebuked the attack on Malchus. He closed the Novatian church, took away its sacred ornaments, and deprived its bishop of his property. The Jews of Alexandria—a powerful body during many centuries—had procured the disgrace and punishment of Hierax, an admirer of Cyril's sermons. Cyril, naturally indignant, menaced the chief of their community; the Jews' revenge was to raise a cry at midnight, "The church of S. Alexander is on fire!" and to massacre those Christians who rushed out to save their church. Cyril appears to have made up his mind that

[p] Theodoret, v. 35, compares it to the Orontes.

[q] Synesius wrote to Theophilus that his pleasure and his duty were to take for a law any mandate from that throne; Ep. 67. Socrates, vii. 11, speaks of the bishops of Rome and Alexandria as resembling princes.

the Christians must right themselves, without expecting justice from the præfect Orestes; and he organized at daybreak a force composed for the most part of the fraternity of Parabolani, so called from *venturing* their lives in attendance on the sick[r]. Their energies were now unhappily diverted from charitable self-devotion to violence in defence of the Church; they attacked the synagogues, expelled the Jews from Alexandria[s], and treated their property as rightful spoil. Orestes, exasperated by this hasty and lawless vengeance, would not listen to the explanations which Cyril offered; and the archbishop, after vainly holding out the Gospel-book[t] to enforce his attempts at a reconciliation, gave up all hopes of peace. Five hundred monks of Nitria, inflamed by a furious partisanship, entered the city and reviled the præfect as a pagan. "I am a Christian," he exclaimed; "Atticus of Constantinople baptized me." A monk named Ammonius disproved his own Christianity by throwing a stone at the præfect, which inflicted a ghastly wound. He was seized, and expired under tortures; but Cyril so miserably forgot himself as to call this ruffian an "admirable" martyr,—a proceeding of which he was speedily ashamed. Then followed a yet darker tragedy. Hypatia was supposed to have embittered Orestes against Cyril; and some fiery zealots, headed by a reader of the Church, named Peter, dragged her to the Cæsareum, and surpassed all the horrors that it had ever witnessed by stripping their victim, killing her with potsherds, and tearing her limb from limb. Cyril was no party to this hideous deed[u], but it was the work of men whose passions he had

---

[r] Their services were especially called forth in time of plague. (See Euseb. vii. 22.) Probably their appellation was suggested by *παραβολευσάμενος τῇ ψυχῇ*, Phil. ii. 30. See Bingham, b. iii. c. 9.

[s] Dean Milman says, (Lat. Chr. i. 147,) "No doubt not without much bloodshed." Socrates, vii. 13, makes no such remark.

[t] Soc. vii. 13.

[u] I infer from Dean Milman's language about Cyril's "barbarities," that he finds Cyril guilty of the murder. "That Cyril had any share in this atrocity," says Canon Robertson, i. 401, "appears to be an unsupported

originally called out. Had there been no onslaught on the synagogues, there would doubtless have been no murder of Hypatia.

A new scene now opened in the Pelagian controversy. Augustine was visited by a young Spanish priest, named Orosius[x], who came to consult him about Priscillianism and Origenism[y]. After replying to his questions[z], Augustine sent him "to learn the fear of the Lord at the feet of Jerome." He also sent by Orosius two letters to Jerome on the difficulties connected with original sin, and on the relative importance of different sins[a]. Jerome had already begun to write against Pelagianism, attacking[b] some "definitions" in which Cœlestius had cast the heresy into a hard dialectical form[c]; and he was employed on a larger treatise, a dialogue between a Pelagian and a Catholic[d], in which he discussed Pelagius' "Testimonies," and exposed the unreal sense in which Pelagians spoke of "grace," meaning thereby the natural powers of the will. He welcomed Orosius at Bethlehem. The "poor unknown foreigner," as he calls himself, was summoned in July, 415, to attend a diocesan synod at Jerusalem. The aged bishop John bade him sit down among the presbyters, and tell all that he knew of Pelagius and Cœlestius. He answered, "Cœlestius tried to

---

calumny." Socrates, vii. 15, says that the murder "brought no small disgrace on Cyril and the Church of Alexandria." But nobody would say that this Church was guilty of the deed.

[x] In Ep. 166 Augustine calls him "a religious young man, his fellow-presbyter in dignity, of quick intellect, ready in speech, and ardently longing to be a vessel of profit in the Lord's house."

[y] See his Consultatio, tom. viii. 665. "Ad te," he says, "per Deum missus sum." [z] Ad Oros., tom. viii. 669. [a] Ep. 166, 167.

[b] Ep. 132, ad Ctesiph.

[c] See S. Aug. de Perf. Justitiæ, written soon after in reply to these same "ratiocinations." The first of these was, substantially, "if sin is avoidable, man can be sinless: if not, it is not sin." Another asked, "whether sin were natural or accidental?" another, "whether man *ought* to be without sin?" another, "how the doctrine that man could not be without sin was clear of the charge of Manicheism?"

[d] It is in this work that he speaks of the clergy as wearing white at Holy Communion.

creep into the priesthood, but was accused, heard, and condemned by many bishops at Carthage. Augustine is now engaged, at the request of two of Pelagius' disciples[e], in making a full answer to a treatise by Pelagius. But I have here a letter written by him to a Sicilian[f], in which he exposes several opinions of the heretics." "Read it," said the priests. Orosius did so; whereupon John introduced Pelagius before the assembly. The priests asked him whether he owned these opinions. "What is Augustine to me?" asked Pelagius. They all exclaimed, "You ought to be excommunicated if you revile the prop of African Church unity." The bishop interposed, bidding Pelagius to take a seat, and observing, "*I* am Augustine here." "If you represent him," said the bold Spaniard, "follow his sentiments:" and he taxed Pelagius with maintaining that a man might, if he chose, easily be sinless. "I cannot deny," said Pelagius, "that I did and do say this." "Well," said Orosius, "this is that which the African synod condemned, which Augustine has opposed, which Jerome in a recent letter has denounced, and is now confuting in his 'Dialogue.'" "Do you appear," asked John, "as the accuser of Pelagius?" "No; I am informing you of the judgment of your brethren. I am a son of the Catholic Church; do not ask me, father, to put myself forward as a doctor, but hear what prelates whom the whole Church honours have pronounced." Pelagius was led to explain his language, so far as to anathematize[g] the proposition that man could become perfect *without God's aid;* a phrase, as he used it, vague and unsatisfactory. "Do you," asked John, turning to Orosius, "object to this?" "Of course not; I have been urging the necessity of God's aid, against

---

[e] Timasius and James. This work of S. Aug., de Naturâ et Gratiâ, (tom. viii. 247,) reclaimed these two young men, who cordially acknowledged its "healing" effect. Aug. Ep. 168.

[f] Ep. 157, to Hilary, who had consulted him as to six propositions, rife among the Pelagians of Sicily, on the possibility of sinlessness, the duty of selling all one's property in order to win heaven, &c.

[g] De Gest. Pel. 37.

the views of the heretics." But Orosius, who spoke no Greek, had been at a disadvantage by having a bad interpreter, and insisted that the heresy was Latin in origin, and should be dealt with by Latin judges; and he carried his point. The conference ended with a resolution to refer the case to Innocent; Pelagius was ordered for the time to keep silence, Orosius to treat the bishop with respect. In September, when the dedication of the cathedral was commemorated, Orosius went to visit John, and was repulsed as a "blasphemer." "I heard you say that not even with God's aid can a man be without sin." Orosius protested that he had never said so, and wrote a pamphlet in his own defence. Three months passed away; and in December fourteen bishops assembled at Diospolis or Lydda, to consider a memorial against Pelagianism, presented by two Gallican bishops, Heros and Lazarus, who had been driven from the sees of Arles and Aix[h]. They were unable to attend in person; Orosius was absent; and Pelagius had to deal with the Eastern bishops only. He brought forward several letters which he had received from bishops, including one which Augustine had written to him two years before, and which combined some affectionate expressions with an implied warning against self-reliance[i]. Various propositions ascribed to him were read from the memorial, on which he made comments. The first was, that no one could be sinless unless he had the knowledge of the law. "Have you put forth this, Pelagius?" "Yes," he answered, "but not in the sense alleged. I mean that he who has knowledge is aided to avoid sin[k]." The Council approved of this. "Next," he was asked, "Have you said, All are ruled by free-will?" "Yes: God assists the will." "Have you said, The righteous have no evil thoughts?" "No; I said we ought to study to have none."

---

[h] De Gest. Pel. 2.

[i] Ep. 146. "Retribuat tibi Dominus bona *quibus* semper sis bonus . . . . ores pro me quo talis à *Domino* fiam."

[k] See the remarks of S. Augustine on this, De Gest. Pel. 3.

"Have you said, The kingdom of heaven was promised in the Old Testament?" The phrase being ambiguous, he explained it by quoting Dan. vii. 18. He was questioned about declarations of possible sinlessness, and about language which directly encouraged self-righteousness; he answered that he had been speaking, in the one passage, of men who, having been converted, could by their own labour and "God's grace[l]" be free from sin; that the other passage was none of his, and that he would condemn it, not as heresy, but as folly. The propositions of Cœlestius, condemned at Carthage, were read to him; five he disowned and anathematized; two, as to sinlessness, he explained. A statement that the Church on earth was spotless, he explained as referring to baptism; other statements, as that grace consisted in free-will, or in law and doctrine, that grace was given according to man's merits, that conquest of sin was not due to grace, and that the need of grace would be the negation of free-will, he anathematized[m]. Upon this the Council pronounced him to be orthodox, but in doing so condemned the errors which, with more or less of disingenuousness, he had modified or disclaimed[n].

The original parentage of his theory has been traced by an ancient writer[o] to Theodore of Mopsuestia. There is no doubt that this remarkable man, who anticipated in many points the Rationalism of modern times[p], was natu-

[l] According to Petavius, Pelagius allowed "grace" in six senses: 1. Nature with free-will; 2. Remission of sins; 3. Christ's doctrine and law; 4. Inward illumination; 5. Baptismal adoption; 6. Eternal life. See De Gest. 47, Ep. 179.

[m] On the whole he condemned fifteen propositions.

[n] Jerome, Ep. 143, speaks of "that wretched synod of Diospolis."

[o] Marius Mercator.

[p] See Mansi, ix. 203 seq., for specimens of his theology, condemned by the fifth General Council in 553. He called it madness to say that God was born of the Virgin; his Christ was a man whom the Son of God united to Himself, in whom Godhead dwelt, "not by essence, but by good-will," and who was rendered spotless by the Spirit. The 22nd Psalm was not, in his view, Messianic; the book of Job was a *Pagan* forgery; the Song was carnal and offensive. "My Lord and my God" was not addressed to Christ, &c.

rally attracted by, if he did not in the first instance suggest, a view which made Christianity less supernatural. He entered into controversy against Jerome, (whom by some mistake he called Haram,) whom he charged with bringing in a new heresy from the West. In some respects he caricatured the Catholic doctrine, as when he said that it made Christ Himself a partaker in sin, because He assumed our manhood. In others he described it accurately enough, as when he said that new-born infants were regarded as inheriting "a sinful nature."

Pelagius contiuued at Jerusalem, and circulated a letter which represented the late synod as having sanctioned the position that a man might, if he chose, *easily* be without sin and keep the commandments[q]. Here "easily" was inserted, and "by God's grace" omitted. Instead of exhibitiug the acts of the synod, he sent to Augustine a defence[r] which gave a false account of it; and he composed a treatise on free-will, in which he maintained that men were aided by God neither in "willing" nor in "working," but simply by receiving from Him a natural capacity to will and to work[s]. The really unchristian uature of his theology was here once for all self-exposed.

Early in 416 Orosius returned to Africa, with letters from Heros and Lazarus. A Council of sixty-seven bishops at Carthage condemned the chief Pelagian errors, and wrote to Innocent on the subject[t]. The heretics, they urged, were leaving no place for the grace of God, were denying that which alone could be called Christian grace: "If we in giving benediction say over our people, 'Grant them, O Lord, to be strengthened with might by Thy Spirit,' they pretend that we deny free-will." It might be, they said, that Pelagius or Cœlestius had denied this or that error; but even in that case, the spread of heresy made it needful to anathematize all who asserted the sufficiency of unaided nature, and denied the salvation of infants to

q De Gest. Pel. 54.
r Ep. 179; De Gest. Pel. 57.
s S. Aug. de Grat. Chr. 6.
t Ep. 175.

come through Christian baptism. Soon afterwards a Numidian Council met at Milevum, and similarly addressed the Pope[u]. All our Christian life, they said, would be subverted by the errors, that God's aid against sin was not to be prayed for, and that the Sacrament of Christian grace did not benefit infants for the attainment of life eternal. Augustine and four other bishops wrote as individuals to Innocent[x], dwelling on the illusory use of "grace" by which Pelagius had deceived the Easterns; insisting that "grace" was not nature, but that whereby nature was saved; and describing the heretics as virtually telling their Maker, "Thou madest us men, but we have made ourselves just." They sent to Rome that treatise of Pelagius to which Augustine's work on "Nature and Grace" had been a reply. Augustine also wrote to bishop John[y], exhorting him to examine the real meaning of Pelagian "grace," and requesting a true copy of the acts of the recent synod. An attack was made by some ruffians on Jerome's monastery, and a deacon was slain, while Jerome himself with difficulty escaped. Innoceut, in a letter to John, implies that Pelagians were the authors of this outrage.

Innocent wrote this year a letter to Decentius, an Umbrian bishop, from which we learn something as to the ritual of the Roman Church, which he derived unhesitatingly from S. Peter. The kiss of peace was not given until after the consecration, in order to express the people's consent to it. The celebration in the cathedral being over, a portion of the Eucharist, called "the leaven[z]," was sent round to all the city churches in token of unity. On Friday and Saturday there was a fast, and no celebration. Priests might anoint the baptized on the crown of the

[u] Ep. 176. [x] Ep. 177. [y] Ep. 179.

[z] See Neale's Introd. ii. 1062; Martene, de Ant. Eccl. Rit. i. 316. There is a question whether *fermentum* was used in a literal sense, and so implies that the early Roman Church consecrated in leavened bread; or whether it was merely a symbolic name for the Holy Sacrament as the bond of unity.

head with chrism episcopally hallowed; but the "holy seal" on the forehead could only be given by the bishop. This letter is the first patristic document which mentions unction of the sick as a regular Church rite; "being a Sacrament, it must not be administered to penitents."

On Jan. 10, 417, John of Jerusalem died, having held the see forty years, since the death of S. Cyril. On Jan. 27, Innocent wrote to the Africans [a], taking occasion to magnify his own see: "As often as a question of faith is debated, I hold that all our brethren and fellow-bishops ought only to refer to Peter, that is, to the heir of his name and dignity, as you, beloved, have done." "From Peter the episcopate itself, and the whole authority of this name, took its rise." The primacy of Rome had not yet become a supremacy, but Innocent interpreted it as an universal refereeship [b]. "The Fathers ruled that nothing should be brought to a close, even in distant provinces, until this see became aware of it." This was a considerable advance from the position held by Julius. Innocent proceeded to denounce the Pelagians: "Lo, this is the man that took not God for his help [c]." He called it folly to say that infants had eternal life without baptism, and in connection with this quoted John vi. 53; probably referring to infant Communion [d], which was then the general practice. He excommunicated Pelagius and Cœlestius, with all their supporters, until they should return from the snares of the devil. "Be they absent from the courts of the Lord!" The true doctrine he stated very exactly. Man had mis-

---

[a] S. Aug. Epp. 181, 182.

[b] Over the West he did claim a virtual supremacy, on the unhistoric ground that the founders of all the Western Churches had been consecrated at Rome.

[c] He evidently loved the Psalter, "throughout the whole" of which, he says, "David proclaims the need of grace;" whereas the new heretics set aside the responsive psalmody.

[d] Theodore had said that the believers in original sin considered both baptism and the Eucharist to be the means of salvation to infants. See, too, S. Aug. de Pecc. Mer. i. 26.

used his freedom, had fallen, and would have been ruined for ever, had not Christ by His grace raised him up. "Through the cleansing of a new regeneration, Christ washed away man's former guilt in the laver of His baptism; and while establishing his condition, that he might walk on more erect and stedfast, yet denied not His grace for the time to come[e]." The Pope also wrote to the five bishops, observing that he could not fully rely on the records of the Council of Diospolis, as far as he had seen them, but that even on their showing, Pelagius had been sophistical and evasive; that he had read through Pelagius' book, and found "many blasphemies, with nothing that he could approve."

This great prelate, who had done less for his see by mere loftiness of claim than by standing up for a righteous sufferer, and loyally guarding an imperilled faith, died on March 12, 417, and was succeeded by a Greek named Zosimus.

---

[e] On the need of watchfulness after baptism, see S. Aug. Serm. 57. 9; de Pecc. Mer. i. 25, 69.

CHAPTER XI.

From the Death of Pope Innocent to the Semi-Pelagian Controversy.

"Nil jucundum, nil amœnum,
Nil salubre, nil serenum,
Nihil dulce, nihil plenum,
Nisi Tuâ gratiâ."

ADAM OF S. VICTOR.

INNOCENT had not been able to procure the vindication of S. Chrysostom's memory at Constantinople. But soon after his death, Atticus, who had resisted his exhortations and those of Alexander, yielded to the popular feeling[a], and to the advice of Theodosius, who thought that "for peace and unity there would be no harm in writing a dead man's name on a diptych." Atticus excused himself for this compliance in a letter to Cyril, in which he observed that, in these Eucharistic commemorations, laymen as well as bishops were included. The nephew of Theophilus was not likely to be thus appeased; and he extracted from the messengers of Atticus the confession that Chrysostom was now commemorated as a bishop. In his view, Chrysostom was simply a man whose crimes had forfeited the episcopate; and he called upon Atticus to "expunge from the sacerdotal catalogue the name of one who was no minister," distinctly intimating that unless he resolved to uphold the authority of the Council of the Oak, and to abandon to their perversity "the few" who clamoured for Chrysostom's name, he would forfeit the communion of the patriarchate of Alexandria[b].

S. Augustine had now finished his great work on the Trinity, and his commentary on S. John's Gospel. When

---

[a] Socrates, vii. 25, says that he hoped to win back the Joannites, who held separate congregations.

[b] See the letters of Atticus and Cyril among the latter's works.

he received the records of Diospolis, he exposed the chicaneries of Pelagius in a narrative *De Gestis Pelagii.* Paulinus of Nola had been very intimate with the heresiarch, and was imperfectly informed on the doctrinal question; Augustine therefore wrote to him on the subject of grace, insisting that it could not be the reward of man's previous deservings[c]. In this letter he put forth a strong view as to predestination. In conjunction with his friend Alypius, he addressed Juliana[d], the mother of Demetrias, on the errors in Pelagius' epistle to the latter. "Would the virgin of Christ learn to be ungrateful to God before her bliss was full, esteem her sanctity her own work, and glory in aught but Him, in whom alone a Christian could glory?" And while thus doing battle with heresy, Augustine kept in view the wild excesses of an incorrigible schism. The Donatist temper had always bred a fierce enthusiasm, and some of the fanatics renewed the old frenzy of suicide. Augustine, in a treatise[e] addressed to Boniface, then tribune in Africa, defended the penal laws against Donatism as having been productive of much good.

Cœlestius, who had procured priest's orders at Ephesus, now came to Rome on the pretext of prosecuting his appeal. He gave in a paper[f] containing his belief, in which, after dwelling at length on points of doctrine "as to which no one had questioned him," he admitted that infants ought to be baptized for remission of sins, quoting John iii. 5; but he explained that in saying this he was not to be understood as admitting the transmission of sin. Sin, he contended, was not born with men, but subsequently committed by them; it was an offence of the will, not of nature. It appears, then, that he was adopting Church language in an unreal sense, and by refusing to acknowledge an inborn taint, was leaving actual sin a more baffling mystery than ever. However, he promised to be

---

[c] Ep. 186.
[d] Ep. 188.
[e] Ep. 185; comp. Ep. 93.
[f] De Pecc. Orig. 5, 26.

guided by the apostolical judgment of Rome. Zosimus held a Council of bishops and clergy in the church of S. Clement[g]; Cœlestius was summoned and examined[h]; and the Pope showed his own perplexity by exhorting him, somewhat in the style of Constantine's letter to S. Alexander and Arius, to avoid "ensnaring questions and idle controversies which sprang from a morbid curiosity." On the case of Heros and Lazarus he went to work more hastily. He had recently declared Patroclus, who had superseded Heros at Arles[i], to be the head of the Gallican bishops; and he pronounced the excommunication of the two accusers of Pelagius. To the African bishops he wrote an account of what had happened, intimating that those who had any evidence to bring forward against Cœlestius must appear within two months.

Soon after the hearing at S. Clement's, Zosimus received a letter from Praylius, who had succeeded John at Jerusalem, in favour of Pelagius, and at the same time a letter and a confession of faith from Pelagius himself, addressed to Innocent. "I am accused," Pelagius wrote, "of two things; of denying baptism to infants, and promising to some persons the kingdom of heaven apart from Christ's redeeming work; and of insisting so much on man's power to avoid sin by free-will, as to exclude the assistance of God's grace[k]." As to the first point, he had no difficulty in repudiating a charge which he characterized as monstrous: "Who is so little read in the Gospel as even

---

[g] Aug., tom. x. 1719. Zosimus speaks of S. Clement as the disciple of S. Peter, and as a martyr.

[h] Ibid. 1724, Paulini Diaconi Libellus. "Do you condemn all the opinions which Paulinus or common fame have imputed to you?"

[i] The claim of Arles to primacy rested on a legend that S. Trophimus was its first bishop. See Burton, Eccl. Hist. i. 282. The Ballerini reject the story. There was another Trophimus, said to have been sent from Rome to Arles in the third century; see Burton, ii. 349.

[k] Aug. de Grat. Chr. 32. In his de Pecc. Orig. 19, he remarks that Pelagius utterly misstated the first point; that he was accused of denying original sin, and of imagining an "eternal life" apart from the "kingdom of heaven."

casually to say or to think of such a thing[l]?" As to the second point; "Let this letter," he said, "clear me in the eyes of your Blessedness, wherein I say, that for sinning or not sinning we have entire freedom of will, which in all good works is always assisted by Divine aid[m]." He added that all men had free-will, but in Christians only was it aided by grace; that others will be condemned for not using that free-will whereby they might "come to the faith and *merit* the grace of God, whereas Christians will be rewarded for meriting it by a good use of their free-will[n]." His "Confession" is a remarkable specimen of elaborate accuracy on matters irrelevant combined with evasiveness as to the real issue. It dilates on the co-equal Deity of Father, Son, and Spirit; speaks of the Three Divine Persons as Hypostases; condemns impartially the Arian and the Sabellian, the Photinian and the Apollinarian errors; affirms that the Son, by taking perfect Manhood of Mary, Ever-virgin, united in His single Person two entire Substances, without any interchange of their properties, which would produce in fact the annihilation of Godhead and of Manhood, and the substitution of something distinct from both; a conclusion "which no heresy has ever yet ventured to propound." Then comes a long paragraph on the actual working of the Personal union; the sufferings of Christ are pronounced to have been really endured, but only by His Manhood, the Godhead remaining impassible[o]. At length, after a statement about the

---

[l] De Pecc. Or. 20. A striking evidence of the universality of infant baptism. He adds, "Who is so impious as to forbid infants to be *baptized and born again in Christ*, and thus to wish to exclude them from the kingdom of heaven?" See also c. Jul. iii. 11.

[m] De Grat. Chr. 33.

[n] De Grat. Chr. 33, 34. S. Augustine observes, 1. "What does he mean by grace? The Christian law and doctrine." But were it otherwise, 2. To make grace, in whatever sense the word is used, a reward of free-will, is to make it no more grace.

[o] This "Confession" is in fact a most valuable document in regard to the doctrine of the Incarnation. It resembles the Athanasian Creed still more closely than does the confession of Braga mentioned above. Augustine, tom. x. 1716, from an old manuscript in the Vatican.

Resurrection, it becomes necessary to face the point on which the question turns, and Pelagius confesses One Baptism, which is to be administered in the same words to infants and to adults, and after which men's lapses may be repaired by penitence; and freedom of will, whereby men are always capable of sinning[p], or, by that Divine help which they always need, of avoiding sin. After this significantly brief and ambiguous statement, Pelagius concluded by saying, "This, most blessed Pope, is the faith which we have learned in the Catholic Church. If in this statement we have by chance used any inaccurate or incautious expression, we desire to be set right by you, who hold both the faith and the see of Peter."

The success of this document is astonishing. Zosimus, and other "holy men who were present" when it was read, agreed in thinking it altogether satisfactory[q]. Some could hardly restrain their tears at the thought of Pelagius and Cœlestius being defamed, when they were, in fact, so orthodox on the question of grace. The Pope, on Sept. 22, 417, struck a heavy blow at the moral influence of Rome by writing to the African bishops in vindication of Pelagius and Cœlestius[r]. He thought fit to remind his brethren that "the Sacrifice and Pontiff who brought salvation to the whole world" had Himself been calumniated; he pronounced a severe censure on Heros and Lazarus, and on the young men James and Timasius, whom Augustine had converted from Pelagianism, for not appearing to make good their charges; and he doubted not that a perusal of the letter and "Confession" would convince the Africans of the orthodoxy of Pelagius.

Aurelius of Carthage and his brethren replied to the

---

[p] This he says in opposition to Jovinian. "To say that man *cannot avoid* sin, is Manicheism."

[q] Dean Milman (Lat. Chr. i. 123) represents the Roman synod as convinced by the mere letter of Praylius. But the document that was "read with joy" was that of Pelagius, which he had mentioned before.

[r] Aug., tom. x. 1721.

Pope's first letter, in behalf of Cœlestius, by desiring him to pause until he could receive fuller information; and Paulinus of Milan wrote to Zosimus on Nov. 8, declining to attend at Rome in order to prosecute a matter which had passed out of his hands, and claiming Pope Innocent, S. Gregory Nazianzen, S. Ambrose, and especially S. Cyprian[s], as opposed to Pelagius. About the same time an African Council showed how freely it could deal, in S. Cyprian's own spirit, with a Pope whom it considered to have lost his way. "We ordain," said the bishops, 214 in number, "that the sentence issued by the venerable bishop Innocent from the see of the most blessed Apostle Peter against Pelagius and Cœlestius shall stand firm, until they explicitly confess that through Christ our Lord we are in every action *assisted, by God's grace, not only to know, but also to do righteousness;* so that without it we can neither have, speak, think, or do aught that belongs to true and holy piety[t]."

Such was the language held by the Church of Africa in a letter formally addressed to a Pope. He replied on March 21, 418, with a magniloquent, and in fact audacious, assertion of his prerogatives[u], followed up by a passage which betrayed his consciousness of a questionable position. "We have taken no new step since we received your letters, but have left everything in its former state." On the 30th of April the men whom Zosimus had pronounced innocent were excluded from Rome, as authors of impiety,

---

[s] Aug., tom. x. 1724. "Pelagius has against him those very infants for whom he ought to feel, if he will not feel for himself; who, in the Martyr's words," (Cyp. Ep. 64,) "receive remission of *non propria sed aliena peccata.*"

[t] Aug., tom. x. 1723, from Prosper, in Collat. 15. They also reminded Zosimus that Innocent had expressed an opinion about the acts of Diospolis, de Pecc. Orig. 9.

[u] "The tradition of the Fathers has ascribed to the Apostolic See so great an authority, that no one can dare to dispute its judgment......ut nullus de nostrâ possit retractare sententiâ...We make this concession to your Fraternity,...non quia quid deberet fieri nesciremus." His deeds refute his words.

by a rescript of Honorius, dated from his palace at Ravenna. The Emperor pronounced on two points of doctrine: God, he said[x], was not so unloving as to create man mortal, and "the whole authority of the Catholic law testified" that Adam in his fall became "the porch of perdition to his posterity."

On the next day, May 1, 418, a great Council of the African Church was held at Carthage. Nine doctrinal canons were enacted, which in substance are as follows[y].

1. Anathema to him who says, Adam was by nature mortal. 2. Anathema[z] to him who rejects infant baptism, or who admits that infants should be baptized for remission of sins, but denies that they derive from Adam any original guilt which must be cleansed by the laver of regeneration; on which theory, the form of "Baptism for remission of sins" is in their case false. The text Rom. v. 12 is to be taken in the Catholic sense, as affirming origiual sin. Infants void of actual sin are said with truth to be baptized for remission of sins, in order that what they have derived by generation may be cleansed by regeneration. 3. Anathema to him who asserts some place of bliss, either in the Kingdom or out of it, for infants dying unbaptized. 4. Anathema to him that denies God's grace to avail prospectively, as aiding us against sin. 5. Anathema to him that explains Christian grace as merely a

---

[x] Aug., tom. x. 1727. The feeble Honorius was doubtless in this case the instrument of advisers who supported the African Church. He is made to express great indignation at the news which had reached "the ears of our Clemency, that within our most holy city the pestilent virus has lodged itself in certain minds," &c.

[y] Some have thought that these decrees were first drawn up at an earlier synod, e.g. at the Council of Milevum, in 416. Petavius, on Pelagian Heresy, ch. i., thinks this a mistake. So the Benedictines. Fleury supposes that the decrees of the Council of Nov. 417 were confirmed by that of May 418.

[z] This is the 110th canon of the African code, received by East and West. All former African canons which had been approved of were in 418 taken into this collection. This canon, and one or two others of this Council, seem referred to in a Greek version of a canon on baptism. Goar's Euchologion, p. 334.

revelation of our duty. 6. Anathema to him who says that obedience is possible without grace, and only becomes easy by means of it. 7. Anathema to him that explains 1 John i. 8 as a mere expression of humility. 8, 9. Anathema to him who explains "Forgive us our trespasses" as not said in literal truth by holy men for themselves.

About this time Germanus, a provincial governor in Gaul, who had quarrelled with Amator, bishop of Auxerre, about a Pagan custom to which he was addicted[a], and for which the prelate had reproved him, was suddenly seized in church by Amator, who gave him the tonsure[b] and the diaconate, and presented him to the people as his destined successor. On Amator's death, which speedily followed this strange ordination, Germain, as he is commonly called, was consecrated bishop, July 7, 418. Forthwith, like Thomas of Canterbury, Germain became another man, and adopted at once the whole extent of ascetic piety.

Zosimus became aware that he had committed the see of S. Peter to a great mistake. Before the acts of the "plenary council" of Africa[c] reached Rome, he began to see how strong was the feeling of the orthodox at Rome[d] against the men whom he had hastily acquitted. The imperial rescript was also a fact of great significance. He summoned Cœlestius to appear again before him; but Cœlestius declined to submit to a second examination[e], and quitted Rome. Thereupon the Pope, in a long epistle called *Tractoria*[f], condemned Pelagius and Cœlestius, assigning to them, in case they recanted, the position of penitents[g],

---

[a] He used to hang the heads of the animals which he slew in hunting upon a pear-tree in the middle of the city. Amator at length caused the tree—evidently one which had been honoured by the Pagans—to be cut down; and the "duke" Germanus threatened his life in consequence.

[b] This *old* tonsure consisted simply in wearing the hair short; long hair being a mark of secularity.

[c] Aug. Ep. 215. [d] De Pecc. Orig. 9. [e] C. Duas Ep. Pel. ii. 5.

[f] Mar. Merc. in Aug., tom. x. 1689.

[g] De Pecc. Orig. 25. "He could not permanently deceive *that see*;" ib. 24.

and entering at length on the whole theology of redemption. All the redeemed, he taught[h], had previously been captives; every one, until he was baptized, was held bound by the "handwriting" against us, derived from Adam. In every condition of human existence, Christ's baptism had the same fulness in a *real* remission of sins. He was equally emphatic on the need of grace. This letter was circulated throughout Christendom, and accepted by bishops of the East and West. In Italy it was rejected by nineteen prelates[i], the chief of whom was Julian, bishop of Œculanum in Campania. He became thenceforward the representative of Pelagianism[k]. He was little more than thirty years old; Augustine had been a friend of his father, a pious bishop named Memor, to whom, in a letter of 408 or 409, he had spoken affectionately of Julian as "his beloved son and fellow-deacon[l]." As a controversialist, he appeared to S. Augustine an embodiment of the faults of youth; fiery, confident, voluble, proud of his argumentative power and his secular learning[m]. But whatever were his faults and errors, he had a kind and generous heart[n]. In conjunction with his adherents he addressed the Pope, giving an account of his faith, and affirming "one baptism, really necessary for all ages," as the means of attaining to pardon and "the kingdom of heaven." All God's laws, they said, could be fulfilled "by the grace of Christ, which assisted every good act, and by free-will." "Grace would neither follow the rebellious nor forsake the obedient." "We are sinners, not because we cannot help it, but be-

---

[h] Aug. Ep. 190. 23.

[i] C. Duas Ep. Pel. i. 3. Sixtus, a priest of Rome, whom the Pelagians had boasted of as an adherent, Aug. Ep. 191, was the first to anathematize them; Ep. 194.

[k] Ven. Bede called him "a very accomplished rhetorician, and the keenest assailant of the grace of God after Pelagius." Pelagius disappears from history after 418.

[l] Ep. 101. Mercator attacks Julian grossly as no true son of Memor.

[m] See Aug. c. Jul. i. 1, 2; ii. 30; i. 12; Op. imp. c. Jul. ii. 36.

[n] Aug., tom. x. 1737. Gennadius says, "Julian in time of famine and want distributed alms to the poor," &c.

cause we are neglectful." "Our nature, as made by God, is good and perfect." They rejected the propositions, that any man could avoid sin without God's grace; that baptism was superfluous for infants; that mankind did not die through Adam, nor rise again through Christ. They declined to condemn Pelagius and Cœlestius in their absence; and cited a passage from S. Chrysostom to the effect that infants were not stained by *sins*. The practical point in their document was their appeal to a General Council[o]. They were successfully opposed on this point by Augustine and the Count Valerius, on the ground that a competent episcopal judgment[p] had already decided the cause. Julian and his friends were deposed[q] by Zosimus; but he circulated through Italy another letter to the Pope, in which he rejected some of the propositions of Cœlestius[r], in language which was charged with equivocation.

Augustine now employed himself in writing treatises[s] on the real meaning of "grace" as used by Pelagius, and on the inconsistency of his language at Diospolis with that of his work on Free-will[t]. He insisted that the controversy was not a verbal or superficial one, but essentially connected with the heart of Christianity[u]. Many questions there were which did not touch the faith: e.g. "where and what was Paradise? where are Enoch and Elijah? why were the antediluvians so long-lived?" But in the question of the two Adams, Christian faith was vitally interested[x]; depending as it did for its very existence on that Mediation which

---

[o] Aug., tom. x. 1732—1736. [p] C. Jul. iii. 5; C. Duas Ep. Pel. iv. 34.

[q] C. Jul. i. 13. [r] Aug., tom. x. 1738. (Mar. Merc.)

[s] De Gratiâ Christi; De Pecc. Originali.

[t] At Diospolis he had condemned the dictum, "Infants are born in Adam's unfallen state." In his book on Free-will he said, "Evil does not spring up with us; when we are born, there is nothing in us but what God created."

[u] De Pecc. Or. 26.

[x] On the memorable words, "*In horum duorum hominum causâ propriè fides Christiana consistit*," De Pecc. Or. 28; compare Olshausen on Rom. v. 12, and Trench on S. Augustine, p. 122 seq.

was the fountain of all grace[y]. He also wrote to Sixtus, priest of Rome, and afterwards Pope, remarking on the secret spread of Pelagian opinions, and supplying him with arguments against them. In this famous letter[z], he not only went over the ordinary topics as to the divine origination of all good in man, the evidence of original sin from infant baptism, &c., but dwelt with earnestness on a view which he had already resorted to in writing to Paulinus, the theory of an absolute predestination. Pelagians objected, "Can God show favour to one sinner and punish another?" Augustine replied, in substance, All were equally deserving of perdition; all formed the "lump" of punishable sin. God might justly have punished all; but He whose dealings are manifoldly inscrutable was pleased, for reasons of His own, irrespective of any foreseen qualities, to exempt some from the common doom, which He allowed to take its course against the rest. This is that Augustinian Predestinarianism, which is his great distinguishing characteristic among the ancient doctors. We shall hear more of it further on; at present it is enough to say that the peculiar intensity of his mental temperament, acted upon by the controversy with an exaggerated doctrine of free-will, led him, unhappily as we may think, to innovate on the older theology by extreme statements on the other side, and to interpret the balanced and indeterminate language of Scripture on this profound mystery as amounting to a definite and unqualified doctrine of Predestination[a].

A case of great importance, in regard to the relations between Rome and Africa, began in this year. Apiarius of Sicca, a Mauritanian priest, who had been twice excommunicated by his bishop Urbanus for gross offences, appealed to Zosimus, who deputed Faustinus, bishop of

---

[y] Hence the emphasis with which S. Leo, as well as S. Augustine, brings the old dispensation under the working of Christ's grace; insisting that this grace was the salvation of all God's servants from the beginning. De Pecc. Or. 31. Comp. S. Leo, Serm. 23, &c.

[z] Ep. 194.

[a] See Mozley on Predestination, pp. 34, 38, 48, 155.

Potentia, and two priests, to visit Carthage[b]. They arrived, and signified to the African bishops in synod that Zosimus was prepared to excommunicate Urbanus, and that he insisted on the observance of a Nicene canon allowing appeals to Rome, or to the bishops of the province nearest to the appellant's. The canon in fact was that of Sardica; but the African Church was unacquainted with any "Sardican" council, save that assembly at Philippopolis which had usurped the title, and had fraternized with the Donatists[c]. In the Nicene canons no mention of this law about appeals could be discovered by the African bishops[d], and the case was adjourned until after a further inquiry. Meantime Zosimus died, Dec. 26, 418. A contested election followed; some of the clergy elected Eulalius the archdeacon, whose cause was largely supported by the people. The majority of the clergy, however, chose Boniface, a priest of high character, whose modest reluctance was an additional recommendation[e]. Nine bishops consecrated him in the church of S. Marcellus; while Eulalius was consecrated in the Lateran by the bishop of Ostia, whose duty it was to officiate on such occasions. Symmachus, præfect of Rome, influenced Honorius in favour of Eulalius. After an attempt to get the question settled by a council of bishops at Ravenna, Honorius ordered both prelates to leave Rome, (March 15, 419,) and summoned a number of bishops to attend another council. He also expressly commanded that Achilleus, bishop of Spoletum, should officiate in Rome at Easter, and that "the Lateran should be open to none but him." But Eulalius boldly returned to Rome, and took possession of the Lateran, where he celebrated the Easter services; a defiance

---

[b] Cod. Can. Eccl. Afr. 134; Conc. Afric. 101.

[c] See Aug. Ep. 44, on his conference with the Donatist Fortunius. Fleury, xxiv. 6.

[d] The Sardican Council, as the great orthodox Council of the West, had been regarded *at Rome* as a sort of supplement to the Nicene, and hence, apparently, the confusion.

[e] See in Baronius, iii. 488, the petition of the Roman priests to Honorius in favour of Boniface. "Et, quod eum magis ornabat, invitum."

of the government which ruined his cause, procured his expulsion, and established Boniface in the see[f].

On May 25 the African Council met at Carthage. The Nicene canons were being read, when Faustinus requested that the late Pope's instructions might come under consideration. They were found to cite, as Nicene, a canon providing for the case of appeals to Rome. Alypius, who represented the province of Numidia, then said,—" We have written about this already, and assured the bishop of Rome that we will obey any Nicene canons. But it so happens that on examining our Greek copies of those canons, I know not how it was, but we found in them not a word of what has been quoted[g]." He moved that Aurelius should inquire at Constantinople, Alexandria, and Antioch, as to the genuine text of the Nicene canons, and should request the bishop of Rome to do the like. Faustinus, not approving of the turn that matters were taking, suggested that an inquiry by the Pope would answer all purposes. In this opinion, however, the Africans did not concur. They resolved that, besides what Boniface might do, their own primate should ascertain the facts of the case by deputies sent to the East[h]. A few days after, Apiarius submitted to the Council, was restored to communion, and allowed to officiate anywhere but at Sicca. The African messengers procured true copies of the Nicene canons; for instance, the priest Innocent obtained such a copy from Cyril, and the words quoted by the Roman legates were found to be absent. These copies were sent to Rome, Nov. 26, 419.

Cyril had now yielded to the exhortations of Isidore of Pelusium, a pious abbat with whom he corresponded, and

---

[f] Boniface soon afterwards wrote to Honorius, expressing his anxiety for the peace of the Roman Church. Honorius replied by a decree that *none should canvass*, and that neither of two rivals should in future hold the see.

[g] "Ista ibi, nescio quâ ratione, minimè invenimus."

[h] See the letter of this Council to Boniface, in which there is a telling hint as to "pride," referring no doubt to the threat of Zosimus about Urbanus. Cod. Can. 134.

who urged him[i] not to make a perpetual schism in the Church by refusing to commemorate Chrysostom. He placed the name of Chrysostom on his diptychs, and immediately received the communion of Rome.

Honorius banished Julian from Italy, and ordered Aurelius to enforce the abnegation of Pelagianism in Africa[k]. The Pelagians wrote two letters, in which they denounced the doctrine of original sin as Manicheism. Augustine, who had already replied to the calumny that he condemned marriage[l], answered these letters in a treatise addressed to Boniface. He insisted that the Catholics kept the mean between the two extremes of Manicheism and Pelagianism, and that these, although opposites, had points in common against the Church[m].

The last work of Augustine against Donatism was called forth by the wild menace of Gaudentius, a Donatist bishop, that if the penal laws were enforced against him, he would burn himself and his people in their church. Augustine wrote two books against this fanatic; urged the criminality of suicide, which had been deemed lawful by Donatists on the ground of a passage in the Maccabees[n], and concluded with a pathetic appeal,—"Let us agree in holding Catholic charity, in growing up with the wheat, in bearing with the tares unto the end, and in living for ever in the barn[o]!" About this time also he wrote a valuable treatise against a nameless "adversary of the Law and the Prophets," whose work was sold and eagerly read at Carthage[p]. In this, as

---

[i] He writes very plainly, though he honours Cyril as the representative of S. Mark. "Put an end to these dissensions, lest you incur the judgment of God;" Ep. 370.

[k] Aug. Ep. 201.

[l] In the De Nuptiis, &c.

[m] C. Duas Ep. Pel. ii. 2, 3. "Separati opinione diversâ, sed propinqui mente perversâ." They agree, he adds, in opposing Christ's grace, making void His (sacramental) baptism, and dishonouring His Flesh, "sed etiam hæc modis et causis diversis."

[n] 2 Macc. xiv. 41—46; the case of Razis. Augustine says that the books of Maccabees are not on the same footing as the Law and the Prophets. C. Gaud. i. 38.

[o] C. Gaud. ii. 14.

[p] Retract. ii. 58.

in other books, Augustine met the objection, then, as now, frequent on men's lips, that the spirit of the Gospel was in absolute contradiction to that of the Law, by showing that the Gospel also had its severe side, that the Law had the germ of Evangelic teaching, that "the Testament was prefigured in the Old, and the Old was unfolded in the New [q]."

The aged recluse at Bethlehem had written [r] to Alypius and Augustine, warmly congratulating them on their successful labours against "the Cœlestian heresy." This is the last of his extant writings. He died on Sept. 30, 420, doubtless in full Christian peace, although the account of his last moments which suggested the picture of "S. Jerome's last Communion" is found in a work which deserves no credit [s]. His age has been variously stated; according to one reckoning, he was ninety-one,—according to another, only seventy-four. The one conspicuous blot on Jerome's character, a controversial fierceness which his religion could not soothe, and which seldom allowed him to be charitable or just, has led many in modern times to forget his better qualities, and the great services which he rendered to the Church by his unwearied labours in the field of Scripture interpretation.

Maruthas again visited the Persian court in 420. King Isdigerdes was favourably impressed, and Christianity would probably have gained another royal convert [t], but for the impetuous zeal of the bishop Abdas, who destroyed a temple sacred to the worship of fire [u]. The king bade him rebuild it, threatening that if he did not, the churches should be thrown down. He persisted in refusal, and was put to death. Isdigerdes kept his word; the churches were destroyed, and a furious persecution set in, which his successor Vararanes carried out in the spirit of Sapor [x]. It lasted thirty years; one of the chief martyrs was a deacon

---

[q] C. Advers. Leg. i. 35: compare de Catech. Rud. 8; de Util. Cred. 9.
[r] Ep. 143. [s] The De Morte Hieronymi, by the pseudo-Eusebius.
[t] Soc. vii. 8. [u] Theod. v. 39. [x] Soc. vii. 18—21.

named Benjamin, who after being thrown into prison, refused to be released on the condition of promising silence as to his faith. "I cannot forbear to communicate the light I have received. I know the doom of those who hide their talents." This answer not being communicated to the king, Benjamin was released, but a year afterwards was put to extreme tortures, and ultimately impaled for refusing to deny his God. Several Christians fled across the frontier into the Roman Empire. Theodosius would not surrender them, and a war broke out. In September 421 the Persians were defeated, and 7,000 Persian captives would have died of hunger but for the noble-hearted Acacius, bishop of Amida. "Our God," he said to his clergy, "does not want plates and cups;" and he melted down his church-plate to ransom these hapless prisoners, whom he maintained for some time, and then sent them back to Vararanes.

Julian had written against Augustine, and then departed for the East. He denounced the Catholics as Manicheans, claimed the Catholic name for his own sect, "gloried in maintaining the truth which others abandoned[y]," and declared that the God of his opponents was not the God of the Apostles[z]. He reproached Augustine with having called in the aid of persecution, and sneered at the Catholic laity as a clamorous and ignoble mob. Augustine in 421 wrote six books against Julian, in the first of which he claimed SS. Irenæus, Cyprian, Hilary, and Ambrose as maintainers of original sin, and showed that S. Basil and S. Chrysostom[a] were really of one mind with the great doctors of the West. In the second book he adduced the earlier Fathers as against the five objections[b] of Pelagian-

---

[y] Aug. c. Jul. ii. 36. [z] Aug. Op. Imp. i. 50.

[a] e.g. that in his Homily to Neophytes he had only referred to *actual* sin, not to original, (τὰ παιδία βαπτίζομεν, καίτοι ἁμαρτήματα οὐκ ἔχοντα·) and that in a letter to Olympias he had said that Adam by his great sin brought all mankind under a common condemnation. Ep. 3.

[b] These were, 1. If God is our Creator, evil cannot be born with us. 2. If marriage is good, it can produce no evil. 3. If all sins are forgiven in baptism, the children of the regenerate cannot inherit original sin.

ism to the Catholic doctrine of original sin, and took his stand, as fearlessly as did S. Athanasius, on the principle of traditionary orthodoxy.

A question as to the election of Perigenes to the see of Corinth had led to a serious dispute between Rome and Constantinople. Boniface, following the example of his predecessors, had made the exarch of Thessalonica his vicar for Illyricum, without regard to the civil separation of a part of Illyricum from the West. Perigenes had been confirmed as bishop by Bouiface and Rufus of Thessalonica; but the opponents of the election procured from Theodosius a decree, trausferring all ecclesiastical cases in Eastern Illyricum to the jurisdiction of Constantinople. Boniface resisted strenuously, insisting that the vicar of the Apostolic see should retain, on behalf of Rome, full authority throughout all Illyricum; and he called in the support of Honorius, who procured from his nephew the recall of the obnoxious decree. Shortly after this success, on Oct. 25, 422, Boniface I. died, and was succeeded by Cœlestine. Very early in his episcopate Cœlestine received a letter from S. Augustine[c] concerning a case which had given the latter much anxiety. Some years before, wishing to strengthen the Church at Fussala, a stronghold of Donatism on the frontier of his diocese, he had established there a bishopric, and fixed upon a priest who understood Punic, and who might well be consecrated for this important charge. The old primate of Numidia had come to officiate; all was ready, when the bishop-elect suddenly refused to be consecrated; and in the perplexity of the

---

4. If God is just, He cannot condemn "the sins of parents" in children. 5. If our nature is capable of perfect righteousness, it cannot have any natural faults. The third objection was ingeniously devised; the Pelagians wished to turn the tables on the Catholics, who made baptism their stronghold in the argument. S. Augustine replies by the distinction between "guilt," which is abolished by baptism, and "weakness," which is left to be subdued by the baptized. This weakness consists of "vicious" tendencies, which must be restrained from breaking out into positive sin. The fourth objection is met by a reference to the sufferings and death of children, &c.

[c] Ep. 209.

moment, Augustine thought that a young reader named Antony, who had been brought up from a child in the monastery[d] which he had established at Hippo, might be presented to the primate. The result showed the grave imprudence[e] of so hasty an elevation; Antony was soon accused of tyranny and other offences, and enough was proved to induce a council of bishops to remove him from his see, though not from the episcopate. This sentence, he complained, was either too much or too little. "I ought either to have been deposed, or permitted to retain my see." He persuaded the primate to write in his favour to Boniface, who replied that he ought to be restored "if his account were correct." The triumphant Antony talked of enforcing this expression of the Pope's opinion by a military force; Augustine therefore entreated Cœlestine with pathetic earnestness[f], not to impose a bad bishop on Fussala, or new temptations on one whom he must still love as a son in Christ. Cœlestine, it seems, had no such purpose; and Antony never regained Fussala.

In the case of Apiarius, this pontiff was less moderate. Discontented, as it would seem, with the position in which he was left by the lenient sentence of the Council of Carthage, Apiarius visited Rome, and secured the favour of Cœlestine, who sent a priest named Leo to Africa, charged with a letter which expressed his satisfaction in regard to the character of the appellant. Faustinus, accompanied by Apiarius, again presented himself before the African hierarchy. Three days were spent in a thorough examination of the charges against Apiarius[g]. Faustinus

---

[d] Like Eusebius of Vercellæ, he organized his clergy on a monastic plan under his own roof. No member of this community retained any property of his own; Serm. 356.

[e] S. Augustine frankly owns that his mistake might be justly complained of.

[f] "By the Blood of Christ, by the memory of Peter, who exhorted prelates not to lord it by force over their brethren." He was so distressed that he even thought of resigning the episcopate. Ep. 209.

[g] Cod. Can. 138; Conc. Afr. 105.

exhibited a vexatious partiality, treating Apiarius as a man whom the judgment of Rome had proved to be innocent. Apiarius himself for a time persisted in a system of "tergiversation;" but at length he broke forth into a remorseful confession of enormities, which filled with horror the judges who had hoped that he might prove his innocence. A sentence of utter excommunication followed inevitably; and the bishops, who at once saw their opportunity, wrote to Cœlestine desiring him never again to show favour to persons condemned by the African Church. "The Nicene canons," said they with significant emphasis, "have committed bishops and clergy to the judgment of their own metropolitan. For, with signal prudence and justice, they provided that all causes should be ended in the places where they began; allowing at the same time of an appeal to the provincial or to a general Council. It is not to be thought that God would inspire one individual with justice, and withhold it from a multitude of bishops in Council." They added that a "transmarine" tribunal would be unable to secure the necessary evidence; while the scheme of a commission sent by the Pope was devoid of sanction from Councils [h], the alleged Nicene canon being found spurious. "If any," they proceeded, "should beg you to send clergy to carry out your orders, do not send, do not consent; lest we should seem to be introducing the gloomy pride of the world [i] into Christ's Church, which exhibits to all who desire to see God the light of simplicity and the clearness of humility." They concluded by trusting that they should no longer have to "bear with Faustinus," since the case of Apiarius was now finally closed. So firmly did the Church of Africa maintain against three Popes the independence of Western Churches outside the proper limits of the Roman patriarchate.

---

[h] This shows their ignorance of the true Council of Sardica; in fact, "the canons of Sardica were not *received* even in the West until the sixth century." Pusey on Councils, p. 144.

[i] See the eighth canon of Ephesus, *infra*.

The letter which Augustine had addressed to Sixtus occasioned great disputes in 426 among the monks of Adrumetum. It was brought to the monastery by a monk named Felix, who read it to the brethren; whereupon some of them exclaimed that it destroyed free-will. At length, in the spring of 427, two young monks, Cresconius and Felix, were sent to consult Augustine, who wrote a letter to the brotherhood, exhorting them to hold together the truths of grace and free-will, salvation and judgment according to works[k]. He composed a treatise "On Grace and Free-will," in which, while contending for the real sense of the former term[l], he himself put an unreal sense on the latter. For he ascribed to grace such a vast controlling power as practically annulled all freedom of choice; the will, under grace, could not choose aught but good; grace, in fact, was simply irresistible. Into this extreme statement Augustine's predestinarianism led him by necessary consequence. The treatise was sent with a second letter[m] to Valentine, abbot of Adrumetum, who had approved of the letter to Sixtus, and who in reply ascribed to Augustine the wisdom of an angel of God. But one of the monks took an objection; "If the will to do good is purely God's gift, why am I corrected for my faults, seeing that He has not given me such a will?" Augustine, in reply, wrote another treatise, "On Correction and Grace;" in which he maintained that those who are "called according to purpose" have an indefectible faith, and an incapacity for sin; whereas the non-elect are the proper subjects of all penal infliction, simply as being what they are. The tone of the argument is at once stern and unreal. We see the great writer condemned by a trenchant theory

[k] Ep. 214.

[l] There is much that is highly valuable in this treatise. Abating the idea of an arbitrary and *irresistible* operation, the truth cannot be better expressed than in the terse passage, s. 33: "*Ut* ergo velimus, *sine* nobis operatur; *cum* autem volumus, et sic volumus ut faciamus, *nobiscum* operatur; tamen sine illo, vel operante ut velimus, vel cooperante cum volumus, ad bona pietatis opera nihil valemus."

[m] Ep. 215.

to have recourse to such a distinction as that between the "free" will of the non-elect and the "freed" will of the elect, each of them being, on the hypothesis, constrained in one particular direction; the former unable to choose good, the latter unable to choose evil. We observe a tendency, the result of a temper which looked always to the fore-ordained conclusion of a man's course, to regard a state of grace as illusory if not predestined to be permanent, and to deny regeneration, or "sonship," in the case of those who do not persevere[n]. And we are amazed by the boldness with which a text that stands right in the path can be disposed of, and God's "desire that all men should be saved," interpreted as referring only to the elect, among whom are specimens of "all" classes[o].

Augustine now became acquainted with a modification of the Pelagian theory, which is technically known as Semi-Pelagianism. Vitalis, a person who had been brought up in the Church of Carthage, maintained that the first step in goodness, the first act of faith, must be from man's own will, unassisted by grace; that after this first step, real grace, in the Catholic sense of the word, was bestowed on the believer. Augustine himself, when he expounded the Epistle to the Romans before he became a bishop, had employed similar language[p]; but he had come to see that unless the first motion of good in the soul were ascribed to God, the self-asserting heresy was not thoroughly repelled. He accordingly wrote to Vitalis[q], insisting on the necessity of prevenient[r] as well as of subsequent grace; arguing from the Liturgic formulas, apparently those re-

---

[n] Compare S. Augustine's peculiar language about Communion, in his work on S. John, and elsewhere. The tendency is not fully carried out; "faith, hope, and love" are admitted to exist for a time in those whom God has not predestined to persevere, s. 18; while in s. 20 we are told that they only who persevere have ever been truly sons of God.

[o] De Corrept. 44. This afterwards appeared among the propositions of Gotteschalk, A.D. 847. [p] See Retract. i. 23. [q] Ep. 217.

[r] Compare the Gregorian original of our collect for Easter-day: "Vota nostra quæ *præveniendo* adspiras, etiam *adjuvando* prosequere."

cited on Good Friday[s], wherein the priest bade the people pray for unbelievers, "that God would convert them to the faith;" and proposing twelve statements as to the doctrine of grace, held by "Catholic Christians through Christ's mercy."

A Gallican monk named Leporius had developed his Pelagian views into a formal heresy on the subject of the Incarnation. Christ, he said, was not God, but a man who had so used his natural free-will as to be sinless, and thus had merited a close union with the Son. The Gallican bishops had been obliged to excommunicate Leporius, who came to Africa, and was there reclaimed by S. Augustine. In the cathedral of Carthage he formally recanted an error which practically numbered the Redeemer among the Saints; and confessed that "God was born of the Virgin," became true Man, and suffered in the lower of His two natures[t]. He sent this document to the bishops who had condemned him, to whom also Aurelius and Augustine sent a touching letter in his behalf[u].

It was in 427 that Augustine carried out a long-cherished design of reviewing all his treatises, and correcting whatever might displease his ripened judgment[x]. This process of "re-handling" was applied, in two books which bear the name of *Retractationes*[y], to ninety-three treatises; the letters were reserved for a subsequent revision.

Atticus of Constantinople had been succeeded in 426 by Sisinnius, who died on Christmas-eve, 427. Nestorius, a Syrian bred at Antioch, of high reputation and great

---

[s] He adds the call to pray "for catechumens, that He may inspire them with the desire of regeneration; for the faithful, that they may by His grant persevere in that which they have begun." It was usual to answer "Amen." See the nine solemn prayers, each preceded by a *bidding* formula, in the Good Friday service of the Gelasian Sacramentary, Murat. i. 560, retained in the Roman Missal. Our third collect for that day represents the intercession referred to by S. Augustine in the text.

[t] He also affirmed that Christ, even in His Manhood, had never been ignorant of anything; a view which appears to go beyond the teaching of S. Athanasius.

[u] Ep. 219.

[x] Retract., prol. I.

[y] Our English "Retractations" has advanced in meaning.

powers as a speaker, ascetic and studious in his habits, was consecrated to the see on April 10, 428. His first sermon indicated a feverish polemical zeal [z]. "Give me," he exclaimed, addressing the Emperor, "give me the earth clear of heretics, and I will give you heaven in return! Help me to overthrow the heretics, and I will help you to overthrow the Persians [a]." He began his episcopate somewhat in the spirit of Macedonius: on his attacking an Arian meeting-house, the Arians set fire to it in their despair; the flames caught other buildings, and the new patriarch received the ominous name of "the Incendiary." Unlike Atticus, he was hostile to Novatians; and his violence against Quartodecimans caused an outbreak in Asia Minor. The early violences of Cyril ought neither to be extenuated nor exaggerated; but there was somewhat less of provocation for the persecuting fury of Nestorius [b].

Valentinian III., the nephew of Honorius, had sat on the throne of the West since 425. He was a mere child, under the guardianship of his mother Placidia, who was herself swayed by the able general Aetius. Count Boniface, who governed in Africa, and whom Augustine had dissuaded from entering a monastery, assuring him that he could serve the Church better in the secular life [c], was a rival whom Aetius longed to ruin. "He persuaded Placidia to recall Boniface;" and then wrote to Boniface, advising him, if he loved his life, to disobey. Boniface disobeyed; and Aetius told Placidia that this undutifulness was proof sufficient of his treasonable designs. Thus led by perfidy into the position

---

[z] Soc. vii. 29.

[a] He obtained from Theodosius the law of May 30, 428, against heretics. But it did not go to the lengths which his sermon had suggested.

[b] "Who," asks Dean Milman, Lat. Chr. i. 145, "would not meet the judgment of the Divine Redeemer loaded with the errors of Nestorius, rather than with the barbarities of Cyril?" Dean Milman, in regard to Cyril, seems rather a prosecutor than a judge; and in p. 143 he shows that Nestorius was guilty of more than "errors."

[c] Ep. 220, written to Boniface after the invasion. Augustine warns him that he is imperilling his soul.

of a rebel, Boniface invited Genseric, king of the Vandals, then dominant in Spain, to come over into Africa; and a Vandal host, professing Arianism, invaded the province in May 428 [d], or in the following year. Arians and Donatists took part with the barbarians: Catholic churches were pulled down, and clergy were tortured, massacred, or reduced to beggary [e]. Two bishops were martyred on plates of red hot iron [f]. It was "the beginning of sorrows" for the Church of S. Cyprian [g]; the moral corruption which had overspread the province was to be chastened by a century of barbarian rule. A bishop named Honoratus asked Augustine whether a bishop or pastor ought not to fly from persecution. The reply was that he ought, when he was specially aimed at, and when others were left to minister to the people; but not in other cases.

Pelagianism had been condemned at Constantinople and at Antioch, and even by Theodore of Mopsuestia, who was however, in all probability, led by policy rather than conviction to abandon it. From the new archbishop of Constantinople Julian hoped for some support; and he had again engaged in controversy with Augustine, before reading the treatise which the latter had written against him in 421. Julian's new work, in eight books, was a verbose attack on part of Augustine's second book, *De Nuptiis* [h]. Augustine began a reply, in which he transcribed his adversary's text, and made a comment of his own on every paragraph; but he did not live to complete the treatise. Another of his occupations was a controversy with Maximin, an Arian bishop in attendance on Count Sigisvult, the Gothic general employed for Valentinian against Boniface. This man held

---

[d] The date is disputed. Gibbon gives 429. The Benedictine Life of S. Augustine gives 428, after the Paschal Chronicle: so Fleury, and Tillemont. [e] Possid. Vit. Aug. 28. [f] Victor de Pers. Vand. 1.

[g] Salvian, de Gub. Dei, vii. In calling Africa "a volcano of impurity," he appeals to "the testimony of mankind."

[h] S. Aug. Op. Imp. i. 34, ii. 127, iv. 5. Julian took credit to himself for brevity; Augustine says he was wearisome to those who despised "superfluous words," iii. 20.

to the creed of Ariminum, and while admitting that Christ was called "the great God" in Titus ii. 13, affirmed that properly speaking the Father alone was God [i], and that the Son and Spirit worshipped Him. "Then," said Augustine at the Conference which he held with Maximin at Hippo, "you either worship two Gods, or you deny worship to Christ [k]." After the discussion, Maximin, on returning to Carthage, boasted of victory; whereupon Augustine wrote two books against him [l], expressly appealing to Scripture only, and employing, as he had done in his work on the Trinity, language which, perhaps, was soon afterwards embodied by a Gallican writer in the "Athanasian Creed."

Cassian had now completed his "Conferences," an account of the practical teaching of the chief Egyptian abbats. One of these, named Chæremon, appears to have taught a doctrine equivalent to the opinion of Vitalis [m]; and the perusal of Augustine's work "On Correction and Grace" brought this doctrine prominently forward. Cassian and other leading Churchmen, at Marseilles, and throughout the south of Gaul,—including Hilary, who had recently been appointed to the primatial see of Arles, and was eminent for devotion, pastoral zeal, and theological ability [n],—took serious exception to Augustine's predestinarian rigour. We learn from letters [o] addressed to Augustine by another Hilary, and by Prosper of Riez, two laymen who agreed with the Augustinian theology, that Cassian and his friends admitted original sin and real grace. But they did not admit an absolute predestination of a fixed number of persons, not based on

---

[i] "The one God, who stooped not to contact with humanity nor to human flesh." Coll. cum Max. 13.

[k] Coll. 14.

[l] In the second of these, c. 22, he gives a mystical interpretation of 1 John v. 8, which probably became the basis of the present seventh verse.

[m] Collatio 13. c. 12. David's desire to build a temple is said to be "both good, and from man," *not* from God; and in c. 11 the devotion of the penitent thief is said to have preceded grace. Such good motions, it is added, need to be *perfected* by grace.

[n] It is well known that Waterland considers the Athanasian Creed to have been composed by him, at the solemn re-admission of Leporius into the Gallican Church.

[o] Epp. 225, 226.

foresight of their perseverance, but making perseverance certain for them, and impossible for all beside. They denounced this teaching on moral grounds, as fatalistic in its tendencies, inciting to carelessness, and discouraging exertion [p]. They insisted on God's offers of mercy to all men [q], on the universality of baptism, on the unlimited efficacy of the death of Christ. But some of them were "Semi-Pelagian" in teaching that grace, as a general rule, was dependent on pre-existing good in man, i. e. on a desire of being healed, which nature could form without Divine assistance. Their zeal for man's responsibility thus led them to take up untenable ground. It was essential to Christian truth that God's restoring grace should be recognized as necessary in aid of the first motions of the will [r]. Augustine, at the request of Prosper and Hilary, wrote two books on "The Predestination of the Saints," and "The Gift of Perseverance." He admitted that the Gallicans were not Pelagians, but repelled their objections as equally applicable to the doctrine of Divine prescience, and declared that there was no real medium between absolute predestination of some out of a guilty mass, and the heresy which made "grace" the reward of human merit. Faith, he urged, must itself be the result of grace. He allowed that great discretion was needful for the preacher of Divine decrees.

The difficulties of the Gallicans were not thus to be disposed of [s]. Augustine, by his own showing, did not acknowledge, on man's part, a real freedom of will—on God's, a real readiness to have mercy upon all men. The truths for which the Gallicans were solicitous appeared in their due place, clear of all "Semi-Pelagian" error, in the

---

[p] Compare Wesley's epigrammatic summary of the Calvinistic doctrine.

[q] Hilary says they would not hear of Augustine's interpretation of 1 Tim. ii. 4. The fifth of the famous Jansenist propositions is, "It is Semi-Pelagian to say that Christ died for all men."

[r] See Aug. de Grat. Chr. 52. Reference has already been made to our Easter collect; and in fact the collects of the Roman Sacramentaries, as a body, show how deeply the doctrine of a preventing grace was fixed in the heart of Western Christendom.

[s] Chr. Remembr. xxxi. 162. (Jan. 1856.)

admirable dogmatic statements of a Gallican Council held a century later, in 529, at Orange. That assembly scanned the mystery of grace and free-will on both sides, and while glorifying God as the inspirer of all prayer and faith [t], proclaimed that "all the baptized, having received grace through baptism, could, by the co-operating aid of Christ, work out their own salvation [u]."

---

[t] Conc. Arausic. ii. can. 3, 5, &c.

[u] It is added, "We not only do not believe that any are predestinated to evil, but if any do hold so evil a belief, we say anathema to them with the utmost abhorrence."

CHAPTER XII.

From the Semi-Pelagian Controversy to the Council of Ephesus.

"God, that came on earth this morn,
In a manger lying,
Hallowed birth by being born,
Vanquished death by dying!"

NEALE'S *Christmas Carols.*

IT was probably in 429 that S. Augustine wrote his work on Predestination in reply to the Gallican objectors. We must now take our stand at the end of 428, to watch the outbreak of a new Oriental controversy, well-nigh as calamitous as the Arian, and as wonderfully overruled for good.

It seems that a well-grounded repugnance to Apollinarianism, combined with more or less of a rationalistic temper, had led some Churchmen so to insist on the distinctness of Christ's Manhood, as gradually to view it in the light of a separate personality. We may be surprised that Diodore of Tarsus, who had done such good service at Antioch, and had enjoyed the esteem of S. Athanasius, should have taken up a line of thought essentially akin to Arianism [a], and said that "the Son of Mary ought not to be regarded as God;" but there is nothing strange in the fact already noticed, that Theodore shook off the burden of so vast a mystery as is enshrined in the confession of the Word made flesh [b]. For that transcendent union of

---

[a] See Bp. Forbes on Nic. Cr., p. 195.

[b] Neander, characteristically enough, defends Theodore as a believer in the Incarnation; but admits that he held a certain "generic identity" between the existence of God in Christ and in the Saints; and that he differed from the Church generally by comparing the union to that which makes man and wife one.

Godhead and manhood in the one Saviour, he substituted such an *association* [c] of the Eternal Word with a man born of the Virgin, as would differ in degree, rather than kind, from the indwelling of God in Saint or Prophet. There was, then, no real Incarnation; the human person co-operated with the Divine, was sanctified by His presence, and enjoyed a reflection of His dignity; but this was all [d]. Such were the opinions of Theodore, which he either implanted or confirmed in Nestorius, who visited him on his way to Constantinople.

Shortly before Christmas a priest named Anastasius, whom the new archbishop had brought from Antioch, was preaching at S. Sophia. In his sermon he said, "Let no one call Mary *Theotocos;* for she was a human creature, of whom God could not be born." Nestorius was present and approved; and on Christmas-day, as it appears, he himself began a short course of sermons, in which he called the title heathenish [e], and spoke of Mary's Son as a mere man, the organ employed, and the vesture worn, by God [f]. Eusebius, a lawyer in the city, stood up in full church, and proclaimed that the Eternal Word Himself was born after the flesh. Nestorius denounced this doctrine; "It was not the Word that was born, but the Man Jesus." Euse-

---

[c] One Nestorian term was *Synapheia*, opposed to the Catholic *Henosis*. The fifth General Council condemns as Nestorian the assertion of an union according to grace, operation, equality of honour, authority, relation, power, good-will, identity of names. An union by indwelling, mutual affection, co-operation, community of name and dignity, is in fact *accidental*. S. Tho. Aq. 3. 2. 6.

[d] In this way men could escape from the overwhelming thought, that the Carpenter of Nazareth was the Creator of the world. "Nestorius shrank from confessing the *condescension* of God." Pusey on Faith, p. 61.

[e] "Hath God a Mother? Then Pagans may be excused for giving mothers to their gods."

[f] "For the sake of the employer, I honour the vesture which He uses." Serm. 1, Mercat. ed. Garnier, ii. 5. In Serm. 2 he denies a duality of sons, and seems only to affirm two natures, until he shows his real meaning in the words, "We call Christ after the flesh God, from His connection with God." His third Sermon is in fact against the assertors of one Person. Garnier ii. 11. "God the Word dwelt in Mary's Son," &c.

bius drew up a paper[g], conjuring all into whose hands it might fall to make known the agreement of Nestorius with Paul of Samosata. "Paul said, 'Mary did not bring forth the Word;' Nestorius says, 'My good friend, Mary did not bring forth the Deity.'" In strictness, the parallel was not accurate; Paul denied the Word's Personality, Nestorius plainly affirmed it. Another layman, Marius Mercator, who had, as we have seen, been zealous against Pelagianism, put forth a pamphlet on the relation in which Nestorius stood to other heretics[h]. This was in January 429. In the same month, Cyril, who had by some means heard of the controversy, set forth the unity of Christ's Person in his seventeenth Paschal homily, without naming Constantinople or Nestorius. He spoke of the Blessed Virgin as *Mother of God*. This title, mostly in the form of "Theotocos[i]," had been used by Tertullian[k], Origen[l], S. Alexander, Eusebius, Constantine, S. Athanasius, S. Cyril of Jerusalem, S. Basil, the Gregories, S. Ambrose, Theophilus, Atticus, and others. S. Hippolytus[m], S. Chrysostom[n], whose preaching Nestorius loved to imitate, not to speak of S. Hilary[o] and S. Augustine[p], had used equivalent language. The word was cherished by Catholics, not primarily for the sake of the Blessed Virgin,—although of course it did express her matchless dignity among human

[g] Mansi, iv. 1007; Garnier, ii. 18. He concludes by anathematizing any who presume to say that the Only-begotten is one, and the Son of Mary another.

[h] Garnier, ii. 17, 307. Mercator admitted that Nestorius had a right faith in the Personality of the Word, although he erroneously held Him to have become the Son at the Nativity.

[i] Cyril here uses Θεοῦ μήτηρ. So Constantine, ad Sanct. Cœt. S. Ambrose has *Mater Dei* in Hexaem. v. 20.

[k] "Nasci se *Deus* in utero patitur *Matris*." De Patientia, 3. Compare S. Ignat. ad Eph. 7, 18; and S. Irenæus, v. 19, "ut portaret Deum."

[l] Soc. vii. 32.

[m] C. Noet. 17, in Routh's Scr. Opusc. i. 75. He says that "God the Word descended into the Holy Virgin."

[n] S. Cyril ad Regin. i. cites his words, "He that sitteth on the throne high and lifted up is laid in the manger," &c.

[o] See De Trin. x. 7.

[p] Serm. 184, 189, 191, &c.

creatures,—but[q] as the symbol of her Son's Divine majesty, as enforcing the reality of the Incarnation, and so maintaining inviolate the Gospel scheme for a world's recovery. For if the Son of Mary were not literally God, He could not bring heaven and earth into unity; to have two Saviours would be equivalent to having none. This, however, is best shown in the words of Proclus, a bishop who could not gain possession of the see of Cyzicus, and who officiated as a priest of S. Sophia. At a festival in honour of the Virgin, probably the Annunciation, he preached in the great church before Nestorius. After speaking of S. Mary in glowing language, e. g. as the bush burning and unconsumed, the cloud that bore "the Cherub-throned," the fleece filled with heavenly dew, he passed on to the practical bearings of the Catholic doctrine. "If the Word had not dwelt in the womb, Flesh had never sat down on the holy throne. It was necessary, either that the doom of death should be executed on all, for all have sinned, or that such a price should be paid in exchange as could fully claim their release[r]. Man could not save, for he was under the pressure of the debt of sin. An angel could not redeem humanity, for he had lacked such a ransom as was needed. One only course remained, that the sinless God should die for sinners[s]...It was God who out of His compassion became Man. We do not proclaim a Man deified, but we confess a God Incarnate. The Selfsame was in the Father's bosom, and in the Virgin's womb; in a Mother's arms, and on the wings of the wind. He was adored by angels while He sat at meat with publicans...The servant

---

[q] Dean Milman, i. 170, and Mr. Greenwood, Cath. Pet. i. 328, do not seem to bring out this point.

[r] See S. Ath. c. Ari. or. ii. 67. "If, being a creature, He had become man, man would have nevertheless remained as he was, apart from God." See, too, the memorable passage on the Atonement in S. Cyril Hieros. Cat. xiii. 33, and the very ancient Ep. to Diognetus, c. 9.

[s] c. 5. In c. 6 he calls the worth of Christ, as a Ransom, not only equivalent τῷ πλήθει τῶν ὑποδίκων, ἀλλὰ καὶ πάσαις ψήφοις ὑπερέχουσαν. This is in effect the doctrine of a *satisfactio sufficiens et superabundans*.

buffeted Him, and creation shuddered...He was laid in the tomb[t], and He spread out the heavens as a curtain...O the mystery! I see the miracles, and I proclaim the Godhead. I see the sufferings, and I deny not the Manhood."

Amid the applause which hailed this sermon, Nestorius rose to make an extemporary reply. He admitted the phrase, "one Son," in the sense, obviously unreal, that the Word was joined to the Son of Mary. He urged that to speak of God as Virgin-born would encourage the Arian notion of an inferior Deity; while the heathen would answer, "I cannot worship a God who was born and died[u]." In another sermon he argued that as the Baptist was filled with the Spirit from the womb, yet Elisabeth was not called the Spirit's mother, so neither could Mary be called Theotocos. No clearer proof could be given by adverse lips of the charge brought against his theory, that it made the Man Jesus, after all, merely the foremost amongst the Saiuts of Scripture. In subsequent sermons he contended that one who was God could not be man's High-Priest[x]; that He who "held the circle of the earth" could uot be wrapt in grave-clothes; that the Sustainer of all things eould not rise from the dead. The Reconciler, he said, was a sinless Man, the living robe of the King, the image of the Godhead. He urged that Scripture never spoke of "God's death;" not seeing that by one such text

---

t "And Thou wast laid within the narrow tomb...
Whom heaven could not contain,
Nor the immeasurable plain
Of vast infinity enclose or circle round."

So Dean Milman, in the "Martyr of Antioch." Few doctrines have held such sway over Christian poetry as this of the Theotocos. In how many of our churches is it hymned forth, every Christmas, in the high strains of *Adeste fideles*, and "Hark, the herald angels!"

u Serm. 4; Garnier ii. 26. S. Chrysostom, in D. Nat. Chr. c. 6, says, "Many Greeks scoff when they hear that *God was born in the flesh*." But this scoff was not to him a proof that the doctrine was in fact foolishness. A living writer says of M. Aurelius, "This strange history of *a crucified God* was not credible to him," &c. Mill on Liberty, p. 49.

x So Proclus had called Him. "God became Priest in Mary's womb." It would be Arianism to say that He was Priest *in His Godhead.*

as 1 Cor. ii. 8 it warranted the general proposition that Christ's acts were acts of God, and the particular inference that S. Mary was God's Mother. Here in truth lay the question as to Theotocos; Nestorius argued that a mother and her child must needs be consubstantial, that a woman could not give birth to what was Divine. The answer was, "Certainly not, in regard to the Godhead; but since the Christ is One, and is a *Divine* Person[y], Christ's Mother is that Person's parent in regard to the Manhood which He assumed. Because God and Man are one Christ, we can ascribe human properties to God[z], and Divine properties to Man[a]; that is, to the one Person of the Saviour, *in His Humanity* and *in His Divinity*[b]." The foundation of his argument, *the real unity of Christ's Person*, was denied by Nestorius; and the discussion of Theotocos did but bring out this denial.

His sermons caused a great excitement at home as well as abroad. Men saw that the question was no strife of words; those laymen who have already appeared as originating the opposition to their patriarch, felt that Catholic truth was their inheritance, no less than that of the clergy[c], and they shrank from the communion of a bishop who made void the Incarnation. Clergy began to preach against him in the church of S. Irene-by-the-sea. When they were silenced, the cry arose, "We have an emperor, but no bishop!" A priest named Philip began to officiate in private; Basil, an abbot, and Thalassius, a monk, told Nestorius to his face that he was in error, and were

---

y Hooker, v. 52. 3. See S. Augustine, Enchirid. c. 36, a passage which shews that *homo* was not used by Latin fathers for a human person.

z 1 Cor. ii. 8; 1 John i. 1; Acts xx. 28? 1 Tim. iii. 16? (The Incarnate Word, *as Man.*)

a John iii. 13; 1 Cor. xv. 47. (The Incarnate Word, *as God.*)

b S. Tho. Aq. 3. 16. 4; Hooker, v. 52. 3; 53. 4; Pearson, i. 324-8; Bp. Forbes on Nic. Cr., p. 209.

c Compare Flavian and Diodore at Antioch, and the faithful at Oxyrinchus. In his seventh sermon, Nestorius says that he regards the threat to throw him into the sea as the croaking of frogs. Garnier, ii. 33.

savagely beaten and imprisoned. A monk who dared to denounce him as one who ought not to enter the church was scourged and exiled. Among his supporters a bishop named Dorotheus was the chief; he surpassed Anastasius by openly anathematizing all who spoke of Mary as Theotocos[d]. The congregation, uttering a cry of indignation, rushed out of the church, but Nestorius proceeded with the service, and administered the Communion to the preacher.

The careful circulation of the archbishop's sermons brought them into the hands of Egyptian monks. Cyril strove to undo their effect by his Letter to the Monks, about the end of April 429. They would have done better, he said, by abstaining altogether from the controversy; but it was necessary, as things stood, to impress on them the positive truth. Since Christ was Emmanuel[e], since He who was in the form of God assumed the form of a servant, since the Son of Man was adorable, since the Lord of glory was crucified, it was impossible to divide His Personality. To sum up all in one simple formula: "If our Lord Jesus Christ is God, how can our Lord's Mother, the Holy Virgin, be *not* Mother of God?" He guarded himself against misrepresentation by clearly confessing a true Manhood in Christ, and clearly denying that Mary could be Mother of Godhead. The confusion between *God* and *Godhead* was a main source of error[f]; all that was meant by "Theotocos" was that the Word was born of Mary, inasmuch as He took flesh of her; He became her Child in virtue of His Manhood.

This letter was forwarded to Constantinople, and wel-

---

[d] There is great uncertainty as to the time of this denunciation. Garnier and Neale connect it with Anastasius' sermon.

[e] The Nestorians made a distinction between God the Word and Emmanuel, by giving the latter name to Jesus.

[f] So in Nestorius' 7th Sermon. "Hear, wretched man (i. e. Proclus), Pilate slew not the Godhead:" again, "James was not brother of the Godhead." Nestorius frequently uses language indicating great confusion of thought. In Sermon 9, "He said not, 'Whoso eats or drinks My Godhead.'" So in Ep. 2. ad Cyr., "Christ said not, This is My Godhead," &c.

comed by persons in high office. Nestorius ordered one Photius to answer it, and set on some Alexandrians whom Cyril had righteously censured, for oppression and other offences, to prepare memorials against their patriarch. Cœlestine, in the name of a Council of bishops, informed Cyril that Nestorius' sermons had been sent to Rome, and asked whether they were genuine productions; but Cyril did not reply until a year afterwards. About midsummer he wrote his first letter to Nestorius[g], beginning, "Men of high character and worthy of credit have come to Alexandria, and informed me that your Piety is leaving no stone unturned against me." The excitement, he insisted, was Nestorius' own fault; he had led some expressly to deny that Christ was God; it was for him to allay the commotion by uttering the single word, Theotocos. Lampon, a priest of Alexandria, took this letter to Constantinople, and prevailed on Nestorius to write in reply. "Though your Piety," thus ran the letter, "has said a good deal that is inconsistent with brotherly love, (I wish to speak in respectful terms,") yet Nestorius is resolved to be gentle and forbearing.

There had been a certain degree of understanding between him and the Pelagians. Julian and three of his companions, had come to Constantinople, and petitioned Theodosius and Nestorius in the character of persecuted Catholics. Nestorius had, in a recent sermon, taken care to testify against Pelagianism[h]; but after Marius Mercator published an account of Cœlestius and of the heresy in general, Nestorius professed in a letter to Cœlestine[i] that he was unacquainted with the facts of the case. He took occasion in this letter to descant on the "corrupt" doctrine

---

[g] Mansi, iv. 883; Cyr. v. ii. 19. From this letter we learn the fact which Neander, iv. 161, seems to have overlooked, that the Roman Council had written to Cyril "as men greatly scandalized."

[h] "From a woman was the debt, from a woman the absolution. . . . . Thou art wroth with me because of the sin of Adam." Serm. 7.

[i] Garnier, i. 66. Easter 429. He wrote two other letters to Cœlestine.

which was held by "some" at Constantinople, who, following in the wake of Apollinaris [k], called the Virgin Theotocos, instead of her true title "Christotocos." In a tone of serene Churchmanship he told the Pope that "many had been brought round;" and that Theotocos was just tolerable in an improper sense, as meaning that from Mary came the temple of the Word. It is evident that by this "temple" he meant a distinct human person, whom the Word employed as His instrument. Cœlestine having received this letter, and other doctrinal writings of Nestorius [l], was advised by his archdeacon Leo to place them in the hands of Cassian for refutation. Cassian accordingly wrote seven books on the Incarnation, establishing [m] the orthodoxy of the disputed title on the simple and strong foundation, "Christ is God." He set forth the connection between Pelagianism and Nestorianism, but apparently in exaggerated terms [n], overlooking the fact that Nestorius did not suppose Christ to have won the Divine title by His holiness [o], but to have possessed it from the first by His association with the Word. He dwelt with the authority of personal knowledge on the faith of Antioch and of his master S. Chrysostom [p], as wholly alien to the Nestorian error.

Basil and other Catholic monks petitioned the Emperor for a General Council, and narrated the sufferings to which

[k] It seems that some Apollinarians adopted the phrase, which in consistency they ought to have abhorred.

[l] They proved to him that Nestorius held the doctrine of original sin. Garnier, however, thinks that Nestorius was in fact a Pelagianizer; ii. 327.

[m] De Incarn. ii. 4. He urges Titus ii. 13, and Rom. ix. 5, and the confession of S. Thomas. In iv. 8 he explains John iii. 13. In v. 10 he cites (as does S. Leo) 1 John iv. 3 as "omnis qui *solvit Jesum* ex Deo non est." He concludes, "we owe so much the more to our God, quanto humilior propter nos factus est à se Deus;" vii. 31.

[n] De Incarn. i. 3; v. 2. See note in Oxf. Ed. of Fleury, vol. iii. p. 24.

[o] As did Leporius, on whose retractation Cassian dwells, i. 5.

[p] He entreats the Constantinopolitans to avoid all fellowship with one who departs from the teaching of "that John who, like the Evangelist, might be said to lean on the Lord's bosom. Remember him, follow him, think of his purity and his doctrine;" vii. 31.

they had been subjected by the heterodox patriarch, who "feared not God nor regarded man [q]."

While the strife was thus raging in the East, and Augustine in Africa was developing Predestinarianism and mournfully watching the Vandals' progress, the British Church had been the scene of a great contest between Pelagianism and orthodoxy [r]. Agricola, a Pelagian teacher, had strengthened the heresy in its founder's native land. If we may combine two accounts, it was by a synod of Gallican bishops [s], on the recommendation of Pope Cœlestine [t], that Germain of Auxerre and Lupus of Troyes were sent into Britain to uphold the doctrines of grace. In a conference at S. Alban's between "divine faith and human presumption [u]," the Pelagians were put to silence; and Bede goes on to tell the noble story of "the Alleluia Victory." The Picts, he says, and the earliest "Saxon" invaders menaced the British host, the largest portion of which had just received baptism, and "shining with the brightness of the laver [x]," took up, under Germain's leadership, a position on some heights which commanded the hostile army. Germain and Lupus then cried out thrice, "Alleluia!" The British took up the sacred strain, which was associated with the Paschal season; and the enemy yielded to a sudden and overpowering panic [y].

Cyril had been blamed, it appears, for not taking stronger measures; he explained that he had not as yet thought it right to retort the anathema of Dorotheus. But in February

---

[q] Mansi, iv. 1101.

[r] Fastidius, bishop of London, appears to have recently composed a treatise, in which he urged that a Christian's hope should be fixed *wholly on Christ*. De vit. Chr. in Aug., tom. vi. Yet he has been suspected.

[s] So Constantius of Lyons, S. Germain's biographer.

[t] "At the instance of Palladius the deacon, Pope Cœlestine sends Germain . . . . . *vice suâ*." Prosper, Chron. See Life of S. Germ. 1844, p. 122.

[u] Bede, i. 17.

[x] So the metrical life of S. Germain.

[y] The Welsh traditions point to "the Field of Germain," Maesgarmon, near Mold in Flintshire, as the scene of this event. But Lingard contends (Hist. Angl. Sax. Ch. i. 11) that this is in more than one respect improbable.

430 he wrote his second letter to Nestorius [z],—the great Epistle which received in subsequent Councils a formal sanction from the Church. "As I hear," so he begins, "some are detracting from my credit." He set forth his faith in the clearest terms, insisting on a real, not a merely moral, union of God and Man in Christ, rejecting the association of a human person with the Word, and disclaiming Apollinarianism, with all notions which would degrade the Godhead. "The Word hypostatically" (i.e. personally) "united to Himself flesh [a] animated with a reasonable soul, and in a manner ineffable and inconceivable became Man. . . . . Diverse are the natures which are combined into this true Union, but from them both is One Christ and Son; *not as if the diversity of natures were annihilated because of the union*, but rather that Godhead and Manhood, through the ineffable and mysterious concurrence into unity, constitute for us the one Lord Jesus Christ." The Godhead did not take its beginning from Mary; the Word was born after the flesh, in that He united Manhood to Himself; Mary must be owned as Theotocos, "because of her was born that holy Body with a reasonable Soul, to which the Word was hypostatically united." In contending against the dogma that a common man was born, and that on him the Word descended, Cyril carefully disclaims the "insane" thought that the Godhead bore the scourge and nails. As in the Nativity, so in the Passion, we must recognize that manhood which the Word had made His own.

Nestorius replied [b], "I pass by the insulting portions of your extraordinary letter." Employing his wonted *ignoratio elenchi*, he contended that the Word as such was im-

---

[z] Tom. v. ii. 22.

[a] Hence came the principle, that the Godhead was never, "not even for the twinkling of an eye," as the Coptic and Ethiopic liturgies express it, severed from the Manhood or from any part of It: that God was in Hades, and God was in the winding-sheet, because the Soul and Body, temporarily parted by death, were still the Soul and Body of God. See Bp. Forbes on Conversion, p. 180.

[b] Mansi, iv. 891.

passible; he treated the terms "God" and "Godhead" as synonymous; he applauded Cyril for admitting the two Natures; he himself appeared to admit the Personal Union, "but it is clear that he means a moral, not a real union [c]." He concluded by assuring Cyril that he had been imposed upon, as to the state of the Church at Constantinople, by persons of Manichean opinions; a phrase which shews that he had learned the phraseology of Julian, who applied that term to all Catholics. These persons, who had united zeal against Pelagianism with zeal against Nestorianism, had recently been deposed at Constantinople from their ministerial offices, in order, perhaps, to console Cœlestius, who had been banished from Constantinople at the close of 429 [d]. About the same time Cyril wrote to some of his own clergy at Constantinople [e]. Throwing aside, as mere sophistry, the Nestorian argument from an impassible *Godhead*, he condensed the whole question into a terse formula of eight Greek words. "What those men aim at is to affirm two Christs and two Sons." Nestorius had said that he had found the people of Constantinople ill-instructed [f]. "What means this superciliousness? Is he more eloquent than John,—is he equal to, or wiser than, blessed Atticus?" Of the Alexandrian calumniators Cyril spoke with lofty scorn. If he were accused, he would not shun a trial; but he would not have "that wretched man" for his judge. As to the name Theotocos, was it more unscriptural than Christotocos? or could Mary be, as Nestorius was willing to call her, *Theodochos* [g], the Receiver of God, unless she were in fact God's Mother? Peace was the thing he most desired, if it could be had without compromise of truth; all that he asked was a plain confession of orthodoxy. For himself, he had resolved on suffering any labour, any torment, in the cause of faith. To a friend of Nestorius

c Neale, Hist. Alex. i. 248. d Garnier, ii. 62. e Tom. vii. 32.

f "Very devout and pious, but blind with ignorance about doctrine. This is not *their* fault," &c. g In his 7th Sermon.

and his own he wrote,—"I care not for distress, or insult, or bitterest revilings . . . . only let the Faith be kept safe[h]!" No one felt more good-will to Nestorius than he did; his anxiety was that a brother-prelate should regain his reputation. He wrote an elaborate letter to Theodosius[i]: "They divide the one Christ into two. . . . . It is not that they distinguish the nature of God from the flesh, or dwell simply on that diversity; for in that case they would not have erred, since *the nature of flesh differs from that of Godhead*[k]; but the point is, that they set the one by himself as a man, and call the other God by nature." They speak, he adds, of the Word as naturally Son, of Christ as Son in an equivocal sense. The question was absolutely vital. If the Word did not become flesh, He could not aid us by His trials; "His work for our salvation comes to nought, —our faith is made void,—the Cross, the world's salvation, perishes." Again, he disowns all "conversion of Godhead into flesh," and dwells on the dignity attained by the Manhood in Christ, arguing from the Holy Eucharist to the Hypostatic Union[l]; since the Flesh of Christ is eaten as life-giving, it must needs be the Flesh of God. Similar treatises were addressed to Pulcheria and the other princesses, enforcing from Scripture[m] the Divinity of Jesus, urging that "Mary, if not Theotocos, must be mother of a mere man, whose death could not profit mankind," and appealing to Fathers who had used this term, explicitly or virtually. About April he answered the letter which he had received from the Pope a year before. After declaring

---

[h] Those who admire the heroism of S. Athanasius, but cannot speak of S. Cyril without bitterness, should consider whether he had not much of the Athanasian spirit in regard to faith.

[i] De Rectâ Fide, and Mansi, iv. 618.

[k] These words show that he did not always use the word "nature" in regard to the *Godhead* in Christ.

[l] So we have seen S. Augustine argue from the received doctrine of baptism to the truth which Pelagius denied as to original sin.

[m] He cited the text about the Spirit, water, and blood, (as all belonging to Christ,) *without* the words as to the heavenly witnesses.

that the main body of the people of Constantinople were holding off from their archbishop's communion, but that their faith was daily receiving injury, he asked Cœlestine to say whether any fellowship should be kept with Nestorius, and to express his mind to the Macedonian and Eastern bishops. He sent withal a series of passages as to Nestorius' own views and the Fathers' teaching, translated into Latin "as well as Alexandrians could do it;" but he charged his messenger, the deacon Posidonius, not to deliver these papers to Cœlestine unless the latter had received documents from Nestorius[n]. He had, in fact, not only received what Nestorius had sent in 429, but another letter, in which the archbishop of Constantinople endeavoured to convince his brother of Rome that Cyril maintained a confusion of two natures. Cyril wrote to Acacius, the aged bishop of Berrhœa, who had been unhappily conspicuous in the persecution of S. Chrysostom, and who replied to Cyril in the tone of a peacemaker, assuring him that John, the much-respected patriarch of Antioch, had heard his letter in a friendly spirit, but that many who had come from Constantinople to Antioch believed the language of Nestorius to be consistent with orthodoxy[o].

Early in August a Council met at Rome. Cœlestine quoted a stanza from the Christmas hymn of S. Ambrose:—

"Redeemer of earth's tribes forlorn,
Come, show Thyself the Virgin-born;
Let every age the marvel greet,—
No common birth for God were meet."

"Thus," he added, "our brother Cyril's meaning, when he calls Mary Theotocos, entirely agrees with *Talis decet partus Deum.*" He cited Hilary and Damasus[p] as teaching the

[n] This, as well as his long delay in writing to Cœlestine, should be considered by those who denounce him on the ground of violence and unfairness.

[o] Acacius observed that Paulinus, though he would not say "Three Hypostases," agreed essentially with those who did.

[p] Damasus, said Cœlestine, had in a letter to Paulinus anathematized the assertors of two Sons.

same doctrine of One Christ; and the council pronounced Nestorius guilty of heresy. On August 11 he wrote to Cyril[q], accepting all his doctrinal statements, and giving him an important commission. "Join the authority of our see to your own, and freely occupying our place, execute this sentence with strictness and rigour; so that unless in ten days from this monition he condemns in writing his unholy doctrine, and assures us that he holds that faith concerning the birth of Christ our God[r] which is held by the Roman Church, and by your Holiness' Church, and by all who belong to our religion, your Holiness may provide for his Church, and let him know that he must needs be cut off from our body." He also wrote to the bishops of Antioch[s], Jerusalem, Thessalonica, Philippi; to Nestorius himself, as to a depraver of the faith who had now received three formal warnings[t]; and to the Church of Constantinople, to cheer up those who might have much to suffer from Nestorius by the example of Athanasius, and the remembrance that no Christian could be exiled from God,—that the thing to dread was exile from the true country of the living. In the close of the letter Cœlestine says, "On account of the distance by land and sea, we have appointed our holy brother Cyril to act in our stead."

Meantime the great saint and doctor of the West was lying on his death-bed. Hippo, one of the three cities which had as yet escaped the common ruin, was besieged by the Vandals in June 430. One day Augustine, while at table, annouuced to the other bishops who had taken shelter in Hippo, that he had prayed God either to deliver the city, or to strengthen His servants to bear His will, or at least

---

[q] Cyr. v. ii. 40, 42; Mansi, iv. 1019.

[r] This phrase, which became a feature of Eastern service-books, was less prominent in Western: but see the responsive hymn on charity in the Roman office of *Lotio pedum* in Cœn. Dom.

[s] Mansi, iv. 1047. Writing to John of Antioch, he says that the question at issue is that of man's salvation.

[t] Mansi, iv. 1025. These letters were entrusted to Posidonius. S. Cyril was to receive and forward them.

to take him out of this world[u]. He ceased not to preach and work, until in August he was prostrated by fever; and as he used to say that even approved Christians and priests ought to die as penitents, he excluded his friends from his room except at certain hours, caused the penitential psalms to be written out and fixed on the wall opposite his bed, and repeated them with many tears. He expired on Aug. 28, 430, in his 77th year. Well might the Church of Paris in after-days commemorate the Doctor of Grace by praying God both to teach men His will, "and to work in them the power to perform it."

John of Antioch advised Nestorius[x] to give peace to the Church, not by an unworthy retractation, but by the admission of a term sanctioned by celebrated doctors, for the expression of an idea which he believed Nestorius himself to acknowledge, which in truth he could not reject without denying that God the Word assumed the form of a servant. Theodoret, the eminent bishop of Cyrus, in the province called Euphratesia,—famous for his eloquence and learning, his zeal in the conversion of heretics[y], and his noble, self-denying generosity[z],—was present when John thus wrote, and approved of the letter. Nestorius replied that he was quite orthodox,—that he had proposed Christotocos as a medium between Theotocos and Anthropotocos,—that he hoped for a general Council,—that the Egyptian's presumption was nothing strange.

The great "Egyptian," after a delay of some weeks, which gives new proof of his reluctance to proceed to extremities, carried out Cœlestine's commission by assembling a Council

---

[u] Possid. Vit. Aug. 29.

[x] Mansi, iv. 1061.

[y] Theodoret, Epp. 81, 113, 145, says that he has converted, and brought to holy baptism, the inhabitants of eight villages, adherents of the Marcionite heresy; another village of Eunomians, another of Arians; in his 800 *parishes* (the word here has its present sense) "no tares of heresy are left:" and in this work he has often been pelted and "shed his blood," has been "brought to the gates of death."

[z] He never bought a house or a tomb; never received an obolus or a coat; nor did his household receive so much as a loaf or an egg. He built porticos, two bridges, an aqueduct, &c. Ep. 81.

at Alexandria in November. The result was a synodal letter, the third letter of Cyril to Nestorius[a]. The bishop of Constantinople was called upon to anathematize, in writing and by oath, his impious dogmas. Then came a long dogmatic exposition of the true sense of the Nicene Creed; in the course of which all confusion of Deity and humanity was denied, while the unity of Person was upheld, and the Eucharistic argument thus set forth. "We approach the mystic Eucharist and are sanctified, being made partakers of the holy Flesh and precious Blood of Christ the Saviour of us all. And we do not receive it as common flesh, God forbid! nor as the flesh of a man who has been sanctified, or connected with the Word according to an union of dignity, or who has God dwelling in him; but we receive it as really life-giving, and as the Word's own proper Flesh. For He, being by nature Life, as God, did, on becoming one with His own Flesh, render it life-giving[b]." To this epistle were appended twelve "articles," or "anathematisms," the teaching of which may be summed up thus:—

The union of God and man in Christ is not simply an association (3) between the Word and a separate "God-bearing" man (4, 5), whose God and Lord the Word is, on whom the Word operates (6, 7), who receives the Spirit *ab extra*, and can be worshipped *along* with the Word (9, 8), and offered sacrifice for himself (10). No! The Word is *hypostatically united* to the flesh, so as to be one Christ (2); Emmanuel, the Son of Mary, is truly God, and Mary is Theotocos (1); all Christ's acts are acts of the Word (4), His Flesh is life-giving as being the Word's Flesh, (11), in which the Word suffered, was crucified, and rose again (12).

In looking at these memorable anathematisms, we may regret that Cyril did not at this time anticipate the objec-

---

[a] Cyr. v. ii. 67; Mansi, iv. 1067; Routh, Opusc. ii. 17. It begins by a reference to Matt. x. 37.

[b] c. 7. This is S. Cyril's explanation of John vi. 63, that "Spirit" is used for Godhead. For the sense of ἀποφαίνειν, as "to render," see Consecr. Prayer in Apost. Const.; S. Cyril, tom. v. ii. 189, vi. 234; Renaudot, i. 241.

tions which were likely to be made to them by men who, without being Nestorians, were exceedingly solicitous for the doctrine of two Natures. The anathematisms by no means denied this doctrine, but they expressed it, to say the least, less clearly than Cyril afterwards found it necessary to do. They were not a full statement of both aspects of the truth.

Two other letters were sanctioned by the Alexandrian synod; one being an exhortation to the clergy and laity of Constantinople, informing them of what had been at last and with difficulty effected, and urging them to play the men in Christ's cause, and to follow those holy fathers who had called His Mother Theotocos, because He was very God; the other a letter to the monks of Constantinople, praising their pious zeal in defence of orthodoxy. Four bishops were sent as the Council's deputies to Constantinople.

But on the 19th of November, before they could reach their destination, Theodosius, at the request both of Nestorius and his opponents, summoned the metropolitans [c] of the Empire to come to Ephesus at the ensuing Pentecost, attended by such bishops as each might select, and there to hold a General Council. Besides the circular letter, Cyril received a private one [d] from Theodosius, which Gibbon supposes Nestorius to have paid for, and the bitter tone of which may at any rate be ascribed to him. "Why have you despised us, and raised all this agitation, as if a rash impetuosity were more befitting than accurate inquiry, or audacity and versatility more pleasing to us than good taste and simple dealing?" The Emperor proceeds to censure Cyril for writing separate letters to himself and to his sister, on the supposition of disagreement in the imperial family, or with the purpose of producing it. The whole subject must be fairly examined in the ensuing Council. Nestorius wrote to Cœlestine [e], speaking lightly of the matter as a verbal dis-

[c] The only simple bishop whom he invited was S. Augustine, of whose death he had not heard. [d] Mansi, iv. 1109. [e] Garnier, ii. 80.

pute, and observing that he understood Cyril to be endeavouring to evade attendance at the Council; that he personally preferred Christotocos as a Scriptural term, but that he would not object to Theotocos if it were not used "to confound the two Natures."

On Sunday, Dec. 7[f], the four bishops entered the cathedral of Constantinople during the time of service, and presented to Nestorius the letters of Cœlestine and Cyril. He instantly sent off a copy to John of Antioch, requesting him to secure Theodoret's aid. Having promised to see the deputies on the Monday, he shut his doors against them. On the Saturday he preached[g], professing his readiness to accept Theotocos in a sound sense, and his belief in the unity of the Son. "What more can be wanted?" cried the audience. "Nothing more," a Catholic might have answered, "except security that he employs the Church's terms in the Church's sense." He framed twelve anathematisms of his own[h], some of which were irrelevant, some tended to confuse the subject, and some betrayed his heresy[i]. He enjoyed the support of John, who thought the anathematisms of Cyril Apollinarian; of Andrew bishop of Samosata, who wrote a treatise against them in the name of the Eastern Church; and of Theodoret, who also composed a "Refutation" of each of Cyril's statements[k]. Theodoret acknowledged Theotocos in the sense of "mother of a man united to God." He could not, he said, understand the phrase "hypostatic union," but he protested against a confusion of the Natures. Some of his criticisms exhibited a really heterodox line of thought[l];

---

[f] Garnier, ii. p. xxi.; Neale, i. 253.

[g] Serm. 12. He says that Arians applaud the word Theotocos. He preached again, Serm. 13, on Dec. 14. Garnier, ii. 93. He also wrote about this time to Cœlestius as a most religious presbyter, &c. Garnier, i. 71.

[h] Marius Mercator translated them into Latin, and replied to them.

[i] In the first he will not allow Emmanuel to be called very God.

[k] Mansi, v. 83. Neander, iv. 167, blames Theodoret for imputing Apollinarianism and other errors to Cyril, who "had expressly enough guarded against them."

[l] He regarded the Son of David as a human person, a man whom God assumed.

others, a singular misapprehension of the points at issue [m]. Cyril replied to both these works; and wrote five books against Nestorius' sermons. In his answer to the Eastern bishops he employed the comparison which we find in the *Quicunque vult*, that as soul and body make one man, so Godhead and Manhood make one Christ [n].

About four or five days before Whitsunday, which fell in 431 on June 7, Cyril reached Ephesus, accompanied by fifty bishops, and found that Nestorius with sixteen had arrived before him. Memnon bishop of Ephesus supported Cyril; whatever may have been his orthodox zeal, he doubtless remembered the humiliation which his see had received from Nestorius' most illustrious predecessor. Juvenal of Jerusalem arrived in Whitsun-week; the Roman legates, Arcadius and Projectus, bishops, with Philip a priest, were on their way. Cœlestine had already expressed to Cyril his opinion, that if Nestorius were minded to repent, he should by all means be received, notwithstanding the sentence already pronounced by Rome and Alexandria. The bishops of the Antiochene patriarchate had not arrived. The suffering Church of Africa could send no prelate; but Capreolus of Carthage wrote, entreating the bishops to maintain the ancient doctrine. Candidian, commander of the imperial guard, was appointed to preserve order in the Council, but not to interfere in doctrinal questions.

Hostilities were in one sense commenced between the two parties before the opening of the Council. Memnon was afterwards charged by the Nestorians with having excluded them from S. John's church, and from other sacred places, so that they had no place wherein to cele-

---

[m] e. g. he thought it relevant to say that Christ must be adored as God and man, in two distinct natures. What Cyril had denied in his 8th article was the notion of two adorable ones; he had insisted that the Incarnate Word was one Person, and must *as such* be adored with "one worship:" the adoration of His Manhood being the adoration of Himself, the God-Man.

[n] See S. Aug. Ep. 137. 3; Serm. 186; Enchir. 36.

brate Pentecost, or to say matins and vespers. They also complained of violence done to them by Egyptian sailors and Asiatic peasants. Cyril doubtless delivered addresses on the great subject which had possession of his mind; but one homily ascribed to him[o] betrays its later origin by the extravagance of its language. Acacius of Melitene preached, and spoke of the cross as honoured "with the altars," and as glittering on the fronts of churches. He endeavoured in vain to convert Nestorius. A bishop of the Nestorian party said to him, "The Son who suffered is one, God the Word is another." Acacius withdrew in horror; but another dictum which fell from Nestorius impressed itself yet more indelibly upon every Catholic heart. On June 19, Theodotus of Ancyra, and some other prelates, were arguing with him on the Divinity of Jesus. "For my part," he said, several times over, "*I cannot say that a child of two or three months old was God.*" This was enough to disprove his fairest professions, and expose to Christendom his profound misbelief.

On Sunday, June 21, a fortnight had elapsed from the time fixed for the Council. A letter had been brought to Cyril, probably the day before, from John of Antioch, to the effect that he had been travelling incessantly for thirty days, and that he hoped in five or six days more to embrace his brother of Alexandria. Two metropolitans of his company also arrived, with a message to the bishops; "If I am delayed, proceed with your business." The

---

[o] Cyr. Op. v. ii. 379. This "encomium" speaks of the bishop of Rome as "archbishop of the whole world," a title not likely to be given him by the "Pope of Alexandria" in 431. The furious attack on Nestorius is totally unlike the language held respecting him by the Council up to the time of his deposition. The long string of apostrophes to the Theotocos appears too elaborate to be Cyril's. There is another homily in Cyr. v. ii. 355, called "When the seven went down to S. Mary's," which is a shorter and more moderate form of the encomium. A writer in Chr. Rem. xxx. 451, calls both "certainly spurious." The latter, if genuine, was preached *after* the deposition of Nestorius. The former says, "God *will* remove thee from...the throne of the pontificate."

question for Cyril and the majority of the assembled prelates was, "Shall we wait until the time which he specifies has expired?" In favour of such a course were considerations such as in a time of controversial excitement are often unpersuasive. It was really most important to avoid the appearance of unfairness or impatience; to put no stumbling-block in the way of a number of prelates who were already prepossessed against the Church of Alexandria, but whose patriarch had addressed Cyril with fraternal respect and cordiality. Having waited so long, the bishops might surely wait until the 25th or 26th; and if John did not *then* arrive, no one could blame them for taking him at his word, and "proceeding with their business." But, on the other hand, they were already weary of waiting; illness, and even death, had appeared among them; they persuaded themselves that John was purposely loitering, in order to avoid taking part in the condemnation of Nestorius[p]. The Egyptians doubtless felt that John, whenever he might arrive, would be hostile to the Alexandrian anathematisms; and the result was that the majority sent a message to Nestorius, warning him to attend next day for the opening of the Council. He replied, "I will see what is my duty." His adherents protested in writing; Candidian supported their view, and on Monday, June 22, when 198 bishops assembled in S. Mary's church, he personally remonstrated against a course which would precipitate division. It was in vain; Cyril and the majority had taken their resolution, and absolutely refused to delay, availing themselves very unwarrantably of the Syrian patriarch's courteous message, which obviously presupposed their compliance with his written request. On

[p] Evagrius says, i. 3, that many think John guiltless of any such intention. In fact, he might be expected, says Tillemont, xiv. 388, to wish to reach Ephesus before the arrival of Cœlestine's legates. His attendant bishops could not leave their churches until after "New Sunday" (Low Sunday) April 26. They could not all assemble at Antioch until May 10. Then, affairs at Antioch prevented John from starting until May 18.

the episcopal throne, in the centre of the assembly, were laid the Gospels; the bishops sat on each side; Cyril, as highest in rank, and as holding the proxy of Cœlestine[q] until the arrival of the Roman legates, presided in the assembly. It would have beeu better if Juvenal or some other bishop had discharged this office; but it appears that Cyril's part in the proceedings was mainly that of a producer of evidence, and that he called on the Council to judge between himself and Nestorius[r]. His secretary delivered a short statement of the priucipal facts. A secoud citation was theu directed to Nestorius; but soldiers with clubs denied the deputies access to his presence, and he sent out word that he would attend when all the bishops had reached the city. A third message was then despatched to him; care being taken to treat him simply as an accused bishop, not as a condemned heretic[s]. Again the rude sentinels thrust back the deputies. "If you stay here all night, you will get no satisfaction; Nestorius has ordered that no one from your Council shall enter." They returned to S. Mary's. "Nestorius," said the bishop of Jerusalem, "shows a bad conscience. Let us now proceed to compare all recent statements with the Creed of Nicæa." The great Confession was then read; the second letter of Cyril to Nestorius was produced, and read by Peter the secretary. "You have heard my letter," said Cyril; "give your opinion as to its orthodoxy[t]." The majority of the bishops, speaking each in turn, and the rest speaking collectively, pronounced it to be thoroughly

[q] This must be distinguished from the commission to "act in Cœlestine's stead," which had been granted and discharged before the General Council was summoned. At Ephesus, as Tillemont says, xiv. 393, Cyril might notwithstanding "bien presumer que Celestin ne le desavoueroit pas sur cela." See Cave, Hist. Lit. i. 391.

[r] Even after the Roman legates came, however, Cyril's name stood first as also representing Rome (Sess. 6); and again in Mansi, iv. 1363, he signs simply as bishop of Alexandria before Arcadius, Juvenal, Projectus, Flavian, Philip.

[s] "Your Piety—the most pious Nestorius."

[t] The Council is here asked to sit in judgment on a document which Rome had approved.

accordant with the Creed. Then was read Nestorius' answer. "Is *this*," asked Cyril, "agreeable to Nicene faith?" "By no means," said Juvenal; "I anathematize those who hold such opinions." Other prelates followed in the same strain; and at length the whole assembly burst forth in vehement anathemas. "We all anathematize Nestorius, the heretic, his impious faith, his letter, his doctrines. Anathema to him who communicates with, who does not anathematize Nestorius." Cœlestine's letter to Nestorius followed, and then Cyril's third letter, to which the twelve anathematisms were appended. Neither of these letters were greeted with express approbation; but it is plain that although the Council might not commit itself to the anathematisms [u], it intended to sanction the third, as well as the second letter [x]. The next evidence was that of the bishops who had carried the third letter, with that of Cœlestine, to Constantinople. After this, the bishop of Joppa conjured Acacius and Theodotus, by the holy Gospels there present, to make known what they had recently heard from Nestorius. They did so; after which a series of passages from the Fathers were adduced in support of the doctrine taught by Cyril; extracts from the sermons of "the most reverend Nestorius" were added, until Flavian of Philippi begged to hear no more of such "horrible blasphemies." The letter of the bishop of Carthage closed the list of documents; its request for the rejection of novelties was echoed by cries of "We all desire the same;" And the prelates proceeded to depose and excommunicate Nestorius, in the name of "our Lord Jesus Christ whom

[u] See Tillemont, xiv. 358, 405.

[x] See the Council's letter to Theodosius, *infra*. Also in the Council of Chalcedon, the magistrates refer to Cyril's *two canonical letters* published at Ephesus. The acts of the fifth General Council say that at Ephesus Nestorius' teaching was compared with *two letters* of Cyril; and that the Council of Chalcedon "accepted the synodical *epistles* of S. Cyril, to one of which the twelve articles were annexed." See Bp. Forbes, Theol. Def., p. 54. Tillemont, xiv. 359, says of the articles, "on n'en parla point dans le Concile de Calcedoine." See also Neale, Hist. Alex. i. 252.

he has blasphemed." The sentence was signed by all the bishops; the first signature being, "I, Cyril, bishop of Alexandria, subscribe to the judgment of the Council." It was now late in the summer evening. The bishops, on issuing from the church, were welcomed with loud applause by the people, who had thronged the streets all day. Torches and perfumes were burnt before them[y], as they proceeded to their several abodes; and thus ended the memorable first session of the Council of Ephesus. It is interesting to think that while the bishops were going home that night, after a day of intense excitement, Paulinus of Nola was calmly giving up his soul. His last words, breathed forth in a low chant at the hour of vespers, were those of Psalm cxxxii., "I have prepared a lamp for my Christ."

On Tuesday, June 23, Nestorius was formally apprised of his deposition, and denounced as a new Judas. Care was taken to placard and proclaim the senteuce; a letter was written to the clergy and church-stewards of Constantinople, admonishing them to take charge of the property of the vacant see. Cyril wrote to Dalmatius, a venerated abbat at Constantinople, who had warned his brethren of comiug troubles before Nestorius had entered on the archbishopric. Candidian protested against the proceeding, encouraged the country-people to insult the bishops, and sent the placard to Theodosius, to whom also Nestorius wrote, asking for a Council to be composed of metropolitans, with two bishops of each province[z]. The Council wrote to Theodosius, expressly declaring that it had compared the doctrinal *epistles of Cyril* with the Nicene Creed, and found them to agree with it both in substance and in words[a].

[y] "Women went before us carrying censers," is Cyril's statement. Mansi, iv. 1241.

[z] His real reason was, that the patriarch of Alexandria was himself the sole metropolitan of Egypt.

[a] Mansi, iv. 1235. This would not necessarily imply an acceptance of the anathematisms. The letter of Nov. 430 might be accepted apart from what was "annexed" to it.

Nestorius' speech as to a child of two months old was referred to; and a request was made for the burning of his books. Letters were also written by the Council to the Church of Constantinople, and by Cyril to the Alexandrians and the monks of Egypt.

On Saturday, June 27, John of Antioch with fourteen bishops arrived. The Council sent deputies to meet him; —this be construed as an annoyance. They followed him to his lodging; after long delay, he consented to see them; but permitted Count Irenæus, Nestorius' friend, to beat them cruelly. Dusty and travel-stained as he was, John proceeded to hold a Council of his own friends and twenty-nine others. Candidian had the assurance to tell this conclave that the Council had deposed Nestorius without any formal investigation. A sentence was drawn up, deposing Cyril and Memnon, and excommunicating the others, until they should condemn Cyril's articles. Forty-three bishops, including Theodoret, signed this document, and sent out letters to Theodosius, and to the clergy and laity of Constantinople. As a specimen of their extraordinary recklessness, it may be mentioned that these adversaries of Cyril imputed to him not only Apollinarian but Eunomian ideas. Theodosius, on June 29, wrote in severe terms to the Council, declared its proceedings null, and ordered that no bishop should leave Ephesus until the doctrinal question had been fairly scrutinized. The Council in reply complained that Candidian had prepossessed Theodosius, and begged that five bishops might be allowed to state the case to the Emperor. John strove in vain to force his way into a church, in order to consecrate a new bishop of Ephesus: a riot ensued, in which some persons were wounded.

And now the Roman legates arrived, and the second session was held in Memnon's house, July 10. Cœlestine's letter to the Council[b], dated May 8, spoke of the episcopal assembly as the visible display of the Holy Spirit's pre-

---

[b] Mansi, iv. 1287.

sence [c], and expressed full confidence that the Council would join with the legates in executing what Rome had already thought good. The bishops answered by applauses. "One Cœlestine, one Cyril, one faith of the Council, one faith of the world!" Next day, in the third session, the legate Philip, having magnified the successor of Peter as inheriting his authority [d], joined with his two companions in affirming the sentence against Nestorius. The Council thereupon wrote to the Emperor that the whole Church was against Nestorius. On July 16, Cyril and Memnon complained of John's proceedings. "His sentence," said Acacius, "is wholly illegal; but we may formally summon him." The first deputation could get no answer; the second was informed that John would give none to persons excommunicate. Cyril had wished the Council to pass sentence on John after the first monition; but Juvenal, whose claims to the primacy of Palestine Cyril opposed, prevented this. Next day, Cyril anathematized the heresiarchs with whom he had been unjustly associated, together with Nestorius, Cœlestius, and Pelagius. Three bishops and a notary were sent to John with a deed of temporary suspension. The soldiers prevented the hostile clergy from insulting the bishops, one of whom they knew of old. John's archdeacon, "a little pale man with a light beard [e]," came down and offered them a paper which they could not receive. They returned to the Council; John and his adherents were formally excommunicated; and letters were written

---

[c] It is certain that Cœlestine knew nothing of the theory which is now called 'ultramontane.' He recognized "apostolic" authority in *all* his brother-bishops alike. See Allies, Ch. of Engl. Cleared, p. 91, ed. 1; Fleury, xxv. 47. Mr. Greenwood ignores this recognition.

[d] Peter, said Philip, was the head of the apostles, and "even now and always lives and judges in his successors." On the whole, what Rome said in 431 amounts to this: "All bishops succeed the apostles, but Cœlestine, as heir of him who was the foremost apostle, has a right to be foremost among bishops." Rome did *not* say, as she now practically says, "The apostolic authority is concentrated in S. Peter's successor." There is nothing strange in Cœlestine's charge to the legates to maintain the authority of Rome.

[e] Mansi, iv. 1321.

to the Emperor and the Pope[f]. The sentence passed by the rival council was characterized as a mere absurdity, which the Council had disregarded; Cyril and Memnon had continued to take part with all their brethren in Divine service. The Council, it was added, had confirmed the Roman judgment against the Pelagians and Cœlestians.

Perplexed, as it seems, by counter-statements[g], Theodosius resolved to send his high-treasurer, Count John, with discretionary powers to Ephesus. While this commissioner was on his way, the Council in a sixth session, July 22, framed a doctrinal Definition, consisting of the Nicene Creed, without the Constantinopolitan additions, and of some passages from the Fathers which might preserve the faith from being explained away. Charisius, a priest of Philadelphia, then informed the Council that two Nestorian priests, James and Antony, had imposed a heretical creed, the work of Theodore[h], on some ignorant Quartodeciman Philadelphians desirous of conforming to the Church[i]. As a sample of heretical subtlety, this document was instructive. It accepted the phrase "one Son," as meaning that He who was inseparably connected with the Only-begotten was called Son in a superior sense to that in which Christians were sons of God. This was quite in accordance with Nestorian disingenuousness. The Council ordained that no one should be allowed to propose,

---

[f] In this letter to S. Cœlestine the γράμματα of S. Cyril, which are said to have been approved, appear to mean his *second* letter.

[g] The adverse party declared that they durst not put their heads out of doors, if they longed for a little fresh air. A count named Irenæus was their advocate at Constantinople.

[h] Mercator criticized it as disingenuously heretical. Garnier, ii. 251.

[i] Some of these poor men, who declared their acceptance of the Catholic Easter, were not able to write; e.g. Rudius, who says, "because I know not letters, I subscribe by the hand of Hesychius," &c. In the deeds of conformity they "anathematize all heresies, but especially the Quartodeciman." Charisius' own formula is not the same as the Nicene; it ends, "and in the Spirit of truth, the Paraclete, consubstantial with Father and Son; and in the holy Catholic Church; in the resurrection of the dead; in the life everlasting."

write, or compile any other "faith" than the Nicene; i.e. that no individual should draw up a creed to be subscribed by converts, and to take the rank of a baptismal formulary[k].

In the seventh session, July 31, three bishops of Cyprus addressed the Council against the claim of Antioch to jurisdiction over their Church, a claim which Innocent had supported in the person of Alexander. Rheginus, one of the three, had been consecrated to the metropolitan see of Constantia, in spite of orders from Dionysius, duke of the East. The Council asked what induced "the most magnificent and glorious duke Dionysius" to put forth this prohibition? "The request," answered the Cypriots, "of the Antiochene Church." "What did he of Antioch aim at?" "An uncanonical supremacy over our island." "Did ever bishop of Antioch ordain a metropolitan of Constantia?" "Never, since the Apostles' time, can a single instance be found of a foreign bishop coming to impart the grace of ordination to the island. The metropolitan has been ordained by the provincial synod of Cyprus." The Council cautiously enacted that *if* these statements were true, and there were no precedents for the claim of Antioch, then the prelates of Cyprus should perform consecrations for the island without disturbance, according to the canons and ancient custom. "The same shall be observed throughout the dioceses and provinces, so that no one of the most pious bishops shall take possession of another province, which was not originally and from the first under his own or his predecessor's power[l]. Or, if he has forcibly occupied and subjected it, he

---

[k] See note in Oxf. ed. of Fleury, vol. iii. p. 111; Waterland, iii. 249, ed. 1843. This canon has been quoted (as by Burnet in 1689) against our use of the Athanasian Creed. The argument mistakes the case, and also proves too much, as it must tell equally against the *Apostles'* Creed, and against the additions made in 381 to the Nicene. Tillemont, however, admits that the terms of the canon have been found embarrassing, xiv. 443. They were discussed in the Council of Ferrara in 1438.

[l] Our divines apply this principle to the case of the old British Church in regard to Roman supremacy; e.g. Bramhall, i. 157.

shall restore it; lest the canons of the Fathers be violated, and the haughtiness of domination [m] glide in under the garb of sacerdotal authority, and so that freedom be gradually and secretly lost, which our Lord Jesus Christ, the Liberator of all men, bestowed on us by His Blood. Every province, therefore, shall retain its original rights, undisputed and inviolate."

Several other proceedings took place, as the condemnation of the Massalian heresy, and the maintenance of the Thracian usage, by which a single bishop had the charge of several sees [n]. The canons of the Council are eight in number:—1. Against metropolitans, (a) seceding from the Council [o], (b) "thinking with Cœlestius." 2. Against seceding bishops. 3. For the restoration of clergy suspended by Nestorius, and against obedience to seceding bishops. 4. For the deposition of clergy who go over to Nestorianism or Cœlestianism. 5. For the permanence of Church censure against those from whom Nestorians would remove it. 6. Censure against enemies of the Council's authority. 7. Against Theodore's "impious creed." 8. On the rights of Cyprus.

Here, properly speaking, the proceedings of the Third General Council came to an end.

---

[m] Compare the Africans' remonstrance to Cœlestine.

[n] Two Thracian bishops were afraid that the bishop of Heraclea, who had turned Nestorian, might strengthen himself by naming bishops to sees which other bishops held *in commendam*.

[o] Such secessions might be looked for so long as the adverse party was strong in court favour.

CHAPTER XIII.

From the Council of Ephesus to the Accession of S. Leo.

"He was God and man in one person indissolubly united,—steeping in the glory of His Divine personality all of human that He wrought."

DEAN TRENCH's *Sermons in* 1856.

A NEW scene was opened by the arrival of Count John at Ephesus[a]. After long discussions he produced an imperial letter addressed to fifty-one bishops, as to one assembly, whom Theodosius gravely informed that he assented to the deposition of Cyril, Memnon, and Nestorius. The Court, it appears, had lost all clear knowledge of the actual position of the two parties. The three bishops were arrested; soldiers were stationed atthe door s of their bedrooms; letters were again written to Constantinople and to Antioch. Those of the anti-Cyrilline bishops prejudiced Isidore of Pelusium, who in consequence admonished Cyril to avoid the errors of his uncle's pontificate[b], and wrote to Theodosius, advising him to visit Ephesus in person. The bishops of the Council, in a little note intended for the clergy of Constantinople, described the distress which they were suffering. "We are killed with the heat; the air is unhealthy,—there is a funeral nearly every day,—the servants are all gone home sick; but if they make us die here, we will not alter what Christ has through us ordained." Many of the bishops were very ill; some had been obliged to sell all that they had, in order to pay their expenses. Cyril

[a] There is some diversity as to the arrangement of events. I have followed Fleury's order. "The last session," he says, xxv. 57, "was held on the last day of July; for so we must read, although the acts place it on the last day of August; since we know that the Council assembled no more after the arrival of Count John."

[b] Ep. i. 310. "Many of those at Ephesus accuse you of gratifying your private quarrels......He is nephew, they say, of Theophilus, and follows his line of conduct."

declared in one of his letters[c] that the "scandalous lies" about his having employed the agency of Alexandrian bath-men, and nuns who had left their convents, had been detected and condemned by Count John. It was vain, he added, to ask the Council to communicate with Antioch; and for himself, he was "ready for the scourge[d]."

But how were these letters to be carried to their destination? The Nestorians of Constantinople beset the ships and the roads, and would allow no ordinary messenger to enter the city. It was determined to give them into the care of a beggar, who might carry them in the hollow of a cane on which he leant[e]. This ingenious device succeeded[f]. The clergy of Constantinople openly addressed Theodosius on behalf of Cyril[g]. There was a great stir among the monks, who were for the most part determined enemies of Nestorianism. The aged archimandrite[h], or abbat, Dalmatius, had not left his monastery for nearly fifty years. The emperor had vainly striven to make him take a part in processional services during earthquakes. But now he felt, as he expressed it, that in a cause which so truly belonged to God he could not be inactive. He issued forth, the head of a solemn train of monks and abbats, including an abbat named Eutyches. Chanting in two choirs, they moved towards the palace; the abbats were admitted to the presence of Theodosius, who, as he had once been seriously alarmed by an impudent monk's informal censure, was not likely to resist a demonstration of this kind. Having read the letter of the Council, he said, "If these things are so, let the bishops come hither." "They are prevented," said Dalmatius. "No, they are

---

[c] Mansi, iv. 1447.
[d] The LXX rendering of our Psalm xxxviii. 17.
[e] Mansi, iv. 1427.
[f] "Que peut l'homme contre Dieu? Un mendiant força toutes ces barrières." Tillemont, xiv. 421.
[g] Tillemont places this address some time after the procession of the abbats, which in his order precedes the arrival of the Roman legates, and the imperial letter about Cyril, Memnon, and Nestorius; xiv. 422, 428, 429, 468.
[h] Literally, chief of a *fold* of monks.

not," said the Emperor. "They are under arrest," persisted the archimandrite. "Will you listen to six thousand bishops, or one impious man?" This rhetorical question he afterwards explained; "I referred to those who are virtually present in their metropolitans." The conference ended to the satisfaction of the archimandrites; they came forth, and directed the multitude without to proceed to a large church at the extremity of the city. Again the procession swept onwards; monks, bearing wax tapers, led the psalmody, without which in those days no great religious movement was conceivable; and the inspiring strain, "O praise God in His holiness!" was being thundered forth as they approached their destination. The church was thronged with eager listeners; Dalmatius caused the Council's letter to be read, and then described the interview with Theodosius. He took no credit to himself, but assured them that if the Emperor had spoken approvingly of the Council, it was because he clung to his father's faith. Dalmatius might well write to the Council, "I have not neglected your wishes." His interposition was a great event; he had proved too many for the Nestorians. By his simple devotion and impressive firmness, the old recluse had given force and unity to a great mass of public feeling, and broken the spell by which a party had bound an Emperor.

Theodosius now ordered both parties to send deputies to his court. The Council chose eight, one of whom was Philip, the Roman legate; among the eight named by their rivals were John of Antioch and Theodoret. Cyril and Memnon remained under arrest, while Nestorius was allowed to retire to a monastery near Antioch. Cyril occupied himself, at the Council's request, in writing an explanation of his anathematisms[i]. Once again he disclaimed all notion of a confusion between Godhead and Manhood. He explicitly taught that the human acts of Christ were

[i] Mansi, v. 1.

not to be ascribed to His Divine Nature, although they must be ascribed to His single Divine Personality. On the eleventh article he said, "We celebrate in our churches the holy, life-giving, and bloodless Sacrifice, not believing That which is present to be the body of a common man, one of ourselves,—nor again, the precious Blood; but rather receiving it as having become the proper Body and Blood of the all-quickening Word. For common flesh cannot quicken; and of this our Saviour Himself bears witness; 'Flesh profiteth nothing, it is the Spirit that quickeneth!'" On the twelfth, he insisted that it was no mere man, "an object of conception as individually distinct from the Word, that bore the precious Cross and tasted death for us; but it was the Lord of glory Himself that suffered in flesh, according to the Scriptures."

The two deputations were met by Theodosius at Chalcedon in the first week of September[k]. He had wisely determined not to expose Constantinople to the risk of such a tumult as their presence might excite. He gave audience five times to the deputies; but he would hear no man plead for Nestorius. Theodoret accused his opponents of identifying Deity with Manhood. He was allowed to preach, and was listened to by large congregations; it was in one of these sermons that he indignantly repudiated the notion of "a suffering God[l]. O our Saviour and Benefactor," he exclaimed, with a confusion of thought which seems absolutely wonderful, "let us not so apostatize from Thy worship, be so ignorant of Thy nature, as to suppose our Deliverer to be passible!" He and his friends had prayers and discourses, but did not read Scripture nor celebrate the Eucharist. It soon appeared that the deputations were powerless to restore unity. The anti-Cyrilline party were prepared to argue the doctrinal question before the Emperor as a qualified judge[m]. Their opponents refused to do so; they insisted simply on the personal question of

k Mansi, iv. 1405. l See Hooker, v. 53. 4. m Mansi, iv. 1401.

Cyril's rights as against Nestorius. The Emperor cut the knot by ordering them to proceed to Constantinople, and consecrate a Catholic patriarch. The schismatic deputies complained loudly. "Such a step would perpetuate the disunion. The Eastern diocese, Pontus, Asia, Thrace, Illyricum, Italy,"—meaning, apparently, the exarchate of Milan,—"would never accept the Cyrilline articles." It is probable that Martinian, archbishop of Milan, who had sent a treatise of S. Ambrose to Theodosius, mistook Cyril's teaching for a form of Apollinarianism. The Emperor wrote to the bishops of the Ephesian Council [n], announcing his final resolve. Memnon was to stay at Ephesus; Cyril and the other prelates to return home. But the Emperor could not condemn the Easterns, because there had been no discussion of the doctrinal controversy. As to the failure of the hope of peace, "God knew who was to blame." The Eastern deputies again addressed the Emperor [o]. They had not expected such treatment. They had *bonâ fide* obeyed his summons; and this was their reward. "You are not only their emperor, but ours; the East is no small part of your realm. The majority of the people are sound. If you continue unmoved, we will shake the dust off our feet, and exclaim with S. Paul, We are pure from your blood!" In a letter to their friends at Ephesus, they denounced the heresy, tyranny, bribery of Cyril [p].

On Sunday, Oct. 25, 431, a pious priest named Maximian, who had been trained at Rome, was consecrated to the see of Constantinople [q]. The event was announced to the various Churches [r]; a letter is extant which communicated it to the bishops of Epirus. Maximian, in writing to Cyril after his accession to "the pontificate of the capital," asked the prayers and brotherly counsel of the great Catholic patriarch. Cyril, who had returned to Alexandria

---

[n] Mansi, iv. 1465.
[o] Ibid., iv. 1405.
[p] Ibid., iv. 1420.
[q] Ibid., v. 1045.
[r] Cœlestine caused the letters which he received from Constantinople to be read in S. Peter's on Christmas-day.

on Oct. 30, compared him, in his reply, to Eliakim succeeding Shebna. Cyril set to work on a defence of his conduct, addressed to Theodosius.

In this year of theological excitement, Cœlestine found time to think of the spiritual needs of that distant Ireland which had been the birth-place of the heretic Cœlestius. He made choice of a Roman deacon named Palladius to undertake a mission to "the Scots who believed in Christ," i. e. according to the language of those times, the Christians in Ireland. Prosper tells us[s] that Palladius was the "first bishop" who had been "sent" to them. This may reasonably be understood in the sense of first in time; there is no occasion for supposing a reference to primatial dignity. In another passage[t], the ardent Prosper, celebrating Cœlestine's zeal against the Pelagians, tells how he "delivered Britain from this pest, when he excluded even from that ocean-solitude certain enemies of grace who were in possession of their native soil; and, having ordained a bishop for the Scots, while he is bent on keeping the Roman island Catholic, he also made the barbaric island Christian." Prosper means to say, "while the Pope sends Germain into Britain, he evangelizes Ireland by Palladius." His enthusiasm for an anti-Pelagian pontiff might easily lead him to ascribe Germain's mission solely to Cœlestine's appointment, and to form too brilliant a conception of the success of the missionary whom Cœlestine sent to Ireland.

It was in the end of 431 that Cœlestine gave a new proof of his fidelity to the doctrine of grace. Being informed by Prosper and Hilary that certain Gallican priests continued to attack the theological reputation of Augustine, he wrote to the bishops of Gaul, rebuking them for their connivance at this presumption[u]. Ten articles, which have been annexed to this letter[x], are chiefly compilations from the writings of Innocent and Zosimus, and from the Council of

---

[s] Prosp. Chron. See Bede, i. 13. [t] C. Collat. 58. [u] Mansi, iv. 454.

[x] Quesnel ascribes them to S. Leo, while deacon; the Ballerini, to Prosper. It is admitted that they were not drawn up by S. Cœlestine.

May 1, 418; and they avoid "certain dark and difficult points" as not essential to Catholic belief[y]. The most striking passage is that in which the Liturgy is appealed to, as formerly by African bishops, in proof of the Church's doctrine[z]. "Let us look back to the sacred forms (*sacramenta*) of priestly supplication, so that the law of prayer may fix the law of belief." The last words, *ut legem credendi lex statuat supplicandi*, have passed into an ecclesiastical proverb[a].

On March 15, 432, Cœlestine wrote to the bishops of the late Council, regretting that Nestorius had been allowed to settle at Antioch, and intimating that it might become necessary to condemn John of Antioch. He urged Maximian in another letter to imitate Chrysostom, Atticus, and Sisiunius, and to resist the followers of Cœlestius. He went so far as to request the Eastern emperor to banish Nestorius. His own work for the Church was done; he died soon afterwards, and was succeeded by Sixtus III., to whom Augustine had written his famous epistle on grace and predestination.

John of Antioch, ignoring the late proceedings, had held Councils at Tarsus and Antioch, condemning anew Cyril and Juvenal, with others. Among those who fell under Nestorianizing censures was Rabbula, bishop of Edessa[b], who had voted at Ephesus for the deposition of Cyril, but had afterwards become a convert to his theology, had anathematized Theodore and his writings, and condemned those of Andrew and Theodoret. John of Antioch suspended

---

[y] Probably alluding to predestinarianism.

[z] The particular prayers referred to were those used on Good Friday; for infidels, idolaters, Jews, heretics, schismatics, the lapsed, and catechumens. For these last, prayer was made "that they might be led to the Sacraments of regeneration, and the door of heavenly mercy might be opened to them."

[a] On the doctrinal value of Liturgic forms, see Bp. Bull, Sermon 13; A. Knox's Remains, iii. 63.

[b] He had been converted while he held the government of a city, by Alexander, founder of a body of "sleepless" monks, who, relieving each other by turns, kept up a perpetual psalmody. Rabbula became bishop of the great capital of Mesopotamia in 412.

communion with Rabbula. Theodoret wrote five books on the Incarnation, and encouraged those at Constantinople who clung to the cause of their ex-patriarch. Catholic bishops, sent to supersede the heterodox, found great opposition. In these new perplexities, Theodosius, by episcopal advice, wrote to John, desiring him to meet Cyril at Nicomedia. He also wrote to the venerable bishop of Berrhæa, and to the famous Symeon[c], surnamed *Stylites*, from the pillars on which he successively took up his abode—every pillar which he ascended being loftier than that which he had left. Fantastic as his devotion was, it must be remembered that he occupied himself not only in prayer and prostrations, but in vigorous preaching to the wild tribes of Syria. Isidore urged Cyril to heal the schism[d]; aud Cyril assured Maximian that he would insist on nothing but the condemnation of Nestorius.

The conference between Cyril and John was found impracticable; but a council was held at Antioch, which framed six articles, expressly rejecting those of Cyril, but accepting S. Athanasius' Exposition of Faith[e]. This document was sent by the hands of Aristolaus, a pious secretary of state, to Cyril, who replied to Acacius with a moderation which did him honour. He had written his twelve articles, he said, simply as against the Nestorian impieties, which he had long refrained from thus denouncing. Nestorius was condemned at Ephesus for practically annulling the Nicene Creed. For himself, he took no heed of personal quarrels; all that he cared for was that the condemnation of Nestorius should be affirmed. He again anathematized Apollinaris; declared the Word to be in Godhead impassible; denied all fusion of the Natures. He could not possibly retract his articles, for he held them to be true; but any further explanation which might be needful could well enough be given when peace was restored.

The Easterns were divided in opinion as to this letter.

[c] Evagr. i. 13. Theodosius called him "the martyr in the air."
[d] Ep. i. 370.
[e] See S. Ath. i. 79.

John and Acacius were satisfied, although John in the recent Council had bound himself to insist on a positive recantation of Cyril's articles, a step which Theodosius and several bishops had deemed a *sine quâ non* of peace. Theodoret said that excepting the point of Nestorius' condemnation, the letter was unobjectionable, and that its doctrine was contrary to that of the anathematisms. Andrew of Samosata was not contented with the letter; but advised a "condescension," or general union on the basis of the formula, "The Son of God is One." Alexander of Hierapolis, with three others, spurned all thought of peace with Cyril. Thoroughly possessed with the belief that a Personal union meant nothing but an unity of Nature, they rejected it as such. "In God's cause," Alexander wrote, "I reverence no man. Cyril is a heretic, who affirms one Nature in Christ." For Cyril to anathematize Apollinaris was an absurdity. He must condemn his own articles. As for the change of mind in John and Acacius, "I prayed, on hearing of it, that the earth might open to receive me[f]." So passed the summer of 432. Meanwhile Prosper was writing[g] against certain propositions in the thirteenth of Cassian's Conferences, which he criticised as injurious to the doctrine of grace.

Palladius, according to the usual story, did not remain more than a year in Ireland, if indeed he landed on its coast[h]. There is great obscurity as to his career. According to Irish tradition, he just lived to pass over from Ireland into Britain[i]. According to Scottish, he found his true vocation in North Britain, and had a successful episcopate of some twenty years among the Cruithne, Deucaledones, or Northern Picts[k]. It is added that he was the spiritual

[f] Mansi, v. 838.

[g] Contra Collatorem. One proposition, which ascribed to God the very first elements of a holy will, he "heartily embraced;" c. 19.

[h] Nennius, c. 50, says that tempests and signs from God prevented his landing.

[i] Hence Bp. Lloyd dates his death Dec. 15, 431.

[k] He died, according to this story, at Fordon, July 6, 450. Joceline in

father of Servanus, or Serf, who became the apostle of Orkney, and of Ternan, who succeeded Palladius, as bishop of the Picts, at Abernethy. S. Ninian, who had converted the Southern Picts, died Sept. 16, 432.

The same year is commonly assigned for the commencement of a more celebrated ministry — that of Patrick, the apostle of Ireland[l]. His real name was Succath; he was the son of a deacon named Calphurnius, and was born either at Kirkpatrick near Dunbarton, or in Cornwall, or in the north of Gaul; as to the time of his birth there is similar variety of opinion. From the age of sixteen to twenty-two he was, according to the touching document called his "Confession," the thrall and cowherd of a heathen prince in Ulster, to whom he had been sold by pirates who had made him a captive. One would gladly believe the beautiful account of his spiritual growth in the midst of utter desolation; the deep conviction of sin which wrung his heart, the glow of devotion which made him rise for prayer before daylight, and continue in prayer all day, on the mountain and in the forest, regardless of "snow, and ice, and rain," because "the love of God" was increasing in him[m]. After he escaped from this captivity, he is said to have been irresistibly drawn[n] towards a missionary life among the people

his Life of Patrick quotes an Irish proverb, (c. 3.) "Not to Palladius, but to Patrick, did the Lord grant the conversion of Ireland."

[l] I follow the ordinary account of S. Patrick. Prosper is silent about him; Bede only names him in his Martyrology; and some would identify him with Palladius. The Irish traditions speak of a Sen-Patrick, or Patrick the Elder, who has been variously regarded as 1. S. Patrick himself--Palladius being Patrick the Younger; 2. Palladius; 3. a precursor of Palladius or S. Patrick; 4. junior to S. Patrick. Amid all this confusion, some deny that S. Patrick is an historical person. Tillemont, who considers the "Confession" to be genuine and worthy of the Saint, dates his mission not earlier than 440 nor later than 460. The Bollandists say that he came to Ireland as bishop in 432, and died, æt. 83, in 460. Act. SS. Mar. 17. They reject the Irish legends about bishops in Ireland before Palladius and Patrick,—Kiaran, Declan, Ailbe, and Ibar.

[m] Confess. 1—6.

[n] His parents begged him never to leave them again; but he seemed to hear the voice of those who inhabited the forest of Focluth in Ireland, "We pray thee, holy youth, come and walk again among us!" Conf. 10. He

who had caused his sufferings; to have studied under Germain of Auxerre, received holy orders, and spent some time in the illustrious monastery of Lerins. He was consecrated a bishop, either by Gallican or British prelates; there is no real ground for ascribing his mission to Cœlestine [o]. He landed, we are told, in Down, and converted the chieftain of the district.

To return to the Eastern troubles. Anxious to secure peace, John of Antioch visited Acacius at Berrhœa; and they agreed to send Paul, bishop of Emesa, an aged and experienced man whom they could trust, to confer with Cyril. John then wrote to Alexander that his impetuous language was uncalled for; that there was no question of abdication or of martyrdom, or of anything but the restoration of unity. When Paul reached Alexandria, Cyril was disabled by illness. At last he had an interview with Paul, who brought a letter in which John spoke strongly against the twelve anathematisms, and against the acts of the Council of Ephesus, but intimated withal his own hopes of peace and unity. Cyril was not propitiated by this letter [p]. "I expected," he said, "an apology for the past, and here is a new outrage." Paul protested, even with an oath, that the bishop of Antioch meant no offence; and Cyril, easily appeased, and actuated, as Paul declared, by a pacific temper "worthy of a pontiff," passed at once to other matters. Paul presented to him a confession of faith, which in its original draft was the work of Theodoret, and which he now exhibited on behalf of John. "We confess [q] our Lord

also heard, in a dream, a chanted strain, of which all that he could understand was, "Who gave His life for thee." The voices seemed to be within his own soul. Ib. 11. He repeatedly protests that he had no other motive for returning to Ireland than the pure love of "the Gospel and the promises." The Confession is full of a deep sense of Divine grace.

[o] The legend was that Cœlestine at first refused to ordain him, when Germain sent him to Rome for that purpose; but that hearing of Palladius' death, he caused Patrick to be ordained in his own presence, and died in a week afterwards. The Bollandists say that the Pope gave a license for his consecration in Gaul. On this see King's Ch. Hist. of Ireland, i. 29.

[p] Mansi, v. 311, 350.

[q] Ibid., v. 291.

Jesus Christ, the Only-begotten Son of God, to be perfect God and perfect Man, of a reasonable soul and a body; before the ages begotten of the Father according to Godhead, but in the last days, Himself the self-same, for us and for our salvation born of the Virgin Mary according to Manhood; of one essence with the Father as to Godhead, of one essence with us as to Manhood. For there took place *an union of two Natures;* wherefore we confess one Christ, one Son, one Lord. According to this notion of the union without confusion, we confess the Holy Virgin to be Mother of God, because God the Word was incarnate and made Man, and from His very conception united to Himself the temple taken from her." It was added that some of the Scriptural sayings about Christ had been referred by theologians to His one Person, others to His Godhead and Manhood respectively. Cyril accepted this formulary as orthodox, and gave Paul a paper framed by himself, which Paul in his turn approved. He and Cyril were thus at one upon the doctrine [r]; as to other points, Cyril required that Paul should anathematize the writings of Nestorius, acquiesce in his deposition, and recognize his successor; nor would he dispense with a recognition of Maximian's sentence against four metropolitans whom the new patriarch had deposed for Nestorianism. Paul drew up, and placed in Cyril's hands, a written statement of their concordat, in the form of a letter [s]. Then, and not till then, he was permitted to attend the Church service, and invited to preach, as a Catholic bishop, on Christmas-day. The scene that ensued was a very striking one. He began with the Angelic hymn, proceeded to Isaiah vii. 14, and then pronounced the momentous words, "Thus Mary,

---

[r] Paul had asked Cyril whether he would abide by S. Athanasius' treatise against Apollinarianism, addressed to Epictetus. "Certainly I will," said the successor of Athanasius; "but is your text of that work free from corruption?" They compared Paul's copy with those preserved at Alexandria, and found that it was seriously corrupt.

[s] Cyr. v. ii. 100; Mansi, v. 287.

Mother of God, brings forth Emmanuel!" The church rang with joyful cries; "Lo, this is the faith! 'Tis God's gift, orthodox Cyril! This is what we wanted to hear! He that says not this, let him be anathema!" Paul resumed, and presently enforced both sides of the true doctrine. "A combination of *two perfect Natures*, I mean Godhead and Manhood, constitutes for us the *one Son*, the one Christ, the one Lord." Again the people shouted applause; "Welcome, orthodox bishop, the worthy to the worthy[t]!" On New Year's day, 433, Paul gave a longer and fuller sermon, citing John iii. 13, Rom. ix. 5, and showing from the prologue of S. John and from the Gospel history in general that the unity of person and the distinctness of natures were coequal and consistent truths. "This," he concluded, "is your ancestral treasure, the teaching of Athanasius and Theophilus." Cyril then briefly expressed his assent to what they had heard. Two Alexandrian clergy were appointed to carry the formulary to John, and to give him a letter of communion with Alexandria when he had signed it: for Cyril would not dispense with his personal signature. Cyril spent a large sum in procuring interest at court; a proceeding which illustrates his unfortunate tendency to "think any means legitimate which seemed likely to make a holy enterprise successful[u]." Both he and Nestorius would doubtless have justified these bribes, which were delicately described by the Scriptural[x] name of "blessings," (*eulogiæ*,) on the ground that ecclesiastics who meant to gain over men of the world for Church purposes ought not to be fastidious as to the way of doing so. Cyril also assured his apocrisiarii, or Church-agents, at Constantinople, that no one need imagine him to have recanted his old principles.

The formulary was accepted by John in a letter to

---

[t] Mansi, v. 293.

[u] Tillemont, xiv. 541. He adds, with great force and truth, "Il ne faut soutenir la justice que par des voies justes," &c.

[x] See LXX, 4 Kings v. 15, τὴν εὐλογίαν.

Cyril[y]. He explained that in doing so he meant not to derogate from the Nicene Creed, nor to fathom mysteries which could not be comprehended in any words of man[z], but simply to bar out assailants of the true belief: and expressly recognized Maximian as the rightful bishop of Constantinople, in the place of Nestorius, sometime bishop, deposed for doctrines meriting anathema. On April 23, 433, Cyril announced this happy reunion in the cathedral of Alexandria. He wrote to John[a], embodying the formulary in his letter, and replying to those who accused him of holding with the Apollinarians that Christ's Body was of heavenly origin; a view, it might well have been thought, which the great assertor of the Theotocos would be the last to entertain. He also commented on the texts, John iii. 13[b] and 1 Cor. xv. 47; and again denied all confusion of the Natures. John wrote to inform his friends of the reconciliation between himself and Cyril. Theodoret refused to abandon Nestorius, to whom he wrote that Cyril's letters did indeed seem clear of heresy. "But certainly," he added, "I do not hate their author less! he is the cause of all the disturbance of the world.—To what was unjustly done against your Holiness, I cannot endure to assent, no, not if both my hands were to be cut off." Alexander wrote indignantly to Andrew; "So,—an union is to be made with the impious Cyril, *not* by his leaving his heresy! Be assured that neither exile nor death, precipices, fire, nor wild beasts, shall make me take part with them." To Theodoret, whose metropolitan he was, he wrote that he would never recognize this union. He would not style John a bishop. John was "a traitor to the faith, and to his own

---

y Mansi, v. 289.

z See S. Aug. de Trin. v. c. 9; vii. c. 4. "Veriùs enim cogitatur Deus quam dicitur, et veriùs est quam cogitatur." Serm. 117. Ath. Treatises, i. 44, note.

a Mansi, v. 303; Cyr. v. ii. 104. "Let the heavens rejoice."

b "Since God the Word descended from heaven, and was called Son of Man while He continued to be God, He is said to descend from heaven as being already considered one with His own flesh."

convictions of Nestorius' orthodoxy." The bishops of his province, Euphratesia, were constrained to act without him in giving a partial adhesion to the concordat. Andrew, who was one of them, tried to win him over, and urged that Cyril had virtually retracted the obnoxious articles. Alexander replied with intense bitterness,—"Enough—you have sought the lost sheep, and it does not wish to be found. We shall meet at the terrible tribunal of Jesus Christ." Andrew thereupon informed the Church-officers of Hierapolis that he was "in communion with the holy bishops, Cyril, Sixtus, and Maximian."

The stubborn old bishop of Hierapolis was not left alone in bearing witness, as he deemed, against an unprincipled compromise [c]. In the two Cilician provinces, where Theodore's influence had been great, Nestorian prelates indignantly denounced all who communicated with the "Apollinarian" of Alexandria. Helladius of Tarsus, one of the four deposed metropolitans,—Maximin of Anazarbus, who insisted that Cyril should, as the one condition of being recognized, sign a recantation of his anathemas,—Meletius of Mopsuestia, who flung back a letter of John's in the bearer's face,—Macarius of Laodicea, who would not name John, his own patriarch, at the altar,—and Eutherius of Tyana [d], who, as it were in desperation, appealed to Sixtus for help against John and Cyril,—may represent the extreme Oriental view which regarded even Theodoret as a tamperer with heretics, and John as a base deserter of his friend. On the other hand, there were among Cyril's old adherents some who asked themselves, whether his acceptance of the Two Natures, a phrase which he had not expressly used before the concordat, were not a deviation from strict orthodoxy. "Theodoret said that it could not be reconciled with his earlier teaching; might not Theodoret be right on this

[c] Mansi, v. 891.

[d] He was especially scornful about the phrase, "He suffered without suffering." "One might as well say, Let us speak without speaking." Could he be ignorant of the sense attached to the words, "The one Christ suffered, but not in His higher nature?"

point, although he blasphemed that teaching? Could a co-existence of Two Natures be in fact maintained without Nestorianism?" Isidore, Cyril's ever-ready monitor, who had formerly taxed him with pressing the Nestorianizers too hard, now blamed him for making terms with them too easily. His patriarch, who had seemed so rigid in 431, was now, in Isidore's eyes, giving signs of weak inconstancy [e]; a criticism which perhaps may diminish the weight of the abbat's former censures. Eulogius, a priest of Alexandria residing at Constantinople, signified to Cyril that some uneasiness was felt; and Acacius of Melitene seems to have done the same. Cyril wrote to Acacius, giving an account of all that had happened, defending the orthodoxy of those who had joined in the concordat, and denying that the new formulary could in fairness be called a new creed. John of Antioch, he urged, was severed from Nestorius by his distinct confession of "Theotocos" and "one Christ." The formulary went beyond a mere association, and asserted a real union. He then employed a phrase which became in after-years a stumbling-block [f]. "While conceiving of the elements which constitute the one Son and Lord, we say that two Natures are united; but after the union, since the separation into two is now removed, we believe that *the Nature of the Word is one, as of one* (Person) *made man and incarnate;*" or, as he expressed it in a letter soon afterwards written to Eulogius, "there is *one incarnate Nature* of God (the Word)."

He had already, in one of the treatises addressed to the princesses [g], cited these words as used by S. Athanasius. The short confession "On the Incarnation of God the Word," in which they occur, has been placed among the dubious works of Athanasius, and been ascribed by some to an Apollinarian forger [h]; while some have gone so far as to conjec-

---

[e] Ep. i. 323, 324. [f] Mansi, v. 319.

[g] Ad reg. i. 9; and in a lost work against Theodore.

[h] See Tillemont, viii. 715: he is doubtful. The Benedictines think it a forgery. "Athanasius......proprietates naturarum semper conservavit."

ture that the text of Cyril's writings has been corrupted by the insertion of the phrase[i]. But taking that text as it stands, and supposing Cyril to have adopted and clung to the phrase, because he believed it to have the authority of earlier Fathers[k], it is incredible that he meant, by using it in 333, to explain away the formulary or his own second letter to Nestorius; and when we look at the contexts in which he used it, we see that the one idea in his mind was to guard the reality of the "undivided" Union[l]. There were those who said, "'One incarnate Nature of the Word' can mean nothing but a confusion of Godhead and Manhood." Cyril's reply in substance is, "It means nothing more nor less than that whereas, apart from the Incarnation, God and Man must be regarded as separate, there is no such separation in the person of our Lord. We are not to think of *a God and a Man*[m], but of *a God-Man;* of one and the same Divine Word, who has become Incarnate, *that is*, has assumed our whole humanity." Thus understood, the phrase was doubtless orthodox; but Cyril's retention of it, however elaborately he might impose a sound sense upon inaccurate language, went far to undo the good which had been wrought by his readiness to conciliate and explain. Though he vindicated the soundness of his new allies, yet the effect of the formulary and of the subsequent letter to John was sadly marred by the re-appearance of language which to minds impatient of glosses would suggest a denial of Two Natures in Christ.

Meanwhile, in the West, Prosper was carrying on the war against the Semi-Pelagians. After writing the *Contra*

---

[i] Leontius of Byzantium; Hypatius bishop of Ephesus; Petav. Theol. Dogm. iv. 330.

[k] "As the Fathers have said;" Ep. 1. ad Successum.

[l] Epp. to Acacius, Eulogius, Successus: especially Ep. 2 ad Succ. Newman takes φύσις here as equivalent to Person, Athan. Treat. i. 155: but see Petavius, iv. 337, who takes it somewhat differently, for Nature, as existing in the Person of the Word, i. e. for the Word Himself.

[m] As he expresses it, a God, καταμόνας, ad Succ. 2, and "a man individually regarded beside the Word," ad Acac. So ad Eulog.

Collatorem [n], he replied to the objections raised against Augustinianism by the Gallicans [o], and to a series framed by one of them named Vincent [p]. The questions debated in this controversy were such as these: whether predestination did not imply fatalism; whether it was consistent with God's good-will towards all men; whether it supposed God to cause directly the ruin of any. He repeatedly declared that no man was predestinate to sin; that no man's life was prolonged in order that he might fall from grace; that to make God the author of any evil will or deed was abominable; that Father, Son, and Holy Spirit had nothing to do with any man's fall from piety. He answered a letter from two Genoese priests, who had found difficulties in S. Augustine's work on predestination [q]. Vincent, whose representations of Predestinarianism he had denounced as a hideous caricature, was apparently the same [r] who in 434 brought out his famous "Commonitory," and is known by the surname of Lerinensis. The "Commonitory" was designed to be a preservative [s] "against the profane novelties of all heretics." The general principle of this famous book, to whose author one opinion would ascribe the *Quicunque*, is well known; the formula in which he states the Catholic rule of Scripture interpretation has taken its place among ecclesiastical proverbs [t]. Among the most striking passages are the application of Deut. xiii. to Christian times, the precise statement of the Personal Union of "two Substances" in Christ, the description of Origen's great gifts marred by "self-reliance" and disregard for traditionary orthodoxy, the paraphrase of

---

[n] Noris, Hist. Pel. 239.

[o] Aug., tom. x. p. 1833.

[p] Ib., p. 1843. In both cases the objectors stated what they considered Augustinianism to imply.

[q] Ib., p. 1849.

[r] Noris, p. 245. He thinks that Vincent went to the monastery of Lerins after writing his book, p. 251. He wrote it in a monastery situated in a secluded *villula*.

[s] Marius Mercator had written "Commonitories" against Pelagianism.

[t] "Curandum est ut id teneamus, *quod ubique, quod semper, quod ab omnibus creditum est;*' c. 3. See Pusey on Rule of Faith, p. 38; Moberly, Gr. Forty Days, p. xliii.

the exhortation to "guard the deposit[u]," excluding all additions to the substance of the faith, and the allowance of an appeal from wide-spread error to the general judgment of the primeval Church. Vincent records the message of Capreolus to the Ephesian Council, that he desired all novelties to be condemned. Capreolus was at this very time assisting two Spanish laymen to maintain the ancient faith against a very bold form of Nestorianism. Christ, he said, was one Person of "two Substances."

There had been for several months an open breach between John and Alexander. John now proceeded to ordain bishops within Alexander's province; whereupon its prelates, including Theodoret, withdrew from their patriarch's communion.

Maximian of Constantinople died on April 12, 434. In spite of the solemnities of Holy Week, the Nestorians of the city, who had abstained from all his ministrations, and numbered among their ranks an abbat and a few clergy, rose in violent uproar, and demanded the restoration of Nestorius. Theodosius ordered Proclus, the titular bishop of Cyzicus, who had preached the great sermon on the Theotocos, to be instantly enthroned; and he officiated as patriarch at the funeral of Maximian[x]. It is refreshing to read the simple eulogy of Socrates on this eloquent and saintly bishop, who "showed himself gentle toward all men, resolved to win them by this means rather than by violence, and refraining on principle from harshness to any sect, restored to the Church the dignity of meekness[y]."

Theodosius, in the latter part of this year, deemed it necessary to enforce the concordat by the civil power. Alexander, Theodoret, Maximin, and Helladius were commanded to communicate with John, and consequently with Cyril, or

---

[u] "Non auctor debes esse, sed custos," &c.; c. 27. And as to the limits of doctrinal expansion, "ut cum dicas *novè*, non dicas *nova*;" ib. "Nihil minuit, nihil addit (ecclesia);" in councils her aim has been, "ut quod antea simpliciter credebatur, hoc idem postea diligentiùs crederetur;" c. 32.

[x] Soc. vii. 41.

[y] Ibid. 41.

to quit their sees. Theodoret laughed at menaces, but was moved by the earnest exhortations of three pious monks, and yielded when he found that John did not insist on his accepting the sentence against Nestorius. John employed him in the work of restoring unity. Alexander, on receiving letters from him, passionately replied that he would never communicate with the betrayers of orthodoxy. Never would he own the abomination of Egypt to be true religion, —no, not if all the dead were to rise up and contradict him, not if John could give him the kingdom of heaven as a reward. "Thank God," the old man added, "with them are synods, and sees, and kingdoms—with us is the Lord our God, and our pure inviolate faith in Him[z]!" Maximin, Helladius, and nearly all the Cilician prelates, followed Theodoret's example; Meletius of Mopsuestia cast in his lot with Alexander, for whom Theodoret entreated John's forbearance. A Count named Dionysius requested Alexander, as a friend, to obey. In reply, he quoted the words of Gal. i. 8, and begged to be "sent away quietly." He was ejected in April 435; his people were wild with grief and rage; but John wrote to them, laying the blame of their loss on the self-will of their pastor. Six bishops in all were dispossessed; and Theodosius, on August 3, forbade the Nestorians, whom he designated as Simonians, to meet for worship or to retain the writings of their master. It was not until some months afterwards that Nestorius himself was exiled to the greater Oasis on the Egyptian border.

The Nestorians now adopted a policy fertile in results for Eastern Christendom. Forbidden to circulate the works of Nestorius, they caused those of Theodore and Diodore to be widely dispersed; the abundant writings of Theodore were rendered into Syriac by a priest of Edessa, named Ibas, and into Persian by Maris, who presided over the college for Persian Christians at Edessa, and to whom Ibas had recently written a letter censuring the Council of

---

[z] Mansi, v. 926.

Ephesus, denouncing the "impiety" of the Cyrilline articles, and describing the reunion as a retractation by "the Egyptian" of his errors[a]. Rabbula was now old and blind, but youthful in controversial energy; he dissolved the Persian college as tainted with heresy, and its members found a home in the Persian Church[b]. Maris became bishop of Ardaschir; and Barsumas, as metropolitan of Nisibis, won the confidence of the Persian king by his hostility to "the faith of the Romans," and became the great propagator of Nestorianism in the remoter East. Thus the Persian Church, "immediately after its glorious confession" in the persecution begun by Isdigerdes, "fell a prey to the theology of Theodore[c];" and through long ages, under the title of "the Interpreter," he has been the oracle of the Nestorian communion.

Cyril believed that several bishops who had verbally condemned the heresiarch were in fact adhering to his doctrine. He therefore procured from the government orders that the bishops should explicitly repudiate Nestorianism. Aristolaus was sent to enforce these orders. Helladius made a full submission; but Theodoret, although he had been in friendly correspondence with Cyril, whose treatise against the writings of Julian the Apostate he had recently read and admired, would neither condemn Nestorianism nor desert Nestorius. Cyril drew up a formula which distinctly affirmed the Personal unity; and sent it to John and Aristolaus as embodying what the Emperor designed to exact. But John was not unnaturally annoyed[d] at this succession of tests, and begged Proclus to obtain for the Churches the repose of which they stood in need.

The Cilician prelates resented Rabbula's attack on Theo-

[a] The letter was grossly unjust to Cyril, imputing to him a confusion between Godhead and Manhood. [b] Asseman, Bib. Or. iii. 2. p. lxix.

[c] Newman on Development, p. 289.

[d] See Tillemont, xiv. 623. He places after this a letter (dated earlier by Fleury) in which Cyril exhorts a zealous deacon of Antioch, named Maximus, to forbear too rigid enquiries into the actual belief of some ex-Nestorians.

dore's teaching; while those of Armenia, having received one of his books, sent it to Proclus with a denunciation of its heretical subtlety. This produced the celebrated doctrinal epistle which has been called the "Tome of S. Proclus[e]." Addressing himself to the bishops, priests, and abbats of Armenia, the patriarch of Constantinople condemned Theodore's opinions without naming him, and stated the Catholic faith as to the One Person and Two Natures. He affirmed "one Incarnate *Person*" (not Nature) "of God the Word[f];" denied any conversion of Godhead into flesh; cited for Christ's Divinity Rom. ix. 5; observed that He never had a human personality; spoke of the swathing bands, the manger, the growth in wisdom and stature, the weariness, the sleep in the ship, as simply proving that true Manhood, which was needful for the work of our salvation[g]. He urged the Armenians to let "no man spoil them through philosophy and vain deceit," and to stand fast in the faith of Nicæa, as taught by Basil, Gregory, "and others like-minded, whose names were in the book of life." He appended to his letter some Nestorian passages which he deemed worthy of condemnation; and he sent both papers in the first instance to John of Antioch, desiring him to accept and subscribe his statements, and to induce Ibas, who had now succeeded Rabbula at Edessa, to do likewise. The bearers of the Tome, without authority from Proclus, inserted Theodore's name as the author of the censured passages; and the bishops of John's patriarchate, assembled at Antioch, while they fully accepted the doctrine of Proclus, declined[h] to condemn a deceased bishop on account of some questionable expressions, quoted, they said, apart from the context, and capable of a sense

[e] Mansi, v. 421.

[f] He also said that "one Person of the Trinity was Incarnate." Fifty years later a great excitement was caused by the saying of Peter the Fuller, patriarch of Antioch, that "one of the Trinity suffered."

[g] "By denying His (human) nature, they disbelieve the Incarnation," (lit. the Economy); "by disbelieving the Incarnation, they forfeit their salvation."

[h] Mansi, v. 1183.

which would harmonize them with the language of eminent Fathers. Still less, they urged, could they anathematize such a man as Theodore, who had done good service against Apollinarianism, and whose memory was so widely honoured. Proclus assured them that he had not wished for a condemnation of Theodore by name; but that he hoped they would condemn the propositions without naming their author. Cyril had thought it undesirable to demand the former, but he urged the necessity of the latter course. He wrote to John [i] that the Antiochene Council had been more indulgent to Theodore's memory than just to the Fathers with whom they had ventured to compare him. Theodore, he said, was a man who had "borne down full sail against the glory of Christ;" the Fathers had written against men whose errors Nestorius had inherited. He composed a treatise on the errors of Theodore, to which Theodoret replied. But the Easterns would not condemn Theodore's propositions, for fear of seeming to put the writer under ban. Cyril and Proclus allowed the matter to drop, and Theodosius signified his wish that the memory of the dead should be safe from censure [k].

Sixtus of Rome was on good terms with Proclus, but vigilantly maintained the position which Boniface had made good as to the Roman claims over Illyricum. He followed precedent by making the bishop of Thessalonica his vicar, and plainly told the Illyrian bishops that they were not bound by the third canon of the Council of Constantinople, to which Rome had never assented. This letter was written in the end of 437. On Jan. 27, 438, a solemn and touching ceremony absorbed the thoughts of the people at Constantinople. The remains of S. Chrysostom, by their desire and the advice of Proclus, were brought with all honour from Comana to a grave beside his ancient home. The Bosporus was in a blaze of light; the whole city seemed

---

[i] Mansi, v. 411.

[k] Theodore was anathematized by the Fifth General Council in 553.

to pour out all its inhabitants; the Emperor, who had been Chrysostom's godson, put his face close to the coffin, and begged the departed soul to forgive Arcadius and Eudoxia[l]. Until that memorable day, a small remnant of Joannites had kept aloof from all bishops of Constantinople, whether Catholic or heterodox; they now, as if satisfied with the reparation made to the Saint, consented to recognize Proclus as their pastor. About a year afterwards, Theodosius made a law forbidding Jews and Samaritans to build new synagogues, disqualifying them for all public offices, and re-enacting the penalty of death against Pagans who should venture to sacrifice.

Genseric had already increased his severities towards the Catholics of Africa by ejecting several of their bishops. Four Spaniards whom he had esteemed, and had vainly endeavoured to allure into Arianism, were first banished, then tortured to death; and a boy named Paulillus, the brother of two of them, having resisted all menaces, was cruelly beaten and reduced to slavery[m]. These events were as the drops before the thunderstorm. Carthage, the city of S. Cyprian, the scene of so many Councils, had become so full of profligacy and violence that the poorer classes, trampled down by their superiors in rank whom Salvian describes as "drunk with sin[n]," sometimes prayed in their agony that God would send them Genseric. A mass of Heathenism held its own amid professions of Catholic Christianity; monks, conspicuous by their short hair and pale faces, could not walk the streets without being cursed and insulted; rich and high-born citizens would pay their homage to the "Queen of heaven," before "ascending to the altar of Christ[o]." Such was the state of that proud city, which Augustine[p] had described as "standing fast in the

---

[l] Theod. v. 36.   [m] Prosp. Chron., A.D. 437.

[n] De Gub. Dei, vii. His language is probably somewhat exaggerated, but we cannot doubt that Carthage was now exhibiting in a very repulsive form that union of godlessness and heartlessness of which Amos gives so vivid a picture.   [o] Salv., lib. viii.   [p] Serm. 105.

name of Christ;" and the terrible suddenness with which the scourge overtook it seemed to bring home the threats of prophet and apostle [q]. Genseric, who had professed friendly relations with Rome, took Carthage on the 19th of October, 439. He committed great cruelties in searching for concealed treasure; drove away the priests, pillaged the churches, and assigned them as lodgings to his men. Quodvultdeus, bishop of Carthage, and several clergy, were compelled to go on board a crazy vessel, which, contrary to expectation, carried them safe to Naples. When some prelates and clergy petitioned the conqueror for leave to dwell in the land where they had been driven from their churches and possessions, he answered in an outbreak of tyrannical passion, that he was determined not to leave in his dominions one of their name or kin [r].

On Nov. 29 a Gallican Council met at Riez, under the presidency of S. Hilary of Arles, to consider the case of Armentarius, a young man of rank, who had been consecrated to the see of Embrun by two bishops, without the consent of the comprovincial bishops or of the metropolitan. He confessed that he had done wrong in accepting so irregular a consecration. The Council forbade his consecrators to appear at any future Council or ordination of bishops. His consecration was pronounced null, i.e. for the purposes of the diocese of Embrun. But any bishop was permitted to assign him a church in which he might officiate, either as a village bishop, or *Chorepiscopus*, under the authority of the diocesan, or as one maintained in "what was called *peregrina communio*," a phrase which in this place appears to mean the position of a foreign ecclesiastic, who resided as a guest where he had no right to officiate as an incumbent, although he might be invited to take part in the services [s]. The Council gave clear proof that it regarded him

---

[q] Isa. xxx. 13; Amos viii. 9; 1 Thess. v. 3.

[r] Victor, i. 5.

[s] Tillemont, xv. 66; Petav. cited by Bingham, b. 17. c. 3. Bingham would explain *peregrina communio* here to mean (as it did mean elsewhere) the charitable maintenance given to a foreign priest who, not possessing

as a real bishop, though he had not had three consecrators; for it allowed him to administer confirmation, and decreed that clergy ordained by him might, if found blameless, be retained at Embrun by the new bishop, or transferred to serve under their ordainer.

One of the last acts of Sixtus III. was prompted by his archdeacon Leo, of whom we have already heard in the Pelagian and Nestorian controversies. Julian, worn with suffering and disappointment, sought to be reconciled to the Church. Leo believed that his professions of sound belief were insincere; and whatever may have been the truth on this point, the chicanery of Pelagius might warrant some suspicions as to Julian. Sixtus, guided by Leo, refused to accept the convert [t], who died—either in 440 or 453—as a schoolmaster in a poor town of Sicily [u]. An inscription on some porphyry columns erected in the baptistery of the Lateran bore testimony to the orthodoxy of Pope Sixtus in regard to the doctrine of "one Baptism for the remission of sins [x]." "Here is the fount of life, which cleanses the whole world, taking its origin from the wound of Christ [y]. This water shall receive the old man and bring forth the new. He that would be guiltless, let him bathe in this laver, whether his burden of guilt be inherited or personal. There is no difference among the regenerate, who are made one by the one fount, the one Spirit, the one faith. Let none be terrified by the number or character of his sins; he will be holy when born in this stream."

Sixtus died either in March or in August 440. This

---

any *formatæ*, or letters commendatory from his own Church, was regarded as a stranger, and more or less under a cloud. But in this case the connection of *peregrina communio* with "the office of chorepiscopus," as forming the other alternative, seems to suggest a milder interpretation.

[t] Prosp. Chronic.

[u] His epitaph, the work of some loving hand, could still be read in the ninth century; "Hic in pace quiescit Julianus episcopus Catholicus."

[x] Baronius, iii. 768. There are sixteen verses.

[y] "The Sacrament of the remission of sins flowed from the opened side of Christ." S. Aug. c. Faust. xii. 16. See Pusey on Holy Baptism, p. 295.

time there was no chance of a disputed election. All Rome looked as one man to the pious, energetic, and Roman-spirited [z] Leo, then absent on a mission significant of his powers, that of reconciling two generals whose feud might be dangerous to the West. Without any show of diffidence, but without any egotistical self-confidence,—knowing "that He who imposed the burden would give His aid for the administration [a],"—Leo the Great, as he has been worthily styled, took possession of the see of S. Peter.

---

[z] "Leo was a Roman in sentiment as in birth." Milman, Hist. Lat. Chr. i. 180.

[a] Serm. 2.

CHAPTER XIV.

From the Accession of S. Leo to the Latrocinium.

"'Every spirit that confesseth not that Jesus Christ is come in the flesh is not of God.' .... Most wonderful prophecy, and surpassing test!"
Christian Remembrancer, vol. x.

JOHN of Antioch died in the same year as Sixtus of Rome, and was succeeded by his nephew Domnus, who had regretted his temporary alienation from S. Cyril.

On Nov. 8, 441, Hilary of Arles presided over the first Council of Orange. Its first canon allows heretics, desiring on their death-beds to be reconciled to the Church, to receive from the priest, in the bishop's absence, not only benediction, but also chrism. Its second canon is remarkable in a similar point of view. Beside the chrism used from the second century[a] at confirmation, and the anointing which had been prefixed to baptism, there had come into use, as confirmation became more and more a separate ordinance, an unction on the crown of the head, administered by the priest immediately *after* baptism. Pope Innocent had distinguished this unction from that which only bishops could bestow. But now the Gallican bishops provided, that if this unction had been administered, no unction in confirmation would be necessary[b]; the bishop was to administer chrism only when informed that the unction after baptism had been omitted. Such, at least, is the generally-received sense of the canon[c], although the reading has been disputed. Another canon shows the germ of patronage in the permission given to a bishop, who founds a church in another diocese, to name, but not to ordain, its clergy[d].

---

[a] Tertull. de Bapt. 7; see S. Cypr. Ep. 70.

[b] "Ut *non necessaria* habeatur repetita chrismatio."

[c] See Sirmond's note; the canon, he says, is a departure "à priscâ ecclesiæ disciplinâ." Another reading, now given up, is, "ut *necessaria*."

[d] Guizot, Civilis., lec. 13. "Ce patronage ecclésiastique amena bientôt un patronage laïque de même nature."

Deaconesses are not to be ordained. Religious widowhood is to be professed before the bishop in his "secretarium," or hall of business [e]. Mention is made of the bondmen of the Church, of slaves emancipated in the Church, and of slaves recommended to the Church by will. Christianity had suggested to its disciples those high thoughts of universal brotherhood in Christ, which were after the lapse of ages to bear fruit in the abolition of slavery throughout Europe [f]. But the time was not yet. The Church was active in softening the hardships of the servile relation, but she did not, even on her own domains, forswear this species of property.

Leo followed up, as bishop, the line of conduct which he had recommended to Sixtus, in regard to the reception of Pelagian conformists. He exhorted the bishop of Aquileia to receive none without an unequivocal abjuration, and a clear admission of real grace. At the same time he showed his zeal against that heresy which Pelagians were wont to associate with the Church.

The Manichean community at Rome had been reinforced by fugitives from Africa. They endeavoured to mingle with Churchmen in public worship; but the eye of Leo was upon them. He found out who the men were that declined to receive the Eucharistic chalice, fasted on Sunday and Monday in honour of the sun and moon, and led some of the faithful, as they ascended the steps of S. Peter's, to turn round at the topmost steps and salute the rising sun. He instituted a search for Manicheans, and detected many, including their bishop; and, assembling a number of bishops, priests, and distinguished laymen, he compelled the captured heretics to confess the infamies which made part of their secret ritual [g]. Some gave token of genuine repentance; with regard to the rest, Leo employed his great powers of terse and vigorous preaching in order to guard his flock from the

---

[e] See Bingham, b. 8. 7. 7. compare Apost. Const. iv. 1.

[f] See Rogers' Eclipse of Faith, p. 363;

[g] Serm. 16.

pollution of their company. In the Ember-week of December 443, and on the Epiphany of 444, he denounced Manicheism with the energy of one to whom the faith of Christ and the Gospel law of holiness were supremely dear. The enemy who had made use of other heresies had built for himself, in this, the very citadel and palace of his empire. The profanity of the Pagans, the blindness of carnal Judaism, the dark secrets of magic, the blasphemies of every form of error, had been poured into one receptacle of foulness. Manicheans, he urged[h], regarded the idea of Incarnation as a debasement of the Deity; they imagined a Christ with a phantom body, which could not really die nor revive; and that the whole truth of the Apostles' Creed might be annihilated, they denied that Christ would come as a Judge. They cast off the Old Testament, they corrupted and mutilated the New; they circulated false Scriptures under sacred names; they strove to ensnare the simple by pretended austerity, by a display of mean dresses and pallid faces, and by fasts which were in truth impure[i]. But he did not conclude without an expression of deep pity for those who had fallen into this Antichristian heresy, yet for whom, as long as life remained, there remained a place of repentance. Some of the Manicheans fled from Rome, and Leo wrote against them to all the bishops of Italy, January 30, 444.

The career of S. Cyril was now drawing to an end. In common with S. Proclus, he had recently given too ready a credence to the aged Athanasius, bishop of Perrha, who, having resigned his see in consequence of heavy accusations, complained that his clergy had plotted his deposition. Cyril and Proclus wrote to Domnus on his behalf. A council was held at their suggestion, but Athanasius declined to attend it. About the same time, Cyril attacked the anthropomorphite notions which were still, as in his uncle's time, taking hold of some monastic dreamers. To his work

[h] Serm. 34.

[i] Compare Serm. 41.

"Against the Anthropomorphites" is prefixed an epistle to Calosirius, bishop of Arsinoe; from which it appears that some of these fanatics insisted on devoting to prayer the time that should have been spent on needful labour, and that others believed the reserved Eucharist to "lose its power for sanctification." "This," wrote Cyril[k], "is an extravagant idea: for Christ is not altered, nor will His holy Body be changed; but the power of the consecration and the life-giving grace is perpetual in it." He died in June 444, after a pontificate of thirty-two years, during the last fifteen of which he may be said to have as truly lived for the Hypostatic Union as his mightiest predecessor for the Homoousion. Doubtless, the fiery spirit which Cyril could not always restrain impelled him, during this great controversy, into some steps which show that he was not an Athanasius. But modern critics of his character have said more than enough on this point, and too little on points of a different kind. Historical justice can never demand that we should take the hardest possible view of his conduct at the opening of the Council of Ephesus, and ignore the noble unselfishness, the patience in explaining over again his own statements, the readiness in welcoming substantial agreement on the part of others,—in a word, the "power, and love, and self-command" which made him a true minister of peace in the Reunion of 433. We need not dwell on other instances in which he showed a remarkable forbearance, as when he bore without irritation the schooling of S. Isidore[l]; on his care for the due probation of aspirants to the priesthood, his depth and acuteness as a dogmatic theologian, his faith and thankfulness when treated as a deposed prisoner. The way *not* to understand him is to substitute a haughty and heartless dogmatist for the ardent, anxious, often the deeply-suffering man, who, against an opponent strong in sophistry, in Court influence, and in Church power, persevered in defending the simple truth of

---

[k] Cyr. vi. 365.

[l] See Tillemont, xiv. 657.

the Scriptural and Nicene mystery, that "the one Lord Jesus Christ was very God of very God, who for us men and for our salvation came down from heaven, and was incarnate, and was made Man." In proportion as Christians of this age confess their faith in the atoning work of this One Christ, they are daily debtors to S. Cyril of Alexandria.

He left a large bequest to his successor, conjuring him "by the venerable and awful Mysteries" to befriend his kindred. The archdeacon Dioscorus, who had accompanied him to Ephesus, was elected; and forthwith, as if suspecting that the family of Cyril and Theophilus had been enriched by nepotism, he extorted from them considerable sums, which he lent to bakers and vintners that they might supply the citizens with good bread and wine. Athanasius and Paul, Cyril's nephews, were imprisoned and otherwise outraged; the houses of the obnoxious family were turned into churches; one which could not be so used was blocked up. Athanasius, after Paul's death, was deposed from the priesthood, excluded from the bath and the market, and reduced, with his aunts and other relatives, to homeless beggary. The patriarch had previously borne a fair character; but his exaltation revealed, or possibly generated, a spirit at once tyrannous and sensual. His life became openly scandalous. He deposed a deacon, named Theodore, whom Cyril had favoured; another named Ischyrion was not only forbidden to officiate, but deprived of his all by agents of Dioscorus, who burned his house, felled his trees, and hacked up his land. His life, he afterwards declared, was twice endangered by the patriarch's malignity.

Nestorius had been banished to the Oasis, whither Constantius had sent some Catholic bishops in 356. It was a miserable place of exile, exposed to the wild nomad tribes; all around were shifting sands, forming a pathless solitude. He was living there when Socrates completed his History in 439[m]; and employed himself in writing a defence of

[m] Soc. vii. 34.

the opinions for which he had lost all. The Blemmyes at length invaded the Oasis, and took Nestorius, among others, captive; then, by what he calls a most unexpected act of compassion [n], released him, and bade him hurry away. He thought it best to proceed to Panopolis in the Thebaid, and voluntarily reported himself to the governor; who, unmoved by his pathetic entreaty that the imperial authorities would not be less merciful than the barbarians, ordered some soldiers to convey him to Elephantine. The journey under such circumstances exhausted the old man; a fall severely hurt his hand aud side; and before he could reach Elephantine, a mandate came for his return to Panopolis. Two more compulsory changes of abode were added to sufferings which remind us, perforce, of the last days of S. Chrysostom; and then the unhappy Nestorius was no more. The exact year of his death cannot be ascertained [o]. Heresiarch though he was, and miserably as he had rent the Church, the first feeling excited by the narrative of his end is indignation at the cruelties of a Catholic government and the shameful rancour of a Catholic historian [p].

We turn to the memorable contest between the two most eminent bishops of Western Christendom. Hilary of Arles was revered for his devotion, his extraordinary euergy as a preacher, his unwearied zeal in converting pagans and heretics; he was beloved for his humility and sympathy, his active compassion for the poor, his readiness to ransom captives even with the vessels of the altar, and the apostolic tenderness with which he administered Church discipline. There was a holy intensity about his character which made him the chief power in the Transalpine Church. Such was the prelate who, while visiting S. Germain at Auxerre, received a complaint against a bishop named Celidonius.

---

[n] Evagr. i. 7.

[o] Tillemont says it was between 439 and 450.

[p] Evagrius, i. 7, "learned that his tongue was eaten through by worms, and that then he departed to the everlasting judgment which awaited him." The remonstrances of the worn-out sufferer are described as a striking with fist and heel!

"He ought not to have been consecrated; while a layman and a magistrate, he married a widow, and he inflicted capital punishment." It was contended, in fact, that he was canonically irregular. A certain degree of morbid formalism had taken hold of the ecclesiastical mind on both these points, and a council of bishops, called together to hear the case, did but carry out the existing law in its literal rigour, by adjudging Celidonius to resign his see.

Celidonius appealed to Rome, apparently in the autumn of 444; and Leo, glad to welcome an appellant, received him without further questioning to communion. Hilary heard of this in the depth of winter. It was characteristic of him to do "with his might," at once and thoroughly, whatever seemed his duty in any matter. Regardless of the bitter weather, he crossed the Alps on foot, and arrived at Rome. His first act was to visit the tombs of the Apostles; that pious office discharged, he presented himself before Leo, and respectfully begged him not to innovate on Church order, but to consider in a friendly and extra-judicial way the statement he had to make. Mindful of his own position, he expressly declared that he was not come to plead before a court, but to give information as to facts unknown at Rome[q]. A council was assembled, in which Hilary had a seat. He was assailed by threats, and urged, apparently, to make a formal accusation of Celidonius, or to communicate with him. He refused, asserting his rights as a Gallican archbishop in language which, as the præfect Auxiliaris expressed it, did not suit "the delicate ears of the Romans," and to which, the Pope affirmed, "no bishop could bear to listen." He withdrew from the council, evaded the guards which had been placed over him, and returned without further delay to Gaul. Leo, who was disposed to take an unfriendly view of all his conduct, regarded this proceeding as a "disgraceful flight[r];" but Hilary had no mind to wait for the judgment of what he deemed

[q] Honoratus' Life of S. Hilary.

[r] Ep. 10.

an incompetent tribunal. That judgment was, that Celidonius had been found innocent of irregularity; and he was formally confirmed in the episcopate.

Here we observe two principles in conflict. The archbishop of Arles was contending, as the African Church before her troubles had contended, and in strict conformity with the canon of Ephesus, for the independence of local hierarchies in regard to a powerful neighbour. Gaul was not within the Roman patriarchate. There was no question of the canons of Sardica; Leo had gone beyond their limits, which were in fact too narrow for his ideas. Whatever thoughts of world-wide supervision and control had passed through the minds of Innocent and Cœlestine, were crystallized in the teaching and the claims of Leo. Africans and Easterns had revered in S. Peter the symbol of unity and the "coryphæus" of the Apostles; and had more or less admitted in the Roman bishop a corresponding primacy of influence and of honour. But Leo held, and it was on the whole a new doctrine, that Peter had *powers* beyond his brethren, which his successors had inherited [s]; and thus he became the founder of that supremacy which subsequent Popes built up in Western Europe. The later assertion of Papal autocracy was a flight which surpassed his proudest dreams [t].

He now gave audience to another complaint. Hilary had suddenly arrived at a city the name of which is unknown, but which was not in the province of the Viennensis, then subject to the see of Arles. Projectus, the bishop of this city, was dangerously ill; and Hilary appears to have thought that it was necessary to make immediate provision for the see. He consecrated another bishop to succeed Projectus, who recovered, and laid his grievance

[s] See Ep. 14, c. 11, Serm. 4.

[t] The confusion of primacy with supremacy is a palpable sophism. The Roman primacy, supremacy, and autocracy may be roughly compared to the respective positions of an older brother, a feudal prince, and a Louis XIV.

before Leo. We do not know the circumstances as they presented themselves to Hilary. Leo was content with an *ex parte* statement, and declared the act of Hilary null. He also wrote a letter [u] to the bishops of Viennensis, denouncing the pride and stubbornness of Hilary, who would not "endure to be subject to S. Peter." He gave his own version of the cases of Celidonius and Projectus, and was so far carried away by hasty injustice as to say that Hilary was "not so much bent on consecrating a bishop as on causing the death of Projectus, and deceiving by a wrongful ordination the man whom he intruded into the see." Such a passage may enable us to judge of other charges against Hilary, endorsed by Leo in this vehement epistle. The ready support given to Hilary in his visitations by the highest civil functionaries, his vigour as a disciplinarian, his rapid movements throughout his province, were represented to Leo in a light sufficiently odious, and probably altogether untrue. The Pope had evidently a foregone conclusion; he had been thoroughly provoked by Hilary's boldness, and now declared him to be excluded from communion with Rome. The powers of the see of Arles over Viennensis, which Zosimus had strongly maintained, were annulled by Leo, who suggested that an aged bishop named Leontius should enjoy a certain kind of primacy in Gaul. This was a high-handed proceeding enough; but Leo, as if apprehensive that the Gallican Church might disregard his bidding, resolved to fortify it by an imperial rescript.

On June 6, 445, Valentinian III. put forth a mandate, for the substance at least of which Leo must be held responsible [x]. "A holy synod [y]," the Emperor is made to say, has ordained that no one shall presume to attempt anything without the authority of that see, which derives its primacy "from the merit of S. Peter, and from the dignity of the city of Rome. For then will the peace of the

---

[u] Ep. 10.

[x] Ep. 11, Valent. Aetio.

[y] The vagueness of the expression is significant.

Churches be everywhere preserved, if they all acknowledge their ruler [z]." Hilary's offences are then recited; that he still retains the title of bishop, is ascribed to Leo's grace alone. The Papal sentence against him "would of itself have been valid; for what could be unlawful in the Church to the authority of so great a pontiff?" But to prevent such disobedience for the future, the Emperor decreed that no bishop in Gaul or in other provinces should be at liberty, "contrary to old usage," to dispense with "the authority of the venerable Pope of the eternal city." All were to hold his ordinances for law; and a bishop, cited to his tribunal, and neglecting the summons, should be compelled by the provincial government to obey. Such was the rescript of 445, which of course could have no reference to the East, but which, considered as a law for the Western empire, must appear a grave offence against historical facts, as well as against the rights of the several Churches. Untruths which Roman ecclesiastics were too ready to believe, became the groundwork of an usurpation which used the imperial power as its instrument. "But the metropolitans were not inclined to surrender their prerogatives [a];" and in this particular case, the Viennese Churches continued in obedience to Hilary, who after doing his best, in vain, to conciliate Leo, sought comfort in his devotions and his pastoral work, and never conceded the point at issue [b].

A few days after this rescript, Leo wrote to the new patriarch of Alexandria, taking care to assume that the Church of S. Mark must have learned her ritual customs from that of S. Peter [c]. In a somewhat authoritative tone he desired that holy orders should be administered on Saturday night, or early on Sunday morning; and that on

---

[z] "Rectorem:" not "lord," as in Milman's Lat. Chr. i. 195.

[a] Hallam, Middle Ages, ii. 228.

[b] Tillemont, xv. 83, does not scruple to say that "in the eyes of those who have any love for the Church's liberty or any knowledge of her discipline, the law of June 6 will be as little honourable to him whom it praises, as injurious to him whom it condemns."

[c] Ep. 9.

great festivals, when the worshippers were too numerous for the capacities of any single church, the celebration should be several times repeated, so that different companies might have in turn an opportunity of offering sacrifice. This was the Roman custom; but it does not seem to have made its way into Egypt[d].

The affair of Athanasius of Perrha was not yet settled. No successor had been appointed to his see, and the clergy petitioned Domnus for a bishop. Domnus assembled a council; Athanasius would not attend, "because he had enemies in the assembly;" judgment was given against him by default, and Sabinian was named bishop of Perrha.

Leo had given to Anastasius of Thessalonica the usual commission to represent him in Illyricum. But Anastasius abused his power. Atticus, metropolitan of Nicopolis, had excused his absence from a synod on the grouud of illness; Anastasius obtaiued an order from the præfect, and caused Atticus to be forcibly conveyed to Thessalonica, "through roads blocked up with snow." Leo wrote a grave rebuke to his tyrannical vicar[e], and expressed his will that the rights of metropolitans should be respected, concluding with the text on the exaltation of the humble.

Germain in 447 paid another visit to Britain, in compauy with Severus of Treves[f]. Again the Pelagians quailed before the Gallicans. On his return, he was appealed to by the Armoricans, who had been driven into insurrection by heavy taxes, and against whom Aetius had despatched the Alani. Germain met the Alan chief upon his way; took hold of the bridle of his horse, and by solemn urgency procured a breathing time for the Armoricans, who thereupon deputed him as their envoy to the Emperor.

The Priscillianist heresy had revived in Spain; Turibius, bishop of Astorga, convicted a great number of its adherents, and wrote an account of the matter to Leo. The

---

[d] Tillemont, xv. 440. [e] Ep. 14.

[f] Bede, i. 21. He connects a miracle of healing with each visit.

heretics, it appears, took pains to conceal their opinions under the cloak of orthodox language and external conformity; at the same time, they circulated apocryphal acts of S. Thomas, S. John, S. Andrew, and a blasphemous memoir of the Apostles which represented Christ as denouncing the Old Testament [g]. Leo replied on July 21, 447 [h]. He spoke of Priscillianism as of the kindred Manichean system; it was a combination of detestable errors. Alluding to Priscillian's execution, he justified it on the express ground that his doctrine was not merely heretical, but a social abomination. The Church, he observed, was too gentle not to "shrink from a bloody vengeance" on her enemies; but when they attacked public morality, and "subverted all laws divine and human, the severity of Christian princes" was well-timed. He entered into a detailed description of Priscillianism, and recommended the Spanish bishops to hold a council against "these impieties." The sufferings of the Mauritanian Church had already given him an opportunity for interfering in its concerns [i]; and he now wrote to the bishops of Sicily, who had been suffering from Arian persecution [k], commanding them to give up their custom of baptizing on the Epiphany, and to confine themselves to Easter and Pentecost [l].

New troubles were gathering round the Eastern Church. A party had been formed, mainly by the zeal of monks, whose watchword was hostility to Theodoret, as being no better than a Nestorian. These men exaggerated the teaching of S. Cyril, or rather, its more conspicuous aspect; using some of his words, and those in a sense not his. From real, though erring reverence, they wished to honour Christ and to bar out a profane heresy by regarding His Manhood as absorbed in His Godhead. Theodoret, on the other hand, although he had worked his way to a real belief in the one Christ, had never accepted the

[g] Turrib. Ep. 5.

[h] Ep. 15.

[i] Ep. 12. He claimed on this occasion a right of confirming the provincial sentence.

[k] Ep. Paschasini ad Leon.

[l] Ep. 16.

Cyrilline articles; and was jealous of any statement that even seemed to obscure that distinction of Natures, on which, as he felt, depended the reality of the Gospel. He wrote about this time a treatise called *Eranistes* or *Polymorphus*, names intended to represent the assertors of One Nature as making up a theory from the "contributions" of "manifold" errors. The book consisted of three dialogues, called "Immutable," "Inconfused," and "Impassible." In the second occurs a memorable passage, wherein the illustration employed by "Eranistes,"—that as the Sacramental symbols are changed by consecration, so is the Lord's Body changed into a divine substance [m],—meets with a direct retort from "Orthodox." "You are taken in the net which you wove; for the mystic symbols do not, after consecration, depart from their own nature; they continue in their former essence, figure, and form, and are visible and tangible as before; but in thought they are conceived, and believed, and adored, as being those things which are objects of faith [n]." Here, as Cyril argued from the life-giving character of Christ's Body to its being the Body of one who was God, Theodoret argues from the co-existence of the outward with the inward part in the Eucharist to the co-existence of Manhood with Godhead in Christ's Person. In the same dialogue he quotes Cyril among other orthodox teachers who had affirmed this latter co-existence. The third dialogue is occupied with enforcing that impassibility of the Godhead, which Cyril had never denied when he spoke of God the Word as having suffered in the flesh.

S. Proclus died on October 24, 447. Flavian, treasurer of his church, succeeded him, and immediately became obnoxious to the eunuch Chrysaphius, by refusing to give any other *eulogia* than a loaf of white bread. Pulcheria sup-

m There were two forms of expressing the same idea: 1. The Godhead was converted into flesh; 2. The flesh, taken from Mary, was changed into something divine.

n See Mr. Owen's Introd. to Dogm. Theol., p. 413, as to this passage.

ported Flavian; and therefore Chrysaphius plotted against Pulcheria. He was the godson of the zealous abbat Eutyches, who was the chief of the monastic and ultra-Cyrilline party at Constantinople. Dioscorus threw himself into the same cause; the Emperor was made to order the expulsion of Irenæus from the bishopric of Tyre, on the ground that he was a Nestorian, and had been twice married. Theodoret wrote to Domnus in his friend's behalf, observing that Proclus had approved of his consecration; that eminent bishops had allowed digamists to be ordained, and that Irenæus had not, to his knowledge, refused to call the Holy Virgin Theotocos. Photius was placed in the bishopric; and Theodoret himself, ostensibly as a disturber of the Church's quiet, was commanded to confine himself to his own city [o]. He obeyed, but wrote in his own defence to high State officers. One letter [p] to the consul Nomus is eminently interesting; he mentions his early dedication to the service of God, and his episcopal labours during twenty-five years. In another [q], to a bishop, he protests that he is so far removed from "that execrable notion of two Sons," that he is offended by some expressions of Nicene writers, who have "made too broad a distinction" between God and Man in Christ. He proceeds to enumerate his commentaries on "the prophets, the Psalter, the Apostle [r]," and his other writings against various heretics, on the lives of Saints, on Providence, on the questions of the Magi, together with one which he calls a mystical book. Dioscorus was violently prejudiced against him by two or more monks who visited Alexandria. He wrote to Domnus in consequence; Theodoret saw the letter, and replied, denying the accusation that he had preached the duality of Sons at Antioch [s]. His sermons,

[o] Tillemont, xv. 275, dates this in 447-8. Fleury dates it in 445.

[p] Ep. 81.

[q] Ep. 82.

[r] i. e. the Epistles; still so called in the Liturgies of S. Mark and S. Chrysostom.

[s] Ep. 83. A fragment of a sermon ascribed to him, and said to have

he said, with a pardonable complacency, had been very acceptable to John of Antioch, who was wont to start up and "clap both his hands." His belief, learned from Scripture and Fathers, was that Christ, the one Lord, had both Divinity and Humanity [t]. Those who denied the difference between His flesh and His Godhead, or who said that either of them was converted into the other, he had been wont to set right by "the medicines of the blessed and admirable Theophilus and Cyril." The latter had written to him as a friend; an epistle which he kept, showed Cyril's estimate of "his accurate belief and his good feeling [u]." He concluded by a solemn imprecation; "Whoso denies the Holy Virgin to be Theotocos, calls our Lord a mere man, or divides the Only-begotten into two Sons, let him be deprived of the hope that is in Christ; and let all the people say, So be it, so be it." Dioscorus, instead of welcoming this letter, allowed Theodoret's enemies to anathematize him in the cathedral, and then, "rising up himself, confirmed their utterance by his own." So wrote Theodoret to Flavian, after hearing of this step, "which, were it not well attested, would be incredible [x]." Domnus took part with Theodoret, and sent envoys to Constantinople in his favour, whom Theodoret charged with several letters, in most of which he protested that he believed in One Christ, truly God and truly Man [y].

---

been preached after Cyril's death, begins, "No one is now forced to blaspheme."

[t] S. Thomas, he says, "called *Him* Lord and God." (Theodore had explained away those words.)

[u] Surely this letter to Dioscorus is in itself a proof of the spuriousness of a letter to John (or, as some would read, to Domnus,) which was produced as Theodoret's in the fifth General Council. It begins, with alleged reference to S. Cyril's death, "So then, at last the bad man is dead." But no extracts could give a due notion of its extreme outrageousness. Neander, iv. 213, thinks it genuine; an opinion which, according to Tillemont, xiv. 705, is equivalent to making out Theodoret to be "un misérable et un méchant." The sentiments, also, are "so mean, ridiculous, and impertinent," that they could not be Theodoret's. "A heavy stone on Cyril's grave will keep him from coming back," &c.

[x] Ep. 86.

[y] e.g. Ep. 104, "I give Him *one* worship...yet I know that Godhead and flesh are distinct; for the union is without confusion."

The exarchate of Ephesus was now held by Bassian, who had been installed under circumstances of some violence, but with the sanction of Theodosius, and had governed his Church four years, in full communion with S. Proclus. During Lent, 448, some troublesome rumours obliged his clergy to write to Theodosius and Pulcheria in his behalf. The application was successful; his peaceable possession of the see was guaranteed; he was one day in the very act of celebrating, when he was suddenly dragged from the altar, beaten, pillaged, and thrown into prison. On the ground of his irregular elevation, Leo and Flavian took part with his adversaries; Theodosius pronounced for his deposition, the priestly robes were torn from him by force, and a priest named Stephen was placed upon his throne. Such was the "tragedy of Bassian [z]." He lay in prison three months, and was released, apparently, just about the time when Germain lay dying at Ravenna, which he had visited as the advocate of the Armoricans. After a life which "many crosses had made one long martyrdom," he could calmly say, "Well do I know what a country it is which God promises to His servants." He died July 31, 448; and his apostolic career was long commemorated in a sacramental preface [a] by the Church of Gaul.

A more important case than Bassian's was that of Ibas of Edessa. He had long been suspected as a Nestorianizer, and we have seen that Proclus was uneasy on this point. Several of the Edessene clergy, who regretted the contrast between their present and their late bishop, accused Ibas of having said, in the hall of his episcopal house, and before his assembled priests, "I do not envy Christ His becoming God; for I can become God no less than He." Ibas excommunicated them as calumniators. After a council at Antioch, which pronounced in favour of Ibas, because two of his accusers were not forthcoming, the Emperor commissioned the bishops of Tyre, Berytus, and Himeria

[z] Tillem. xv. 465.

[a] Murat. ii. 698.

to hear the cause. This commission was granted on October 26, 448. A few days afterwards, on Nov. 8, a council of bishops was sitting in the synod-room of Flavian's palace. One of them, the bishop of Dorylæum, was that Eusebius who had denounced Nestorius twenty years before, while yet a mere layman. He now showed his unchilled fervour of orthodoxy by attacking an error in the opposite extreme[b]. In a memorial which he presented to his brethren, Eutyches was characterized as a frenzied blasphemer, who applied the name of heretic to those whose faith agreed with that of the Saints. Eusebius protested that, for himself, he held the faith of Cyril; and he begged the Council to summon the archimandrite, whom he undertook in that case to convict of heresy. When the paper was read, Flavian observed that an accusation against one so respected was simply astonishing. Could not Eusebius visit Eutyches, before invoking the Council's judgment? Eusebius, who was greatly excited, declared that Eutyches had been once his friend; he had repeatedly warned him to desist from heterodox language; he could not, after these vain remonstrances, "go and hear him once again blaspheme." It was therefore agreed that Eutyches should be summoned; the Council adjourned to the 12th, and on that day read the second letter of Cyril to Nestorius, and his letter to John after the concordat. The patriarch then declared his belief that Christ was perfect God and perfect Man, consubstantial with the Father as to Godhead, with Mary as to Manhood; that *from* the two Natures, united after the Incarnation in one Person, there resulted one Christ. Other prelates followed in the same strain; Basil of Seleucia still more expressly, "I adore one Christ, acknowledged *in* two Natures after the Incarnation." Again the Council adjourned to Nov. 15; when the messengers who had been sent to Eutyches reported that he had long ago resolved never to leave his monastery; that he con-

---

[b] Mansi, vi. 653.

sidered Eusebius to be his personal enemy; that he admitted Christ's perfect Manhood, but not that His flesh was consubstantial with ours, nor that He was of two Natures. He acknowledged, they said, *one Nature* only of God Incarnate; he accepted the teaching of the Fathers, but looked to Scripture as being the safest guide. Two priests, Mamas and Theophilus, carried to him the second summons. At first they were denied admittance. When he did receive them, he bade them say that he was an old man, as good as dead; he was, in fact, seventy. "Where," he added, "does Scripture speak of two Natures [c]?" "Where," retorted his visitors, "does Scripture speak of Homoousion?" "It is in the Fathers." "Very well! the Fathers are good interpreters of Scripture, and they also speak of two Natures." There were, in fact, many such testimonies, as Theodoret had shown in the second of his dialogues; the priests were doubtless thinking especially of S. Chrysostom, who, for instance, had said that S. John, in the words "Jesus wept," intended to show "that He was truly clothed in our nature [d]." Eutyches replied by a phrase which showed that his temper was not like that of Theodore's school, irreverent and rationalistic; "I do not speculate on the nature of the Godhead." Theophilus drew from him the admission that the Word was perfect God, and, as incarnate, perfect Man also. "If, then, the two perfects make up one Son, why do you refuse to confess two Natures?" Eutyches repeated that he would not speculate, nor affirm Christ to be of two Natures; he would stay in his cloister; and, if deposed, he would make it his tomb. It appeared that he was stirring up the monastic party, by sending a doctrinal treatise to be subscribed in all the

---

[c] Mansi, vi. 725.

[d] In Joan., hom. 63. 2. See also S. Melito, in Routh, Rell. Sac. i. 121; Tertull. de Carne Chr. 5; S. Greg. Naz. ad Cledon. "There are *two natures*, but not two Sons;" S. Amphilochius; "Distinguish the natures of God and Man;" S. Basil, c. Eunom. i.; "Our Lord was born in the essence of the Manhood;" S. Aug. Enchir. 12, &c.

monasteries of Constantinople. He also sent a brother abbat to inform the Council that he was very ill. "He could not sleep all night, but groaned; and his groans kept me awake." Flavian answered kindly, "We have no idea of pressing hardly upon him. We are old friends of his; we will wait until he is better, and then let him come and confess that he has erred." He added, after the sitting was broken up, that "fire itself seemed cold to Eusebius," whose vehemence he had endeavoured to calm down. A third summons was followed, on Nov. 27, by the personal attendance of Eutyches. His great influence and position were shown by the officers, soldiers, and monks who escorted him, and by an imperial order that the patrician Florentius should have a seat in the synod[e]. Eusebius declared that he had much to fear from Eutyches: "I am a poor man without property, he is rich; he menaces me with exile, he already depicts to me the Oasis." The patriarch asked if Eutyches confessed an union out of two Natures. He replied that he did. "My lord archimandrite," asked Eusebius, "do you confess *two natures after the Incarnation*, and will you say that Christ is cousubstantial with us according to the flesh?" Eutyches attempted to fence with the question, by putting in a paper which averred his belief in the doctrine of Cyril and other Fathers, and anathematized Apollinaris as well as Nestorius. When called upon for a verbal statement, he freely admitted, 1. That S. Mary was "consubstantial with us;" 2. Although he had "never before said it," that Christ was so likewise, as Man. Here, then, were two points gained; the second not without protestations on his part that he was afraid to speculate, and that he only said what he did in deference to the Council. The chief question remained; it was repeated by Florentius. "Was Christ of two Natures after the Incarnation, or of one only?" Appealing to the

---

[e] Florentius disclaimed all idea of dogmatizing. Mansi, vi. 809. But he took an active part in the dispute with Eutyches.

authority of Cyril and Athanasius, Eutyches replied, "Of two Natures before the union; *but after it I acknowledge one.*" Basil endeavoured to show him that he was mistaking S. Cyril: "Do not say absolutely, One Nature, for that is to confound Deity with humanity; but say what S. Cyril really said, One Nature incarnate. There is one Lord Jesus Christ, but His Godhead is one thing, His flesh another. If you hold *this*, you agree both with us and with the Fathers." It was kindly meant, but the old man would not or could not heed. A narrow mind, stiffened by seclusion and bewildered by harassing excitement, was in no state to appreciate a qualification or a paraphrase. Eutyches had, apparently, one single thought—how best to contradict Nestorianism. To him it seemed that unity of Person could only be preserved by unity of Nature; and thus, ignoring S. Cyril's statement, he clung, as for life, to a formula which his judges deemed intolerable. They all rose, and exclaimed that no one could be forced into faith; and Flavian, in the name of the synod, passed sentence of deposition and excommunication against Eutyches. This document professes that the bishops shed tears over his spiritual ruin. Such was the Eastern style in condemning a heretic; it had been used at Ephesus in regard to Nestorius, and it is probable that the doom of Eutyches was spoken with more than usual sorrow. But the bishops were less than just in saying that he "adhered inflexibly to Valentinus and Apollinaris." What he held fell short of the wild theory that Christ's Body was of a celestial substance; although, in truth, it might lead others to that theory, and was not less incompatible with a right faith in the Incarnate Mediator than the Nestorian view from which it was a reaction. If Christ were to be really owned as the Second Adam, as a true Example, a true Sacrifice, a sympathizing and brotherly High-Priest, whose Very Manhood was the basis of the Church and the medium of His brethren's renewal, the condemnation of Eutyches was an inevitable duty.

After the Council had broken up, Eutyches said in a low voice to Florentius, "I appeal to Rome, Alexandria, and Jerusalem." He wrote at once to Leo[f], sending the paper which the Council had not allowed him to substitute for an oral statement, quoting a passage against two Natures, wrongly ascribed to Julius of Rome, and entreating Leo to protect him from being "shaken out of the number of the orthodox at the close of his days." It seems, although the point has been debated, that Flavian wrote to Leo soon after the Council[g], as he did to other leading bishops, and sent a record of what had passed. As Eutyches' monks disowned the archbishop's sentence, he prohibited any celebration of the Eucharist within their monastery, where he had recently hallowed a new altar. Christmas and Epiphany were no festivals for them.

The trial of Ibas began at Berytus, Feb. 1, 449. He indignantly disclaimed the blasphemy imputed to him: "Anathema to any one who said it, and to the author of this slander! I would rather die a thousand deaths." "He did say it; we have witnesses here." Three men came forward. "They are incompetent," said Ibas; "they have been living with my accusers." This was not denied; the judges sustained the objection. Ibas then produced a document, signed by fourteen priests and many other clergy, protesting that they never heard him utter such words, or any words contrary to faith. The accusers went on; "He has called the blessed Cyril a heretic." They brought forward his letter to Maris. Ibas declared that he had never thought Cyril a heretic after his reconciliation with John. The accusation came to nothing; but the matter was revived very soon afterwards at Tyre, where the judges succeeded in setting it at rest by a concordat between the parties, Feb. 25. They promised to forget past quarrels; and Ibas bound himself to respect, not only the doctrine agreed upon be-

---

[f] Ep. 21.

[g] Ep. 22, Nihil.

tween John and Cyril, but the decisions of the Council of Ephesus [h].

On Feb. 18, before Flavian's letter, which was unaccountably delayed, had reached Rome, Leo wrote to Flavian [i], marvelling at his silence, and requesting him to explain the grounds on which Eutyches had been thus severely punished. Eutyches had written to Peter, surnamed Chrysologus, the pious and eloquent bishop of Ravenna, who replied [k] by deprecating the continuance of strife, and urging submission to the "living" presence of "blessed Peter in his own see."

Dioscorus was forward in espousing the quarrel of Eutyches. He admitted him into his communion, and worked in conjunction with Chrysaphius in support of his petition for a General Council. It was rumoured that Theodosius would grant this request. Flavian now replied to Leo's letter. He entreated Leo to give a written approval of the sentence against Eutyches, and thereby to preserve Christendom from any fresh disturbance [l]. Before Leo could receive this letter, Theodosius wrote on March 30 to Dioscorus, announcing his will that a General Council should meet at Ephesus on August 1. Each patriarch or exarch was to bring with him ten metropolitans and ten bishops. A preliminary council was held at Constantinople in April, in order to examine the records of the council of November, which Eutyches taxed Flavian with having falsified. No inaccuracy of importance was discovered; but the statement made on behalf of Eutyches, that he had lodged a formal appeal to other great bishops, was proved untrue. The bishops had heard no such words fall from him: he had but spoken informally to Florentius. About this time Flavian,

---

[h] This is according to Tillemont's arrangement. [i] Ep. 23.

[k] Ep. 25, Tristis. One feature of his episcopal character was his impassioned energy as a preacher; another, his zeal against the heathenish rejoicings on Jan. 1. Compare the Gelasian collect for that day, in reference to these unholy revels, Murat. i. 501.

[l] Ep. 26, Pietate.

at the Emperor's bidding, gave in a confession of faith[m], in which he "did not refuse[n] to say, One incarnate Nature of God the Word," in the sense of personal unity. Theodoret, on hearing of the proposed Council, expected that it would enforce the Cyrilline articles, and urged Domnus to withstand such a course. He himself was forbidden to attend, unless he should be specially called for by the bishops; but Barsumas[o], an Eutychian archimandrite, was summoned with the prelates as the representative of his order. A military force was to be at the disposal of the Council; Elpidius and Eulogius, two counts, were ordered to attend on behalf of the Emperor; and the Patriarch of Alexandria was appointed to preside.

S. Hilary died on May 5, at the age of forty-eight. He was, like Meletius, a man of acknowledged sanctity outside the Roman communion. On the day of his funeral a touching evidence of his large-hearted charity was given by the Jews of Arles, who chanted mournful psalms in Hebrew. Ravennius was elected in his stead, and Leo, on hearing of the election, expressed his satisfaction that "Hilary of holy memory" had been succeeded by a well-tried man[p].

Leo adhered to the custom of his predecessors, who had never attended a council at a distance from Rome. He appointed three legates, Julius bishop of Puteoli, Renatus a priest, and Hilarus a deacon. On the 13th of June he wrote several letters. One of them was his famous *Tome*[q], a doctrinal epistle addressed to Flavian,—"a clear, forcible, intelligible text-book[r]" on both aspects of the Incarnation-

[m] He begins by quoting 1 Peter iii. 15, and ends with, "Christ, my Lord and God, help me." He anathematizes Nestorianism.

[n] Theodoret had admitted the phrase, Dial. 2, with this explanation; "The nature of the Word, we know, is one; but we have learned that the flesh wherein He was incarnate is of another nature."

[o] He must be distinguished from the Nestorian Barsumas.

[p] Ep. 40.

[q] Ep. 28, al. 25, Lectis.

[r] Greenwood, Cath. Pet. i. 364. He bestows on the Tome some very warm and just praise. It is, indeed, one of the most precious documents in Christian literature. It was afterwards read during Advent in the Italian and Gallican Churches.

mystery, the most important passages of which will be found in the Appendix. Other letters were addressed to Theodosius and Pulcheria, to Julius, to some anti-Eutychian abbats, and to the Council. This last epistle insisted on S. Peter's confession as implying belief in both Natures.

On the 8th of August, 449, the Council met in that same church of S. Mary at Ephesus which had witnessed the condemnation of Nestorius. About a hundred and thirty bishops were present. Dioscorus presided; next to him was Julius; then Juvenal, who renewed his claim to patriarchal dignity by taking precedence even of Domnus, who himself was seated above Flavian. The deacon Hilarus sat last of all; Renatus had died on the way to Ephesus. Barsumas was attended by a crowd of violent monks. After the writ of convocation had been read in due form, Hilarus explained the reason of Leo's absence, and announced that Leo had sent a letter. "Let it be received," said Dioscorus[s]. The letter was handed in[t]; but by a preconcerted scheme the secretary interposed, suggesting that another letter of Theodosius to Dioscorus deserved the attention of the assembly. Dioscorus thus prevented the reading of Leo's words; and shortly afterwards, Eutyches himself was introduced.

"I commend myself to Father, Son, and Holy Spirit, and to the true sentence of your justice; and I take you as witnesses of my faith." Such were his opening words. He gave in a statement, containing the Creed as settled at Nicæa, and rejecting all heretics, especially those who said "that the Flesh of his Lord and God Jesus Christ had descended from heaven." He added that Flavian had exposed him as a "Manichean[u]" to a mob outside the church. Flavian de-

[s] Here and elsewhere the ponderous forms of ceremonial speech, which so weary a modern reader of the Councils, have been omitted.

[t] According to Leo, Ep. 45, it was the Tome addressed to Flavian; to which Leo refers the Council in the letter addressed to them, Ep. 33.

[u] Deniers of Christ's distinct Manhood were long afterwards branded with this odious name.

sired that Eusebius might be heard. "No," said Elpidius; "the accusation which he preferred is a thing of the past; it is on the sentence which followed it that the Council is adjudicating;" as if the sentence could be appreciated without inquiry into the accusation. The records of the trial were read, Dioscorus promising that afterwards the Council should hear the Pope's letter. When the reader came to Basil's words about "one Christ in two Natures," a bishop sprang forward, exclaiming, "This language turns the Church upside down." Barsumas raised the cry, "If he says two Natures, cut him in two." The recitation of Eusebius' demand, that Eutyches should own two Natures after the Incarnation, produced a still more furious outbreak. "Divide the divider! burn him alive! cut him in two!" "Will you endure," asked the president, "to hear of two Natures after the Incarnation?" His adherents responded with "Anathema." "I want your voices, and your hands too," said Dioscorus; "if any one cannot shout, let him hold up his hand." Then, confident of succeeding by terrorism, Dioscorus put the question, Was Eutyches orthodox? The prelates, speaking one after another, voted in the affirmative; Juvenal was followed in this weak submission by Domnus; and Basil, whom the uproar had wholly unnerved, consented to retract his obnoxious language.

Eutyches being now rehabilitated, his monks were formally absolved from censure. The reader went on to the acts of the sixth session of Ephesus. Hilarus again vainly attempted to procure a hearing for Leo's letter; and Dioscorus, on the ground that Flavian had infringed that decree of Ephesus which forbade any tampering with the faith of Nicæa, gave his judgment for the deposition of Flavian and Eusebius. "I disclaim you," said Flavian. Hilarus uttered one emphatic word—*Contradicitur!*

The scene was really terrific. The bishops, who had acquitted Eutyches against their consciences, struggled hard to escape this new degradation. Several started up, and clasped the president's knees; Onesiphorus of Iconium cried imploringly, "By the feet of your Piety, I pray you forbear; he has done nothing worthy of condemnation. If he deserves rebuke, rebuke him; but do not condemn a bishop for the sake of a presbyter." Dioscorus rose from his throne, and standing upon the footstool, made a signal with his hand and exclaimed, "Look you, he that will not sign the sentence has to deal with *me*. If my tongue were to be cut out for it, I would say, Depose Flavian. Are you making a sedition? where are the Counts?" A body of soldiers, with clubs and swords, rushed in; monks and parabolani followed, ready for any violence; the bishops were reviled as heretics, menaced with fetters, assailed with blows. Flavian himself was brutally kicked and trampled on; Barsumas stood over him, and cried, "Stab him!" By sheer extremity of bodily terror, bishop after bishop was made the tool of Dioscorus. They voted as he bade, but this was not enough; they must sign a blank paper on which the sentence was to be recorded. Several were shut up in the "secretarium" of the church [x], and only yielded on the evening of that miserable day. Hilarus escaped from Ephesus without having compromised his fidelity; nothing is known as to the conduct of Julius. Eusebius and Flavian were sent into exile; Flavian died of his recent injuries, on August 11, in a village of Lydia. Theodoret and Ibas were deposed; and Domnus received the same treatment from the tyrant before whom he had quailed. Three days after the sentence against Flavian, he was deprived of the see of Antioch, on the ground that he had called Cyril's articles obscure, and had allowed Theodoret to preach in his presence a sermon which insulted Cyril's memory [y].

So closed the assembly which has received its name from

---

[x] Stephen, exarch of Ephesus, was one of these. The secretaries of Dioscorus fell upon his secretaries, tried to pull away their inkstands, and nearly broke their fingers. Mansi, vi. 624.

[y] This sermon, already alluded to, was in all probability an invention of the Eutychians.

an indignant letter of S. Leo; "it was no court of justice, but a gang of robbers[z]." This *Latrocinium*, like the Ariminian synod, is a proof of the statement of our Article, that the formal convocation of a General Council cannot ensure to it rectitude of proceedings, freedom from error, or subsequent œcumenical acceptance.

---

[z] Ep. 95.

CHAPTER XV.

From the Latrocinium to the Council of Chalcedon.

"The Christ shall come again
Even as He goes; with the same human heart,
With the same godlike train."
Christian Year.

IT was S. Leo's custom to hold an annual synod on Sept. 29[a]. This assembly was sitting when Hilarus arrived: he had eluded the pursuit of the Eutychians by choosing the most unfrequented routes[b], and he now described the horrors which had taken place, excepting Flavian's death, of which he was unaware. Leo wrote, on Oct. 15, four synodical letters. The first was to Theodosius[c]; he assured him that the Christian faith would be ruined, unless the decision of the late Council were reversed. Flavian, he said, had solemnly appealed to Rome; and in accordance with "Nicene canons," such an appeal ought to be heard by a General Council held in Italy. Here we observe, on the one hand, that Leo repeats the mistake of his predecessors as to canons really Sardican; on the other hand, that he does not quote them as ascribing a sole jurisdiction to the Roman pontiff[d]. To Pulcheria he declared that at Ephesus one furious man had carried his point by force and terror[e]. He exhorted the Church of Constantinople to own no other bishop than Flavian, and denounced alike Nestorius and the deniers of Christ's true Manhood. He reminded the anti-Eutychian abbats of Constantinople —doubtless a minority—of Gal. i. 9. Other letters he wrote in his individual capacity; one being addressed to Flavian.

---

[a] Ep. 16.
[b] Ep. 46, Hilarus to Pulcheria.
[c] Epp. 43, 44. Leo was in the habit of making more than one draft of his letters, as in this case, and when he wrote in June to Pulcheria.
[d] See Fleury, xxvii. 43.
[e] Ep. 45.

There were many at Constantinople who loudly proclaimed their attachment to their patriarch[f], and Pulcheria was stedfast in the same cause. Her brother, deeming himself consistently anti-Nestorian, put forth an edict confirming the late Council, which he expressly associated with the former Council of Ephesus.

Dioscorus now ruled in the East. He consecrated for Constantinople an Alexandrian named Anatolius, who seems to have had little religious earnestness[g], but ranged himself at this time on the side of Eutyches, and boldly assumed the office of consecrating one Maximus to the see of Antioch. Athanasius came back to Perrha; Nonnus was installed at Edessa; Theodoret appealed for help and advice to the first bishop of Christendom. In this remarkable letter[h] he traced the primacy of Rome to her civil greatness, her soundness of faith, and her possession of the graves of Peter and Paul. He eulogized the exact and comprehensive orthodoxy with which the Tome of Leo conveyed the full mind of the Holy Spirit. He dilated on his own wrongs, and his exertions as a bishop, entreating Leo not to despise his old age in its affliction, but to decide whether he ought to submit to the recent sentence. "I await the judgment of your apostolic throne." He expressed a desire to visit Rome, and earnestly begged the assistance of Leo's prayers.

It was probably in the February of 450 that a festival of S. Peter attracted to Rome the Emperor Valentinian, with his wife and mother. They attended the service at the Vatican basilica. A number of bishops were then visiting the Pope, and stood around him, when, from the steps of the altar, he addressed the imperial personages, and besought their intervention for the restoration of Flavian and for the assembling of a General Council in Italy. They wrote to Constantinople accordingly[i]; Valentinian magnifying the

---

f Ep. 59.

g Ep. 113.

h Theod. Ep. 113; the 52nd in the Leonine collection.

i Epp. 55—58.

primacy of Leo, and ascribing to him a right "to judge about faith and bishops." The answer of Theodosius was wholly unpromising[k]. He assured his relatives that he adhered to his hereditary faith, that the recent Council had been righteous and orthodox, that Flavian had but received his due. Meantime Leo wrote again to the orthodox of Constantinople, insisting on the deeply practical nature of the controversy[l]. "They must be held aliens to the mystery of man's salvation, who, by denying the nature of our flesh to exist in Christ, contradict the Gospel and withstand the Creed." He proceeded to argue from the Eucharist, not, like S. Cyril, to the Divinity of Christ's Person, but to the reality of His Manhood, as to a truth so familiarly known that "not even the tongues of little ones[m] are silent at the Sacrament of Communion, as to the truth of the Body and Blood of Christ;" alluding to the Amen, repeated by all communicants[n]. He added that original sin could only be remedied by a real Second Adam; and that any one who disbelieved this assumption of our nature "neither recognized the Bridegroom nor understood the Bride, and must therefore be excluded from the marriage-feast."

The contest between Arles and Vienne had not been closed by the Pope's letter of 445. The bishop of Vienne complained that Ravennius of Arles had invaded his jurisdiction; but nineteen suffragans of Arles requested Leo to confirm their mother-church in her rightful primacy. S. Peter, they said, had sent Trophimus to Arles, which had thenceforward been a centre of unity to three provinces;

---

[k] Epp. 62—64. He calls Leo "the most reverend *patriarch*."

[l] Ep. 59.

[m] The Eucharist was given to infants and children by the Western Church for many ages; "in France until the twelfth century," Newman's Fleury, vol. iii. p. 223. The East retains the custom.

[n] On this solemn Amen see Tertull. de Spectac. 25; Euseb. vi. 43, vii. 9; S. Cyr. Hier. Cat. Myst. 5. 21; S. Aug. Serm. 272, &c. In the Lit. of Apost. Const. the form is—"The Body of Christ. *Resp.* Amen. The Blood of Christ, the Cup of life. *Resp.* Amen." The Amen is retained in the Scottish Communion Office.

the claim of Vienne they set aside as "impudent." Leo replied on May 5, by dividing Viennensis between the two metropolitans of Vienne and Arles, and allotting to Arles the wider jurisdiction [o]. He appears to have felt that in Hilary's case he had been more imperative than successful. He requested Ravennius to circulate his Tome, with the second epistle of S. Cyril to Nestorius [p].

Theodosius had desired him to recognize Anatolius. He answered, July 16, that "the person who had begun to preside over the Church of Constantinople" must first of all make a public avowal of orthodoxy. He named Cyril's second epistle as a standard, and added that his own letter might deserve consideration, and would be found in harmony with the ancient faith [q]. He sent legates to ascertain the mind of Anatolius on this subject, and wrote to the orthodox and sympathizing Pulcheria.

And now the main difficulty was suddenly removed. Theodosius died on July 29, having reigned forty-one years. The sovereignty passed from the feeble and obstinate brother to the sister who might well have ruled alone, but that a female reign was without a precedent. Pulcheria made the senator Marcian at once her husband and her colleague. Eutychianism was now a losing cause. In a solemn council, which was attended by the Roman legates, Anatolius subscribed the Tome, and anathematized both Eutyches and Nestorius. Rome and Constantinople were now again at peace; the enthronement of Maximus at Antioch was tolerated by Leo [r], the rather that Domnus had retired no one knew whither. That unhappy ex-patriarch was, in fact, bewailing his guilty weakness in the Syrian monastery where he had spent his youth; and he never claimed restoration to his see. The body of S. Flavian was brought to Constantinople, and buried in the church of the Apostles; the bishops who, for adhering to his cause, had been exiled

[o] Epp. 65, 66. [p] Ep. 67. [q] Ep. 69.

[r] Ep. 104. He speaks of this consecration as a presumptuous act, unprecedented and uncanonical.

by Theodosius, were permitted to return home[s]. Among these was Theodoret, who, however, declined to leave the monastery where he had dwelt since his expulsion from Cyrus. He appears to have signified to Leo, through one of the legates, that he had signed the Tome; and Leo, some time afterwards, formally recognized him as an orthodox bishop. Marcian was perfectly willing to grant a Council, and proposed that Leo should hold one in the East; but added that if such a journey should prove inconvenient, he himself would summon the bishops to some place of his own choosing[t].

The early spring of 451 was "a cloudy and dark day" for the Gallican Church. Attila, with his savage Huns, invaded Gaul. On Easter-eve, April 7, the people of Metz became his victims, and the clergy were butchered at the altars. Genoveva, a holy woman of Paris, inspirited her fellow-citizens, and successfully predicted that the storm would pass them by. It laid waste other cities, and menaced Orleans, where Anianus the bishop was active both in prayer and in procuring succours from Aetius, which arrived when the walls were tottering under the assault. Then followed the great repulse of "the Scourge of God" at Chalons.

Eusebius spent this Easter at Rome, in happy intercourse with Leo, who on April 13 replied to a letter from Anatolius, by recommending[u] that Dioscorus and Juvenal should not be commemorated among worthier bishops at the altars of Constantinople; and that any prelates who repented of their submission to Dioscorus should be received to communion on condemning his acts. "For in God's Church, which is Christ's body, there are neither valid priesthoods nor true sacrifices, unless we are reconciled by a true High-Priest in our very own nature, and cleansed by the true Blood of a spotless Lamb; who, though set at the Father's right hand, is carrying out the mystery of propitiation in

[s] Ep. 77. [t] Ep. 76. [u] See Ep. 80.

that same Flesh which He took of the Virgin, as the Apostle saith,"—Rom. viii. 34.

Leo had formerly requested that affairs might remain *in statu quo* until the meeting of a new Council. But his demands now rose with his hopes, and he boldly urged on Marcian, April 23[x], that the question for discussion was not whether Eutyches were "impious," or whether Dioscorus "had decided perversely;" those points were already settled. The Council would have simply to determine the conditions on which pardon should be granted to those whom Dioscorus had scared into wrong-doing. This, however, was not Marcian's view. He would neither allow the Council to meet in Italy, nor exclude the doctrinal question from its province. He issued a summons to the greater prelates, on May 17, desiring them to attend on Sept. 1 at Nicæa, with as many of their suffragans as they chose to bring; and expressly announced that the Council would have to enter thoroughly into an examination of the *truth*. Disappointed, as he must have been, both as to the place and scope of the Council, Leo was also vexed by the promptitude of the summons. Before he received the circular he had asked Marcian to defer the synod until the cessation of warfare in the West should allow the bishops to leave their sees[y]. This letter and the circular crossed each other on their way; Leo, on finding that Marcian had taken his own course, professed to ascribe it to a pious zeal[z]. He had recently sent to Constantinople, in order to confer with Anatolius, Lucentius a bishop, and Basil a presbyter. He now appointed these two, with Paschasinus bishop of Lilybæum, and a priest named Boniface, to preside in his name at the synod[a]. They were charged with a letter announcing this commission, referring to the Tome, and exhorting the assembled prelates to put down heretical disputatiousness, and to maintain the authority of the *former*

[x] Ep. 82. [y] Ep. 83. June 9. [z] Ep. 89. June 24.
[a] They were to consult Julian of Cos; Ep. 92.

Ephesian Council. "The impiety then condemned must derive no advantage from the just excommunication of Eutyches[b]." Nothing, in fact, more vividly displays S. Leo's theological greatness than his impartial solicitude for both sides of the sacred truth. His Tome, so full of this solicitude, had been already welcomed by Gallican bishops; and he received, about August, from Eusebius archbishop of Milan, a synodical letter comparing it to the statements of S. Ambrose[c]. It was also signed by many Oriental bishops.

Five hundred and twenty bishops—traditionally reckoned as six hundred and thirty by including those whose proxies were held by their metropolitans—assembled at Nicæa. It was then, probably, that Dioscorus took the daring step of excommunicating Leo, and inducing ten bishops to sign the sentence. After the bishops had awaited the Emperor's coming for some time, he desired them to proceed to Chalcedon, where he could attend with more convenience by simply crossing the Bosporus from Constantinople. Many of the bishops were apprehensive of danger from the excited Eutychians of the capital; but the Emperor assured them of perfect safety, and on the 8th of October they opened the synod in the stately church of S. Euphemia at Chalcedon. As at the first Council of Ephesus, the presence of Christ was symbolized by the Gospel-book in the midst of the assembly. The Roman legates sat in the highest place; next to them Anatolius, then Dioscorus, Maximus, and Juvenal. In front of the chancel-screen sat nineteen high civil dignitaries, commissioned to represent the Emperor, and to exercise a general control.

---

[b] Ep. 93. Compare Sermon 28, c. 4, where S. Leo says that he hardly knows of any error which did not begin by denying the One Person and Two Natures. Against Nestorianism see also Serm. 30, 65, 69, &c.

[c] Ep. 97. Eusebius refers to S. Ambrose, De Incarn. Dom. Sacr., where the unity of Person and the distinctness of Natures are both affirmed; just as in his fourth hymn, together with "Talis decet partus Deum," we find "Geminæ gigas substantiæ."

The legates opened the proceedings by standing forward and demanding, in Leo's name, that Dioscorus should not have a seat in the Synod. This was so far granted that Dioscorus was obliged to take his seat apart in the midst. Eusebius then entreated, with passionate eagerness, that his petition to the Emperor might be read; and he, too, sat in the midst while this was done. Next, he begged the Council to hear the records of the Latrocinium. Dioscorus, at first, joined in this desire; but suddenly changing his mind, strove vainly to obtain a discussion of doctrine. The reader came to that imperial letter which forbade Theodoret to appear at Ephesus. The commissioners then ordered that he should enter the Council, because Leo had annulled his deposition, and Marcian had willed his attendance. The moment that he appeared, there arose the vehement cries and counter-cries which disturbed so often the order of this Synod. The clamour of the adherents of Dioscorus is at once intelligible; and those over whom he had tyrannized were agitated by the loss of self-respect, and by their loathing of a heterodox persecutor.

"Pity us, the faith is ruined! the canons expel him! drive him out!" Such were the shouts of the Egyptian, Illyrian, and Palestinian bishops; to which Dioscorus added, that to admit Theodore was to "cast out Cyril." The bishops of the East and Pontus, of Thrace and "Asia," exclaimed, in words which showed a wounded conscience, "We signed a blank paper under blows. Drive out the Manicheans!" and then, alluding to Flavian's death, "Drive out Dioscorus the murderer!" Theodoret stood calmly in the midst, and desired that his petition to Marcian might be examined. The commissioners repeated that as he had the approbation of Rome and Antioch, he was in a position to accuse, as well as to be accused by, any other person present. They meant, of course, not that Leo's judgment in his favour was all-sufficient, but that, especially when combined with that of his own patriarch, it removed any obstacle to his appearance as a bishop in the assembly. He sat down beside Dioscorus and Eusebius, as one of the parties in the cause. The confused uproar broke forth again around him: "He is worthy!" "Call him not a bishop!" and some voices, taking up a frequent by-word against Nestorianism, shouted, "Turn out the Jew!" The commissioners interposed with dignity. "These cries beseem the populace, not bishops. They serve no one's cause. Be pleased to let the records be read through." The Egyptians, after protesting that they were shouting in the interest of true religion, allowed the reading to proceed; but presently, when the Easterns repeated that they had been coerced by clubs and swords, in an assembly which could not be called a synod, and their attendant clergy joined in their exclamations, the Egyptians remonstrated: "This is a synod of bishops; turn out those who have no business here." Stephen of Ephesus and others described the outrages of the Latrocinium in detail. "Christians are not cowards," was the bitter comment of the Egyptians; and Dioscorus had the assurance to remark that no man ought to have signed a blank paper. His opponents called attention to the suppression of Leo's letter. "He swore seven times," said the archdeacon of Constantinople, "that it should be read. It was not read, and he is forsworn." Dioscorus, with danger thickening around him, showed a dauntless front; when a reference was made to Eutyches, he exclaimed, "If Eutyches holds any view contrary to Church doctrine, he deserves not only to be punished, but to be burned. I care not for any individual, but for the Catholic and Apostolic faith." Basil of Seleucia reiterated his assertion of "Christ *in* two Natures," and quoted his words addressed to Eutyches. They suggested a question to the commissioners: "How came you, who had spoken so soundly, to subscribe the condemnation of Flavian?" "I could not but submit to a hundred and twenty or thirty bishops; had I been dealing with magistrates, I would have suffered martyrdom." The Easterns exclaimed, "We all did wrong; we all ask foriveness." Dioscorus was asked why he had excluded ̃usebius from the Latrocinium. He pleaded an imperial rder; the commissioners made a remarkable answer,— That is no excuse when faith is in question." The reader ent on to Cyril's letter to John of Antioch. The Illyrians ried out, "We believe as Cyril;" and the whole Council choed the acclamation, "We believe as Cyril; we have so elieved, we do so believe. Anathema to him that does ot!" Theodoret professed his belief in the unity of the on. There were cries of "Flavian suffered for this—Leo s of this mind—Anatolius of this mind;" and the commissioners joined with the bishops in exclaiming, "So the Emperor and the Empress think." The Easterns observed hat Eusebius, the denouncer of Eutyches, had also been he denouncer of Nestorius. Dioscorus, when a reference as made to Cyril's language about the "one incarnate Nature," anathematized all notions of change or fusion. Eustathius of Berytus testified that Flavian accepted Cyril's nguage. They proceeded to discuss the statement of belief nade by S. Flavian at the trial of Eutyches. The commissioners put the question, Was that statement orthodox? Paschasinus called it pure and complete, and accordant ith the Tome of Leo. Anatolius, Lucentius, Maximus, nd others, followed; the Easterns declared that "the martyr Flavian had well expounded the faith;" Juvenal nd the bishops of Palestine, leaving that side of the hurch on which the Egyptians sat, crossed over to the ther, amid shouts of "Welcome, orthodox!" Peter, bishop f Corinth, on approving Flavian's words, was greeted with Peter is of *Peter's* mind." Dioscorus declared that he id passages from the Fathers against the dogma of Two atures. "I am being driven out with the Fathers." I admit," he added, "the phrase, '*of two Natures*,' but ot '*two Natures*,'" which was as much as to say, "I deny at He *is now* in two Natures[d]." "Regard for my soul

[d] Contrast S. Cyril, Ep. 2 ad Nest., "Not as if the diversity of natures ere annihilated because of the union."

compels me to be outspoken." Eusebius reproached him for his violence at Ephesus. "I will answer for it to God," said Dioscorus, "both here and above." "Ay, and to the laws too," said Eusebius, in a spirit of vindictive exultation. "Why have I come forward? Assuredly to exact penalties from you. Did you come here merely to salute us?" "Had Flavian," pursued Paschasinus, "such freedom of speech as this man has enjoyed?" "No," said the commissioners; "*this* synod follows the principles of justice;" and Lucentius added, "Let a just sentence be awarded to both parties." Evidence was given as to the violence with which Dioscorus enforced Flavian's condemnation; cries of "Anathema to Dioscorus" arose, together with "Many years to Leo and Anatolius." The commissioners proposed the deprivation of Dioscorus, Juvenal, Basil, and three other bishops, who had taken a prominent part in the Latrocinium. Shouts of applause were mingled with the solemn hymn of Trisagion,—"Holy God, Holy and Mighty, Holy and Immortal, have mercy upon us!" and with the passionate denunciation, "Christ hath deposed Dioscorus the homicide." But as yet there was no formal voting. The commissioners desired the bishops to prepare individually declarations of their faith, and signified Marcian's adherence to the teaching of Nicæa and Constantinople, of Fathers Eastern and Western, and of "Cyril's two canonical epistles, promulgated and confirmed at Ephesus," i.e. the second and third to Nestorius.

So ended the first session; the latter part of its business had required the aid of lighted tapers. In the second, the bishops declared that they could have no other Creed than that in existence, which had been illustrated by the doctors from Athanasius to Leo. The Creed was read, not as at Ephesus in its Nicene, but in its Constantinopolitan form. The second letter of Cyril to Nestorius was read, the third being passed over. Then came his letter to John, and the Tome of Leo. In regard to three passages of the latter, the bishops of Palestine and Illyricum expressed some doubt, whether the idea of duality were not carried too far; but Theodoret and the archdeacon of Constantinople read equivalent passages out of S. Cyril. The letter was finished amid loud applause; "Thus we all believe; *Peter hath spoken by Leo; Cyril and Leo have taught alike.* Why was not this read at Ephesus? Why did Dioscorus hide it?" "Has any one still any difficulties about the letter?" asked the magistrates. "No one has," cried the bishops impatiently. But Atticus of Nicopolis requested a little time for quiet study of the letter, and added that Cyril's third letter to Nestorius, "in which he bade him accept the twelve articles," ought to be placed before the synod. It was agreed that the discussion should be resumed in five days.

Three days later, another session was held for a different and more formidable business, the trial of the patriarch of Alexandria. The magistrates and Dioscorus were absent. He was accused by Eusebius, and evaded two citations. Theodore, Ischyrion, Athanasius, and a laic, appeared with their complaints; and denounced him not merely on account of their personal wrongs, but on other grounds of more public interest. He was, they declared, a shameless profligate, an Origenist, a man of blood and violence. He had aimed at secular supremacy throughout Egypt; he had perverted a charitable bequest, and had bought up, in order to sell it at a high price, the supply of corn sent by the Emperor to Libya; whereby "the awful and bloodless Sacrifice" was not celebrated, and the poor and the stranger were deprived of their relief. These petitions were addressed to Leo the "*œcumenical patriarch* of great Rome," and to the œcumenical Synod; but for the former title the Council itself gave no authority [e]. A third summons was sent to Dioscorus, who again refused to attend. "What I have said, I have said; I can say no more."

---

[e] Bramhall, i. 253, says that in one sense this title was lawfully given to any one of the patriarchs. See the petitions in Mansi, vi. 1006.

This he repeated several times. Paschasinus asked the bishops what such contumacy merited. "We wish to learn the pleasure of your Holinesses." The Council answered, "We say what the canons say." "We assent," said Maximus, "to what you may propose." Thus encouraged, the legates gave their judgment. Dioscorus had uncanonically communicated with Eutyches; he had refused to repent of his offences committed at Ephesus, i. e. in regard to Leo's letter; he had dared to excommunicate Leo; he had refused to stand a trial. Wherefore Leo, by his legates, and by the Council, in conjunction with Peter, the rock and foundation of the Church and Faith, "deprives him of episcopal and sacerdotal dignity." Rome had thus pronounced; but her sentence needed to be confirmed by the vote of the Council. The legates desired the synod to vote what it pleased. Anatolius said, "Being of one mind with the Apostolic see, I vote with it on the deposition of Dioscorus." Maximus and the other bishops followed. After the votes had been given, the sentence was regularly subscribed. A formal intimation of it was made to Dioscorus; and letters were sent to his clergy then at Chalcedon, to Valentinian and Marcian, to the empress, and to the people of Constantinople and Chalcedon [f].

On the 17th of October the doctrinal question was resumed according to agreement. The Tome was hailed by acclamation as in accordance with the Baptismal faith. Each bishop then in turn made a personal statement, accepting the Tome on the express ground of its ascertained conformity to orthodox standards. "It agrees," said Anatolius, "with the Creed of Nicæa and of Constantinople, and with the acts of Ephesus under Cyril; wherefore I gladly subscribe it." Some bishops expressed this judgment laconically, but distinctly; "It agrees, and I

---

[f] The "excommunication" of Leo is not mentioned in three of these documents. But in the fifth session Anatolius said that Dioscorus was condemned, 1. for excommunicating Leo, 2. for contempt of citations.

subscribe." Theodoret specified its agreement with "the letters[g] of blessed Cyril." The Illyrians said that they had met the legates at the house of Anatolius, and had heard them anathematize "all who separated the Flesh of our Lord God from His Divinity[h]," and who did not predicate of Him both human and divine properties, without confusion, change, or severance. This had convinced the Illyrians of Leo's thorough sonndness. Thus did the Council sit in judgment on the Tome, and stamp it, after due examination, with the approval of a superior authority[i].

The bishops now expressed their wish to deal indulgently with the five prelates, whom the commissioners had proposed to include in the sentence on Dioscorus. The commissioners at first objected, and also remarked that the actual deposition of Dioscorus had been carried out in their absence, and without the knowledge of the Emperor[j]. "It was God," cried the bishops, "who condemned Dioscorus." The court acceded to the Council's wishes as to the five, who re-entered and took their seats amid a shout of welcome. "This is all God's doing; many years to the Emperor, to the magistrates, to the orthodox. This is the peace of the Churches."

Thirteen Egyptian prelates, headed by one Hieracus, had addressed the Emperor, professing fidelity to the teaching of S. Mark, and of their most eminent patriarchs, and especially condemning those who denied the Lord's Flesh to be from S. Mary. They came before the Council; their petition was read; they were ordered to anathematize Eutyches, and subscribe the Tome. After some delay, they yielded the first point; as to the second, they im-

[g] Meaning, the 2nd to Nestorius, and the letter to John. Mansi, vii. 19.

[h] Compare Leo's Serm. 65, "The flesh of our race is become the flesh of the Godhead;" and on the glory given to Manhood by the Ascension, Serm. 73.

[i] In accepting the Tome, the Council solemnly affirmed S. Mary to be Ever-Virgin; see its second chapter.

[j] Dioscorus was banished into Paphlagonia. Evagr. ii. 5.

plored the Council, in abject terms, to excuse them until they had a new archbishop. If they took any such step without such authority, they would be murdered on their return. Prostrate on the floor, they cried, "Let us die by your hands, not in Egypt; give us an archbishop, and we will subscribe; but spare men whose lives are at your mercy." They had been trained to regard "the Evangelic throne" as an oracle; and they appealed to Anatolius as knowing their Church's usage. The Council, remembering what a part had been played in the Latrocinium by suffragans of Alexandria, were disposed to treat the terrified men with sternness; but the commissioners pronounced that they should be allowed to stay in Constantinople, and not be required to subscribe anything until they received a new patriarch.

The monastic order contained many Eutychians; and eighteen persons professing to be archimandrites, and belonging to that party, had petitioned Marcian against Catholic ecclesiastics who were "seeking to expel them from their monasteries and churches." They also were admitted; their memorial was read; but one man's face seen among them filled the Council with wrath and horror. "Barsumas stabbed the blessed Flavian; he brought a thousand monks upon us. To the arena with the murderer[k]!" Another petition was read, in which the eighteen applied to the Council for the restoration of Dioscorus. This, of course, was not granted; the petitioners were ordered to submit to the Council, but allowed a month for due "consideration."

In the fifth session, Oct. 22, the magistrates desired to hear what had been decided as to the faith. A "definition" was read, and all but the legates and some Easterns approved of it, declaring that those who were not satisfied with it must have tendencies in an opposite extreme to the Eutychian. "Send out the Nestorians; add to the Creed that S. Mary

---

[k] Barsumas propagated the Eutychian heresy in Syria, and died in 458. Samuel, his disciple, carried it into Armenia.

is Theotocos." The legates and the magistrates united in observing that a formula which defined Christ as being *of* two Natures was ambiguous, and therefore inadequate. Dioscorus had said as much, in a sense of his own. He had condemned Flavian for saying, "There *are* two Natures." Leo had said the same, and nothing short of this unequivocal confession that Christ had, ever since the Incarnation, been truly existing *in* Manhood[l], as well as in Godhead, would meet the emergency. Would the bishops, after all, ignore the Tome of Leo? "If so," said the resolute legates, "let us return, and have a synod held in Italy." Loud murmurs arose, even from the Illyrians; "Let the malcontents be off to Rome!" But strength of will and clearness of perception carried the day. Backed by an imperial order, the magistrates appointed a committee of twenty-two to discuss the question in a chapel attached to the church, and reminded the synod that they must choose between Dioscorus and Leo. This produced a cry of "We believe with Leo." The committee, which included the legates, retired to revise the Definition, and brought it back in a form which secured the whole truth[m]. It recited the Creed of Nicæa, and that of Constantinople, and then referred to the recent errors, the denial of "Theotocos," and the confusion of the Natures, which had obliged the Council to vindicate the true sense of the Creed. As a safeguard against Nestorius, the Council received the synodical letters of S. Cyril to Nestorius and to the Easterns; while it combined with these, as against Eutyches, the letter of "Archbishop Leo." The following opinions were then condemned; 1. Duality of Sons; 2. Suffering in the Godhead; 3. A confusion of Natures; 4. Christ's lower Nature not of our substance; 5. Two Natures before the union, but one after it. "Following, then, the holy Fathers, we confess one and the same Son, our Lord Jesus Christ; and we all with one ac-

[l] See his Tome, c. 3, and Serm. 27.

[m] Mansi, vii. 107.

cord announce Him, the self-same perfect in Godhead, the self-same perfect in Manhood, truly God and truly Man, the self-same, of a reasonable soul and a body; of one essence with the Father as to Godhead, of one essence with us as to Manhood, in all things like unto us, sin excepted; before the ages begotten of the Father as to Godhead, but in the last days, for us and for our salvation, the self-same (born) of Mary, the Virgin Mother of God, as to Manhood. One and the same Christ, Son, Lord, Only-begotten, recognized *in* Two Natures[n] without confusion, change, division, separation; the difference of the Natures being nowise removed[o] by reason of the Union, but, on the contrary, the property of each Nature being preserved, and combining into one Person and one Hypostasis; not as it were parted, or divided into two persons, but One and the self-same Son, Only-begotten, God the Word, Lord Jesus Christ; even as we have been instructed concerning Him by the prophets from the beginning, and by our Lord Jesus Christ Himself, and as the Creed of the fathers has handed down (the truth) to us." After this comprehensive statement, penalties were again, as at Ephesus, denounced against those who should compile a new creed. The Council received the Definition, thus perfected by the well-timed persistency of the legates and the commissioners, with the acclamation, "This is the faith of the fathers, the faith of the Apostles; we all follow it!" In the next session, Oct. 25, Marcian and Pulcheria visited the Council; not to "exercise power," as he expressed it, but "simply to confirm the faith." The sovereigns were hailed as a Constantine and a Helena, and the Definition was ratified anew.

The subsequent sessions were less important. In the seventh, Juvenal made good his claim to patriarchal authority over Palestine; but his extravagant pretension to

[n] The Armenians, who had only one word for Nature and Person, unhappily misunderstood this formula as meaning "two Persons."

[o] From S. Cyril; see above. See Evagr. ii. 4.

superiority over Antioch was laid aside. In the eighth, the case of Theodoret occupied the Synod. Acknowledged by Rome as orthodox, he was not the less called upon to satisfy his brethren by anathematizing Nestorius. He never had done this; he had resolved never to do it; but as the clamours became menacing, he said, "Anathema to Nestorius, and to every one who calls not the Holy Virgin Theotocos, or who divides the one Only-begotten Son into two. I subscribe the definition of faith, and the epistle of the most holy archbishop Leo; and this is my mind. God save you!" The commissioners declared that all doubt was now removed; the Synod exclaimed that "Theodoret was worthy of his throne;" and then several bishops in succession pronounced the same judgment, Maximus declaring that from the first he had been assured of Theodoret's orthodoxy. Yet the anathema was a plain confession that in the Nestorian contest he had greatly erred.

In the ninth and tenth sessions the Council took up the case of Ibas, on his appeal. He complained that Eutyches had caused him to be arrested, and committed to a succession of guards; he had been deposed in his absence by the Latrocinium. The records of his trial at Berytus were read, including the offensive letter to Maris. The commissioners proposed that certain parts of the records of the Latrocinium, which related to Ibas, should be read; but the legates and the Council would not hear of it. They pronounced him orthodox, evidently on the ground that his letter to Maris, which they distinctly took into consideration, was now to be read in connection with his recent language [p], and his acceptance of the Tome and Definition: to which he added an oral anathema against Nestorius. They must have considered him virtually to retract his censure of the Ephesian Council, whose authority they held sacred [q].

Other cases which came before the Synod were those of

[p] The Fifth General Council condemned the letter to Maris, as a document. The Council of Chalcedon was dealing with the author personally.

[q] See the acts of Chalcedon epitomized, Evagr. ii. 18.

the ex-patriarch Domnus, for whose maintenance his successor was permitted to apply some portion of the revenues of the see; of Bassian, who asserted his claim to the throne of Ephesus, a claim which, with that of Stephen, was set aside [r], the Council ordering a new bishop to be appointed; and of Sabinian, who was restored to the see of Perrha, pending the trial of the charges against Athanasius.

The canons of Chalcedon have been variously referred to the seventh, eleventh, and fifteenth sessions. The first canon ratifies those of earlier synods, meaning Nicæa, Ancyra, Neocæsarea, Gangra, Antioch, Laodicea, Constantinople, Ephesus. Others refer to the regular convocation of provincial synods, to the authority of the bishops over religious communities, to the ordination of deaconesses, and to the prevention of clerical or monastic disorders. Simony, disobedience to, or conspiracy against superiors, a relapse from the monastic to the secular life, needless undertaking of worldly business, translations of bishops or priests, "vain-glorious" removal from one cure to another, and haunting the capital for factious purposes, are all forbidden. The sixth prohibits ordination without a title; the fourteenth recites that readers and chanters are in some provinces allowed to marry, and forbids them to marry heretics. The twenty-ninth rules that a bishop who merits degradation from the episcopate shall not be allowed to officiate as a priest. The twelfth is against the division by mere civil authority of one province into two. The ninth forbids a clerk to appeal to a civil court, and orders him to appeal first to his bishop, or to arbitrators approved by his bishop; then in appeal from a bishop, to the provincial synod; in appeal from a metropolitan, to the exarch, or to the throne of Constantinople. This canon appears to be connected with the famous twenty-eighth. In the fifteenth session, October 31st, Aetius, archdeacon of Constantinople, announced that his Church had some

[r] In the discussion, the bishop of Magnesia said that from the time of S. Timothy there had been twenty-seven bishops of Ephesus.

business to bring forward, and requested the legates to attend to it. They declined on the ground that they had no instructions to do so. Thereupon the commissioners directed the Council to take up the business; and thus, after the legates had withdrawn, the Council enacted a canon which recited and confirmed the third of Constantinople, and proceeded thus: "For to the throne of Old Rome, because that was the imperial city, the Fathers with good reason gave privileges, and the hundred and fifty bishops," (i. e. the Council of Constantinople in 381,) "acting with the same view, awarded the same privileges to the most holy throne of New Rome; judging with reason, that the city dignified by the monarchy and senate, and enjoying equal privileges with the old imperial Rome, should also in ecclesiastical matters be honoured like her, holding the second place next to her; and so that the metropolitans only of the Pontic, 'Asiatic,' and Thracian dioceses, (but also those bishops in the said dioceses who dwell in barbaric districts,) should be ordained by the said most holy throne of the most holy Church of Constantinople." This canon, although it professed to be a confirmation of the canon of 381, was in fact a considerable advance beyond it. The canon of 381 gave a pre-eminent *dignity* to Constantinople. Since 381, and mainly by means of S. Chrysostom's pontificate[s], the bishop of Constantinople had acquired a patriarchal *jurisdiction*, not only in Thrace, but in the Pontic and "Asiatic" dioceses. This usurpation, which had broken in upon the Nicene arrangements, the Council of 451 thought good to legalize, but spoke, in so doing, as if it were no usurpation at all[t]. The account of the Roman Church's position was naturally borrowed from the canon

[s] Atticus, also, obtained an imperial order that no consecration should take place without his leave. Soc. vii. 28.

[t] We are not in the least concerned to defend whatever in this case was unfair, or proceeded from Constantinopolitan ambition. Tillemont drily says, xv. 710, that Anatolius "might well have excused himself from signing the canon." After all, it maintained Rome's primacy.

of 381. Although the civil greatness of Rome was only one cause of her ecclesiastical precedency[u], it was that cause which would serve the purpose of a Constantinopolitan argument, and in fact had greater force for the Eastern than for the Western mind.

The next day, Nov. 1, Paschasinus complained[x] in full Council of the enactment of this canon, as contrary to the law and discipline of the Church. Aetius gave his account of the circumstances under which, "not in a corner, nor by way of fraud," the business had been transacted. Lucentius said that the bishops had been compelled to sign. A cry arose, "No one was forced!" Again he asked, and with some show of reason, why the Nicene canons had in this instance been set aside, and preference given to those of Constantinople? "If Constantinople has enjoyed this privilege, what does she want now? If she has not enjoyed it, why does she now ask for it?" Aetius parried this question by desiring the legates to produce any instructions which they might have received from Leo on this matter. Boniface quoted Leo's order, that the legates were to maintain inviolate "the rule of the holy fathers;" to uphold the dignity of the Pope; and to resist usurpations attempted by prelates of distinguished cities. "Let each party produce the canons," said the commissioners. Paschasinus read his version of the sixth Nicene canon, beginning, "The Roman Church *has always held the primacy*[y]; therefore Egypt also holds (this right), that the bishop of Alexandria should have authority over all," &c. He also read the seventh canon as part of the sixth. But Aetius produced the genuine text of the sixth canon, in which the first words quoted by the legate were wanting; it began with "Let the

[u] The Council, in fact, repeatedly refers to the connection of Rome with S. Peter.

[x] Mansi, vii. 425.

[y] "Quod ecclesia Romana semper *habuit* primatum." Another reading, given by a Latin version, is *habeat*; and another version is paraphrastic, "Antiqui moris est ut urbis Romæ episcopus habeat principatum."

ancient customs prevail." To this rebuff [z] the legates could make no answer. The first three canons of Constantinople being read, the commissioners called upon the Pontic and "Asiatic" bishops to state whether they had voluntarily signed the new canon. They answered one after another, to the following purpose; "In the presence of God I say that I signed of my own will." "I take pleasure in being under the throne of Constantinople." "Three bishops before me were ordained by this throne, and I have followed the custom which I found." "The glory of the throne of Constantinople is our glory." Eusebius even declared that, when at Rome, he had read the canon of 381 to Leo, who had approved of it. The commissioners pronounced that the primacy and the pre-eminent dignity ought before all things to be secured, according to the canons, to the archbishop of Old Rome; but that the archbishop of Constantinople ought to enjoy the same privileges of dignity. They added the provision as to the consecration of metropolitans for Asia, Thrace, Pontus, such metropolitans having the sole right to consecrate their suffragans. "We have considered these matters, but let the holy œcumenical Synod be pleased to declare its mind." The bishops exclaimed, "This is a just judgment. By the safety of the sovereigns, dismiss us! We all adhere to this decision." Lucentius made another attempt. "The Apostolic see ought not to be degraded in our presence. We desire that what was done irregularly in our absence be rescinded, or else that our protest be recorded, that we may know what report we ought to make to the apostolic Pope of the Church Universal, so that he may be able to declare his judgment as to the injury done to his see, or the subversion of the canons." The commissioners replied with laconic emphasis, "What we have said has been approved by the whole Council."

---

[z] Compare the case of the canon on appeals, as quoted to the African bishops, and found not to be Nicene.

The bishops, before separating, drew up a letter to Marcian, expressing their thankfulness for a zealous Emperor, and for a bishop of Rome who strove like S. Peter for the truth. They stated their principle as to dogmatic formulas; "The Creed could receive no new elements, but it was vindicated, not injured, by definitions which asserted its only true meaning." They referred to portions of the Creed, and expanded them. "Incarnate" implied a real assumption of our flesh. "He was made Man;" therefore He had a rational Soul. Some had been led by "a professed solicitude for the Saviour's dignity," to deny His Mother the title of Theotocos. Others had been tempted to ascribe the Passion to His Godhead. Some had divided the mysterious Union, and reduced the Lord to a merely human Prophet; others had recoiled from the diversity of Natures, and imagined a fusion which destroyed the properties of both. The Council proceeded to enforce the truth on both sides, and defended the promulgation of Leo's Tome by weighty precedents [a], and its theology by extracts from Athanasius, Basil, Gregory, Amphilochius, Ambrose, Chrysostom, Atticus, Proclus, and Cyril. To Leo himself was sent a letter which carried diplomatic courtesy to an excess [b]. The bishops address Leo as their head and father, the appointed guardian of the Vine; they are confident not only that he will confirm their canon in favour of Constantinople, but that the opposition made to it by his legates proceeded simply from a wish "that this good work also should begin from his thoughtful care."

So ended the Fourth General Council. The relation in which it left the East and West exhibits very clearly what could, and what could not be done, in the fifth century, by the greatest man who had ever held the greatest of bishoprics. Leo could preside by his legates at Chalcedon; he could secure abundant expressions of reverence; his

---

[a] The Epistles of S. Athanasius to Epictetus, of S. Cyril to the Easterns, of S. Proclus to the Armenians.

[b] Ep. 98.

teaching could be hailed as worthy to rank with that of S. Cyril and S. Athanasius; his legates, with the co-operation of State officers, could persuade the Council to amend its definition of the faith. But his judgments, whether as to an individual or as to a doctrine, were first reviewed, and then confirmed; his version of the Nicene canons was rejected as corrupt; a canon which he could not but dislike was enacted in spite of his legates' protest, and enforced throughout the East in spite of his own; and he himself was content to denounce it[d], not on the ground of "S. Peter's prerogatives," but simply in the name of the Council of Nicæa.

---

[d] Epp. 104, 105, 106.

APPENDIX.

I.

THE CANONS OF NICÆA.

1. Against a misinterpretation of Matt. xix. 12.

2. "Whereas in many cases, either through necessity, or otherwise through men's urgency, the rule of the Church[a] has been transgressed, in that men who had but just come over to the faith from a Gentile life, and had been but for a little time catechumens, have been at once brought to the Spiritual Laver, and immediately after their Baptism promoted to the episcopate or the presbyterate; it seems good that no such thing take place in future. For the catechumen needs time and a longer probation after Baptism. For the Apostolic Scripture plainly says, "Not a neophyte, lest being puffed up he fall into condemnation and the snare of the devil." But if in process of time any sensual fault be discovered respecting the person, and be proved by two or three witnesses, let such an one cease from his clerical function. He who acts against this, will do so at the peril of his clerical function, as having dared to resist the Great Synod.

3. The Great Synod strictly forbids any bishop, presbyter, or deacon, or any other clergyman whatsoever, to retain a female inmate, (συνείσακτον,) excepting mother, sister, aunt, or other person free from all suspicion.

4. That a bishop should be appointed by all the bishops in the province, is the most proper arrangement. But if it be encumbered by difficulties, either through urgent necessity or the length of the way, then three must in any case meet, and the absent ones give the same vote and assent in writing, and so the ordination must be performed. In each province, the ratification of the proceedings must be allowed to the metropolitan.

5. Respecting those who, whether clergy or in the laic rank,

---

[a] See Church of the Fathers, p. 305.

have been excommunicated by the bishops in every province, let the sentence hold good according to the rule which prescribes that those who are excommunicated by some be not received by others. But let it be inquired whether their exclusion has proceeded from any petty jealousy, or party feeling, or any such frowardness, in the bishop. Accordingly, that this may receive the due examination, it seems good that twice every year Synods be held in each province, that such questions may be examined before a public assembly of all the bishops of the province; and so they who have confessedly offended the bishop may be reasonably held excommunicate in the sight of all, until the episcopal body think fit to pronounce a more indulgent sentence respecting them. Let one of the synods be held before Lent, that all petty jealousy being got rid of, the Gift[b] may be purely offered to God; and the second about autumn.

6. Let the ancient customs prevail, which exist in Egypt, Libya, and Pentapolis; so that the bishop of Alexandria have authority over all these countries[c]; since this is also customary for the bishop of Rome[d]. Similarly also at Antioch, and in the other provinces, let the privileges of the Churches be preserved. This also is altogether manifest, that if any one be made a bishop without the consent of the metropolitan, the Great Synod ordains that such a one ought not to be bishop. But if two or three through their own party feeling contradict the common vote of all, when it is reasonable and according to the rule of the Church, let the vote of the majority prevail.

7. Since a custom and old tradition has obtained, that the bishop in Ælia[e] should receive honour, let him hold the second place, the metropolitan[f] being secured in his own dignity.

8. Concerning those who call themselves Cathari[g], (the pure,) if they come over to the Catholic and Apostolic Church, the Holy and Great Synod ordains that they, being in orders, shall so continue among the clergy. But it is meet that they should first of all give

---

[b] The Holy Eucharist. Compare Matt. v. 23.

[c] i.e. let him be metropolitan as well as "pope." Allies, Church of England Cleared, p. 19. See Meyrick's Papal Suprem., p. 7.

[d] Ruffinus' version of this is, "And that in Alexandria, and in the city of Rome, the old custom be preserved, so that the one bishop have the care of Egypt, the other of the *suburbicarian* Churches."

[e] Jerusalem. [f] Of Cæsarea. [g] The Novatians.

a written promise that they will consent and adhere to the decrees of the Catholic and Apostolic Church, that is, that they will communicate with the twice-married, and with those who fell away in the persecution, and in whose case a time has been fixed, and a term defined (for their penance), so that they will follow in all things the decrees of the Catholic Church. Whenever they are the only ordained men to be found either in villages or in cities, those who are found in the clergy shall keep their own rank; but if any come over where there is a bishop or a presbyter of the Catholic Church, it is clear that the bishop of the Church must have the dignity of bishop, and he who was named a bishop by the so-called Cathari must have the honour of a presbyter, unless it should please the bishop to impart to him the nominal honour (of a bishop); otherwise he shall provide him with the place of a chorepiscopus or a presbyter, in order that he may at any rate have a clerical position. This rule is to secure that there be not two bishops in one city.

9. If any have been promoted to the presbyterate without scrutiny, or on being examined have confessed themselves guilty of offences, and men, moved to act against rule, have laid hands on them in spite of such confession; these men are not received by the canon, for the Catholic Church vindicates (only) what is irreproachable.

10. If any lapsed persons have been ordained through ignorance, or with the knowledge of their ordainers, this does not prejudice the rule of the Church, for when they are found out they are deposed.

11. As to those who transgressed without compulsion, or without loss of property, or without danger, or such like circumstance, which took place during the tyranny of Licinius; it seems good to the Synod to treat them kindly, although they are unworthy of indulgence. All such, then, who sincerely repent, shall, if they were among the faithful, spend three years among the hearers, and seven among the prostrate: and for two years they shall communicate with the people in the prayers [h], without (receiving) the Oblation.

12. Those who were called (to the Church) by grace, and gave token of early zeal, and laid aside their (military) belts, but afterwards returned as dogs to their vomit, so that some even spent money and won their re-admission to the army by presents, must be among the prostrate ten years, after spending three among the

[h] i. e. the Eucharistic service. Their position was that of *consistentes*.

hearers. But in the case of all these, it is fitting to scrutinize their purpose of mind and the character of their repentance. For as many as by reverence, tears, patience, and good works manifest their conversation in deed and not in show, shall, after fulfilling the fixed period of being hearers, with good reason take part in the prayers, it being lawful for the bishop to take yet more indulgent measures respecting them. But those who bore (their penance) with indifference, and deemed a merely formal entrance (as penitents) into the Church sufficient for their conversion, must by all means go through their whole time.

13. Concerning those who are at the point of death, the ancient and canonical law shall be still observed; that whosoever is dying shall not be deprived of his final and most needful *Viaticum*[1]. But if, having been given over and re-admitted to Communion, he be again found among the living, let him take his place with those who have fellowship in prayer only. But in every case, and with regard to every one who is dying, and asks to receive the Eucharist, let the bishop, having made due enquiry, impart to him the Oblation.

14. Concerning the lapsed catechumens, it seems good to the holy and great Synod, that for three years they be auditor-(catechumens) only, and afterwards pray with the catechumens.

15. By reason of the great disturbances and factious movements which take place, we ordain the total abrogation of the usage which has been found to exist irregularly in some parts; so that no bishop, presbyter, or deacon shall remove from city to city. But if any one, after this regulation made by the holy and great Synod, attempt such a thing, or lend himself to it, the proceeding shall be absolutely annulled, and he shall be restored to the Church of which he was ordained bishop or presbyter.

16. All presbyters or deacons, or others at all enrolled in the (clerical) list, who in a rash mood, not having before their eyes the fear of God, not knowing the rule of the Church, shall remove from the church (to which they belong), ought by no means to be received in another church, but to be absolutely compelled to return to their own; or if they do not return, it is fitting that they should be excommunicated. But if any one ventures surreptitiously to take (a clerk) who belongs to another (bishop), and to ordain him

---

[1] Ἐφοδίου—alluding to 1 Kings xix. 8. S. Mark's Liturgy applies it to every Communion.

in his own church, without the consent of the proper bishop from whom he who was enrolled in the list removed, let his ordination be void.

17. Whereas many enrolled in the list, following the love of gain and filthy lucre, have forgotten the Divine Scripture, which saith, "He lent not his money upon usury," and lending it, demand the hundredth part; the holy and great Synod has thought it just, that if any after this regulation be found to take usury, going about the matter by unfair management or otherwise, either exacting half as much again, or devising any other scheme at all for filthy lucre's sake, he shall be deposed from the clerical office, and excluded from the list.

18. It has come to the knowledge of the holy and great Synod that in some places and cities the deacons give the Eucharist to the presbyters, whereas neither the rule nor custom have handed down such a proceeding as that those who have no authority to offer, should give the Body of Christ to those who do offer. Further, this was ascertained, that even now some deacons touch the Eucharist before the bishops. Let all this, then, be done away; and let the deacons remain within their proper limits, knowing that they are attendants on the bishop, and inferior to the presbyters. And let them receive the Eucharist according to their order after the presbyters, either the bishop or the presbyter giving it to them. But let not the deacons be allowed to sit among the presbyters; for this practice is irregular and disorderly. If any one refuses to obey, even after these regulations, let him cease from the office of a deacon.

19. Concerning the Paulianists who may hereafter flee to the Catholic Church, a regulation has been promulgated that they must by all means be rebaptized[j]. If some of them in time past have been enrolled in the list, then, if they should appear blameless and irreproachable, let them be rebaptized and ordained by the bishop of the Catholic Church. But if the inquiry should prove them unfit, they ought to be deposed. Similarly concerning the deaconesses, and generally concerning those who are enrolled in the list, the same form shall be observed. We refer to those deaconesses[k] who are found (only) to wear the garb; since they have

---

[j] Strictly speaking, *baptized;* for the Church, by enacting this rule, declares their Paulianist baptism to be invalid.

[k] The Paulianist deaconesses. See Routh, Scr. Op. i. 414.

not had any imposition of hands, they must certainly be ranked among the laity.

20. Whereas there are some who kneel on the Lord's day, and even in the Pentecostal days[l]; in order that all observances in every parish[m] may be uniform, it has pleased the holy Synod that the prayers be offered to God standing."

---

[l] From Easter to Whitsuntide inclusive. Tert. de cor. 3.

[m] i. e. diocese.

II.

FROM THE TOME OF S. LEO.

"THE properties of both Natures and Substances being preserved, and combining into one Person, humility was assumed by majesty, weakness by strength, mortality by eternity; *and*[n] *in order to discharge the debt of our condition, the inviolable Nature was united to the passible one; so that—and this was the fitting mode of our cure—one and the same Mediator between God and men, the Man Christ Jesus, could die from the one element, and could not die from the other.* Thus, in the entire and perfect Nature of very Man, true God was born, thoroughly God, thoroughly one of ourselves[o]..... He assumed the form of a servant without the stain of sin, dignifying humanity, not abating Divinity..... The Self-same who, abiding in the form of God, made man, was made Man in the form of a servant. Each Nature retains its own properties without defect..... The Self-same who is very God, is very Man; and there is no deceit in this Union, while the lowliness of man and the loftiness of God are interchanged. For as God is not changed by the compassion (exhibited), so Man is not consumed by the dignity (given). *For each form discharges its proper work in fellowship with the other; that is, the Word*[p] *working what belongs to the Word, and the Flesh executing what belongs to the Flesh. One of these is radiant with miracles, the other stoops under outrages.....* To be hungry, thirsty, weary, asleep, is clearly human. But to satisfy five thousand men with five loaves, and to give to the Samaritan woman living water, ... to walk on the back of the sea with unsinking feet, and by rebuking the storm to still the uplifted billows, is unquestionably divine. As then .... it is not of the same Nature to weep with tender pity for Lazarus a deceased friend, and by the

---

[n] The passages in italics are those to which some bishops, in the second session of Chalcedon, made objections which Theodoret and Aetius removed.

[o] "Totus in suis, totus in nostris."

[p] The Word is here used for the Godhead of our Lord.

mandate of a voice to raise him up alive . . . . . so it is not of the same Nature to say, 'I and the Father are One,' and to say, 'The Father is greater than I.' *For although in our Lord Jesus Christ there is one Person of God and Man, yet that from which both undergo contumely is one element, and that from which both derive glory is another. For His Manhood, inferior to the Father, is from our side; from the Father is His Godhead, equal to the Father.* Therefore on account of this Unity of Person to be considered in both Natures[q], we read both that 'the Son of Man descended from heaven,' since the Son of God assumed flesh from that Virgin of whom He was born; and again, the Son of God is said to be crucified and buried; while He underwent this, not in the Godhead itself, wherein the Only-begotten is co-eternal and consubstantial with the Father, but in the weakness of human nature. Wherefore we all in our very Creed confess that the Only-begotten Son of God was crucified and buried, according to the words of the Apostle, 'For had they known it, they would not have crucified the Lord of majesty.' . . . . If, then, Eutyches accepts the Christian Faith, and turns not away his ear from the preaching of the Gospel; let him see what Nature it was that hung transfixed with nails on the wood of the Cross, and let him understand whence the blood and water flowed, after the side of the Crucified had been pierced by the soldier's lance, that the Church of God might be freshened both by the Laver and the Cup. . . . . This is the faith by which the Catholic Church lives, by which she advances; that we must neither believe Manhood to exist in Christ Jesus without very Godhead, nor Godhead without very Manhood."

It may not be out of place, in connection with S. Leo's Tome, to notice a recent disparagement of the orthodox formulas of the age of the Councils. "The Creeds," says Professor Jowett, (*Essays and Reviews*, p. 353,) "are acknowledged to be a part of Christianity;" (this phrase, it may be observed, is ambiguous;) "they stand in a close relation to the words of Christ and His Apostles; nor can it be said that any heterodox formula makes a nearer approach to a simple and Scriptural rule of faith. Neither is anything gained by contrasting them with Scripture, in which the germs of the expressions used in them are sufficiently apparent. Yet it does not follow

[q] See S. Augustine, c. Serm. Ari. c. 8, from which S. Leo took the substance of this passage.

that they should be pressed into the service of the interpreter. The growth of ideas in the interval which separated the first century from the fourth or sixth makes it impossible to apply the language of the one to the explanation of the other. Between Scripture and the Nicene or Athanasian Creed a world of the understanding comes in," &c. The language of the Creeds, it is allowed, "has a truth suited to its age, and its technical expressions have sunk deep into the heart of the human race;" but "it is not the less unfitted to be the medium by the help of which Scripture is to be explained. If the occurrence of the phraseology of the Nicene age in a verse of the Epistles would detect the spuriousness of the verse in which it was found, how can the Nicene or Athanasian Creed be a suitable instrument for the interpretation of Scripture?"

Surely that may be serviceable as a comment which could not pass itself off as part of the text. It is no objection to a commentator that he has his own "ideas," and his own modes of speech, which cannot be looked for in the original. The question is, How does he employ them? Do they stifle and thrust aside the sense of the original, or do they express and illustrate it? In the present case, no one dreams of making the old Church formulas a substitute for the actual study of Holy Scripture. But considering that, e. g. the Nicene Creed was framed by men most anxious to guard the literal meaning of the Scripture language respecting Christ, and familiar with the interpretation which it had traditionally received in the several Churches, there appears to be *primâ facie* ground for regarding their statement as the representative of the primitive belief. And when Professor Jowett observes that although S. Paul "looked to his Lord as the Creator of all things,—high above all things in heaven and earth, —he does not speak of Him as equal with the Father, or of one substance with the Father," one may ask, 1. Whether a Person of such dignity could be less than very God? and if not, (i. e. if Arianism is untenable,) then 2. In what point does the idea of our Lord's *real Divinity* fall short of the idea of His *Consubstantiality*, as proclaimed in 325? Is it not matter of history that the Nicene Council employed the Homoousion as meaning simply this,—The Son is very God, of and with the Father?

It is satisfactory to hear from Professor Jowett that a "sound instinct prevented the Church from dividing the humanity and Divinity of Christ." But did not an equally sound instinct prevent her from confounding them? Professor Jowett quotes 1 John i. 1, in proof of Christ's *humanity;* yet he considers that we do violence to "the natural meaning and connection" of such texts as Phil. ii. 6, Mark xiii. 32, Matt. xxvi. 39, xxvii. 46, &c., when we "insist on reconciling them with the distinctions of later ages." But if we really believe our Lord to be *God and Man,* then, quite apart from all Church formulas, "distinctions" of some sort are inevitable. We may object to those of the Athanasian Creed and the Fourth Council; but, in that case, we must make others of our own. Systematic theology did not create the "difficulties" of the subject, and to abandon it is not to escape from them. No sooner do we call Christ "God and Man," than they confront us with "a presence which," in this world, "is not to be put by."

III.

PRINCIPAL EVENTS.

	A.D.
EDICT of Milan	313
Councils of Arles, Ancyra, Neocæsarea	314
Constantine decides against the Donatists	316
Rise of Arianism. Persecution by Licinius	319
Council of Alexandria condemns Arius	321
Council of Nicæa	325
S. Athanasius, archbishop of Alexandria	326
The Eusebians depose Eustathius of Antioch	331
Council of Tyre. First exile of S. Athanasius	335
Death of Arius	336
Constantius, emperor	337
Council of the Dedication. Second exile of S. Athanasius	341
Sapor of Persia begins to persecute	343
The Macrostich refused by first Council of Milan	345
Council of Sardica	347
Paul and Macarius in Africa	348
Constantius recalls S. Athanasius	349
Constans slain. S. Cyril bishop of Jerusalem	350
First synod of Sirmium deposes Photinus	351
Liberius succeeds S. Julius	352
Constantius sole emperor in East and West. Rise of Homœan Arianism	353
Third Council of Milan, overawed, condemns S. Athanasius	355
Third exile of S. Athanasius. George in Alexandria. Liberius, Hosius, and S. Hilary in exile	356
Fall of Hosius and Liberius. S. Basil in Pontus	357
Semi-Arian Council of Ancyra	358
Councils of Ariminum and Seleucia	359
Eudoxius succeeds Macedonius at Constantinople	360
Meletius at Antioch. Anomœan Council of Antioch; Constantius succeeded by Julian	361
Council of Alexandria. Schism at Antioch increased. Donatists recalled. Fourth exile of S. Athanasius	362

	A.D.
Jovian succeeds Julian	363
Semi-Arian Council of Lampsacus	365
Semi-Arian Deputies satisfy Liberius; Damasus succeeds him	366
Edict of Valens. Fifth exile of S. Athanasius	367
S. Hilary dies	368
S. Basil, archbishop of Cæsarea	370
S. Athanasius writes against Apollinarianism	371
Consecration of the two Gregories, and of S. Martin	372
Death of S. Athanasius. Peter driven to Rome	373
S. Ambrose, archbishop of Milan	374
Gratian, emperor of the West	375
Ulphilas becomes an Arian. Controversy on "Hypostasis"	376
Death of Valens; close of Arian persecution	378
Death of S. Basil. S. Gregory Nazianzen at Constantinople	379
Edict of Theodosius. Council of Saragossa	380
Council of Constantinople. Council of Aquileia	381
Gratian murdered. Augustine at Rome	383
Execution of Priscillian	384
Siricius succeeds Damasus. First contest of Justina with S. Ambrose	385
S. Jerome at Bethlehem. Second contest of Justina with S. Ambrose. Conversion of S. Augustine	386
Tumult at Antioch	387
Jovinianism	389
Penance of Theodosius	390
Murder of Valentinian II. Great anti-Pagan edict	392
Origenistic controversy begins	393
Death of Theodosius. S. Augustine, bishop of Hippo	395
Death of S. Ambrose: mission of S. Ninian. S. Martin dies	397
S. Chrysostom, archbishop of Constantinople	398
Theophilus persecutes the Tall Brothers	401
Epiphanius at Constantinople. Council of the Oak	403
Final ejection and exile of S. Chrysostom	404
Jerome attacks Vigilantius	406
Death of S. Chrysostom	407
Taking of Rome	410
Conference at Carthage	411
Pelagianism condemned at Carthage. S. Cyril, patriarch of Alexandria	412
Close of Antiochene schism	414
Conference at Jerusalem. Synod of Diospolis	415
Zosimus succeeds S. Innocent; is deceived by Pelagius	417
Council of Carthage, May 1. S. Germain, bishop of Auxerre. Case of Apiarius begins	418

	A.D.
S. Jerome dies. Persecution in Persia	420
Predestinarian question arises	426
Semi-Pelagianism. Vandals in Africa. Heresy of Nestorius	428
S. Germain and Lupus in Britain	429
S. Cœlestine declares against Nestorius. S. Augustine dies	430
Council of Ephesus. S. Palladius' mission	431
S. Patrick's mission	432
Re-uuion of S. Cyril and John	433
S. Leo, pope	440
S. Cyril succeeded by Dioscorus	444
Quarrel of S. Leo with S. Hilary. Edict of Valentinian	445
Eutyches condemned by S. Flavian	448
The Latrocinium	449
Pulcheria and Marcian succeed Theodosius II.	450
Council of Chalcedon	451

INDEX.

Abdas, 297
Acacius of Amida, 298
——— Berrhæa, 241, 245, 323, 350
——— Cæsarea, 34, 69, 89, 95, 101, 105
——— Melitene, 330, 333, 336, 355
Acesius, 21, 26
Aerius, 107
Aetius, heretic, 66, 91, 100
——— general, 305, 377
Agelius, 85, 135
Agricola, 319
Alaric at Rome, 257, 261
Alexander of Alexandria, 10, 12, 17, 28
——— Antioch, 272
——— Constantinople, 17, 44
——— Hierapolis, 348, 353, 359
——— Thessalonica, 40
Alexandria, councils of, 12, 20, 64, 115, 126, 326
Alypius, 193, 219, 295
Amator, 290
Ambrose, S., election of, 154
——— death of, 293
Amphilochius, 153, 156, 172
Anastasius, pope, 232
——— priest, 311
Anatolius, 395
Ancyra, councils of, 6, 91
Andrew of Samosata, 328, 348, 354
Andronicus, 262
"Anomoiou," the, 66
Anthimus, 147
Anthropomorphites, 235, 370
Antidicomarians, 158
Antioch, councils of, 47, 79, 105, 128, 347, 361
——— sedition of, 196
Antoninus, 238
Antony of Fussala, 300
——— S., 36, 75
Apiarius, 293, 300
Apollinaris, early life of, 63
——— heresy of, 146, 158, 181
Aquileia, council of, 179
——— battle of, 218
Arbogastes, 112
Arcadius, emperor, 220
Arcaph, John, 28, 38, 45
Ariminum, council of, 94, 98
Arius, heresy of, 11
——— death of, 44
Arles, councils of, 7, 70
Armentarius, 364
Arsacius, 246
Arsenius, abbat, 221
——— Meletian, 38, 40
Asterius, 43
Athanasius, nephew of Cyril, 317, 405
——— of Anazarbus, 15
——— Perrha, 369, 377, 395

Athanasius, S., early years of, 12
——— election of, 31
——— death of, 148
Atticus, 251, 283
Attila, 398
Augustine, S., early years of, 182
——— conversion of, 193
——— death of, 325
Auxentius, 73, 94, 105, 129, 154

Barsumas, Eutychian, 389
——— Nestorian, 360
Basil, abbat, 315
—— of Ancyra, 68, 91, 101
——— Seleucia, 383, 391
—— S., early life of, 88, 113
——— election of, 141
——— death of, 163
Bassian, 382
Benjamin, martyr, 298
Beziers, council of, 81
Boniface, count, 305
——— pope, 294, 299
Bonosus, 211
Brothers, the Tall, 239

Cæcilian, 4, 21, 266
Cæsarius, 112
Candidian, 329
Capreolus, 329, 358
Carthage, councils of, 60, 226, 231, 236, 279, 289
——— conference of, 263
Cassian, 221, 258, 307, 318
Catechumens, 187
Celidonius, 373
Chorepiscopi, 6, 364
Chrysaphius, 378
Chrysostom, S., early life of, 171
——— election of, 229
——— death of, 255
Circumcellions, 14, 59, 267
Cœlestine, S., 299, 323, 346
Cœlestius, 258, 269, 285, 321
Colluthus, 12, 20
Collyridians, 158

Consistentes, the, 6, 187
Constans, 56, 58, 64
Constantine, religious position of, 18
——— death of, 45
——— II., 46
Constantinople, councils of, 101, 172, 180, 181, 243, 383, 388
Constantius, emperor, 46
——— death of, 108
Cyriacus, 247
Cyril, S., of Alexandria, election of, 272
——— death of, 370
—— of Jerusalem, election of, 65
——— exile of, 90

Dalmatius, 334, 341
Damasus, S., election of, 132
Demetrias, 272, 284
Demophilus, 87, 142, 169
Dianius, 114
Didymus, 125
"Dioceses," 176
Diodore, 62, 142, 171, 310
Dionysius of Milan, 70
Dioscorus, election of, 371
——— deposition of, 406
Diospolis, council of, 277
Domnus, 367, 377, 392, 397
Donatus of Bagai, 59
——— Carthage, 58
——— Casæ Nigræ, 5
Dorotheus, heretic, 316
——— priest, 159

Eleusius, 85, 97, 101, 130
Ephesus, councils of, 238, 331, 390
Ephrem, S., 65
Epictetus of Centumcellæ, 73
——— Corinth, 146
Epiphanius, S., 158, 216, 240
Eudoxia, 238, 241, 245, 247
Eudoxius, 35, 90, 96, 100, 102, 130, 135, 140
Eugenius, 213
Eulalius, 294

Eunomius, 80, 91, 102, 158
——— chamberlain, 46, 73, 92, 110
Eusebius of Cæsarea in Palestine, 15, 17, 24, 35, 39
——— in Cappadocia, 114, 131, 135, 137, 140
——— Dorylæum, 311, 383, 391, 398, 401, 415
——— Emesa, 48
——— Milan, 400
——— Nicomedia, 15, 24, 33, 42, 46
——— Samosata, 153, 162
——— Vercellæ, 70, 73, 103, 115, 118
Eustathius of Antioch, 21, 35
——— Sebaste, 88, 91, 96, 101, 107, 131, 152, 157, 166
Eutropius, chamberlain, 228, 234
——— Joannite, 246
——— of Hadrianople, 36
Eutyches, heresy of, 380, 383
Euzoius, 25, 33, 105, 108, 150

Fastidius, 319
Faustus, 184
Felix, Manichean, 248
——— of Aptunga, 4
——— of Rome, 74, 86
——— treasurer, 122
Flavian of Antioch, 62, 66, 142, 173, 196, 211, 233
——— Constantinople, 379, 383, 388, 392
Fortunatian, 72
Fortunatus, 213
Fortunius, 231
Frumentius, S., 32, 82

Gallus, 70
Gangra, council of, 166
Gaudentius, Donatist, 296
——— S., 251
Genseric, 306, 363
George of Alexandria, 79, 115
George of Laodicea, 34, 91, 105
Germain, S., 290, 318, 377, 382
Germinius, 93
Gervase and Protase, relics of, 92
Gratian, emperor, 156
Gratus, 58, 60
Gregory of Alexandria, 48
——— Armenia, 21, 27
——— Elvira, 103
——— Nazianzum, consecration of, 147
——— at Constantinople, 164
——— of Nyssa, 147

Helena, S., 29
Helladius, 354
Helvidius, 180
Hilarus, legate, 389, 394
Hilary, anti-Pelagian, 307
——— deacon, 70, 117
——— S., of Arles, 307, 364, 367, 372, 389
——— Poitiers, 66, 73, 81, 87, 92, 95, 102, 104, 118, 129, 139
"Homoion," the, 69, 93
"Homoiousion," the, 68, 91, 130
"Homoousion," the, 20, 24, 127, 131
Honoratus, 223
Honorius, emperor, 221
Hosius, 20, 53, 86
Hypatia, 259, 274
"Hypostases," the, 116, 159

Ibas, 359, 382, 387
Innocent, S., 240, 250, 282
Irenæus, 335, 380
Ischyras, 20, 37
Ischyrion, 371
Isdigerdes, 272, 297
Isidore of Pelusium, 295, 340, 355
Ithacius, 186

James, S., of Nisibis, 65
Jerome, S., early life of, 160
——— death of, 297

John, count, 337
—— of Antioch, 323, 335, 353
—— Jerusalem, 215, 275
Jovian, emperor, 125
Jovinian, 204
Julian, apostasy of, 109
—— Pelagian, 291, 306, 317, 365
Julius, legate, 389
—— pope, 47, 54, 61, 67
Juvenal, 329, 332, 390, 410
Juventinus, 121

Lampsacus, council of, 130
Laodicea, council of, 138
Leo, S., election of, 366
Leontius, Arian, 35, 62, 66
—— of Cæsarea, 21
Leporius, 304, 307
Libanius, 125
Liberius, 67, 73, 87, 103, 118, 131
Licinius, 9
Lucifer, 70, 117
Lucius, 115, 150
Lupus, 319

Macarius, envoy, 58
—— of Jerusalem, 15, 30
—— Laodicea, 354
—— priest of Alexandria, 37, 44
Macedonius, 45, 65, 85
—— heresy of, 103
Macrostich, the, 52
Majorinus, 4
Manicheism, 183, 203, 369
Marcella, 231, 261
Marcellinus, 263
Marcellus of Ancyra, 43, 57, 147
—— Apamea, 209
Marcian, emperor, 397
Marcus, pope, 43
Marinus, 7
Maris of Chalcedon, 25, 110
—— Edessa, 359
Marius Mercator, 269, 312
Mark of Arethusa, 93, 111
Martin, S., early years of, 104
—— death of, 227
Martyrs, the Forty, 9
Maruthas, 250, 271
Massalians, 210
Maximian, Donatist, 214
—— of Bagai, 248
—— Constantinople, 344
Maximin, Arian, 306
—— emperor, 5
—— of Treves, 43
—— Anazarbus, 354
Maximus, Cynic, 164
—— emperor, 182
—— of Jerusalem, 39, 63
Melchiades, 5
Meletius of Antioch, 104, 128, 148, 162, 172
—— Lycopolis, 10, 25, 28
—— Mopsuestia, 354
Memnon, 329
Milan, councils of, 52, 56, 70
—— edict of, 4
Modestus, 142
Monica, S., 184, 199
Mursa, battle of, 67

Nectarius, 174, 207, 228
Neocæsarea, council of, 6
Nestorius, heresy of, 311
—— death of, 372
Nicæa, council of, 21
Nicè, conference of, 97
Nina, S., 32
Ninian, S., 225, 227, 349
Novatians, 26, 85, 182, 305

Oak, council of the, 241
Olympias, 247
Olympius, philosopher, 209
Optatus, Donatist, 231
—— S., 120, 141
Orange, councils of, 309, 367
Orders of clergy, 232
Orestes, 274

Origenism, 215, 224
Orosius, 275

Pachomius, 33
Paschasinus, 406
Palladius, Arian, 180
——— biographer, 169, 193
——— S., 345, 348
Paphnutius, 21
Paris, council of, 104
Patrick, S., 349
Patroclus, 285
Paul, envoy, 58
—— of Constantinople, 45, 50, 65
——— Emesa, 350
——— Neocæsarea, 8
Paula, 180, 244
Paulinus, biographer, 154, 193, 269, 288
——— of Antioch, 107, 117, 162
——— Nola, 219, 284, 334
——— Treves, 70
——— Tyre, 9, 16, 35
Pelagius, 249, 269, 276, 279, 285
Perigenes, 299
Peter of Alexandria, 150, 165
Petilian, 265
Pherbutha, 51
Philagrius, 41
Philip, legate, 336
——— præfect, 65
Philippopolis, council of, 53
Phœbadius, 87, 98, 153
Photinus, 57, 66, 113
Pistus, 47
Porphyrius of Antioch, 247
Portian church, the, 187
Posidonius, 323
Potamius, 86
Potamon, 21, 39
Prætextatus, 134
Praylius, 285
Primian, 215
Priscillian, 168, 186
Proclus, S., 313, 358
Projectus, 374
Prosper, 307, 345, 348
Pulcheria, 256, 379, 397
Pusices, 51

Quartodecimans, 21, 337
Quodvultdeus, 364

Rabbula, 346, 360
Ravennius, 389
Restitutus of Carthage, 97
Rheginus, 338
Rhodanius, 81
Riez, council of, 364
Ruffinus of Aquileia, 215, 234, 230, 235, 240, 262
Rufinianus, 73

Sabas, martyr, 147
Sabinian, 377
Sapor, king, 50
Sardica, council of, 52, 294
Saragossa, council of, 169
Saturninus, 70, 81
Secundus, Arian, 13, 47
——— priest, 79
Seleucia, council of, 95
Serapion, archdeacon, 238, 252
——— monk, 235
Severus, 192
Siderius, 144
Silvanus of Cirta, 14
——— Semi-Arian, 90, 100, 131
Simplicianus, 236
Siricius, pope, 186, 204
Sirmium, councils of, 66, 86, 93
Sisinnius, 304
Sixtus III., 346, 365
Sophronius, 95
Stephen, hermit, 82
——— of Antioch, 57
Stilicho, 223, 257
Sylvester, S., 5, 21
Symeon, S., martyr, 50
——— Stylites, 347
Symmachus, 184
Synesius, 259, 262
Syrianus, 75

Telemachus, 248
"Thalia," the, 17
Theodore of Mopsuestia, 171, 278, 306, 337
——— Tabenne, 82, 125
Theodoret, 325, 328, 343, 378
Theodosius I., emperor, 164
——— death of, 220
——— II., emperor, 256
Theophilus of Alexandria, 209, 229, 235, 272
——— the Indian, 51, 91
Theophronius, 48
"Theotocos," the, 17, 165, 181, 312
Thessalonica, massacre at, 205
Timothy, 173, 189
Toledo, council of, 236
Turibius, 377
Tyana, council of, 135

Ulphilas, 101, 157
Unilas, 234
Ursacius, 42, 56, 63, 67
Ursinus, 132
Usthazad, 50

Valence, council of, 153
Valens, Arian bishop, 35, 56, 63, 67, 93, 98
——— emperor, 129
Valentine, 302
Valentinian I., emperor, 129
——— II., emperor, 185
——— III., emperor, 305
Valerius, 222
Vararanes, 297
Vincent of Capua, 57, 70, 103
——— Lerins, 357
Vitalis, 303
Victor, Donatist, 15
Victorinus, 111
Vigilantius, 224, 252

Zenophilus, 14
Zosimus, pope, 285, 290

ERRATA.

Page 67, line 5, *for* proceed, *read* proceeded.
„ 69, „ 25, *for* Homæan, *read* Homœan.
„ 70, „ 5. *for* Anomæan, *read* Anomœan.
„ 141, „ 28, *for* Milevis, *read* Milevum.
„ „ note, *for synacti, read syneisacti.*
„ 159, „ *for* 843, *read* 243.
„ 172, „ *for* S. Mel. i., *read* S. Melet.
„ 226, line 1, *for* northern part of, *read* north-west part, or.
„ „ „ 7, *for* Strath-clyde, *read* 'Cumbria.'
„ 233, „ 17, *for* 388, *read* 398.
„ 246, „ 32, *for* Arcacius, *read* Arsacius.
„ 297, „ 5, *for* the Testament, *read* the New Testament.

Printed by Messrs. Parker, Cornmarket, Oxford.

The Practical Christian's Library—continued.

SUTTON.—Learn to Live. By CHRISTOPHER SUTTON, D.D. *A new Edition.* 18*mo.*, 1s. 6d.

——— Learn to Die. By CHRISTOPHER SUTTON, D.D. *A new Edition.* 18*mo.*, 1s.

TAYLOR.—The Golden Grove; a choice Manual, containing what is to be believed, practised, and desired, or prayed for. By BISHOP JEREMY TAYLOR. 18*mo.*, *cloth*, 9d.

——— The Rule and Exercises of HOLY LIVING; in which are described the means and instruments of obtaining every virtue, and the remedies against every vice. 18*mo.*, *cloth*, 1s. 6d.

——— The Rule and Exercises of HOLY DYING; in which are described the means and instruments of preparing ourselves and others respectively for a blessed death, &c. 18*mo.*, *cloth*, 1s. 6d.

The above two volumes in one, 2s. 6d.

WILSON.—A Short and Plain Instruction for the better understanding of THE LORD'S SUPPER, with the necessary preparation required. A new Edition, reprinted entire. By BISHOP WILSON. 32*mo.*, *cloth*, 1s.

Also an Edition with Rubrics in red, *cloth*, 32*mo.*, 2s.

——— Sacra Privata. Private Meditations, Devotions, and Prayers. Adapted to general use. 32*mo.*, 1s.

With red Rubrics, *cloth*, 32*mo.*, 2s.

THE PENNY POST.—A Church of England Illustrated Magazine, issued Monthly. Price One Penny.

That this Magazine is wanted, a circulation of 22,000 copies of each number testifies. It is *the only Penny Magazine* upholding sound Church principles. That it does good, and is appreciated, testimony whence it would be least expected, abundantly proves. But at the same time it must be borne in mind, that this is a small circulation for a Penny religious periodical. Those who differ depend much upon their periodicals for inculcating doctrine hostile to the Church, and circulate thousands, where the Church of England, unfortunately, circulates only hundreds.—Monthly, One Penny. Subscribers' names received by all Booksellers and Newsmen.

Vols. I., II., III., and IV., of the Old Series, crown 8vo., cloth, may be obtained, price 1s. 6d. each.

Vols. I. to V. of the New Series of the "Penny Post," 8vo., in handsome wrapper, 1s.; or in cloth, 1s. 8d. each.

The Literary Churchman.

To the Clergy and Laity generally, to Heads of Families, to Authors and Publishers, and to all who are interested in Religious Literature.

IN an age of great ecclesiastical and polemical activity, when theological and religious publications occupy a most important rank in literature; when Romanism and Dissent are modifying their developments, and resorting to the Press for the dissemination of their principles; and when on the Continent, and especially in Germany, Theology is undergoing many important changes, it can hardly be doubted that there is a wide opening for a learned, impartial, and exclusively critical Journal, conducted on true Church-of-England principles.

Such a Journal is the LITERARY CHURCHMAN. Commenced in 1855, it has pursued its course to the present time, and has succeeded in attracting the approbation and support of a considerable number of Churchmen, including bishops, clergy, and some of the most influential laity.

To Authors it presents an effective means of making the merits of their publications known; while, from the fact of its appearing so frequently, it becomes a better medium for advertising new books than any of the monthly or quarterly periodicals.

Communications to be addressed to the Editor, 377, Strand, London, W.C.

Published on the 1st and 16th of each Month, price 4d.; free by post, 5d.

SUBSCRIPTIONS.

	s.	d.		s.	d.
For Six Months	4	0	For the year	8	0
„ Ditto free by post .	5	0	„ Ditto free by post .	10	0

A specimen Number sent gratuitously on application.

It will be seen on comparison with the various Reviews and Magazines connected with Religious Literature, that this, while giving the most complete and full information, is still by far the cheapest.

www.ingramcontent.com/pod-product-compliance
Ingram Content Group UK Ltd.
Pitfield, Milton Keynes, MK11 3LW, UK
UKHW041429200326
11397UKWH00027B/202

9 789353 975029